Please return/renew this item by the last date shown
on this label, or on your self-service receipt.

To renew this item, visit **www.librarieswest.org.uk**
or contact your library

Your borrower number and PIN are requ

Librar

4 5 0011394 7

ALSO BY MIKE TYSON WITH LARRY "RATSO" SLOMAN

Undisputed Truth

MIKE TYSON

WITH LARRY "RATSO" SLOMAN

IRON AMBITION

LESSONS I'VE LEARNED FROM THE MAN WHO MADE ME A CHAMPION

sphere

SPHERE

First published in the US by Blue Rider Press,
an imprint of Penguin Random House LLC in 2017
First published in Great Britain in 2017 by Sphere
This paperback edition published in 2018 by Sphere

1 3 5 7 9 10 8 6 4 2

The author gratefully acknowledges permission to reprint excerpts from the following:
"Ten Thousand Words a Minute" by Norman Mailer, originally published in *Esquire*.
Copyright © 1963 by Norman Mailer, used by permission of The Wylie Agency LLC.
Zen in the Art of Archery by Eugen Herrigel, copyright © 1953 by Pantheon Books, a division
of Random House, Inc., and renewed 1981 by Random House, Inc. Used by permission
of Pantheon Books, an imprint of the Knopf Doubleday Publishing Group, a division
of Penguin Random House LLC. All rights reserved.

Photography credits are found on page 467.

A CIP catalogue record for this book
is available from the British Library.

ISBN 978-0-7515-5962-0

Printed and bound in Great Britain by
Clays Ltd, St Ives plc

Book design by Lucia Bernard

Papers used by Sphere are from well-managed forests
and other responsible sources.

MIX
Paper from
responsible sources
FSC
www.fsc.org   FSC® C104740

Sphere
An imprint of
Little, Brown Book Group
Carmelite House
50 Victoria Embankment
London EC4Y 0DZ

An Hachette UK Company
www.hachette.co.uk

www.littlebrown.co.uk.

In memory of Cus D'Amato, who inspired me
to be more than I could ever be

IRON
AMBITION

'm staring out the window of my suite at the Ritz-Carlton in Battery Park City in New York. In the other room my wife, Kiki, is looking after our two babies. Milan is doing an arts and crafts project, and Rocco, as usual, is rampaging around the room. I'm in town to make a special appearance at the Barclays Center, where Deontay Wilder is defending his WBC heavyweight title against Artur Szpilka. Wilder? Szpilka? They used to say that the heavyweight division was all that mattered in boxing. Those days are long gone.

I look out on the Wall Street area and my mind goes back to the days when I was growing up in Brownsville, Brooklyn. Every time I talk to my wife about my childhood, she thinks I'm just stroking my ego. I say, "Baby, I just can't believe the shit that happened in my life." My wife doesn't understand the degree of how fucking poor I was. Then I point out the streets where, as a nine-year-old, I slammed people against the walls of buildings and snatched their chains.

If I crane my neck a little, I can look uptown toward 42nd Street. That was our playground. I'd hang out in the arcades or sneak into Bond's International Casino to pick the pockets of the people who went to listen to music. Every night was like a weekend on 42nd Street. But things have changed in Times Square. Now you got Disney characters walking around hawking pictures with tourists and the Naked Cowboy strumming a guitar. Everybody's got their cameras out taking selfies with strangers. Imagine trying to do that with the people I was hanging out with in Times Square. "Hey, man, let's take a selfie!" A fucking selfie, nigga? Back in the seventies, taking any kind of picture around strangers was a no-no. You didn't even say hi to people you didn't know. Motherfucker would start beating on you and leave you in a coma on the street.

I was part of a vicious cycle back then. I would rob and then go buy nice things and then the bigger kids would steal my sneakers and my jacket and my jewelry. How do you beat those big monsters? Everyone was scared. But somehow I never died in those situations. "That's Mike, man," one of my older hip friends would say, and the bad guys would let me go. I began to think that I had a special destiny. I always knew that I wasn't going to die in the gutter—that something was going to happen to me that was going to be respectable. I was an insecure street rat but I wanted glory, I wanted to be famous, I wanted the world to look at me and tell me that I was beautiful. I was a fat fucking stinking kid.

It's funny that one of the things that made me feel special was that there was a white baseball player named Mike Tyson. He was a journeyman infielder for the St. Louis Cardinals, but because I had this guy's name I just knew that I was different and that I would go places.

Then I met another white guy, an old Italian gentleman who also thought I was special. His name was Cus D'Amato and he filled my head with visions of glory. Without this man I wouldn't be sitting here, looking out the window of a fancy hotel. I might be living in some crummy apartment building back in Brownsville or eating chicken wings in a greasy spoon uptown instead of ordering penne pasta from room service. Or I might be dead.

Back when I was a kid, I'd be scared to go back to 42nd Street because a motherfucker might recognize me from the day before and start chasing and beating the shit out of me. Now I can't walk down 42nd Street because someone might love me to death. Isn't that crazy? I'm on 42nd walking around and so many people will slap me five, I got to get in the car.

And not just on my old stomping grounds. I can't walk the streets most anywhere in the world. Ain't that some bullshit? I'm in Dubai and we can't go shopping for jewelry. I can't leave the hotel or I'll get mobbed.

This is all because of Cus. Don't think I'm whining—I'm very grateful for my situation. But I don't understand how it all happened. How did this boxing manager and trainer who was in exile in upstate New York watch me spar for less than ten minutes when I was thirteen years old and predict that I would be the youngest heavyweight champ ever?

This book is about our relationship. Cus D'Amato was one of the most unique men ever to walk the planet. He touched the lives of so many people and helped them become a better version of themselves. He took the weak and made them strong. And he took a fat, frightened thirteen-year-old and made him into a guy who can't walk the streets because I'm the most recognizable face on the planet.

1

Before Cus, pigeons saved my life. I was a fat Poindexter when I was growing up, the kind of kid who gets his change stolen, his meatball sandwich knocked to the ground, and his glasses broken and shoved down into the gas tank of a truck parked outside his school. I was bullied every day until I was brought up onto a roof near where I lived and told to clean up the pigeon coops by the older, cooler guys who kept their birds there. It didn't make sense to me. The birds were so small, so insignificant looking. Why would fly guys be so interested? But you could see by the smiles on their faces that these pigeons meant the world to them.

When people saw me up there with those guys, they said, "Don't fuck with this guy anymore. He knows those guys." You don't fuck with pigeon guys. They were known to deal with people messing with their birds by throwing them off the roof.

From being a pigeon gofer I got into a life of petty crime. I never hung out with anybody my own age. I was schooled by my older friends like Bug and Barkim. Because I was smaller, they'd have me climb through a window and unlock the door so they could rob a house. One time I got locked up with Bug. He joked that he would be going to the big house while I got a vacation with cookies and milk at juvie. I was like a professional student, soaking up all these street moves from these older guys.

As I got older, I got bigger but I still felt like that small four-eyed guy who got bullied all the time. I never thought I would be a fighter, but I used to hang out with my friend Wise, who was an amateur boxer. We used to smoke weed and shadowbox. Wise always used to do the Ali shuffle while he shadowboxed. My first fight happened by accident. By then I had used some of my pilfering money to buy my own pigeons. I kept them in an abandoned building next to mine. This guy named Gary Flowers stole one of my birds, and when I confronted him to get it back he pulled it out of his coat and twisted its neck off and rubbed the blood on me. I was furious but I was scared to fight, until one of my friends egged me on. "You've got to fight him, Mike." So I hit with a right and he went down and I was stunned. I didn't know what to do. Then it dawned on me how cool Wise looked doing the Ali shuffle, so I started shuffling and everybody started clapping. My first taste of applause.

Fighting was big in my neighborhood. If you were a good fighter, you had respect. Nobody would ever try to rob you. So I began to get a rep for my street fighting. I was especially good at that sneaky sucker punch shit. If I was fighting someone and they slipped, I would attack him on the floor. But I didn't win all my fights. I got beat up a lot because I was fighting older men. I was eleven or twelve and I was fighting guys in their thirties because when I beat them in a dice game, they didn't want to pay a little kid. And if one guy didn't pay, then nobody paid. So I attacked the guy. Those men might have had guns, but I didn't care. They knew I wasn't a punk and they had to fight or pull out a gun and hit me with it.

When we were young, I thought that all my friends would be together forever. But then life goes on and people start dying. I never knew people who got married and stopped robbing and went on the straight and narrow. I just thought that we'd keep on our life of crime until somebody would kill us or we'd kill them. Sometimes we would go hustle and one of our friends would die—somebody would stab him or shoot him. You would think that we would run home, go and tell his mother what happened, but we were still looking to rob some more shit. We didn't go home until we got some more money. We were like fucking sharks, just kept moving.

My mother was getting more and more fed up with my petty-criminal life because I was spending more and more time in Spofford. The actual name of the place was Bridges Juvenile Center, a rat-infested hellhole on Spofford Avenue in the Hunts Point section of the Bronx. Going in there was like a class reunion, like in *Cheers*, where everybody knew your name. And while there might not have been air-conditioning, at least you were getting your three hots and a cot. And your cookies and milk.

One of the times while I was in there, just after I had turned twelve, they were showing the movie *The Greatest*, a 1977 movie where Muhammad Ali plays himself. I liked Ali's style then but I wasn't a boxing fan at all. I used to love watching wrestlers like Bruno Sammartino and Killer Kowalski. The only time I saw an Ali fight was when he was fighting Leon Spinks for the second time. I was hanging out on a corner in Brownsville with my friend when we saw a guy going into the corner store. Somebody told us that the guy had food stamps and money on him so we went in after him. I went in the back and got some chips and then made sure I got in front of the guy. Everybody's eyes were glued to the television that was showing the Ali fight. So I dropped my bag of chips and then bent over to pick it up and the guy stopped and my friend, who was behind him, went into his pockets—boom. I loved Ali but I wasn't a bit interested in the fight.

But watching his biopic in a room filled with hundreds of kids at Spofford was great. And when the movie was over, the lights came on, and all of a sudden Ali walked out on the stage and the place just exploded. Whoa. Ali started talking to us about being in detention and he was saying how he had been in jail and he had lost his mind. He was saying beautiful, inspirational stuff. That speech was a game changer for me. It's not that I wanted to become a boxer after hearing him. I just knew that I wanted to be famous. I wanted the feeling that when I walk into a room, people bow down and lose their fucking minds. But I didn't know what I was going to have to do for people to do that shit.

I was back in Spofford for a burglary rap. I was in my sixth month of an eighteen-month sentence. Spofford is a holding facility, and they were getting ready to transfer me to another juvenile center, so I was hustling to make some bank before I left. You have to be savage and make sure you rob some stuff you can trade when you get to the next place they send you. If you leave broke, then they're going to think you're a pussy at your next stop.

I used to team up with my boy Darryl "Homicide" Baum, who was in there with me. The guys from Brownsville all stuck together. They'd tell me that there's a nigga from the Bronx in the next dorm with some gold on and we'd go get it. I was the robber guy. Everyone knew Brownsville Mike the Robber. Now, to get that gold chain, we'd wait until we had gym with the guy. Most of these guys didn't take their gold off, they wore it. Homicide and me went to the gym and Hommo spotted him. The guy was cool, though, and I went up to him and he punched me right in my face, boom! I wasn't expecting it, and then Hommo just jumped on him, boom, boom, boom, boom. We beat that nigga's ass and took his jewelry.

I was always in trouble in Spofford. Right before they were going to send me out, our dorm was fighting with another dorm and I got caught with a knife. The CO who ran the place came in and read the report from the shift before and then he told me to get up and take my punishment. For being caught with a knife, I had to get ten hits in the head with a half pool stick.

POP. POP. POP. POP . . . Those guards were brutal. They'd beat you like a dog.

A few days after that thrashing, my caseworker came in and told me that I was being sent away to finish the last year of my sentence. They don't tell you where you're going so you can't tell your peeps where you'll be. The next morning two guards handcuffed me and put me in the backseat of a car and drove me upstate to Johnstown, New York. I was going to a place called Tryon but I had never heard of it. So I'm thinking, "If I don't know anybody up there, I'll have to start stabbing some people. That's just how it is."

The Tryon School for Boys was light-years away from Spofford. It was in the woods an hour northwest of Albany. All the kids lived in different cottages. There was an indoor swimming pool, a nice gym, and programs that included raising pheasants. Because they didn't consider me a violent offender, I was initially placed in the Briarwood Cottage, which was an open cottage. I had my own room with no lock on the door.

I immediately began acting out, attacking kids, attacking guards, attacking everyone. I began to get a rep. Mike Tyson—the psycho crazy guy, the sick fuck who would walk up and punch you in the face or throw hot water on you. The final straw came when a kid passed me in the hall as I was walking into one of my classes and he tried to snatch my hat and I pulled it back. I had to wait forty-five minutes for the class to be over and all I could think about was what I was going to do to this guy. When the class was over, I found the guy and beat his ass.

That was it for my freedom. Two guards came and got me and escorted me to Elmwood, the lockdown cottage. Elmwood was a place where you needed to straighten out, because if you didn't, those huge redneck guards would fuck you up. Elmwood was where the badasses go. For me it was a badge of honor.

Once we got to Elmwood, they locked me in a room, took off my clothes, and took the mattress out of the room. I was on some kind of suicide watch. Every half hour a staff guy would check up on me. I was in isolation but there was a tiny window in the door and I'd hear some inmates walking by. "Hey, what's going on out there?" I yelled. One of the guys told me that they had just finished sparring with Mr. Stewart, one of the guards at Tryon. I had heard about Bobby Stewart. He had a boxing program and everyone who was in it was always laughing and happy. He'd make the kids miss with a punch and they'd fall down and everybody would crack up. I decided I wanted to get in on that program.

Every time the staff came to check on me, I begged to see Mr. Stewart. Then they'd pick up a phone and call Stewart. "He's completely calm. He's polite. He ate and asked to clean up. All he wants to do is talk to you," they told him. Stewart waited until everybody was in bed, because if I started a commotion he didn't want any of the other kids involved. Then he came to my room. He smashed the door open and ran into the room.

"What do you want with me?" he yelled.

Just writing that sentence still gives me a chill to this day.

"I want to be a fighter," I said.

"So do the rest of the guys," he barked. "If they were fighters, they wouldn't be here in the first place. They'd be out in the street, going to school, getting a job. We deal with losers here."

"All I want to do is be a fighter. I'll do anything you ask me to do," I said.

Mr. Stewart kept screaming at me and then he changed his tone.

"All right, lookit, let's see your behavior change. Let's see you go to your classes with no incidents. Let's see a month of good behavior and we'll see what happens."

Later Stewart told me that he'd been working there for ten years and he had never seen anybody as insecure as me when I came in. He said that he could see me stealing a pocketbook if no one was looking but he couldn't see me confronting someone. I couldn't even look him in the eye when he barged into my room. For all my street bravado, I was a shy kid. I was really just a follower, not a leader. All I knew back then was how to cheat, steal, rob, and lie.

Stewart would check the daily logs to see if I was behaving myself. He saw that not only was I doing everything I was supposed to do, but I was actually asking the staff if there was extra work I could do. I'd ask them to write in my request so Stewart would see it. In six days, I got up to the top level for my class. Look, my family is from the South. They taught me how to be calm, how to talk to people, like "Yes, ma'am. No, sir."

Mr. Stewart started reading my files and he saw a notation that said I was borderline retarded. He went to the staff psychologist and said, "What is this?" She told him that I was intellectually handi-capped. "How do they determine that?" he asked. "Well, they give him tests." "Tests! He can't read and write properly. How can you deter-mine he's retarded? I've seen this kid for a while now. He's smart. He just doesn't know how to read or write. I can't read or write that good but I'm not retarded!" The psychologist started waffling and Stewart lost his cool and told her that she was retarded. He got written up for that. I love Bobby. He's one of those Irish guys who talks and doesn't have any filter.

So I kept behaving and getting good reports and Mr. Stewart seemed impressed. I know he was impressed when he came into the weight room one day. I was about to use the Universal bench press machine.

"What are you doing?" he said to me. "You've got two hundred fifty pounds on that machine."

"The other guys said I can't do this," I said.

"Don't you do it! Take the weight off and start with a hundred thirty-five pounds," he said.

He turned his back on me, and when he looked back I was press-ing the 250 pounds, ten times—without warming up. I was so fuck-ing strong back then. I guess my feat got back to his boss, because when Stewart finally decided he would let me spar with him, his boss was worried.

"Jesus, I know you're in good shape, but this kid is stronger than all of us put together. You be careful," he told Bobby. "The staff can't be seen getting beat up by the kids."

I was so excited the day we sparred for the first time. The other kids knew about my reputation as a street fighter back in Brooklyn, so they were psyched. We started boxing and I thought I was doing well, because he was covering up and I was getting some punches in. Suddenly he came out of a clinch and the motherfucker hit me in the stomach and I went down. I had never felt pain like that before in my life. I felt like I was ready to throw up everything I had eaten for the last two years. I got right up but I couldn't breathe.

"Walk it off," he barked. "Walk it off." I got my air back and we started boxing again. When we finished, I asked him if he could teach me how to punch a guy in the stomach like that. That was going to be my robbing punch.

Even though he had manhandled me like that, I never quit. The whole dorm, most of the staff, they'd all come out to watch us box. I was so happy to be getting attention. I wanted people to look at me and adore me but then I got mad when they did! I was so crazy then.

Once he saw that I kept coming back even though he was beating my ass, he started to teach me. We'd wait until the other kids went to bed at nine p.m. and then we'd go to an empty dorm room and work from nine-thirty until eleven, when it was time for me to turn in. Mr. Stewart would stand there and throw punches at me and I'd move, then we'd reverse it. I'd never had any goals in my life except for robbing but Bobby gave me something to focus on. I turned the same desire I had for robbing into fighting. When we finished I'd go to my room and, in the total dark, I'd practice what he'd shown me that night until three a.m. I know that Stewart was impressed with my work ethic and that he had a good feeling what we were doing was going to help me outside the ring.

I was so excited that I put him on the phone with my mother one of the times that I was allowed to call her. He told her how much progress I had been making and that if I could continue doing good, I could make something out of myself. She just laughed and thanked him. I had never given her any reason to be hopeful about me.

Mr. Stewart was excited by my progress but he began to worry about what would happen to me when I was released. He knew that if I went back to Brooklyn I might fall back into a criminal mind-set. He thought about finding a gym down there for me to work out of but then he had another idea.

One day, after we sparred, he sat me down.

"Listen, man, my wife is mad. I'm coming home with a broken nose and black eyes. I can't box with you no more, but I'm going to take you somewhere where they're going to take you to the next level. Do you think you want to do that? Because I believe when you get out of here, you're going to get killed or locked up again."

"No," I protested. "I don't want to go. I want to stay here with you."

"I want you to work with Cus D'Amato. He's a famous trainer. He took Floyd Patterson to the heavyweight title. He made José Torres into a light heavyweight champ. He takes kids in if they behave and work hard. Maybe you could stay at his house with him."

Before Bobby called Cus, he showed me a few moves that were meant to impress the old trainer. One was a diagonal side step that enabled me to swing coming out of the corner. I practiced that and got good at it. Then Stewart called Cus and asked him if he'd take a look at me.

"Absolutely," Cus said. "If you think he's got potential, then bring him down tomorrow."

On the way there, Stewart tried to tamp down my expectations.

"Cus may not even like you the first time, I don't know," he said. "But maybe he'll say we can come back. If he does, then we'll work harder and then we'll come back and come back until he sees we can do it."

Cus's gym was on top of the police station in Catskill. Inside it was old and musky and there was a small ring. There were also a lot of weather-beaten newspaper clips on the wall. There were a few older white guys there along with a younger guy named Teddy Atlas who was assisting Cus. I was introduced to Cus and in a second I could see that he was totally in control of everything there. He just sucked up all the air in the room. He shook my hand and there wasn't a trace of a smile on his face. He showed no emotions.

Right away Teddy Atlas took one look at me and said, "We've got nobody to box with him." Stewart said that he was going to box me and we got in the ring. I was really good that first round, pressing Mr. Stewart and banging away at him. We did that spinout move that we had been practicing and I looked over and saw Cus smile for the first time. "Wow! Wow!" he said. "That's beautiful."

I kept pressing Stewart in the second round and he got me with a couple of shots and my nose started bleeding profusely. It looked a lot worse than it felt and Atlas jumped into the ring.

"All right, Bobby. We've seen enough," he said.

"No, no," I protested. "Mr. Stewart says we don't quit. If we start, we have to go three rounds."

Bobby looked over at Cus, and he said it was like watching a movie. Cus's face turned red and he looked over at his friends who were there and everyone was smiling. Bobby later told me it was like Cus's body had miraculously transformed. "His whole face lit up. You ever see a guy who gets scared and his hair stands up? Well, Cus had no hair but that's what it reminded me of. His eyes opened wide and it was like 'I have life again.' "

Cus let us go a third round and I did pretty good. Teddy took my gloves off and Cus started helping Mr. Stewart with his gloves.

I saw them talking but I couldn't make out what they were saying. I couldn't get a read from looking at Cus's face. He was impassive. I wouldn't find out until later that Cus asked Bobby, "Would he be interested in working here?" Bobby knew I wanted to do that but he played it cool and said he'd have to talk to me.

On the way to our car I was almost bursting with anticipation.

"Can I come back? How did he think I did?" I peppered Bobby.

Bobby pushed me. "Guess what he said?"

"He said I can't come back?" I said. I was such a low-esteem schmuck.

"No! He said, 'Bobby, barring outside distractions, that is the heavyweight champion of the world and possibly the universe.' But only if you continue to work like you've been working."

I pushed him back. "Come on," I said. And then I started crying.

"I'm telling you, that's what he thinks of you," Bobby said. "See, you're not a scumbag. You're not a loser. He said all that about you the first time he saw you. Do you realize what that means? But you can screw it up in one second. You've gotta work."

"I'm ready," I said through my tears. "I'm ready to work."

2

On the ride back to Tryon, I just knew I was going to be a success. Even though I talk negative and project myself as a bum, my inner core thinks I'm a god and I know I'm going to be successful. Every time I say, "I'm a piece of shit," or "I want to kill myself," that's all confusing the enemy. Everything I say is for a reason: to confuse the enemy. That's a concept that I would soon learn from Cus.

When I saw Bobby the next day, he said, "Now we really got to work." We worked out every day and then he'd call Cus on Sunday and report on my progress. Every second week we'd drive down to Catskill and have a session with Cus. Cus would talk to me and tell Teddy what new moves to show me. Then, back in Tryon, Bobby and I would work on those moves. We'd spar three nights a week and on the other nights Bobby would throw punches at me and I'd move from side to side to avoid them, practicing what Cus showed me.

I was doing well in my classes too. Bobby told me, "I don't care if you flunk every subject, but you try and behave yourself in class." A few weeks later he got a call from one of my teachers. "What the fuck happened to this kid? He went from a third-grade to a seventh-grade reading level. He's doing great!"

On one of the early visits to Catskill, Cus took Bobby and me aside.

"Listen, most kids don't want to go to the grown-ups' prison, so they say they're younger than they really are," Cus said. "He's too strong, too big, too coordinated, and too fast. He's got to be an older guy."

Bobby looked confused.

"Mike, listen. I'm talking to you. How old are you for real?" Cus asked me.

"I'm thirteen!" I said. But I didn't look it. I was only five-six then, but I weighed 196 pounds.

The next time we came up, Bobby brought some documentation from the state that proved I was thirteen years old. Cus almost had a heart attack.

"Listen, you will be the national champion. You will be the Olympic champion. That's who you are. Do you want to do this?" Cus asked.

I didn't know if I wanted to do all that. I was scared. But I didn't want Cus to think I was a punk.

"Yeah," I said.

"Okay, let's get to work," Cus barked.

From that day on, Cus began to talk with me along with giving me boxing instructions. "Do you realize why you're doing this?" "Do you feel good doing these things?" "Don't just do something because I tell you to do it." One day he looked at me and said, "Would you like to change your life?" I nodded yes. "From what I've seen and if you listen to me, with no distractions and not allowing people to mess your head up, you will be the youngest heavyweight champion of all time." I was thirteen years old and he thought I was invincible! Of course, I told him that I wanted to be the world champion, and he liked that. But mostly it was Cus doing all the talking. He'd talk to me about my feelings and then he'd tell me why I was feeling that way. Cus wanted to reach me at the root. It wasn't just about the physical aspects of boxing; it was getting at the mental side—why a fighter got bubble guts, why our minds play tricks on us so that something seems more difficult than it is. I didn't understand everything he was saying, but I did. Cus knew how to talk my language. Cus was really a street kid who had improved himself as a person.

After a few more months of these gym visits, I was getting close to being paroled. Bobby Stewart came to my room one day.

"Listen, do you want to stay with Cus? I don't want you to go back to Brooklyn. I'm scared you're going to get killed or go right back to prison."

I didn't want to go back to Brooklyn either. I was looking for a change in my life. I liked the way these people made me feel good, made me feel like I was part of a society. Before you're released from Tryon you get three home visits. For my first home visit I went to Brooklyn to see my mom.

"Just remember, if you get in freakin' trouble, that's the end of everything," Bobby warned me.

I was home for an overnight visit and nothing much happened. I might have smoked some weed and gone up to Times Square with my friend App, but other than that I didn't do anything. I talked to my mom and she was drunk, hanging out with her friends. My brother wasn't around and my sister was with her friends. But I told everybody I was going to be a fighter.

My second home visit was down in Catskill. This one was for three days and two nights. It was the first time that I saw Cus's house. I couldn't believe my eyes as Bobby drove down the long, winding driveway. It was like coming up on Diamond Jim Brady's driveway. They had named the road for the family who initially lived in the house, the Thorpes. The house itself was a big-ass white Victorian with something like fourteen bedrooms. I'd never seen anything like that. There was a path out the back of the house that led right to the Hudson River.

"I'm going to stay *here*?" I asked Bobby. He nodded.

"What am I going to have to do, take the garbage out?" I asked. I was a real sarcastic kid.

Cus wasn't home but I got to meet Camille Ewald, his companion, who actually owned the house. She was a strong-looking Ukrainian lady but she seemed real sweet.

"Hey, sit down and have tea with me," she said. "Talk to me."

It was just like some girl talk. Where was I from? Have I been

other places before? Was I excited? After a while she showed me my
room and I just sat on the bed waiting for Cus. He came in with some
of the other kids who lived there and we ate something and I did some
chores and then we all went to the gym.

I spent the three days just training and reading boxing magazines
and watching old fight films with Cus. I didn't even feel different being out of prison, because after I got involved with Cus, even when I
was in prison, I was out of prison. Do you feel me? Cus had been putting gasoline on a raging fire that was consuming me. When I left to
go back to Tryon, I had a large book that Cus had lent me. I'd been
looking through the books in the living room and I'd stumbled on Nat
Fleischer's *Ring Boxing Encyclopedia and Record Book*. I started
reading it and I was just overwhelmed. I fell in love with all those old
fighters. The book had all their records and their bios. There were
pictures of some of them that showed their bodies and, wow, they
fucking looked beautiful! They were ripped to shreds, ready to fight.
I don't care if they were 119 pounds—they were ripped. It was so im-
pressive knowing how much work went into looking like that. When
you went to a boxing match or a weigh-in, the people were more excited looking at the fighters' bodies than at the pretty girls around
them. That's why, ever since, I'd do the old-school turn-of-the-century
shit and go up there in my underwear, because that's the impression
those boxers left on me—they're beautiful. That gave me motivation
to work hard too, because I knew I had a tendency to get fat. I wanted
to have that six-pack. Every time they threw punches in that book,
the frame stopped and every muscle, every vein in their body, was
showing. I fantasized about me being that guy.

Cus saw me thumbing through that book. "Do you like that? Take
it with you," he said.

That was it. Once he gave me that book, it was like looking at a
Penthouse magazine. By the next time I came down to Catskill I had
memorized that whole encyclopedia. And I began to barrage Cus with
questions about the fighters. I'd say a name like Freddie Welsh, and
Cus would tell me everything about him. If I mentioned a name like
Armstrong or Canzoneri or Ray Robinson, Cus would go, "Whoa!

Now, that's a fighter!" and then my fucking senses would go out of this world. I wanted to learn all about these ancient champions and master their philosophy. They worked hard but they played hard too, and people looked up to them like they were gods. These guys were immortals to me. And Cus was my conduit to them, so I wanted to impress him. I looked forward to going to the store for him, cleaning the gym, carrying the bags, being his servant. I was Cus's slave. Whatever he told me to do, I would do it. And I was happy to be his slave. I wasn't as close to the other boxers in the house at first. I would walk around the grounds and go down to the river and just stare out at it. This country living was new to me. I talked and participated in the goings-on in the house but I had a weird attitude. I wasn't confrontational. It was more that I just spoke a different language than the rest of them.

My mother didn't like the idea of me going up to Catskill. She went for it because I wanted to go but I could tell that she wasn't thrilled. My sister said, "Why are you going up there with those white people?" And I would reply, "Because I'm going to be champ of the world." As my release came closer, we had to make plans for me to come under Cus's supervision. My mom felt bad about me moving upstate but she signed over the papers. Maybe she thought she had failed as a mother.

I was helped out by a wonderful social worker named Ernestine Coleman. She was a big black lady from Hudson, New York, which was just miles from Catskill, and she went out of her way to smooth my transition. She had a lot of empathy for me and I knew how to play on that. She was a little easier to deal with than Bobby Stewart but she was no pushover.

I think Cus immediately realized that I suffered from low self-esteem and had been scarred by years of being bullied and abused, so from the very first time that I started coming up to Catskill he began to work on building up my ego.

"You've got to believe in yourself," he'd tell me in the gym. "Tell yourself that every day. Look in the mirror and see how handsome you are. Look at your powerful hands." At first I was thinking that he's a fag. From the world I come from, older guys do that shit when they want to suck your dick. Anybody that tells me I'm good-looking, that sends off triggers in my head. I didn't think I was good-looking, I felt ugly from being abused all my life. I felt so ugly I couldn't even look at myself in the mirror. But there he was, every day, "Listen, you're a good-looking guy." And when I'd protest and say, "Get out of here!" he'd come back, "No, you go look in the mirror and tell yourself how good-looking you are. Go shadowbox and say, 'Look how beautiful I look!' You're looking more handsome every day—you might just turn into an actor!"

But there was no loving feeling when he was saying this. He was dead serious. It was all about a mission—the heavyweight championship of the world. He didn't treat me like a kid. He was making me feel that I was worth something, that we had a mission together.

Bobby Stewart used to say that I was a born follower, and it's true. Back in Brooklyn, I followed Barkim into a life of crime. Barkim lived in my building and taught me how to rob and steal but I always had to watch out because if he was doing bad and I had money, he might flip on me too. But Cus was a much different mentor. Barkim didn't put the law down like Cus. Cus put it down that we were on a mission to the crown and at the end of the road there was going to be some good shit. When I would go into the ring and fight, I had to fight until I had nothing left. You can't quit, you've got to fight until you die.

Cus promised me that nobody would ever bully me again. He'd tell me about old fighters who had been beaten up in life and were able to overcome their feelings. As I got older, I realized what Cus's psychology boiled down to. He gave weak people strength. You give a weak man some strength and it becomes an addiction. Cus didn't want boys who were well-adjusted—he wanted to work with the kids who were flawed. He wanted the dregs of society who came from the worst neighborhoods. He was so happy when I told him I was from Brownsville. "Oh man, a lot of tough fighters came out of there. Al 'Bummy' Davis, Floyd Patterson grew up nearby."

Cus told me he thought the best fighters were the guys who had endured the most. José Torres told me later that Cus was sure I'd become champion when he heard that I used to get on public buses and wait until the passengers were warned about pickpockets and then I would go ahead and pick their pockets. He saw I had a native intelligence and that I could transfer my antisocial skills into the ring.

Cus would listen to me talk about my street escapades. Then he would look at me with no emotion, cold as steel, and say, " 'No' will be a foreign word to you." Cus was totally consumed with what he was capable of doing. "Will you listen to me, boy? Do you hear what I'm saying to you? People of royal descent will know your name. The whole world will know who you are. Your family name will reign, people will respect your mother, respect your children. Do you understand what I'm saying to you? Are you going to do this?" Can you imagine a thirteen-year-old kid hearing that?

WE TALKED A LOT about Cus's childhood. Costantino D'Amato was born on January 17, 1908. His father, Damiano D'Amato, left Italy in 1899 and arrived in New York. Six weeks later his wife, Elisabetta, arrived with Rocco, Cus's oldest brother, and the family settled in Manhattan, where Damiano began a coal and ice delivery business. Cus didn't remember much about his mother because she died when he was five years old. By then Cus had three older brothers, Rocco, Gerry, and Tony, and one younger brother, Nick. Cus seemed to take his mother's death in stride. "I was lucky," he told a reporter. "My mother died when I was five years old, so I had to learn to think and act on my own at an early age."

Cus said that he was named Costantino after his maternal grandmother, Costanza, but his father didn't get along with her so he told Cus that he was named after the first Christian emperor, Constantine. That was probably the first time that Cus thought that he was special. The family legend that they were somehow related to Napoleon through his maternal line only added to Cus's sense of being unique.

When Cus was six, the family migrated to the Frog Hollow section of the Bronx. The neighborhood was tough and became infamous for spawning gangsters like Dutch Schultz. Even though Damiano couldn't speak English, he became a community leader among the Italian immigrants and people would come to him with their business problems. He was known for his honesty and impressed that trait on all his children. He was also very generous, and while the family never had much money, Damiano would always share with neighbors who were having a hard time.

Cus told me that his dad was a very accomplished Greco-Roman wrestler and a big fan of boxing. He also had a great voice and after his work was done he'd light up a pipe and play mandolin and sing old Italian folk songs.

Damiano was also color-blind. One time, after he brought back another wife from Italy, Damiano invited a black friend of his, a coal miner, to have dinner. Cus's stepmom asked, "Do you think your friend wants to go to the bathroom and wash up?" She had never seen a black person before and she thought he was just dirty from the coal dust. Damiano's attitudes about race had a big impact on Cus. He never judged people by the color of their skin. He also became close to his Jewish neighbors. When he was sick, they'd send over some chicken soup for him. Cus returned the favor by turning on the lights for his Orthodox Jewish neighbors on Saturdays.

By all accounts Damiano, with his old-school emphasis on discipline, wasn't the easiest guy to get along with, and Cus's older brothers all left the house as soon as they could. It was hard on Damiano to raise all the boys alone, and when he found himself without a wife for the second time, he made a trip to Italy to get a new wife, his third. Cus was twenty-one by then, and usually he and Nick would stay with a relative when Damiano made his frequent trips back to Italy. But this time his brother Tony found both Cus and Nick sleeping in a doorway. He took them to his home. It was Christmastime and Tony had a young daughter. He and his wife woke up on Christmas morning to the sounds of Cus and Nick playing with their little niece's Christmas toys.

Whenever I'd tell Cus about my lousy childhood, he'd tell me he went through similar experiences. They never had much money and sometimes he'd steal apples and share them with friends. "Nowadays, they say you can't eat behind somebody, you'll get germs," he told me. "When I was a little boy, my friends and I shared apples. Give him a bite, I'd eat after. We got sick all the time." One time he starved himself for five days as a test to make sure that nobody could ever intimidate him with threats of starvation. He concluded that he could abstain from food for a couple of weeks "if you don't ask too much of your body."

Cus was also bullied growing up. He got picked on by neighborhood kids because his parents would dress him up "like little Lord Fauntleroy." His older brother Gerry was a tough guy and he had given Cus some fighting lessons. One time one of their neighbors was getting the shit kicked out of him by seven guys and Gerry just plowed into that melee and knocked out six people with seven punches. Gerry was Cus's hero and he was the first of Cus's brothers to join a gang. Cus followed in his footsteps and joined a gang and used to fight in the streets all the time.

Cus would talk about the time when he was in his twenties and he was sitting outside his house. Vincent "Mad Dog" Coll, a notorious gangster affiliated with Dutch Schultz, came up to Cus and put a gun to his head.

"You'd better tell me where so-and-so is," Cus recounted the story.

"I don't know where he is. You're just going to have to kill me."

Mad Dog realized that he had the wrong guy and left. It was only then that Cus began shaking.

Cus told me that he had lost his eyesight in one of his eyes in a street fight. But here's where it gets murky. Over the years, Cus told about four different versions of what happened. He told me that he lost his eye defending a neighborhood kid who was getting bullied by a guy with a knife. In 1958 he told *Sports Illustrated*, "I could and should have boxed. But I had a street fight when I was a boy, just 12 years old. It was with . . . one of those men who push kids around because they know they can't push men around. He gave me a bad eye, my right eye. I was blind in it for years but I made the man run and I chased him." But then he told Gay Talese in *The New York Times Magazine* that he had lost the vision in his *left* eye after he was struck by a stick in a street fight. The stick version was elaborated on as he told of staring at himself in shop window with his eyeball hanging out. Yet another time he said that he had lost his vision when he tried to stop a kid from tormenting a kitten.

The real story may be a lot more horrifying. One of Cus's nieces said that her father, on his deathbed, revealed that Cus lost the sight in his eye when Damiano disciplined Cus with a belt buckle. Cus always told me stories about his father beating on him.

"No one got beatings like me, I got the worst beatings in the world, but I deserved them," he told me. Cus would come home late and before he'd even open the door, he'd cover up, and as soon as the door opened, BOOM, BOOM, BOOM, his father would attack him and beat the shit out of him. Cus would refuse to say he would never be late again. That was Cus's whole thing—you can kill me but you ain't gonna break me. His father would cry as he hit him. Then one time Cus couldn't take it anymore and he gasped, "Maybe I won't do it again." Damiano started crying and the two of them embraced.

"It's a lot of nonsense when I hear people say that beatings crush a child's spirit," Cus told a reporter. "I never lost respect or love for my father, and it didn't crush my determination." I wonder if the reason Cus told me all about his beatings was because he knew that I had been beaten by my mother continually when I was young. We had those horrific experiences as a bond.

Cus was never interested in school. He quit high school in his sophomore year. He also had no interest in getting a job. Cus's father would constantly be on his case to get out and look for work. He didn't want to lie to his father, so once a week he would go to a local icebox factory and stand in the back of the room filled with job applicants so he would never get called. The place was run by religious Jews and one week one of the owners went to the back and told Cus how impressed he was by Cus showing up to look for work every week, so he hired Cus and put him on the assembly line. Now, Cus was never meant to work for anyone and he was so mad at actually having to work that he worked twice as hard as anybody there. The owner wanted to make him assistant foreman. Cus came up with new methods to increase productivity, which didn't sit so well with the ex-cons and Hispanic immigrants who didn't want to be bossed around by a seventeen-year-old kid. After a year and a series of brutal fights, Cus left the job.

Cus seemed to hate authority figures, but for a few years while he was a teenager he was fascinated by Catholicism. Even though his father was never religious, Cus started going to Sunday school because one of his friends went and Cus won prizes in his Bible classes. He would never think of committing a sin, and he obeyed the Ten Commandments to the letter. He was even thinking of going into the priesthood. Around the same time, he became preoccupied with death. He would watch funerals go through his neighborhood and he would think, "The sooner death, the better." If someone he knew died, he would consider them lucky because now they could be happy all the time. He told me that he would go into cemeteries at random and look at all the names on the headstones.

Then someone gave him a book and it turned his mind around. It was Thomas Paine's *The Age of Reason*. Paine hated organized religion and challenged the legitimacy of the Bible. That's what got his book on the Catholic Church Index, which meant it was a sin to read it. So in Cus's mind he was no longer a Catholic.

He wouldn't be a priest but, in his own way, Cus began a true life of service. He always said that he learned by example from his father and I guess he was impressed by his father's selflessness. Suddenly Cus became the neighborhood fixer, the go-to guy if you had a problem. He would translate for people, he would fix things, he would intercede with their landlords if they were having trouble paying their rent. He even became a youth counselor to the kids in the neighborhood. Of course, he refused payment for any of his services. Otherwise, he wouldn't consider what he was doing a favor.

More than anything else, he hated to see rich people get over on poor people. Cus found out that his friend Angelo Tosto's father-in-law was getting ripped off by phony land developers in Deer Park, Long

Island. The scammers targeted recent immigrants from Slovakia and swindled them out of their life savings by selling them land that they didn't have title to. Cus spent years researching the scammers. Finally, one Friday he went down to the company's lawyer's office, pretended he was a son-in-law to Angelo's father-in-law, and waited there until he was seen. He told the lawyer that if the family didn't get a check for a full refund he was going to go straight to the DA's office and have them charged with fraud. On Monday morning there was a check for the full amount. But that only infuriated Cus more. Now he knew the outfit was fugazi so he went to Riverhead, where the Long Island land transaction records were kept, and found proof that it was a scam. By the end of December 1937, thirty-nine individuals and twelve corporations had been indicted, and on July 7, 1938, the ringleaders were sentenced to jail terms of three to six years for swindling over $2 million from 1,800 Slovaks. His pal Angelo must have been incredibly grateful to Cus for his help, because twenty years later he was acting as Cus's chauffeur and driving him around town.

Cus always was a creative guy. But he had a strange explanation for his creativity. He once told a reporter, "It's almost like I never was a kid. I didn't learn very much in my lifetime because of these things I understood when I was young. How did I get so wise? I don't know. I used to think everybody was like that. I found out later in life it wasn't so. I don't talk about it usually. What's the sense of talking about something people don't understand?"

Cus was always inventing things but he never bothered trying to make money off his creations. He came up with a toy plane that was outfitted with a firecracker in a heavy metal cap on the nose of the plane. When the plane's nose hit the ground the firecracker would go off, sending the plane back into the air, and then it would descend through a series of loops and dives. His greatest invention was a sanitary sheet to use on public toilet seats. He even patented it when he was thirty years old. But Cus never pursued this, perhaps because a lady from Louisiana had filed her own patent for a sanitary toilet seat cover sixteen years earlier.

Cus's ingenuity was helpful to his family during the Great Depression. Cus was almost twenty-two when the Depression started. He told me about reading in the papers about old people starving to death because they were too proud to go and beg for help, but I think that they weren't too proud. It was Cus who was too proud. He made it so he knew how they were feeling, but I think it was that he wanted to look at people that way. He was coming from an antiquated place. Cus was living his life like a chivalrous knight and projecting his feelings. He was very morally conscious.

The food riots in lower Manhattan made a lifelong impression on him. Sometimes twenty thousand people would cram into Union Square and riot because they had nothing to eat. Cus was there once when he saw a guy in a lumber jacket standing on a tailgate making a speech. He found out that this guy was a member of the Communist Party. Cus watched as he made a speech and then got the shit beat out of him by the cops on horseback. But what was amazing to Cus was that as soon as one guy got beaten unmercifully, another guy would spring up on that tailgate, knowing that in minutes he was gonna get the beating of his life. Cus admired their guts and dedication. His dad kept telling him to stay away from those people, that they were going to get him in trouble, and I'm sure that added to his fascination.

One thing that never wavered in Cus's life was that he was pro-Italian like a motherfucker. He was fanatic about that heritage. Beatrice, his brother Tony's wife, was Irish. Right after Betty, their daughter, gave birth to twins, she was rushed back to the hospital. Cus called her to see how she was doing, and the nurse told him Betty couldn't get on the phone because she was getting a blood transfusion. Cus rushed over to the hospital and stormed into her room. "I had to get here fast to make sure your mother's Irish relatives weren't giving you blood," he said. "I didn't want your blood diluted further."

Man, Cus thought that the Italians were the niggas of the world. He was still bitching about the execution of the Italian anarchists Sacco and Vanzetti when I got up to Catskill. They did get a lousy deal, being framed for an armed robbery, and convicted for first-degree murder, and then frying in the electric chair in August of 1927. It took until 1977 for Massachusetts governor Michael Dukakis to issue a proclamation that they were unfairly convicted and "any disgrace should be forever removed from their names." But Cus would still go around the house and grouse about them.

One outlet for Italians and Jews, who were both marginalized in society when Cus was growing up, was boxing. Cus came from a boxing family—his brothers, his cousins, they all got turned out by boxing. Both his older brothers Tony and Gerry were fighters who rode the rails and fought in the streets, earning some money from the proceeds of the bets that were wagered. Lots of times if Cus got into trouble, it was Gerry or Tony who would bail him out. Tony was so tough that he used to sit on the stoop of their building with knitting needles and defiantly knit away, challenging anybody who passed by to fuck with him.

Gerry eventually became managed by Bobby Melnick, and Cus used to carry his bag to the gym. Back then boxers were heroes to every young kid. *The National Police Gazette* was in every barbershop and the magazine had a section devoted to boxing. Every neighborhood had a local hero who was a boxer, and whenever he left his house for a fight he'd be trailed by kids as if he were the Pied Piper.

Cus was enthralled by the atmosphere of a boxing gym. He told the story of having met Jack Dempsey and then going back to his neighborhood and having his friends line up to "shake the hand that shook Jack Dempsey's," but that might have been a stretch. According to his niece Betty, her father, Tony, met Dempsey at a fight club one day when he was sixteen. Dempsey asked Tony to be his sparring partner, but after Tony saw the vicious way that the Manassa Mauler destroyed his sparring partners, he nixed the job offer but managed to shake Dempsey's hand. Then he came home and told everyone, "I'm not going to wash my hand because I shook hands with Jack Dempsey."

Cus told one interviewer that it was his brother Gerry and not Tom

Paine who dissuaded Cus from considering the priesthood. Gerry took Cus under his wing and taught him how to defend himself. And then, when Cus was sixteen, a tragedy struck the family that rocked everybody to their core. Gerry was shot dead by an Irish cop.

Throughout his life Cus didn't like to talk publicly about the murder. He did tell me that Gerry had been the star of the family and that his death "broke my father's heart." Cus was there when Damiano found out about his death and he said that he could never forget his father's piercing wail. He told a close friend who was preparing a biography of Cus that Gerry and his wife were at a social function and an off-duty cop started getting "fresh" with his wife. A struggle ensued, they broke through a plate-glass window, and instead of the cop "receiving his just punishment," he shot Gerry. It was a strange way to describe a fight. The official police report tells a different story.

"Gerald De Matto—White—Married—Italy—Bartender was arrested & charged with Felonious Assault by Patrolman George Dennerlein . . . while resisting arrest, struck the patrolman several times with his fist, took his night baton from him and threatened to strike him with it." Then Dennerlein shot Gerry and he died at Lincoln Hospital at seven p.m., October 21, 1924, six days after the shooting. The report goes on to say that Gerry was drunk walking home, and when told by the officer to go home and get some sleep, he grabbed the officer, was arrested, and then knocked the officer to the ground and attempted to strike him with his own baton. "The officer sensing his life was in danger, drew his service revolver and discharged one shot the bullet entering the left groin of De Matto."

The night Gerry was shot, his brother Tony gathered together some friends and, armed with bats, marched on the police station seeking revenge. Luckily Damiano rushed there and calmed down the mob. After Gerry died, Cus visited the local parish priests and demanded to get answers as to why his brother had been killed by a "corrupted" cop, but the priests told him to "have faith and stop questioning." It was then that Cus finally decided that the path of the priesthood was not for him and that he had to, as he said, "train myself as a warrior and train other men to become warriors too."

Patrolman Dennerlein was transferred to Staten Island but the story didn't end there. Years later, when he had the money, Cus hired private investigators to investigate the case. Cus even told me that he knew where the cop lived right now, and that freaked me out. But he never tried to get revenge. I always wondered about that. Tony's daughter Betty said that the cop wasn't on patrol, he was off duty, and he and Gerry were in a bar when the altercation happened. But the fight was over Gerry's wife. She had been having an affair with the cop. Perhaps that was what Cus meant with his cryptic statement that the cop should have just received "his just punishment."

CUS WAS A BELIEVER in destiny. Even as a young boy, he felt that he'd be famous someday; he always had a feeling that "there was something different" about him. I had the same exact feeling. So it felt right that I would move in with Cus and Camille. Cus was so happy. I couldn't understand why this white man was so happy about me. He would look at me and laugh hysterically. Then he'd get on the phone and tell people, "Lightning has struck me twice. I have another heavyweight champion. He's only thirteen."

One of the first nights that I stayed over at the house on one of the home visits, Cus took me into the living room, where we could talk alone.

"You know I've been waiting for you," he told me. "I've been thinking about you since 1969. If you meditate long enough on something, you get a picture. And the picture told me that I would make another champion. I conjured you up with my mind and now you're finally here."

3

My whole life changed on June 20, 1980. Actually it was a week later. I had been going up to see Cus for a few months and I was listening to his promises of wealth and fame, but I wasn't all in. I didn't know how to be that guy Cus was talking about. But then while I was back at Tryon we watched the replay of the first Sugar Ray Leonard–Roberto Durán fight. And everything just clicked. I finally understood fighting. Both these guys were aggressive yet elusive and they were fighting their asses off. It was breathtaking.

People were applauding and going crazy and my dick got hard. I wanted people applauding me. The whole energy in my mind and my body coalesced. I knew what happened with my life was going to happen in that ring. I thought, "I'm going to dedicate my life to this. If I don't do this, I'd rather die."

I wasn't supposed to be released from Tryon until October but Cus got together with Mrs. Coleman, my social worker, and since I was fourteen and so big they decided it would be better for me to start school with the rest of the class in September. She loved Cus to death. He was one of those white guys who knew how to talk to the minorities. I should have been in the seventh grade but they put me in eighth because I was too damned big and scary.

It was hard to adjust at first. I'm from the gutter, from an institution, and all of a sudden I'm a middle-class kid in a white neighborhood. You come from hell and the next thing you know, you're in heaven but you're still the devil. Can you believe I was fourteen and I'd never seen a rose in my life, only on television? I thought only rich people had roses. The first time that I stayed over at the house, I asked Camille if I could have some and I cut them and took them back to reform school. Is that some poor black motherfucker shit or what? I didn't know I could buy a rose for two dollars. I saw a rose and I thought I was at Fort Knox. Right after I moved in, I stole money from Teddy Atlas's wallet. It was just a reflex. Teddy would go to Cus and say, "He's got to be taking the money. Nothing was missing until he got here." Cus said, "No, it's not him." In the back of my mind I probably was planning to rob Cus too. But as I settled in and got with Cus's mission, I got that filth out of me.

School was pretty awkward for me. I was so much bigger than my classmates. I was up to 210 pounds by then. When I went into my new classes, they thought I was the teacher. I felt like shit. School wasn't where I wanted to be. I was never part of that system. I only wanted to be a fighter. I didn't know many black kids at school. Maybe 20 percent of the school was black and the black kids were the ones rejecting me because I was with this white family. They called me Mighty Joe Young because I was so big. I knew a couple of kids from the gym but it wasn't easy making new friends because I was a shy guy. I made friends with some of the other outcasts there, the stoners. I'd go hang out at their houses and smoke pot. Then I found out my roommate Frankie was into weed and we'd smoke together.

The main reason that I hated school was that it was distracting me from my gym work. I'd wake up around four in the morning and do some running. Then I'd go back up to my room and do around five hundred sit-ups and push-ups. Then I might do ten sprints on the property, just running back and forth. This was all before school.

The first time that Bobby Stewart came down to spar with me after I had moved in, Cus told him, "Don't fool with Mike. Believe me, he's improved immensely." I didn't know until later, but Bobby had been working out twice a day just to keep up with me. We started sparring and he was doing a lot better than I was and I started crying.

I was a perfectionist. If things don't go my way, my life is over. Pull the plug. That's my mentality. I was so desperate to achieve. Plus I wanted to succeed for Cus. For the first time in my life someone was telling me that there was no one better than me.

Cus was as obsessive as I was about boxing. He really didn't think of anything else. He never went to movies. He didn't watch TV shows. He didn't know who the famous entertainers of that era were. If your name wasn't John Wayne, Judy Garland, or James Cagney, he didn't know about you. All he wanted to talk about was boxing. And I was happy to pepper him with questions about all the fighters that I was reading about in the *Boxing Encyclopedia*. As I settled into the house, Cus began to tell me how he got into boxing.

In 1936, when he was twenty-eight, Cus opened the Gramercy Gym on 14th Street in Manhattan. He wanted to perpetuate the memory of his brother Gerry, but he also wanted to have a champion. One of Cus's heroes was "Slapsie" Maxie Rosenbloom, the then light heavyweight champ of the world. He saw that Maxie traveled around town in a chauffeured Rolls-Royce and people treated him like a king. "After you're champ, you're going to have a chauffeured Rolls too," Cus told me. All of a sudden, my life was mapped out after this Jewish guy Maxie.

Cus found a big loft on 14th Street and started figuring out how to pay the forty dollars a month rent. Years earlier, after he saw the plans to create a big highway in the Bronx called the Bruckner Expressway, Cus had helped one of his friends. Knowing that there would be a lot of traffic, Cus told his friend, who opened four gas stations along that stretch and made a ton of money. He was happy to pay Cus's rent every month. There were probably ten other gyms in town but Cus felt that his knowledge of boxing was considerably more than any of the other trainers, so he was confident that he'd be a success.

Cus got a used ring from an old boxer and his brothers helped him build out the rest of the gym. But it was smack in the Depression and at first nobody came to the gym. Then one day a committee of about six mothers came up to see Cus. They pleaded with him to get their kids off the streets and out of trouble. Lower Manhattan was a tough area at that time and there was no Police Athletic League or any positive influence in these kids' lives. The mothers had no money to pay Cus but he didn't care. In fact, he never charged anyone a nickel to spar in the gym for the next thirty years. One of the reasons Cus picked that location, aside from the cheap rent, was that he knew the best fighters came out of tough neighborhoods. And Cus had one rule: if you did well and went pro, then he would manage you.

The gym was up three flights of rickety stairs. If you stood at the bottom of the stairs, you could see all the way up to the top. It was like you were climbing a stairway to heaven. Once you got up to the top, there was a big hole in the door, patched up with mesh wiring, and there was a huge watchdog that would smash up against the mesh, barking like crazy. Cus always said he could determine a lot about the character of a kid who made that trek up the stairs. He even called that walk "the trial." If a kid came up alone and wasn't deterred by the dog and pushed the door open and said he wanted to be a fighter, Cus knew he had something to work with. But if someone brought a kid there, it was a different story. "Now, if they were brought up by somebody, I knew I had my work cut out for me," Cus said, "because that fellow didn't have the discipline or a desire strong enough at the time to come up there by himself and open the door and say, 'I want to be a fighter.' "

Right from the beginning, Cus wasn't satisfied with just being a trainer. He also aspired to be a manager. "To be a real manager one must know all aspects of boxing. He must know emotions, publicity, management, fighters, how to train. A chain is only as strong as its weakest link. A manager must control the situation so even if he doesn't do the thing himself he can direct how the thing gets done," Cus told an interviewer once. Part of that job description was matchmaking. Cus was incredibly cautious with his fighters and he always tried to match them up with someone they could beat, because an early defeat could be devastating to a boxer's psyche. "I'm not in this business to get my guys massacred," he told *The New York Times*.

Picking opponents wasn't always easy. One time Cus was tricked and agreed to a fight with a guy from Long Island he hadn't heard anything about. "Almost as soon as the bell rang I realized my guy wasn't fighting no preliminary fighter. My guy got hit with everything and was knocked down ten times and I kept yelling to the referee, 'Stop it, stop it!' not wanting to get my guy ruined. After the fight I went into the locker room and my guy looks up and says, 'Cus, I'm sorry I let you down.' 'You didn't let me down. I let *you* down. I overmatched you.' Then I went over to collect the money and I heard the phone ring and somebody says it's a long-distance call asking for the result of the match. I knew then that this white boy wasn't no amateur from Long Island; he'd been brought in from another part of the country." Cus was furious and smashed his right fist into his left palm. "I don't make many mistakes like that!"

Cus was happy to teach anyone how to box. At one point he even trained some showgirls and taught them some boxing moves for a show that was being mounted. But Cus first got a reputation for training deaf and dumb boxers, or "dummies," as they were called back in those politically incorrect days. He thought they were great fighters because their sense of vision was so acute. "The ability to see is a fighter's biggest asset and dummies are so much better in interpreting things and responding to them instantly—those little signs that a punch is going to be thrown. They are very hard to hit," Cus said. To work with them Cus learned sign language. I watched him do it. It was so weird because he did it so hard and fast, almost violently. It looked like he was fighting. He also used his ability to read lips. That came in handy, because by the time I got with Cus, he was nearly deaf. He used to say to me, "Let me look at you. Talk to me right now." He told me that he used to look across the ring between rounds and if the other trainer didn't have his back turned to Cus, he would figure out what the guy was telling his fighter.

Cus was so known for his work with deaf and dumb fighters that boxing people started calling him Dummy D'Amato. But Cus still hadn't made a dent in the boxing business, and in 1942, after six years at the Gramercy, he was drafted into the Army. Before he even entered the Army, Cus began a strict regimen of self-discipline. Cus told Gay Talese, "I went into the Army prepared to die," but I'm sure he must have known that his bum eye would have kept him out of combat. He still began to put his body through some pretty heavy shit just to be prepared for all eventualities. He started by sleeping on the floor of his gym. Half the time he was sleeping on a cot in the office there, so that wasn't such a deprivation. But then he set his alarm clock to ring at random times during the night so he conditioned himself to waking up refreshed no matter the hour. He walked out in freezing weather without a coat.

Once he got in the barracks he continued his self-mortification practices. He slept on the floor, which was handy if they did a sneaky inspection. He shaved using only cold water. Cus used to have an expression that would pop into his mind when he was in the Army: "I will execute any command!" And he took it to the moon. He stood at attention for hours at a time and he practiced his salute like a madman until it was perfect. When his troop found themselves out on bivouac and flies were swarming them, making it impossible to eat, Cus made up his mind to not swat away the next insect. It turned out to be a spider, not a fly, and Cus put a piece of bread over it, closed his eyes, and ate it! Listen, I'm a weird dude today because of this guy. His whole thing was to discipline yourself to the point of rejecting pleasure.

His bad eye eventually did get him out of any dangerous combat and Cus wound up as a military police officer stateside for three years. He was assigned to guard some Russian deserters who were fighting for the Germans and became POWs. After a few shifts he refused the assignment because he had compassion for the Russians who were being tormented by American soldiers. Cus was such a model soldier that they allowed him to get out of it.

But Cus was even more incensed by the horrible way that black American soldiers were treated by both southern soldiers and northern civilians. Cus was coaching a boxing team, composed mainly of black GIs, and he took them to a restaurant in Trenton, New Jersey, for a bite to eat before going to Fort Dix, where the fights were to take place. Cus asked for a table for a party of ten. Six of the ten were black. The cashier pulled Cus aside and said, "We can serve you but not them," indicating the black boxers who were in uniform. Cus freaked out and started screaming how the black soldiers were protecting people like the cashier and that he better serve them. By now, the whole restaurant was looking at him and he had to be restrained by his fighters. They pulled Cus out of the restaurant with him still screaming at the customers who continued to eat.

When the team went to the South for exhibitions it was worse. Hotels refused to let the black boxers get a room and Cus wound up sleeping with his black fighters in a public park. Those black fighters never forgot what Cus had done for them. That kind of segregation was par for the course then, even for pro fighters. If black champions found themselves in a town where they didn't know anybody, then they had to sleep in the park and defend their title the next night.

Cus was most upset by the racism of southern soldiers. He told me a story of how he rescued his friend, a sergeant named Murphy, who was actually Italian, from a bunch of rednecks. Cus was getting some money from managing the boxing team so he had enough to have a steady supply of cigarettes and cookies. These rednecks would come by and bum cigarettes and cookies and Cus always gave them some. One day, the rednecks got drunk and showed their true colors by singing lynching songs. Cus was irate that his friend Murphy was cornered by the rednecks. So Cus got some of his black boxers and planned a mission to rescue his friend. "Do you hear what they're singing?" he told them. "We got to go get Murphy." The black soldiers were scared but Cus persuaded them and they "rescued" Murphy. Cus was so proud of that. He made it sound like he was a general and he had rallied his troops and got Murphy back home safe.

Cus told me he got nothing out of the Army because he was already self-disciplined. At one point while I was living with him I got a weird idea that maybe I should join the Army.

"What, are you crazy?" he shouted. "You want the military to think for you? You want to do everything they say? You want to go back to slavery?" That was the last time I ever mentioned that idea.

———

CUS WAS ALWAYS ACKNOWLEDGED as being one of the first trainers to concentrate on the psychology of his boxers. At various times
during his career he said that boxing was 50, 60, and once even 85
percent mental. So early in his career he began developing psychological theories of behavior that could be applied to boxing. One of the
first places he looked was the work of Sigmund Freud. "People talk
about me reading Freud, but all I ever read of him was ten chapters
in one of those paperback books I picked up somewhere," he told
Sports Illustrated. "I read those ten chapters [and then] it was getting technical so I put the book away." Freud "hadn't told me anything I didn't know already," he told another reporter.

Cus began my psychological training for real once I moved into
the house. The first thing he did was to give me a book by Peter
Heller called *"In This Corner . . . !"* It was a great book because it
was interviews with all-time great fighters. Cus thought that this
was essential reading because all these immortals were admitting
their fears in the book. Controlling fear and making it work for you
was the cornerstone of Cus's philosophy of life. Giants like Jack
Dempsey were as scared as I was. He's a Cancer like me, very emotional. But once he got into that ring, you would never think that he
was a frightened guy. Deep down he thought he was a coward, same
as me. Yet he was the face of ferocity when he was fighting. Ain't
that something?

Henry Armstrong was another guy who, like Dempsey, was a hobo
during the Great Depression. Riding the rails, getting to a new town,
fighting for food, getting beat up—that's how they learned to fight.
Armstrong would get up in the morning and run fifteen miles to
work and then run fifteen miles home and then he would train. You
know what his job was? Hitting spikes into railroad rails for eight
hours a day. Man. He was the only guy with three championships simultaneously, three out of twelve. Cus thought he was the epitome of
determination and will, who crushed his opponent's spirit.

But the best example of learning about fear was the Willie Ritchie story. That's how I learned to have steel nerves. Ritchie was a Polish lightweight who had the championship in 1912. He fought a guy who was a little bigger and it was a tough fight but they called it a draw. The promoter smacked Willie on his back and said, "Hey, you got lucky tonight, kid. You've got to fight a rematch in two weeks." Ritchie was petrified. He thought the guy had kicked his ass and he had gotten a gift. He was so scared that it took him an hour to tie his fucking shoes and put his shorts on and get in the gym and work out. At the weigh-in he was sweating. He couldn't eat, he thought he was sick, he thought he was going to get killed. As he was about to weigh in his opponent's manager came up and smacked him on the back and said, "Okay, we took it easy on you last time, tonight we're knocking you out quick." Ritchie was an emotional wreck, but he didn't show his fear to anybody. He was about to call the fight off but somehow he summoned up his discipline and got up on the scale. Then he waited for the other guy. After a few hours it was clear that his opponent wasn't showing. Ritchie got the whole purse. What Ritchie learned from that was no matter how frightened he was—and he was frightened like he was about to see Satan—his opponent was more afraid of him. When I read that story I knew I had that advantage, I knew how they felt and they didn't know how I felt. Even though I was afraid when I was fighting, I thought, "They're more afraid of me than I am of them."

Besides making me read the book, Cus gave me what he called "The Talk." Cus felt that most kids who want to be fighters hadn't learned how to cope emotionally. He thought that to teach a fighter, you had to first solve his emotional problems and do it in a way that the pupil is no longer embarrassed about feeling things like fear. Cus called that peeling away the layers of personality. His theories were very similar to those of Wilhelm Reich, a pupil of Freud's, who talked about a person's essential life force, orgone energy, getting bound throughout the body by an armoring process that had to be manipulated until the life force could be released. Once you peeled away the layers of childhood trauma and embarrassment, then you could be receptive to Cus's teachings.

I've heard a hundred different versions of Cus's fear rap, but the way he laid it out in the sixties when he was interviewed for a video that was produced by Jim Jacobs—who would go on to be my first manager—is really special.

"When I have a new boy, the first thing I do is give him a lecture. And although I don't expect him to remember, fully, the things I tell him, by repetition once I give him the complete lecture, I expect him, when circumstances present themselves related to the lecture, that they might possibly recall what I have said and therefore not be intimidated by the circumstances they come to face with," Cus said. "Now, the lecture of fear goes something like this: All people are afraid. Being afraid is a very normal, healthy thing. If an individual was not afraid, I would have to send them to a psychiatrist to find out what was wrong. Nature gave us fear in order to survive. And of course fear is our best friend. Without fear we would all die, we'd do something foolish or stupid, which would cause our death, or being crippled. But also, fear is something which has to be controlled. I always compare it to fire. Fear, like fire, must be controlled and, once it gets out of control, like fire, could destroy everything around, not only the individual—everything around you. So once you control fear like fire, you could make it work for you. Without fire we wouldn't have the civilization we now recognize, or recognize today. But the fighter who controls his fear can now function in a manner far over and beyond anything he was capable of before.

"No matter how ugly a person is, no matter whether he bathes or not, if he saves my life—if he's always there when I'm in trouble—then I forget about how obnoxious he is. I look upon him as my friend and accept him as such. Well, that's what fear is. Fear is your friend and nature gave us fear in order for us to survive. And I give the example of the deer crossing an open field and coming to the forest and instinct telling him danger is present in the trees, perhaps in the form of a mountain lion. At that moment the adrenal gland injects adrenaline into the bloodstream, the heart beats faster, enabling the deer to perform an extraordinary feat of agility. In the first leap, [the deer can] possibly jump thirty, forty feet, sufficient to get out of the immediate danger, and the natural asset of speed which nature gave it would save it. Now, we, as human beings, in my opinion, we tame these qualities, so they are somewhat dormant because we live in a civilized atmosphere, but nevertheless, faced with a situation that intuition tells us danger is present, these natural assets that nature gave us to survive come to the surface and if we don't panic, if we maintain the discipline and the control over it, we can use them and they not only will help us survive the particular instance, but continued success will give us a comfort that is so strong and a foundation so powerful that in time we can get to overcome almost anything."

"So you explain to your fighter that this feeling of fear, prior to a fight, is normal and healthy and that he shouldn't be apprehensive about it?" Jimmy asked.

"Not only that but before they have a fight, I tell them what they're going to experience. The night before his first fight, just say it's an amateur fight, he won't be able to sleep all night. I say, 'When you wake up in the morning, you're going to say, "How in the world am I going to fight? I didn't sleep last night."' The only consolation I could offer him is that his opponent went through the same thing. So in effect, it's an even fight. Secondly, when he gets in that corner and looks across the ring at his opponent, that fellow is going to be the biggest, most powerful person in the world. When he gets in the corner and loosens up, that fellow is going to look like the most experienced fighter, although it's his first fight. This is the imagination at work, exaggerating the obstacles. But if he remembers the things I tell him, he knows that I told him this was going to happen and then he faces this with confidence. And when he knows this and understands this, and confronts the type of situation I explained long before he gets into the ring, his opponent now is less intimidating. Hopefully some of my words will reach him in that fearful state, just before the bell rings."

Cus did get something out of his time in the Army. He was issued a paperback to read called *Psychology for the Fighting Man: What You Should Know About Yourself and Others*. It was published by the

National Research Council's Emergency Committee on Psychology and some of America's leading psychologists contributed to it, among them Gordon Allport and E. G. Boring of Harvard University. The book focused on the psychology of ordinary GIs, not their higher-level officers, and it was full of practical information on boosting morale and adjusting to Army life.

The book contained a frank discussion about fear. When you read it, you can see how it helped hone Cus's theories about both fear and the importance of traumatic childhood experiences. "The mental habits of childhood are usually carried on in more or less disguised form all through life. This is sometimes good and sometimes bad for the adult, depending on what sort of childhood he had." In chapter 9, the authors talk about how habit formation is an excellent stage of learning. "No action ever becomes automatic by learning in words how to perform it but without actually practicing it. But by repetition the operation of a machine or a rifle gets itself reduced to habit so that it becomes almost or entirely mechanical." This would form the basis of Cus's insistence that boxing is best learned through repetition and was echoed in Cus's training innovation called the "Willie Bag," which I'll get to later.

Cus didn't make these lectures seem abstract. He always brought in his own life experience and told his pupils that he, too, experienced fear. When he was about fourteen, there was a man in the Bronx who hid in lonely places and jumped out and attacked people. The newspapers called him the Gorilla Man. One night, Cus was late getting home and he decided to take a shortcut through a vacant lot with grass as high as Cus's head. He was walking down the path when he saw a murky figure in front of him. It looked like a giant with its arms spread out, ready to attack. Cus was sure it was the Gorilla Man. His first instinct was to get the hell out of there but then he checked himself. "If I run now, I'll never be able to take this shortcut again," he thought. So he confronted his fear and marched straight ahead. And the "Gorilla Man" was only a tree that had most of its branches cut off. In the darkness, its silhouette looked just like a gorilla's. Cus said that proved that there is nothing as bad as imagination. From then on, anytime he was confronted with an obstacle in life, he would say to himself, "That's just a tree in my path."

When Cus was twenty, he had his first fight in a gym. He was hanging around a gym, hitting the heavy bags, when a manager who was there seemed impressed and asked him if he'd like to box. He put Cus in with Baby Arizmendi, a Mexican fighter who trained at that gym. Arizmendi had beaten the great Henry Armstrong twice! "While I was waiting I experienced fear in the ring for the first time in my life," Cus told a reporter. "I couldn't understand what was making me feel this way. My heart was pounding. I thought it might be that I was afraid, but I wasn't sure. Going into that ring was like going to the electric chair."

Arizmendi beat the crap out of Cus, breaking his nose and closing his one good eye. He asked Cus if he wanted to go another round and Cus confronted his fear and they sparred some more. At the end Baby went over to Cus. "What a tough monkey you are!" he complimented him. It was an acknowledgment that Cus had learned to conquer his fear. Cus used that incident to make sure that his fighters were never ashamed of being afraid, that it was normal to feel fear.

Cus told me that in all his years in boxing, there were only two fighters who never experienced any fear. The first was a deaf mute Cus managed who would routinely take a horrible beating. The other guy was a Jewish boxer named Artie Diamond. Diamond was discovered when, on his first day as a newspaper peddler, he beat up an older man who had the corner Artie wanted. After a stint in the Navy, Artie came back and started training under Cus. But Cus realized he was not a normal guy when he was on the way to the ring for his first amateur bout. "I come into the ring and I'm holding the rope down and all of a sudden I hear a dog growling," Cus told one of his pupils. "I'm like, 'Who the hell has got a dog?' And I look around and it's Artie coming under the bottom rope, growling, frothing at his mouth." The bell rang and Artie charged out and gave his opponent a savage beating.

"Artie got hit to prove he wasn't afraid," Cus said. "Not that he was a macho man. He was just a maniac." Despite Artie's 18–2 amateur record, including fifteen straight KOs, Cus forced Artie to retire at twenty-two after a few years as a pro because he was taking too much unnecessary punishment. A few weeks later Artie and a few friends took out an armored truck in the South Bronx. In the struggle, Artie shot the guard in the head, paralyzing him for life. He was sent to Sing Sing to serve a seven-and-a-half-to-fifteen-year sentence. On his first day in prison, Artie was strolling through the yard smoking a cigar, when a big black inmate approached him.

"Hey, come here, good-looking." The black guy hissed.

Artie couldn't believe he was talking to him.

"White boy, I'm talking to you."

"How can I help you?" Artie said, playing dumb.

The black guy pulled Artie toward him and told him that he'd have a pleasant stay with all the cigars and contraband food he could want—as long as he'd be the black guy's number one bitch. Artie nodded agreement and took the black guy's head in his hands. He leaned over as if he was going to whisper sweet nothings in the guy's ear but he suddenly let out a bloodcurdling shriek and bit a large chunk of the guy's ear off. As the black guy ran away in pain, Artie calmly looked at his huge audience in the yard, spit out pieces of the ear, and snarled. Years later Artie would say, "Everybody was sitting there laughing and I turned around and I spit it at them. That was my only regret in my life. I should have chewed it and swallowed it and showed them how vicious I really was."

Artie was sent to the hole for a month, and on the day he got out he asked around to find out who were the bosses among the various ethnic groups in the prison. He then proceeded to beat the shit out of each one of them in one day. After eight years, Cus was able to get Artie out of jail by hiring him as José Torres's conditioning coach. I bet José listened to everything Artie said. Artie did a few more stints in jail and then he came out and got a job as head of security for a Spanish nightclub. He got involved in a dispute with a patron and he was shot once in the heart and died. Artie never had any fear. "He couldn't have died any other way," Cus said.

Besides learning to control his fear, Cus had a very unusual experience that first time he boxed the great Mexican Arizmendi. During the second round of that sparring session, suddenly Cus got what he called a "picture in my mind." He saw himself stepping to the side and throwing an uppercut that landed square on Baby's chin. He had become detached from his body in the middle of the fight. He became impervious to the blows that Arizmendi was landing, as if they were hitting someone else. It was like his mind was directing somebody else in the ring. Cus told me that he had another out-of-body experience like this one when he was lying down on his bed and suddenly he felt he was up in the ceiling looking down at himself.

From these experiences Cus realized that a key element for a fighter being successful was for him to act intuitively and impersonally, to rid himself of the baggage of his emotions in the ring. It wasn't just being alert, as his deaf and dumb fighters were because they didn't have the distractions of sound. More important was to develop an intuitive sense of what your opponent was going to do. If you know that a punch is coming at you a split second before it's thrown, then you can respond almost casually. You can start moving and the punch will miss you. Cus was all about projecting what you want to project. You always have to appear to be what your opponent can't be. You have to set the rules. He was all about abusing your opponent psychologically, confusing the enemy.

When Cus would talk to me about all this, he stressed that what he meant by "intuitive thinking" was acting unconsciously. Intuitive thinking wasn't distorted by any emotional interference. You became like a robot or a computer. Like Nike used to say in that commercial: Just do it. Or like Cus used to tell us: the body knows things that the mind doesn't know it knows. You have to do it in a split second—you can't have a chance to think about it. If you do, you'll get hit.

Years after Cus had developed this theory of controlling your emotions and getting to an intuitive state, he talked to Norman Mailer about it one day in Mailer's house in Stockbridge. Cus recounted that conversation to a Mailer biographer. "We talked at length and probably more deeply about the mind and emotions in boxing than we had before. I gave him my definition of a real pro: a man who can be completely impersonal, who doesn't allow his emotions to get involved with anything he does, who's able to be constantly objective. I don't like to say a lot of these things to just anyone, because people say, 'He's some kind of screwball.' But with someone like Norman it's okay. Anyway, while we were talking he suddenly excused himself and came back with a book, *Zen [in] the Art of Archery*. He asked if I'd read it, and I told him, no, I'd never heard of Zen. He said, 'Are you sure? Because you don't know it, but you practice Zen.' Later, having read the book several times, I realized that the principles I use do involve that kind of thing, developing an impersonal state without interference from any emotions. We talked about fear, because when you become impersonal you control fear, separate it from your mind and body. Because of my concentration I've been hit by blows and never felt them. I was there but outside my body: I could see myself throwing punches, just like I was watching somebody else, and it happens automatically, intuitively."

By the time I came to Cus, he was using that Zen book as part of his curriculum. Cus probably thought it was too hard for me to read when I was fourteen, so he read it to me. The book is the account of a German philosophy professor who studied a form of Japanese archery for six years in Japan in the 1920s. And in listening to Cus read the book's introduction, by Daisetz Suzuki, a famous Zen scholar, I knew that this wasn't just some lessons to apply to boxing but that they were life lessons as well.

"One of the most significant features we notice in the practice of archery, and in fact of all the arts as they are studied in Japan and probably also in other Far Eastern countries, is that they are not intended for utilitarian purposes only or for purely aesthetic enjoyments, but are meant to train the mind; indeed, to bring it into contact with the ultimate reality. Archery is, therefore, not practiced solely for hitting the target; the swordsman does not wield the sword just for the sake of outdoing his opponent; the dancer does not dance just to perform certain rhythmical movements of the body," Mr. Suzuki wrote. "The mind has first to be attuned to the Unconscious. If one really wants to be master of an art, technical knowledge of it is not enough. One has to transcend technique so that the art becomes an 'artless art' growing out of the Unconscious. In the case of archery, the hitter and the hit are no longer two opposing objects, but are one reality. The archer ceases to be conscious of himself as the one who is engaged in hitting the bull's-eye which confronts him. This state of unconsciousness is realized only when, completely empty and rid of the self, he becomes one with the perfecting of his technical skill. . . . Zen is the 'everyday mind.' . . .

"Man is a thinking reed but his great works are done when he is not calculating and thinking. 'Childlikeness' has to be restored with long years of training in the art of self-forgetfulness. When this is attained, man thinks yet he does not think. He thinks like the showers coming down from the sky; he thinks like the waves rolling on the ocean; he thinks like the stars illuminating the nightly heavens; he thinks like the green foliage shooting forth in the relaxing spring breeze. Indeed, he is the showers, the ocean, the stars, the foliage. When a man reaches this stage of 'spiritual' development he is a Zen artist of life. He does not need like the painter, a canvas, brushes and paint; nor does he require, like the archer, the bow and arrow and target. He has his limbs, body, head and other parts. His hands and feet are the brushes and the whole universe is the canvas on which he depicts his life for seventy, eighty, or even ninety years. This picture is called 'history.' "

CUS USED A VARIETY of methods to implement these theories. One time an amateur boxer of his named Paul Mangiamele was doing well in a fight and he got a little cocky, tied up his opponent and looked over to his corner, where Cus was sitting ringside. He winked and mouthed the words "I got this." When the fight was over, Cus let him have it.

"Don't you ever do that again!" Cus screamed. "You don't go into the ring to fuck around. You keep your focus. You take your mind off what you're doing and you're going to get hurt." That was the last time Paul pulled something like that.

My roommate Frankie Mincelli used to get all worked up before his fights. So Cus used one of our communal dinners to try to calm him down. "You got to tell yourself to completely relax, to be able to see everything that's going on. A man who is thinking and worrying about getting hit is not gonna have a good sense of anticipation," Cus said. "He will, in fact, get hit. And when you get hit, that's when you gotta be calmest. A professional fighter has got to learn how to hit and not get hit, and at the same time be exciting."

Cus used to give me lessons on how to have out-of-body experiences. I would be sitting down and watching television and he'd say, "Let's do a session." And he'd sit next to me and then he'd say, "Transcend. Focus. Relax until you see yourself looking at yourself. Tell me when you get there."

Learning how to detach yourself from your feelings was essential for me. It's like teaching yourself to be a professional liar. If I can't separate from my emotions in the ring, then I'm just a punk. I'm too emotional out there. I might hit a guy with a hard punch and then I get scared if he doesn't go down. So learning that Zen detachment was definitely a survival skill for me.

Besides controlling your fear and detaching your emotions in the ring, Cus was a big believer in using your mind to bolster your confidence. Cus pushed the idea of doing affirmations, of not only thinking positively but affirming it daily. Near the end of the Depression there were two authors who wrote about how you could use positive thinking to succeed in life. In 1936, Dale Carnegie wrote a bestseller called *How to Win Friends and Influence People*. A year later a guy named Napoleon Hill wrote a self-improvement book called *Think and Grow Rich*. In the early fifties Dr. Norman Vincent Peale wrote a huge bestseller that was a Christian version of positive thinking titled *The Power of Positive Thinking*. But Cus didn't think much of those guys. He believed that any positive thinking had to begin in your unconscious mind, just like in the Zen archery exercises.

Cus had unearthed a book, *Self-Mastery Through Conscious Autosuggestion*, by a French pharmacist named Émile Coué, that was published in the United States in 1922. It's easy to see why Cus loved this cat. Coué was a brilliant guy who ran his pharmacy from 1882 until 1910, when he retired and opened up a clinic where he treated people for free using optimistic autosuggestion. As a pharmacist, he had seen how the placebo effect worked on some of his customers, so he figured that a steady diet of affirmations could do the same. "I have never cured anyone in my life. All I do is show people how they can cure themselves," Coué said.

Coué thought that to cure disease, a person's imagination had to be tapped and directed. "You possess within you an unlimited power, your unconscious being, commonly called imagination. It acts on matter if we but know how to domesticate it. The imagination may be compared to a horse, improperly harnessed to your carriage, and without bridle or reins; that horse may perform all sorts of foolish tricks and cause your death. But, harness him properly, drive him with a firm hand, and he will go where you want him to. It is the same with your unconscious self. You must direct it for your own good." Sounds a lot like Cus's fear rap.

The way that you direct your imagination is by repeating a simple affirmation. " 'EVERY DAY, IN EVERY WAY, I AM GETTING BETTER AND BETTER.' This formula must be repeated in a low voice (with eyes closed, body in a position that permits of relaxing the muscular system—say in bed or in an easy chair) and in a monotonous tone, as if one were reciting a litany. The words must be repeated twenty times, morning and night. You may use a string with twenty knots on it which serves as an aid in counting just as a rosary does. This material aid is important; it insures mechanical recitation, which is essential. While articulating these words which are registered by the unconscious, you must not think of anything in particular, neither of your illness nor of your troubles. You must be passive, with only the desire that all may be for the best; the formula in every way has a general effect. Your desire must express itself without passion, gently and without exertion of your will, but with absolute faith and confidence. . . . The will must not be exercised at all at that moment! Imagination only must come into play; that is the great motive power, infinitely more active than will power which is usually invoked. Have confidence in yourself. . . . Believe firmly that all will be well with you.

"Autosuggestion is *implanting an idea in one's self through one's self.* . . . Autosuggestion is nothing else but hypnotism and may be defined as *influence of the imagination on the moral and physical being of man.* THE WILL MUST NOT BE BROUGHT INTO PLAY IN PRACTICING AUTOSUGGESTION because it is not in accord with the imagination. . . . The key to my method is in the knowledge that the *imagination is superior to the will.* If both go together in the same direction, as in saying for instance: *'I will* and *I can'* they are perfectly in accord; otherwise the *imagination always wins* over the *will.* . . . We possess in *ourselves* an *incalculable force* which is often prejudicial to us, if we handle it unconsciously. If, on the contrary, we direct it in a *conscious and wise* manner, *it gives us the mastery of ourselves* and enables us, not only to save ourselves from physical and mental ills and ailments, but also to help others; and to live in comparative happiness under any and all conditions."

I started in with the affirmations as soon as I moved in with Cus. "Day by day, in every way, I'm getting better and better. Day by day, in every way . . ." (That was Cus's English translation of Coué's phrase. Some people said "Every day" instead of "Day by day.")

Coué was adamant that a parent should start his child on this course very early in life. "Parents should wait until the child is asleep; then father or mother should noiselessly enter the room, approach the bed, and murmur to the child twenty times over, all the things you want the child to do or to be as regards health, sleep, work, application, conduct, etc.; then retire as noiselessly as you came, taking great care not to awaken the child. . . . When the child sleeps his body and his conscious being are at rest; his Unconscious self, however, is awake. You speak therefore to the latter alone and, as it is very credulous, it accepts what you say without contradiction and little by little the child becomes what the parents desire it to be," Coué wrote. And that's what Cus did! He used to come into my room when I had just fallen asleep and repeat the affirmations to me.

Coué spent his life curing his patients with his affirmations. But

Cus was using them to build up his fighters' confidence. I used to do my affirmations all day long. I loved hearing myself talk about myself. Cus used to say, "You take a guy who has all the greatest qualities of success, beautiful body, beautiful looks, great sexual endowment, everything is perfect. But you take away his confidence and you put him out in life and he will fail. On the other hand, you take somebody who has nothing, absolutely nothing, and you give them confidence and you throw him in the world, he will succeed. Confidence breeds success and success breeds confidence. Confidence applied properly will supersede genius." I'm sure all this is why I've got some issues going on right now. He was making me think I'm God.

Cus wasn't the first manager to realize how important confidence was in building up a fighter. Jack Dempsey was managed by Jack "Doc" Kearns, a hustler and a con man. The origin of the term "con man" is confidence man, a person who gains your confidence and then rips you off. Kearns realized the fragile nature of Dempsey's ego and he went out of his way in building it up. "If Kearns said I could beat a polar bear, I'd know that it was true. That's how Kearns affected me in those days," Dempsey said later. "I had talent, I know that. But I had the greatest confidence a man could have. I got it from Doc Kearns."

Cus didn't stop with affirmations. He plastered the walls of our gym with self-empowering sayings and poems. One of those was a poem called "Don't Quit." It was originally titled "Keep Going," and it was credited to the poet Edgar Guest, one of the first widely syndicated newspaper writers in America. He had a feel-good column, "The Breakfast Table Chat," and on March 4, 1921, he published the poem:

When things go wrong, as they sometimes will
and the road you're trudging seems all uphill,

When the funds are low and the debts are high
and you want to smile, but you have to sigh;

When care is pressing you down a bit,
rest if you must—but don't quit.

Life is queer with its twists and turns,
as every one of us sometimes learns.

And many a failure turns about
when he might have won had he stuck it out;

Don't give up, though the pace seems slow—
you may succeed with another blow.

Often the goal is nearer than it seems
to a faint and faltering man.

Often the struggler has given up
when he might have captured the victor's cup,

And he learned too late, when the night slipped down,
how close he was to the golden crown.

Success is failure turned inside out—
the silver tint of the clouds of doubt.

And you never can tell how close you are.
it may be near when it seems afar;

So stick to the fight when you're hardest hit.
It's when things seem worst that you mustn't quit.

Cus was constantly on me about strengthening my mind. "Your mind is not your friend, I hope you know that, right?" he'd say. "You have to fight with your brain, you have to put it in its place." For Cus, a person's mind was a muscle. The more you exercised it, the stronger it got. He also said that your mind would constantly play tricks on you. A guy could be in great shape but if he doesn't want to fight or he's afraid of his opponent, he'll convince himself that he's tired and find a convenient spot on the canvas to lie down.

Cus always said that the best way to teach was to teach by example, and he did that in dealing with the cataract that had developed in his bad eye. Every day he'd do his affirmations and concentrate on healing his eye. Then he'd cover his good eye and say, "I can see certain things. It's getting better." Cus was totally against conventional medicine. He agreed with Coué that the mind could cure any illness.

For Cus the key to controlling your mind was to develop a great sense of discipline. He would always say that discipline was "doing what you hate to do but doing it like you loved it." He was like a monk! That must be why I'm crazy today, living my life like that, suppressing my desires, just working out and jerking off. Man. When you develop that level of discipline, then you become a professional in Cus's eyes. It's fascinating to listen to an exchange between Cus and Muhammad Ali discussing the definition of "professionalism" for a show that Jim Jacobs produced.

ALI: We're talking about different fighters and you say that Floyd Patterson was a professional. I mean, ain't everybody who works for a salary or who makes money boxing considered professionals? CUS: Well, they may be considered professional, but I don't think so. The average man associates professionalism with confidence. If he's a good fighter, he has skills, he's a professional, that person fights for money. But my opinion of a professional is entirely different. I believe a person is a professional when they can make themselves do what needs to be done in order to accomplish the objective he sets out to deliver, in boxing or anything else. If I go in to fight you and I'm afraid of you and as long as I have the discipline to make myself do what my intelligence, my experience and my training have taught me to do, in order to beat you, regardless of how I feel within, I will beat you, if I'm able to do this. This requires discipline and the type of discipline I've just described is what makes a professional. So long as a man can do what is required to be done, regardless of how he feels within, that man is a professional in whatever field he is in. Once a man becomes a professional, he requires a certain amount of experience in order to know all the different facets of the sport or competition that he may be in, in this case it's boxing. Well, after he acquires these, then he must be professional enough, in other words he must have the discipline to apply these things in the manner that's necessary to get the results that he wants. With one opponent, he may use one or more of these things.

ALI: Would you consider me a professional? CUS: Well, I think you became a professional, I think you became a professional the night you fought Chuvalo, this is my opinion.

ALI: You mean all the Sonny Liston fights, the Floyd Patterson fights and all of the Olympics and all of this, wouldn't make me a professional? CUS: Positively not. But I'll tell you why I think you became a professional that night. That night you deliberately absorbed punches without flinching, which indicated a well-developed discipline. You didn't react in the way you normally would have reacted. You did exactly what you wanted to do without regard to the physical effect on your person.

Cus was also a strong believer in creative visualization. A person who aspired to being a champion should be that entity he wanted to achieve. If I wanted to be a heavyweight champion, I had to start living the life of a heavyweight champion, even if I was only fourteen years old. I was a champion in my mind at fourteen because I lived the life of a champion fighter! Training hard every day, thinking like a Roman gladiator. Cus told me that I had to be in a state of war, but I always had to be calm and relaxed—to not let people know you're in a state of war, because you don't act as if a state of war exists until war is at hand. At the same time, Cus also used to warn me about being too calm and confident. "The greater an individual is, the more insecure he is," he told me. Security was death. "If a man is secure in his position, then he's in the position to lose his position." Cus was so deep.

Cus was teaching all of us how to train our minds but every once in a while he'd start talking about the extent to which he had been able to train his own mind. And it was some far-out stuff. He would always tell me that he knew what I was thinking better than I did. He said that he could see the wheels go round in almost everyone's mind who he had studied sufficiently. To him it was like playing poker with a guy for a weekend. By the time he'd gone through hand after hand for that amount of time, even if his opponent was trying to hide his thinking from Cus, he was unintentionally revealing it by the way he was playing and the way he would bet.

Cus said that when he was working with fighters he'd been with for a while and he knew how their minds worked, he would get calm, go into that state of being outside, watching himself, and he'd get a picture in his mind and he'd know exactly how any of his fighters would respond to a situation. He'd see those wheels going around in his head and it was as if he was his fighter—that he was inside his head! This is one heavy dude.

But Cus went even further with his black magic shit. When Cus had his gym on 14th Street, he would take his binoculars and look out the window and pick out someone at random who was walking on the sidewalk below. Then he'd give them what he called "The Look." And with his powers of concentration he would be able to make that guy stop, look around, cross the street, whatever he wanted them to do. He was practicing telepathy. I actually saw him do this shit. Cus was a very enlightened guy. He wanted to know why, when you're thinking about someone, they just show up. He wanted to be able to make that connection at any time.

Cus also claimed that he could get his fighters to throw punches by telepathy. He told Al Caruso about the time that Rocky Graziano was fighting with his mother and brother and sister in the crowd. Rocky had his opponent down with his first shot, but when the round was over, Rocky wanted to quit in his corner. He had no confidence. Cus knew that with his relatives there, Rocky would continue the fight if Cus pushed him back into the ring. He did that and in the second round Rocky knocked the guy down twice. And when the round was over, Rocky came back and said, "Cus, I can't do it. I'm too tired. I want to quit." And Cus said, "Get the hell out there" and then he pushed him out again. But he saw that Rocky was too timid to throw some serious punches so he used his will and got Rocky to throw his right and his opponent was knocked out.

I thought it was strange that for a guy who was so into you

controlling your own destiny by working on your mind-set, Cus believed in astrology. Cus was convinced that he could tell if you were going to be a good fighter from your astrological sign. Al Caruso brought a friend of his to the Gramercy one day and right away Cus asked the guy his sign. "Gemini," the guy said. "Well, what do you do for a living?" Cus asked. "I'm a carpenter," the guy responded. "Go back and be a carpenter," Cus said, and walked away. But when he met Matthew Hilton, the Canadian light middleweight, he popped the question to Hilton. "I'm a Capricorn," Matthew said. "You're going to be a champion," Cus predicted. And he was right. I passed Cus's test. I'm a Cancer, and every heavyweight champion was born under only three signs and Cancer was one of them.

Another irony was that for a guy who was so into controlling your fear, Cus was well-known for his aversion to flying. Whenever he'd have to go to one of my tournaments, he'd always take the train. But he had a very rational answer when the guys would kid him about his fear of flying. "Look, Cus, when it's your time to go, it's your time to go," my housemate Tom Patti once said.

Cus just smiled. "Yeah, but when it's the pilot's time to go, then we all go."

4

With my psychological training in full swing, Cus began to work on my boxing skills. And he brought the same innovation to the physical side of boxing. Cus devised a new style of boxing, a style that his enemies dismissed with the name "peekaboo." The style was based on Cus's admiration for the way Slapsie Maxie Rosenbloom boxed. Slapsie fought 274 times and he was knocked out only twice, while winning 207 times. He learned fighting the old-fashioned way; at first he got his ass kicked, so he became a technical fighter and kept his hands up to protect himself. He'd stand in the middle of the ring and his opponents would throw punches but he'd slip every single one of them. He wasn't a hard puncher, but he would slap the shit out of great fighters, just slap them to death.

Maxie made good fighters look bad but he was a boring fighter. So Cus modified Maxie's style to enable his fighters to go forward and become aggressive counterpunchers. In 1959, Cus told a *Life* magazine reporter the origins of the peekaboo style. It came out of the fear that every boxer exhibits. "To stop that fear you gotta be protected— not part of the time, not most of the time, but all of the time. You can't gamble by using the open stance. Because every time you gamble and lose you get hurt. And when a fighter gets hurt, he's intimidated, he thinks he's tired, pooped. He covers up. Now, in my style you cover up from the start. You never gamble. The right arm is always protecting the liver, the left the solar plexus. The hands are protecting the chin. When you flick out with your left, the arm works like a piston. When you move, you move like an owl. Then suddenly you're not being hit and that means you're not being hurt. And when you're not being hurt is when boxing becomes fun. As soon as it's fun for a fighter, nothing's going to stop him."

Cus was mocked in the press and dubbed "Cautious Cus," but his niece Betty said that caution was a family trait, along with being prepared for any event. Al Caruso, one of the first fighters to learn this style from Cus, attributed it to Cus's cautious nature too. But he also recognized the aggressive component Cus added. "The peekaboo style is not designed to make a guy miss, miss, miss, miss. You make them miss once and twice and then you get in," Caruso said. When a guy keeps missing punches, Cus knew it would have devastating effects on their psyche. A monstrous puncher who can't connect with anything and then is on the receiving end of a counter becomes intimidated. And their greatest asset all of a sudden becomes a weakness.

Some people compared the style to that of a turtle. But Cus got his inspiration from cats. Cus told Eugene "Cyclone" Hart, a pro fighter he was training, "I would wake up sometimes and think about how a cat fights. I used to have a cat. The cat would claw at me and I'd try to grab his paws and he'd hit me with three hundred punches before you can grab him." Cus equated everything with fighting. He'd watch two roaches fight, and he'd say, "Did you see that? He's jabbing." Cats are very agile. They move side to side, they feint. They're the best killing machines on the planet. Cus said I moved like a cat.

It's not easy using the peekaboo. It's a lot of hard work because you have to keep moving your head to slip punches. "Move your head, move your head"—that was his mantra. And not every fighter found it easy to keep their hands up. My housemate Tom Patti's father, Anthony, first trained with Cus in the forties. When Anthony kept bugging Cus for a fight, Cus said, "You haven't learned how to keep your

hands up yet. The day you learn to hold them up, I'll get you a fight."
And then he had Anthony train in front of a mirror with his right
hand tied around his neck so he wouldn't keep dropping it.

You never knew where Cus would get his inspiration from—cats,
cockroaches. When Cus was down south trying to put together a fight
for Floyd Patterson, one of his opponent's rich backers introduced
Cus to an amazing guy named Bobby Lamar "Lucky" McDaniel, who
had a unique talent. McDaniel took a BB gun with the sights removed. Then he'd take a metal washer that had a hole in the center
like a doughnut. He'd throw that up in the air and he was able to hit
all around the outside. Then he was able to take the washer and hit it
around the inside of the hole with the BBs. Then he would take a
piece of membrane or tissue and put it on there and he was able to put
the BB right through it. But the amazing thing was he could teach
anyone to do this within an hour and they'd never miss. That was
some *Matrix* shit. It turned out that McDaniel was training the unconscious mind of his pupils, similar to how a Zen monk taught
archery.

Cus realized that if you did that in an area with a dark background you could watch the BB go through the hole. The human
brain was that amazing. A BB moves somewhere around four hundred feet per second. No human hand moves that fast. So Cus's theory was that if your eye could see the BB, then why can't your eye see
a punch coming? You get hit with it because you haven't trained your
body in sequence with your brain to move from that punch. You want
the guy to be already in motion with that punch; then, as it's coming,
he can't pull back, and he'll miss and you'll counter him. Cus then
understood that he could train a fighter to slip punches, and he came
up with something he called the slip bag.

Actually Cus's brother Nick, a chiropractor who lived on a farm on
Long Island, devised the slip bag. Floyd Patterson described the bag
in his autobiography: "Nick took a regular leather speed bag, but instead of having it blown up, he filled it with about ten pounds of sand.
It was hung from a chain from the ceiling so that it was suspended
about at the height of my own face when I crouched. I'd push the bag

forward and wait until it swung back toward me. I'd try to wait until it almost touched my face. The idea was to 'slip' the bag, just as a fighter slips a punch being thrown at him."

Cus started me on the slip bag right away. You had to both slip and weave so you wouldn't get hit by the bag on its way back. It was a U-shaped movement. It was hard to do at first, but I got used to it and became pretty proficient at it.

Besides the slip bag, Cus also hung a clothesline between two walls and the fighters had to bob and weave, up and down, back and forth, crouching low to get underneath it. One of Cus's favorite moves to counterpunch was a move where you'd jump to the left and then throw an uppercut. Cus told Al Caruso that he got that move from sidestepping into a revolving door in an office building in Manhattan.

But the most innovative training invention of Cus's was what he called the Willie Bag. He came up with this device when José Torres was training to fight Willie Pastrano. The Willie was five mattresses strapped to a frame. The front mattress had an outline sketch of a man on it, and various parts of the body were numbered as targets. Number 1 was a left hook to the jaw, 2 was a right hook to the jaw, 3 was a left uppercut, 4 was a right uppercut, 5 was a left hook to the liver, 6 was a right hook to the spleen, 7 was a jab to the head, and 8 was a jab to the solar plexus. Cus then made a tape of his voice calling out numbers. The boxer would deliver a punch to the corresponding number on the Willie. At first, Cus's voice would call out one punch every five seconds. But as the tape progressed, the tempo increased. Again the idea was to get to a Zen state where by sheer repetition you'd act on instinct, you'd be on the outside, doing it without thinking about it.

Cus first thought about creating this when he came across a European pianist who developed a system for teaching piano. The Willie Bag was also inspired by Cus's trips to racetracks, where jockeys would whip their horses in sensitive areas and the horse would react to the whipping and run faster. Back in the forties, a friend of his developed a technique for improving the typing speed of office secretaries. He recorded an album that dictated sentences, slow at first, and then increasing the tempo as the typists improved their speed. Cus spoke about his innovation in a documentary about José Torres.

CUS: This apparatus develops the speed, power, accuracy, coordination, and stamina. As a result of using this apparatus, it took about six weeks to two months to build up, so that Torres was able to throw a six-punch combination in two-fifths of a second. INTERVIEWER: That's so hard to believe. CUS: Of course, but I had the stopwatch and in the presence of all the newspapermen, I timed him five or six times consecutively. Now the question was brought by a reporter, What good is this when Pastrano is not stationary? So I pointed out to him that Pastrano must remain stationary at least for one second sometimes, and if Torres is in a position to punch, all he needs is two-fifths of a second to get up four or five blows.

What was great about this system was that it could be used during a fight. Cus could be in his boxer's corner yelling out random numbers and the other trainer and fighter would have no idea what the numbers meant.

Cus was very big on throwing short punches. They have to travel shorter distances and they have more impact when they connect. Cus thought that punching hard didn't have anything to do with a person's physical strength. He thought that it was all about precise, controlled emotion. Another technique Cus taught was throwing combinations in rapid succession. He used to tell me, "The biggest effect you'll get out of your punches will be when you make two punches sound like one." He thought speed was energy. The closest you can get to that *POP*, where two punches sound like one—that was perfection to him. Cus also thought that people only got knocked down by punches that they didn't see. So the element of surprise was also a big component of boxing. Speed, timing, movement, precision, and the element of surprise, all delivered with a relaxed, confident demeanor while under fire. That was the ultimate.

Cus was so ahead of his time. He hung around with Dr. Robert Gross, who, with his wife, Joy, cofounded the Pawling Health Manor in upstate New York. Cus learned about state-of-the-art nutrition and supplements from them. He also learned some elementary chiropractic techniques from his brother Nick. I was working so hard once that I threw my back out. Cus had me hang my leg over the staircase and told me to relax, and he cracked my back and then my neck. One time Cus worked on me so hard that I couldn't walk the next morning, and then I had to go to a licensed chiropractor.

NOW THAT I WAS LIVING in the house, I had access to all the old fight films 24/7. Some days I would watch them for ten hours at a time. I was getting my Ph.D. in boxing history. And I started to idolize some of those old-time fighters. I loved Dempsey. I loved that he was extremely aggressive, but what attracted me more to Dempsey was that he was very famous and very rich at the time. Dempsey was a great dresser and all the prominent women of his time were fans of his. He was bigger than boxing, bigger than sports back then, bigger than Babe Ruth.

I also admired Joe Gans. Gans was the first African American world champ in the twentieth century. He was considered one of the greatest lightweights of all time and was known as the "Old Master." But what impressed me the most about him was the way that the white racist reporters around the turn of the century wrote about him. They considered him a god because no one could beat him. He never lost a fight legitimately until he contracted tuberculosis, which eventually killed him. All the other losses on his record were because he threw fights to take care of his family. But everyone knew no one could beat him. Every now and then you would have white fighters who had pride and believed in themselves and said, "No man is going to take a dive for me. I can beat any man in the world in a fair fight." And he would knock them out so easy it was funny. Gans was less threatening than Jack Johnson. He knew how to get around—he knew his place, so to speak—but he was masterful.

Benny Leonard was another lightweight I adored. He was a real arrogant prick who transcended boxing. Leonard didn't take shit from anyone. During World War I all the big boxers trained at a gym owned by a German guy who claimed that the Jews caused the war.

Plenty of tough Jewish boxers trained there and they didn't say shit, but Benny was the man. He left the German guy's gym and went to Stillman's to train, which was owned by a Jewish guy but it wasn't doing well. But when Leonard left, everybody, even the non-Jews, followed him to Stillman's. I was attracted to fighters who weren't only great technicians but were leaders too. Guys like Gans and Leonard were only 130 pounds but they were big boys, little giants, in and out of the ring.

Cus and I would talk about the old fighters for hours and hours. You know what we talked about a lot? Fighters who were child champions, guys like Jimmy McLarnin and Georges Carpentier, guys who fought as babies. Georges Carpentier fought his first pro fight when he was fourteen years old. He fought anybody and everybody. He was champion in every weight division in Europe by the age of nineteen.

Cus loved Henry Armstrong. "Constant attack, no letup, moving his head with a good defense. That's what Armstrong would do, break his opponent's will, destroy his spirit, make all his causes a fucking lie," Cus said. Cus knew him very well. He knew all the old fighters. When all the old fighters saw him, they called him "Mr. Cus." Take Beau Jack. Cus loved that guy, he was his favorite lightweight. He was fighting one time and he slipped and dislocated his knee. The referee went to talk to the other guy's cornermen and Beau Jack jumped up, hopping to the guy, ready to fight. So every time Beau Jack would walk by Cus, Cus would take his hat off and say, "Listen, I take my hat off to that man. He fought on one leg, hopping to his opponent. I've never seen bravery like that."

Cus was so in love with these old fighters that he would make excuses for some of their behavior. Jack Dempsey would smoke a cigar when he fought and Cus would say something like "Back then they liked to have a cigar in their mouth as a symbol of success, but he never lit it." I knew that was a lie. He would use only the qualities of a champion that would inspire me and make me do the right thing. They didn't have any bad qualities, they were perfect. He would impress on me how vicious and mean they were in the ring but they were so calm and relaxed doling out punishment. I used to get so excited hearing him tell these stories—how this guy went over here and fought this great guy. How this black fighter went there by himself, even with all these white guys saying they were going to kill him, and he goes there and he wins.

Cus was always about me being a warrior. "If you don't have the spiritual warrior in you," he said, "you'll never be a fighter, I don't care how big or strong you are." He was constantly reinforcing that theme by talking about great warriors from antiquity. I didn't know who they were so I'd hear Cus mention a name like Alexander the Great or Genghis Khan and talk about them like they were the shit so I'd be interested in finding out who they were and I'd look into them. We'd talk about history and he would mention names like Hannibal and say he conquered Italy and I'd run to the encyclopedia. These figures from antiquity became my role models. I read about the Punic Wars, I read about the Venetian wars, I read about how these guys conquered by force and they fought among their brothers, and sisters too, for power. I quickly learned that power was worth dying and killing for.

I heard people talking about Machiavelli and quoting him and I got into him. I read about Charles Martel, Clovis, Shaka Zulu, the Jugurthine War. I admired Vercingetorix. He never got his shot because Caesar killed him, but before that he was a magnificent warrior. Cus talked to me about Spartacus. He explained to me that the Africans and the Italians had been fighting wars since the beginning of time. He said that's why Sicilians got the reputation of being black, because they interbred with a lot of African warriors in antiquity.

Cus was a great storyteller. He would talk about such minute things but he would make it sound like an earth-shattering event. He'd get all of us so excited, so engrossed in every word he was saying. And Cus talked with such enthusiasm because enthusiasm is contagious and people will do things when they get enthused. To the day he died he was so enthusiastic. He would talk about a shitty little slice of pizza from Catskill like it was cooked by Wolfgang Puck. "I've been all over the world, and this is the best pizza I ever tasted!"

Everything was the best in the world. He made the tiniest thing so big. He could take the most boring subject and make it exciting. He had that power.

Cus was a master salesman. That guy made me believe I was the heavyweight champion the first time I met him. What kind of salesman is that? He put me on this fucking mission. I'm just this dumbass kid, I don't know how I'm going to do this shit. But it was so adventurous I romanticized it. And why not? I'm reading about all these boxing legends and he's telling me that I could be one of them. He told me, "You'll make everybody forget them and the only reason people will know them is that you'll have to tell them about them." He used to tell me that all the fucking time. This guy had me hungering for glory like a mad dog. I would do anything—cheat, lie, steal—I had to get there, to that place.

One of the reasons I was so devoted was that I knew Cus had my back. Cus was hard and cold and talked about racism in this country as if he were a bitter black man. He considered himself a nigga as an Italian kid who grew up with a lot of prejudice directed at him from the Irish in his neighborhood in the Bronx. Cus had a big chip on his shoulder. He used to say even slaves were worth some money but "an Italian ain't worth two dimes. At least the slaves ate. They didn't feed the Italians. They starved to death." When his father got sick, they couldn't take him to a real doctor. They had to wait for some little Italian medicine man to come to the house carrying his little box on the top of his bicycle.

Nobody made me more conscious of being a black man than Cus. "They think they're better than you, Mike," he told me about white people. And he backed up his words with action. A few months after I moved in, Cus was hosting the South African boxing team, which, during apartheid, was all white. The first thing Cus did was to go to them and say, "There's a young black boy in this house and he's our family member. You treat him with the same respect you treat us, you understand?" He said it respectfully but he said it deadly. And they said, "Yes, sir."

That touched me to my heart. How could I not love this guy? All he talked about was how great I could become, how I could improve myself day by day, in every way.

You know what Cus found out about me early on. "Oh, you're a chameleon, aren't you?" he said to me one day. He said that because when I would come downstairs after hours and hours of watching the old fighters that he knew, I started talking like them and I would imitate their fighting styles. I even morphed into Cus's personality. I didn't play—I was dead serious about training.

Many nights Camille would be upstairs while Cus and I sat downstairs and plotted out our conquest of the world. We hadn't done shit. I hadn't even had an amateur fight yet, but we're talking about traveling to Europe as royalty, how "no" will be a foreign word to me, if I just listened to Cus. Who talks like that? This was some sick shit. Imagine a kid hears, " 'No' will be a foreign word to you." A white guy telling him that shit too. And the white guy seems to have some juice because you got guys like Norman Mailer, who's constantly on TV and in the papers, and guys like Budd Schulberg all showing him mad respect. Can you believe that shit? Two bums, a has-been and a fucking slum dweller, sitting in a room in upstate New York, plotting world domination.

5

October 2, 1980, was a black day for Cus. A few of us had driven up to Albany to watch the Ali–Holmes fight on closed-circuit TV. Muhammad Ali was like a god in the house. Cus thought that nobody in the world had the same competitive spirit as Ali. He was the quintessential fighter, not just because of his skills but because of his whole psychological perspective. "Ali is the greatest because he loves himself," Cus said. Cus loved people who were outrageous and unbelievable, guys who would shit talk like he did. He would have loved Kanye West. "This guy knows what he's talking about," he'd probably say.

Every day Cus would tell me I'm the most fierce, ferocious fighter the world has known, that if I would just listen to him, I'd be invincible. That word struck me to my core. Cus would talk about mean fighters but he would talk about pedigree fighters too, like Beau Jack. But when he talked about Ali it was on a whole other level.

"Ali looks more like a model than he does a heavyweight champ, right?" he'd tell me. "But if I take my shotgun and hit him with both barrels, BOOM, if he's got anything left, I had better get the hell out of the way because he's coming straight at me."

I would hear that kind of talk a lot between Cus and his older friends who were in their seventies. "That guy? You gotta kill him to beat him." We don't talk about fighters that way anymore.

As much as Cus loved Ali, he disliked Holmes. Holmes was a great fighter, but he came after Ali and he just wasn't Cus's type. Maybe Cus had some kind of vendetta with the people who represented him. All I know is that Cus told me that nothing else mattered except training and being the best fighter in the world. "That's your main objective," he'd say. "We have to knock Larry Holmes out. I don't want to hear any excuses; I just want to see results." Your value as a human being meant nothing. The only thing that mattered was winning. "Best fighter in the world." That's all he talked about.

"Your brain is not your friend, Mike," he lectured. "Your brain wants pleasure but it's not time yet for you to deserve pleasure. When it's time for you to work, your brain wants to do something else. It works when you want to work too, but it doesn't work all the time when you want to work, so you've got to get out of your own way and not allow your mind to be your enemy."

Cus had a theory that when you put fire to any substance, you can find out what it will turn into. Would it dissolve into ashes or form itself into an iron sword that could penetrate the most impenetrable force? This is the way Cus talked. The fire could be adversity or psychological diagnostics or your own opinion of yourself. Cus was all about using that fire to succeed. We'd see a champion bike racer on the news and Cus was coming up with ways to surpass that guy, figure out how he could be beaten.

"I would let you fight Larry Holmes right now. You could beat him. But you don't believe it. Confidence applied properly will surpass genius. Nothing surpasses confidence."

Ali had been in retirement but he came out of it to fight his former sparring partner Holmes. And he still seemed to have that old Ali swagger. "I'm so happy going into this fight," he said. "I'm dedicating this fight to all the people who've been told, 'You can't do it.' People who drop out of school because they're told they're dumb. People who go to crime because they don't think they can find jobs. I'm dedicating this fight to all of you people who have a Larry Holmes in your life. I'm gonna whup my Holmes, and I want you to whup your Holmes."

There was some doubt that Ali should even have been fighting that night. Three months before the fight he was ordered by the Nevada State Athletic Commission to undergo neurological exams at the Mayo Clinic. The results weren't made public then but they were released later and they were scary. Ali was a bit off when he was told to touch his finger to his nose. His speech was slurred. He couldn't even hop on one foot satisfactorily. It didn't matter—they approved the fight.

We cringed the whole fight long. Ali's legs were gone, his punch was nonexistent. All he could do was absorb punishment for ten rounds, until his trainer Angelo Dundee threw in the towel. It was a massacre. In the ninth round Ali was driven into the ropes with an uppercut that was followed by a right to the body. It was the first time that Ali's cornermen ever heard him scream.

It was like a funeral driving back to Catskill. I had never seen Cus that upset before. Cus and Ali went way back together. When Ali was still a young boy he and his brother Rahman borrowed their uncle's car and drove from Louisville to Cincinnati to see Floyd Patterson work out before an exhibition bout. Cus was Floyd's manager, and for Ali it was like meeting God, because he'd heard so much about Cus.

"Mr. D'Amato, I'm Cassius Clay and I'm going to be a fighter and we came here to see Floyd Patterson," Ali said.

"Well, I've got two tickets for you," Cus said.

After the fight Ali went to thank Cus.

"If I become a little bit famous, I want you with me," he told Cus.

Cus smiled. "Well, we'll talk about it when that time comes. How are you getting back to Kentucky?"

Ali told him they were driving.

"How much money do you have?" Cus asked.

"We've got enough," Ali said.

"Show it to me," Cus insisted. Ali pulled out a twenty-dollar bill.

"That's not enough," Cus said, and gave him two hundred dollars.

That made a big impression on Ali. Years later, when he was champ of the world and had his training camp in Deer Lake, Pennsylvania,

Ali would repeat all of Cus's questions to young fans who had driven up to see him spar and then he'd give them money himself.

Over the years Ali made a few other overtures to Cus to manage him but Cus was busy with Patterson. And Ali loved Cus but he didn't want to hurt Angelo Dundee's feelings. Dundee was his trainer in theory even though Ali really trained himself and had Dundee on a salary. Cus had a strained relationship with Dundee. He was jealous of the notoriety that Dundee was getting because he thought that Dundee was basically a glorified cheerleader. Cus was so bitter about that. I was confused by all this because Angelo always liked and respected Cus.

But Ali maintained a close relationship with Cus. They were always strategizing, talking about how to win in the ring and in life. When Ali fought Liston, Cus told him that if Ali fought his fight and avoided fear he could win. When the first Liston–Ali fight was postponed because of Ali's emergency hernia surgery, Cus was on the scene at the hospital in Boston, and as Ali was being wheeled into surgery, Cus was outside, briefing reporters, telling them that if the doctors handled the operation correctly the fight could still go on as scheduled.

After Ali won the title from Liston, he went to Puerto Rico to watch Cus's fighter José Torres fight, and when he saw Cus he pointed at him and told the reporters who were following him, "Best teacher of boxing in the world!"

No one supported Ali more when he had his title stripped for refusing to fight in Vietnam than Cus. Cus and his friend Jim Jacobs produced a documentary on Ali and shot a TV program called *The Battle of the Champions* featuring Muhammad Ali and Cus D'Amato. From the footage that exists you can see how much mutual respect and love there was between the two men.

ALI: Cus D'Amato can be seen from a great distance, especially when the sun is shining, because his head shines. Cus D'Amato—the genius of boxing. He knows all about boxing. He can tell you about all the fighters from the first fighter up until myself. He don't look like a boxing coach or a boxing manager, he's a conservative-looking fellow. He looks like a senator or a congressman. He's the bible of boxing. Plus, he's ugly. Say, Cus, I was just wondering, if I have to find me a new trainer, somebody told me you didn't work for a salary.

CUS: Me work for salary, me? ALI: I mean, what's wrong with a salary? CUS: Me, I don't work for a salary. I'm no worker. I'm not an employee. ALI: I could get you a hundred and fifty dollars a week. CUS: Me? A hundred and fifty dollars a week, me? ALI: Two fifty a week, that's the best I could do. CUS: You couldn't give me two fifty a minute, much less by the week. I don't work for salary. ALI: That's pretty good money. CUS: Then you take the job. ALI: I'm the employer. CUS: You're my employer? You, my employer!? The only thing you could hope to be is my partner. ALI: Three hundred dollars a week. CUS: I wouldn't care if you gave me three hundred dollars a minute! ALI: Three fifty a week. CUS: Three hundred and fifty a minute, I wouldn't take it, a minute, never mind a week. A minute, I wouldn't take it. ALI: We're not going to get along. CUS: That's right, I agree.

Two proud Capricorns. Coincidentally, they shared the same birthday—January 12. But Cus turned serious when he talked about Ali in the movie *a.k.a. Cassius Clay.* "It is the mark of a great fighter when he has character, plus skill, because a fighter with character and skill will often rise and beat a better fighter because of this. Character is that quality upon which you can depend, under pressure and other conditions. Character makes the fighter predictable, character helps them win." For Cus, no one had more character than Ali.

Ali was inactive for over three and a half years and Cus came up with many creative scenarios in which Ali could fight Frazier without having to be sanctioned by the boxing commissions that had suspended Ali's license. Cus's first idea was to have the fight take place on a Mississippi riverboat before a small audience who paid a huge amount to get on the boat. The live audience meant nothing, since the closed-circuit audience would have been phenomenal. When the logistics didn't fall into place he changed the idea and wanted to get a barge that would be moored in the ocean ten miles offshore, beyond the territorial limits of the United States. Another idea was to have the fight on an Indian reservation or in the District of Columbia, which was not a state so there was no state commission to sanction the fight. But the most creative idea of them all was to have his friend Norman Mailer write a play in which the final act was a prize fight between Ali and Frazier.

Ali lost his linear title to Joe Frazier when he resumed boxing, and after defeating Frazier in their second fight he was ready to take on George Foreman, who won his title from Frazier. But Foreman was a massive guy with a massive punch and Ali was worried about the outcome of the fight. Right before he boarded his bus that was to take him from his Deer Lake camp to New York for the flight to Zaire, Ali had his right-hand man, Gene Kilroy, call Cus up in Catskill.

"Cus, how do I fight this guy?" Ali asked.

"You take his strength and make it his weakness," Cus said. "Foreman has no respect for you. He does not think you can hurt him. What you need to do is go out there in the first round, set yourself, throw a hard right hand and hurt Foreman. Your first punch must be a right thrown with bad intentions."

That was a strange instruction. No one throws right-hand leads in a championship fight in the first minute of round one.

"I don't know what to do. Tell Gene," Ali said, and turned the phone over to Gene Kilroy.

"Cus, look what George Foreman did to Joe Frazier. Look what he did to Kenny Norton," Kilroy said.

"THAT'S NOT ALI!!" Cus yelled so loud they almost heard him in Deer Lake.

They hung up and Ali told Gene that was what he was going to do.

Just read how Norman Mailer described the first round of the Ali–Foreman fight in Zaire:

"The bell! Through a long unheard sigh of collective release, Ali charged across the ring. He looked as big and determined as Foreman, so he held himself, as if *he* possessed the true threat. They collided without meeting, their bodies still five feet apart. Each veered backward like similar magnetic poles repelling each other forcibly. Then Ali came forward again, Foreman came forward, they circled, they feinted, they moved in an electric ring, and Ali threw the first punch, a tentative left. It came up short. Then he drove a lightning-strong right straight as a pole into the stunned center of Foreman's head, the unmistakable thwomp of a high-powered punch. A cry went up. Whatever else happened, Foreman had been hit. No opponent had cracked George this hard in years and no sparring partner had dared to. Foreman charged in rage. Ali compounded the insult. He grabbed the Champion around the neck and pushed his head down, wrestled it down crudely and decisively to show Foreman he was considerably rougher than anybody warned, and relations had commenced . . . Ali was not dancing. . . . Maybe fifteen seconds went by. Suddenly Ali hit him again. It was again a right hand. . . . Champions do not hit other champions with right-hand leads. Not in the first round."

CUS WAS STILL FURIOUS the next morning after Ali had been brutalized by Holmes. Sure enough, the phone rang and it was Kilroy. Ali wanted to talk to Cus. I sat nearby, listening in.

"How did you let that bum beat you, Muhammad? HE'S A BUM! A BUM!" Cus was yelling and we were both hurt to the core. There was so much sincerity in Cus's words they cut right through me. It was as if an explosion rocked the house every time he said the word "bum."

They talked a bit more and then Cus changed the topic. "I have this young black kid who is going to be heavyweight champ of the world. Make sure you tell him to listen to me, Ali, all right? He's almost fifteen and he's going to be champ of the world."

Cus handed me the phone. I was still crying and I told Ali that I was sad that he lost. Ali told me that he was taking medicine that got him sick and that he was going to come back and knock Holmes out. Then I said, "When I get big, I'm going to get him for you." It took me a little over seven years but I fulfilled my promise.

I saw another fight that rocked my world a few months later. My hero Roberto Durán was going to fight a rematch against Sugar Ray Leonard. Their first fight solidified my passion for boxing and now I was looking forward to the second. But Cus was raining on my parade. "Durán won't win the second fight. He can never get up that high again. He's dead right now."

Cus was right. We watched the fight on TV and Leonard used his speed to elude Durán for six rounds and sneak in flurries and then make Durán miss. During the seventh round, Leonard started taunting Durán. At one point he began winding up his right hand for a bolo punch and then fooled Durán and hit him on the nose with a left jab. Durán was so humiliated that near the end of the next round he turned his back on Leonard, waved his hand, and told the referee he couldn't go on. Though Durán denies it, legend has it that he said, *"No más."*

I started crying. I was hurt because everybody was saying bad things about my hero. To a guy like Cus you don't wave your hand and quit a fight. You have to give every last ounce you have in you. If you quit, Cus won't go in the ring and get you, he'll leave you there like a fucking dog. Years later, the wife of Durán's legendary trainer Ray Arcel said that Durán quitting like he did broke Arcel's heart and took years off his life.

Durán's loss affected me for days. I was moping around the house and Cus started getting alarmed. Eight months later, when Durán returned to the ring against a Jersey kid named Nino Gonzalez, Cus pulled me aside.

"I want you to watch the fight with me tomorrow afternoon," he said. "Durán is fighting this Puerto Rican kid from Bayonne, Nino, and he has the heart of a lion." Cus kept pumping up this Gonzalez guy. It was a pretty even fight and Nino even cut Durán. It took me a long time to realize Cus wanted me to watch Nino fight because he didn't want me to be too infatuated with a quitter. But I stayed loyal to Durán and he came back and won three more titles, so it just went to show that you can never give up, even after you do.

Now that I was living with Cus I started working out at the gym seven days a week, no exceptions. Besides the occasional visits from

Bobby Stewart, Cus had me sparring with some local kids who were heavyweights. We never used headgear. Cus thought that headgear gave a fighter a false sense of security and that if you didn't have it on, you'd have a keener awareness of where the punch was coming from and you'd be more careful to make sure you could avoid it. Early on, I learned a neat new trick. It was a punch known as the Blinder. You put your jab out and leave it in your opponent's face for a split second before the ref can warn you. Your glove blinds the guy for a second and then you instantaneously spring to the right, set your weight properly, and launch a six-five-two. It was lethal.

After the Ali–Holmes fight, Cus thought I was ready for my first fights. Every week, Teddy or Lennie Daniels, another older student of Cus's, would drive a few of us down to the Bronx to fight at Nelson Cuevas's gym. Nelson had learned how to box from Cus back at the Gramercy Gym and he was so impressed with Cus's dedication to the neighborhood kids that he decided to do the same thing for the kids of the Bronx. He saved up $14,000 and opened up the Apollo Boxing Club in the Fort Apache section, the most crime-ridden part of the Bronx. The fights at the Apollo were called smokers, which were un-authorized bouts attended by a loud, crazy crowd of locals who stepped over discarded needles, walked up three flights of urine-soaked stairs, paid $3 at the door, got drunk on rum served in paper cups, smoked stinky cigars (hence the name), and bet on the fights.

I had to fight in these unsanctioned bouts because I was too physi-cally advanced to fight in the younger version of the Golden Gloves, called the Silver Gloves. They were for kids eight to fifteen, but when John Condon, from Madison Square Garden, took one look at me, he immediately banned me from the Silvers. I just looked scary. "I can't let you fight in the tournament," he told me. "You're going to hurt these kids." He was a good man and he knew what time it was so I understood.

The first night I went down to the Bronx all I could do was watch because there was nobody there that night who was in my weight class. They had only two heavyweights and they were already matched up. So they made sure that one of those guys would come back the

next week and I was set for my first fight. That whole week I prepared for the fight, but when I got to the Bronx I was scared to death.
I had seen this guy fight the week before and I knew that I could beat
him but I was an insecure kid. I started to freak out and I went downstairs to get some air. There was a subway stop right across the street.
I sat on the steps leading up to the elevated line and thought that
maybe I should hop on that car, get out at Rockaway Avenue, and
walk three blocks to my mom's house.

I was scared of getting beat up, I was scared of letting people
down, but it all came down to the fact that I didn't want to be humiliated. So I thought about that book *"In This Corner . . . !"* and remembered that all the greats were scared too, and all of Cus's lessons
about discipline came back to me and I pulled myself together and
went back up to the gym.

I got in the ring with a tall Puerto Rican guy with a big Afro. He
was eighteen, four years older than me. We went at it pretty good for
two rounds but in the third I knocked him into the ropes and followed
up with an uppercut that knocked his mouthpiece into the sixth row.
He was out cold. I was a real emotional kid so while he was out cold I
stepped on the guy and raised my arms in the air. If you talk to Nelson today, he'll tell you that the only reason I stepped on the guy was
that I knocked him out in my corner and I had to step over him to get
to a neutral corner. That's bullshit! I stepped on him intentionally.
The whole crowd started booing. To avoid a riot Nelson called the
fight a draw.

Cus had asked Nelson to give him a report on my fight so he called
Cus and said, "I'm sorry I have to tell you but Mike knocked out his
opponent but then he did something that the people didn't like so I
had to give the fight a draw." He told Cus what had happened and
Cus wasn't concerned at all. Cus always loved my enthusiasm.

I always did well at Nelson's. I never lost a fight and most of them
ended in spectacular knockouts. After a few times, it was hard to
find opponents for me to fight. So sometimes I'd just watch the crazy
proceedings. Nelson often had to change the scoring so our kids
didn't win all the fights. A lot of times a guy who had a nice robe

would come out and he'd look professional, so he'd be heavily favored, but if he got his ass kicked in the first round, they'd change the odds in the middle of the fight! One time Teddy got into a major fight because he didn't like the way a guy scored a fight and Nelson smashed a trophy over the head of the guy who was fighting with Teddy, then pulled out his gun. It was the Wild West.

I went all around the country fighting at these unsanctioned smokers. The fights sometimes were in a barn in someone's backyard. Cus always told me, "You've got to be confident. You can fight a guy in his living room and the family could be the officials and you'll still win." Any place we could get a fight, we'd take it. Most of the time Cus didn't come with me, but whether he sent me to Massachusetts or Rhode Island or Ohio, before I left, Cus would sit me down and bark in a very flat, staccato tone, "Listen, I'm going to have some friends watching you tonight. They're going to call me after the fight and I expect them to be ranting and raving about you." Oooh, how that fired me up. I might be on a plane for three hours and I wouldn't rest for a minute, my heart would be pumping so fast. I couldn't wait to get to the ring and start beating the motherfuckers in an explosive fashion, doing what Cus taught me. I may have been a major-league dickhead but I was caught up with this shit. He sold it to me and I bought it.

Now I was getting a chance to test out Cus's theories about fear. I had never experienced that in a ring unless it was when I was sparring with Bobby Stewart. So when I started sparring with new people that was also scary. Cus used to get turned on when I told him that I was afraid and I might be a coward. He loved that. He knew that would feed into my fear base and he worked everything off fear. Cus wanted you to react like a robot so that when he said something, you'd do it on command. Cus showed me the difference between fear and intimidation. Being intimidated prevents you from performing at the highest level you're capable of. But fear can help you ascend to great heights. "Be afraid of your opponent personally but don't be afraid to hurt him," he told me. What people don't realize is that when controlled properly fear can take you to a level of euphoria where you believe you're invincible. Very few people can get to that level. But when you do, a weird aberration of nature takes place and you're sent to a level of invincible proportion.

In some way, when I got in that ring, I was getting retribution for all the people who fucked me up as a kid. Being bullied stays with you your entire life. No one was going to pick on me ever again. Whenever I got in the ring I pictured that the people I was fighting were the people who bullied me when I was younger. I was dead serious. I wasn't doing this to motivate myself. I was a glutton for power and fame.

AFTER HEARING REPORTS about my emotional reactions to winning my first smokers, Cus began to implement a new technique to get me to relax and to focus on my goal. He had told me about using hypnosis when I first started coming up to train with him and now it was time for me to experience it. I was excited to do it because I was afraid that my nerves and my insecurities would overwhelm me. So Cus and me and a few other fighters would pile into Cus's old ragged station wagon and drive down to Manhattan to see John Halpin. Halpin had been a social worker with the NYC Department of Welfare who was taking pre-med courses but abandoned them when World War II started. After the war he went into hypnosis and opened an office on Central Park West, where he worked with dieters, smokers, drinkers, and narcotic addicts.

Cus had heard about Halpin through a chiropractor friend of his and the two men immediately bonded over their knowledge of and respect for the subconscious mind. When we'd get to Halpin's office, he'd have us lie on the rug on his floor and he'd put us under. Once we were hypnotized, he'd turn the conditioning over to Cus and Cus would address each of us individually and go over the areas where we needed improvement. Cus thought it was important that he talked to me while I was under because he wanted me to internalize his own voice.

Cus would say, "You are a fighting machine, Mike. You're the best fighter that God has created. The world has never seen a fighter like you, because when you throw your punches in combination, you are ferocious. Your intention is to inflict as much pain as possible."

Cus would go on for an hour, with his words just washing over me. It was like I was transcending, watching him in the chair and me on the floor. When Halpin would take me out of my trance, I'd wake up and we'd drive back upstate. I didn't feel any different after the experience but I performed better and so did the other guys who got hypnotized. The next day in the gym, you'd go, "Holy moly, what a difference. That guy is so much calmer in the ring." And it wasn't something that went away after a few days. People were making breakthroughs.

Of course, hypnosis didn't work for everyone. One time I went with Matthew and Alex Hilton, who were fun-loving crazy Canadians. Alex had been out all night before we went to see Halpin so he immediately went under and fell asleep. He was sound asleep, snoring, but Cus was hard of hearing so he didn't realize what was going on. "Look, look, he's hypnotized," Cus said, all excited.

Cus started putting me under in the house. It might be before a training session or even before a fight. He'd have me lie down on the floor of the living room or sit in a big comfortable chair and he'd start in with the heel method of relaxation—the head, the eyes, the arms, the legs, the heels all getting heavy. Once I was totally relaxed he'd go into his rap about me being the most ferocious and elusive fighter the world has ever produced.

Sometimes he'd give me more specific instructions. "Your jab is like a weapon. Like a battering ram. Your objective is to push his nose into the back of his head. You throw punches with bad intentions. You move your head after every punch. You are a scourge from God—the world will know your name from now to the eons of oblivion. I'm not telling you all this because you are incapable of doing these things. This is not a séance. This is what you are capable of doing. I need you to relax, this is going to help you."

It was deep shit. And I believed all of it. Cus didn't even have to be there. I might be in my room and his voice would come to me, almost telepathically. I learned to hypnotize myself, and before a fight, in the dressing room, I'd go under and repeat what Cus had told me.

Cus had everyone who trained with him doing affirmations. He would say to each fighter, "Not everybody becomes champion, but if you apply the same principles and techniques that I will teach you, you'll become successful no matter what the endeavor. My objective is to develop the person's character so that they have the ability to transcend and succeed, no matter where they've come from or no matter how difficult the task." He told us that we could personalize our affirmations so that besides saying "Day by day, in every way, I'm getting better and better," we could say "Day by day, in every way, I'm getting calmer and see more in the ring and I'm getting better and better" or "Every day, in every way, my swollen ankle is getting better and better."

Cus had me integrate my hypnotic suggestions into my affirmations so instead of the less intense "Day by day, I'm getting better and better," now I was affirming that day by day I was becoming the most ferocious fighter that the world has ever seen. All day long I'd be saying to myself, "The best fighter, nobody in the world could beat me, the best fighter in the world, nobody in the world could beat me." The more I said it, the more I believed it.

Cus began to reward me for any accomplishments inside the ring. He'd dangle things in front of me. Clothing was my weakness then, so Cus would say, "You want that leather jacket? You want those nice sneakers? Win the tournament. Remember, you have to look at your opponents like they're food." So if I won a local or regional tournament, he'd find rewards for me, even if they were things I didn't even know if I wanted. "Don't you think this is beautiful? I bet you'd like that." Of course the ultimate prize he was dangling was the heavyweight championship. Being the heavyweight champion of the world was more important to Cus than being the president of the United States.

Cus had no money and we were all living on a shoestring budget, but as far as Cus was concerned I was to be treated like a king. He was getting a small amount of money from New York State for me, and if I spent 90 percent of my allotment for school clothes on a fly leather jacket Cus would complain a little and say, "You put all that money on one coat? I've still got to get you socks and underwear," but then he'd shell out the money. Cus's whole operation in Catskill was being funded by his close friend Jimmy Jacobs and Jacobs's business partner Bill Cayton.

Another tactic Cus used to inspire me was to bring world-class fighters up to Catskill. Wilfredo Benitez came up and trained there and I felt like I was looking at the Holy Grail when he showed me his championship belt. Another time Gerry Cooney came up to Catskill to see Cus and I was thrilled to get his autograph.

All this was part of Cus's attempts to build up my ego. I had so little self-esteem when I came to Catskill. I was never jealous or envious of anyone before I met Cus but he brought those feelings out of me. "You should have this." "You could beat this guy, you're better than him." It wasn't like, "You could be better if you work hard," it was more like, "Why should he have that and you don't?" And the way he said it was intimidating.

I was a sneaky little conniving guy back in Brooklyn with no ego who was hustling. I looked up to the other kids who were older and more charismatic than I was. But now Cus was telling the whole world that I was going to be the youngest heavyweight champ of the world. And I deserved it. I had to live up to that shit. I had to build up so much venom for somebody that you want to hurt them so bad just for your notch in the world. I wanted to be the best on the planet at what I did. Cus told me about our plan and I had no doubt it was going to happen. I'm bragging and I'm an arrogant motherfucker not even knowing that I'm offending people telling them that I'm going to be the youngest heavyweight champ.

So I adopted a persona. I was a chameleon. Look, Cus had me reading Nietzsche when I was fifteen years old. I can barely spell my name but I think I'm a fucking Superman. I used to go to the smokers and club fights. These places were disgusting cesspool rooms populated by all these thug-looking tough street guys, real hard people. I'd walk into the rooms and they'd look at me and I'd look at them and we're nothing but a bunch of scumbags, yet I'm thinking in my mind that I'm noble, I'm this great gladiator, ready to do battle. I'm a fucking schmuck. I'm fifteen years old. This is my whole life. I'm watching cartoons, karate movies, and boxing films and jerking off incessantly. But I'm noble!

I couldn't wait for my fights. I couldn't wait to stride into those crowded rooms because I knew that when I came out people would be applauding me. They'd never seen anybody like me. They must have thought I was crazy, glowering at everybody. I wouldn't talk to nobody. If Cus would be talking to somebody and he didn't introduce me to them, I wouldn't talk to them, I'd just stare at them. They'd put out their hand to shake and I'd ignore them. I wouldn't bathe before a fight. I wanted to be in the worst state of anarchy I could be in, but under control. Cus loved that I was a mean little kid. He was all about creating chaos and confusion but staying cool under it all.

The psychology of fighting was in Cus's bone marrow. I couldn't get enough of him. I absorbed this old bald-headed man. I was so desperate. Cus made me believe that I should be treated like a god anywhere I went, because I was the greatest. And I was trying to make this guy happy by acting out his vision. He tells me I'm the greatest, okay, I'm the greatest. I'm running with that. But now I'm a megalomaniac with low self-esteem because this guy was such an artful manipulator. It was great that Cus helped me stop feeling like a piece of shit, but now I'm taking it to the moon. I wasn't just vain, that would have been an understatement. Cus told me if all the prophets had a son and the son was a fighter, they couldn't beat me, because I was Cus's fighter. I would tell people that I'd be the Olympic champion and then I'd have a few pro fights and then I'd be the heavyweight champ of the world and then I'd be the greatest champ ever. They couldn't understand me saying this, but Cus had brainwashed me.

My first big test on the road to Olympic gold was my first Junior Olympics tournament. I was fighting smokers right up until I entered the tournament because Cus's theory was that I should go in battle-ready. My first fight in the New York Junior Olympics was in

Saratoga but my opponent pulled out. That would be a common occurrence as my name got more and more out there. I won my next three fights by KOs, so on June 24, 1981, I went to Colorado Springs for the Nationals. I was going to have to win three fights in four days to get the title. Before I left, Cus reminded me, "Just remember, the other guys are going through the same thing as you."

I plowed through my first two fights, Jesus Esparza and Randy Wesley, with first-round KOs. After each fight I'd call Cus. He told me to keep calm and that with each win I'd get more and more acknowledged. He told me about fighters who won this tournament and went on to become champion. Sometimes he reminded me to use my jab and punch to the body. I was a little nervous because I'd never experienced anything like this before but I wanted to win so bad. I wanted that trophy.

I didn't sleep much the night before the final. The morning of the fight, I ran, worked out a bit, and then took a nap. Teddy Atlas and I had something to eat and then we went to the arena. I shadowboxed a bit in the dressing room and then the officials came in and checked my hands and then you just go out there. I could see the ring from the corridor outside our dressing room so I'd watched the earlier fights. I loved to do that, it got me so in the mood. Then I was up. I was fighting a big Mexican kid named Joe Cortez. I didn't know much about him other than he had knocked out all his opponents too. He had more fights (his record was 13–4), but I had better form. I just looked like I knew how to fight.

I went into the ring with confidence. I had boxed grown men and he was just a kid like me. The bell rang and I charged after him. I drove him to the ropes with a left and after a quick flurry I caught him with a short right to the chin and he was out. I had just set a Junior Olympics record with an eight-second KO. I jumped up and started crying like a dickhead. It felt real good. I got my trophy and we went back to the hotel and called Cus. He was all excited, calling me "champion." Setting the record for the fastest knockout in history didn't hurt.

"I'm going to relax tonight," I told him. "I don't want my head to swell any more than it is."

When we got back to Catskill, Cus convinced the town to put a big banner up congratulating me on my victory. Plus he had a nice cake waiting for me at home. Cus liked his cake and ice cream. The fight was televised a week later on ESPN and Cus's friend at the local newspaper put a notice in the paper about the replay. We had a viewing party at the house and Cus invited all the kids from the gym and their parents and some local leaders. Everyone was pleased that the town was mentioned on TV. Cus, of course, said that I was going to put the town on the map.

I became a bit of a local hero. I got more popular at school. Locals would come up to me on the street and pat my back. "Hey, you're going to be champ one day," they'd say. I got a similar reaction when I went back to Brooklyn to visit. Strangers would say, "Hey, you're Mike Tyson. I saw you on television." I was just a kid and it was a little overwhelming that fight fans across the country knew who I was.

A few days after I got back, Cus came to my room. "You're going to need to find a hobby," he said. "Every day is not going to be exciting like it's been lately when you're the champ. There'll be some boring days too. You have to have something to occupy your mind."

As a present for winning my first Junior Olympics, Cus gave me money to build a pigeon coop and stock it. Cus used to fly birds himself back in the Bronx and he was very adamant about me getting pigeons up in Catskill. He was shrewd, though. I killed a lot of time with those birds. I loved my birds.

Now that I was back from the Nationals, Cus upped my training regimen. And it was all about sparring. Cus wasn't a big believer in running. "Waste of time," he'd say. "For Christ sakes you're not going to be running in the ring, you're going to be fighting!" He was all about sparring and combat every day. I had been sparring with Bobby Stewart when he could come over and then with local kids but I was too much for the local guys. Then Cus started hiring sparring partners but a lot of those guys didn't stay—I was too fast and too rough for them. Cus wanted me to go all out in sparring. So if I hit a guy, boom, and he's hurt, oh, he'd also get a boom-boom-boom-boom-

boom-boom! I'm not going to stop until he goes down. As I started getting better I'd go through two or three sparring partners a day.

A few times, a new guy would stay for one session and leave on the next train, abandoning all his stuff at the house. Tom Patti and I would go through his stuff, and we got some slick-ass Nike leather jackets and great alligator boots once. That guy called back and said his boots were worth fifteen hundred dollars and the leather jacket was three grand and he had to get the clothes back. Tommy and I were at the table eating away, and Cus said, "We don't know nothing about any bags of clothes. You took everything when you left." Cus was so pissed off that the guy left. When you do something like that, Cus didn't care if you died! Cus respected "Hey, Cus, I'm not feeling good, I'm hurting today, I don't think I could go." But he didn't respect leaving in the middle of the night. If the guy said he was hurt, Cus would massage the guy, and then the next thing you know Cus would start telling the guy, "Do this." He's training the fucking sparring partners! He did that to make it difficult for me. When I was doing something wrong, he'd tell them, "Hey, when he makes those mistakes, you throw this punch as hard as you can at him. As hard as you can, you hear me?"

I'd get in the ring and Cus would stand on the apron of the ring, holding the top rope. "Move your head," he'd bark. "Hands up, move your head. Hands up when you pull out." When the round was over, I'd go back to the corner and Cus would give me more detailed instructions, like "Stay close to him so he can't uppercut." I would be breaking in a new sparring partner and while we sparred, he'd yell over to Cus, "Strong boy, Cus." "Oh, I told you that." Cus beamed. "I told you so it wouldn't take you by surprise. He knows how to fight, he knows what it's about."

When a session was finished, I'd come over to get my gloves unlaced. "They say you're strong but they don't say how smart you are. If you weren't smart you would have gotten hit more," Cus would say. "I didn't do so hot today," I'd say. I was always down on myself. "Yes, you did," Cus would say. "You may not be able to understand and appreciate what happened in there. We did, all of us here."

Cus usually had one of his friends watching my sessions with him. He'd yell out encouragement to me and then he'd whisper things to his friends like "I'll give him a strong body and he's gonna have to get strong in other ways. He's not as tough or as hard as people think he is. When they see me, they say, 'Oh boy, you got that Tyson. He just loves to fight. He just loves to hurt people. He's afraid of nothing.' That's not true, but when we're done with him, he'll look like he is anyway."

Now Cus thought I was ready to spar with professionals. Five amateur fights and he's got me fighting pros! It was usually on short notice. Frank Bruno came through one time and Cus had to call the school to get me out of classes. "There's an emergency here at the house. Someone is sick and Mike needs to come home," he'd say, and I'd get out so I could spar with Bruno.

Of all my sparring partners, my favorite was Marvin Stinson. He was a highly talented amateur boxer who fought the great Cuban Teo Stevenson, fought all the great Russians too. At that time he was Larry Holmes's chief sparring partner. Cus wanted me to go to Larry Holmes's camp to train and Larry Holmes said, "I won't train with amateurs." More fuel for Cus's hatred of Holmes. After I'd trained a week with Marvin, Cus said, "What do you think?" and Marvin said, "He could box with Larry."

Marvin was such an awesome guy. I reached a whole other level sparring with him. He was very difficult to hit at first, and I had to get comfortable with him before I could time him and score. He was kicking my ass; there was no doubt about it, he was more experienced, he was setting me up, he hit me a lot. It bothered me all that day and all night. I couldn't wait for the next day because I wanted to do better. But still I'd be very nervous inside because I knew he was going to be tough. Cus would talk to me about what I did the day before, and Marvin would tell me, "This is what you do when you get in there. When I do that move, you've got to do this." They were both schooling me.

I went to Brooklyn to visit my mom shortly after my victory in the

Junior Olympics. I was so excited. I was a different person then. My confidence was sky-high. I had an ego now and I knew I was the best fighter in the world. Before I met Cus I wouldn't have dreamed of saying that—somebody would've beat my fucking ass in the street if I did. As soon as I got in the apartment, my mom looked me up and down. "Wow, you look good," she said, admiring my physique.

"I'm going to be the youngest heavyweight champion of the world. My manager says that I'm going to be the best ever, nobody in the world can beat me," I bragged.

"Well, they got Joe Louis one time. They got Cassius Clay too," she warned me. "You have to be careful, there's always someone better. You always have to remember to handle your defeats as well as you handle your victories."

I didn't want to hear that corny shit.

"I'm not going to have time to handle the defeats because I'm going to be accepting so many victories," I said smugly. I'm just repeating all this shit that Cus told me. Then I pulled out all these clippings about me winning the Junior Olympics and put them on the table in front of her.

"There's always someone better, son," she said firmly.

"You know that person you're talking about who's always better than somebody? That's me. I'm right here. I'm that person." Cus had contaminated my mind with these notions of grandeur. Oh, why did I say that! My mother pushed away from the table, ignored my clippings, and went in another room. She probably couldn't have dreamed her son could be this guy. She thought I was going to die in the streets.

The rest of my stay in Brooklyn was pretty uneventful. No robbing, no jostling. Just a grim reminder that a lot of my friends were getting swept up into serious crime and paying the price. After I got back to Catskill I got a phone call from my friend John. He had shot someone and it was too hot for him stay in the neighborhood and he had nowhere to go. I invited him to come and stay with me at Cus's until things cooled down. He took the train up, Cus talked to him for a minute, and everything was cool. Cus had no idea he was harboring a fugitive.

I SUFFERED MY FIRST DEFEAT at a smoker in Rhode Island in November of 1981. I was fighting an older guy named Ernie Bennett who was the local champ. He was twenty-one and about to turn pro. The place was packed and we fought hard for three rounds. The crowd cheered the entire time, even when we were in our corners between rounds. I thought it was the best performance of my life, especially when I knocked him through the ropes in the last round. But it was a hometown decision and I felt robbed.

I cried all the way from Rhode Island to Catskill. But Cus was waiting up for me and he had a huge smile on his face. "I heard you fought a great fight. Stay home from school today and rest." There was no way I was staying home. Bennett had given me a black eye and I wanted to show it off at school.

"Mike, what happened?" everyone said.

"I lost," I said.

"Wow, you lost!"

"It's okay. I lost to a good fighter. Don't worry. I'm going to be champ one day, guys."

Cus was at his best after his fighters were defeated. This was the time when we needed his reassurances the most. Cus's whole rap was about not getting discouraged. You can cry, you can complain, you can whine, but don't get discouraged. You go back in the ring like you knocked the guy out instead of him knocking you out.

I was so sensitive back then. I'd explode from left field. Cus loved my emotional side, but he wanted me to control it, especially in school. He was a Bruce Lee–type mentality guy. Cus wanted you to be ready at all times. In the ring and out. Cus was into keeping people street-fight tough, just as much as he was into the fight shit. He repeated the story of how Mad Dog Coll put the gun to his face when he was a kid. "I was scared to cry, because I thought if he didn't kill me, everybody else would think I was a coward, but if he killed me, everyone would talk about me forever, because I was a man and stood up to the gun."

I was pretty quiet and reserved and moody, even after I won my first Nationals. I was also battling an eating disorder at the same time I was hitting puberty. I was always a fat kid. Everybody in my family was obese. I used to eat a ton of food after my fights and gain a lot of weight. I guess it was a lot of growing pains. I was dealing with them and my desire to achieve at the same time. I was getting acne, I was getting horny, I had no girlfriend. I just had that goal of being champion.

I was trying to internalize Cus's directives to control my mind but it wasn't easy. Sometimes in the dressing room before a fight, I'd have a crying fit. I'd bawl until I was finished and then I would come out and kill the guy like nothing had ever happened. I did what I had to do to get the job done. Maybe I was overly dramatic.

It was one thing to have these outbursts in the dressing room but when they started happening at school, then it got dangerous. Cus always rushed to straighten out these incidents because he was deathly afraid that the authorities might try to take me away from him. It took a while for Cus to even realize I was acting out in school because whenever they'd send a progress report to the house, I'd intercept the mail and tear it up. Finally, one day they called the house. Cus didn't need to see a report card, just hearing that shit was bad. He started giving me the third degree. We could be happy and chummy and then, boom, it's just not funny anymore.

One day I got into an altercation on the school bus as it pulled into the school grounds. A teacher came on board and I refused to listen to him. I wasn't used to anybody but Cus telling me anything. Cus had told me that no one could tell me anything but him. So I didn't have any respect for authority figures if they weren't Cus. Another time I threw an eraser at a teacher and they were going to suspend me. Cus went down to the school to see Mr. Bordick, the principal, who was also Italian. Cus immediately got into that Italian stuff.

"You're from Italy? Where's your family from?" That's the first thing Cus says, "Where's your family from?" He doesn't even say "Hey, man, what are you doing?" It's "Where's your family from?" because if he knows your family, he knows who you are. That's how Cus judged people, from their family's reputation. That was all he needed to know to gauge whether or not you were a good person.

Cus was a control freak to begin with. When Camille came home with the groceries only Cus could organize them and put them away. And they'd fight if Camille hadn't bought at least fifteen cans of tuna. Cus loved his tuna. But with me getting cited at school, his control over me was ratcheted up a notch.

"What did you do in school today?" Cus would come up to my room in the afternoon and begin his interrogation. "You had to do something. You were in school all day. Where's your homework?"

Sometimes all I had to do was make some noise in my room and he'd yell up from the stairs, "Hey, what are you doing up there?" "Cus, I *live* here," I'd say. If I used a new word I had learned at school, he'd be all over me. "Where'd you learn that word from? I don't use that word; I've never said that word. Who have you been hanging around?"

Outside influences were the nemesis of his world. One night I was at a school dance and I called Cus and told him that I was going to be late coming home, I had to wait for a cab. He freaked out. "We've got to go to sleep. We don't have time for you to wait for a cab. Run home now, run!" So I took off. It was three miles back to the house and I'm running with a two-piece suit and dress shoes on.

Whenever I came home, Cus would be there waiting. "So how was the movie? Who did you go with? What are their last names? What does their family do?" He didn't want anybody influencing me and putting ideas in my head. He'd tell me to stay away from certain people because I was too special for them.

But one time I pushed Cus a little too far. Cus had told my junior high principal that I was "special" and that "allowances" had to be made for me. But I was fifteen and uncomfortable in my skin. I didn't know how to talk to girls. They would tease me and I would fight with them. I was used to men and women fighting, that happened all the time in Brownsville. So one day at school I got into a fight with some girls and I started chasing them and I chased them right into the girls' bathroom.

When Cus found out about that, he called me into the living room.

"If you're going to keep acting like that, you're going to have to leave here. You're wasting my time."

Those words cut through me like a knife. I started busting out crying. Oh man! Cus looked so uncomfortable. Even if it killed him to do it, he put his arms around me and hugged me. "It's going to be all right. It's okay," he mumbled. He turned from that mean guy to that nice old man in a second.

I had a meltdown. It was a traumatic moment for me. I didn't want to leave that house. Besides all that champion stuff Cus had put in my head, I loved being in a family environment that I'd never experienced before. I was making new friends, I was beginning to feel that I belonged. Where would I go? Back to Brownsville? I was losing friends there every day, especially around Christmas and New Year's. That's when most people die in the hood because they're hustling, trying to get money for the holidays. Every year when the holidays were over, my friends and I would get together and go, "What happened?" And it was always, "Homeboy robbed someone, they had a gun, boom, he got shot." "What? The little guy who was laughing with us last night? He got killed?"

I needed a while to decompress from Cus's threat. Camille saw me moping around and she went to Cus. "What's wrong with Mike? Why is Mike crying? Is everything all right?"

"What do you mean what's wrong with Mike?" Cus said. "Nothing is wrong with Mike."

When she found out what Cus had said she came to my defense. "Where's he going? He has nowhere to go."

After that incident, I started training even harder, if that was possible. I'd get restless and do more every day. When I got home from the gym I literally had to crawl up the stairs. I never had any major altercations with Cus after that day. I knew that I was there for a purpose and that I was not going to die until it was accomplished.

f Cus had thrown me out of the house after that incident at school, it wouldn't have been the first time that he had fired a fighter. Burt Young, who got his start in boxing before he went on to star in the *Rocky* films, was always amazed that Cus fired his neighbor Vic Campo shortly after he had gone pro. Cus felt that Campo had no future. "I never heard of a manager firing a fighter," Young said. "If they have any ham and eggs, they keep them on the books. They don't care, managers would have seventy fighters." But Cus was never about money. Cus was about developing a plan for a fighter and instilling enough discipline in the boxer so that they could execute the plan. For Cus it was all about creating champions.

In 1945, when Cus returned from the Army, he found the Gramercy in a state of disarray. While he was gone, his friend and partner Harry Davidow had been left in charge of the gym but didn't do a good job, and the ten main-event fighters that Cus was developing, including Tony Johnson, had developed bad habits. But Cus had two fighters who he felt could go the distance given the proper supervision. One was named Joe Juliano, who boxed under the name Joe Sulick. Juliano was a great welterweight prospect. He had a strong defense and he was one of the best punchers under the heart.

But Joe had one major weakness—he loved to gamble. When he was flush he'd drive around Manhattan in a 1933 Packard touring car complete with a chauffeur. He'd disappear from the gym for months. Anthony Patti asked Cus where Joe was. "He won't be back until he runs out of money," Cus said. Juliano was one of those talented guys who don't even train, just go in the ring, fight, win, and then buy a car and gamble.

Cus didn't want to put his time into boxers who had weaknesses like that. Eventually Juliano left Cus because other managers told him that he'd never be a champ with Cus representing him because Cus didn't have the right connections. But Joe remained friendly with Cus for the rest of his life. I got to meet Mr. Juliano and he was an awesome guy.

Early in Cus's career, the closest he came to developing a champ was when he discovered a neighborhood Italian kid named Thomas Rocco Barbella. Barbella and his friends had come up to the gym one day and Cus found out that Barbella had a fearsome reputation as a street fighter. But when he sparred with one of his friends, Cus saw that he didn't know how to box at all. He asked another one of the friends why that was and he told him that Barbella would disarm his victims by dropping his hands to his hips and then he'd suckerpunch them with a devastating right. When Cus asked him to train and become a boxer, Barbella was deathly afraid. Cus worked with him secretly and, after a year, he was ready to fight.

But Cus found out that Barbella was never able to conquer his fear and cowardice. One time Cus and some of his fighters were going to a fight but not everyone could fit into the cab, so Cus decided to walk to the arena. By the time he got to the dressing room, he found Barbella having a meltdown because he wasn't there yet. That's when Cus realized that his fighters were too dependent on him.

Barbella was ready to turn pro but Cus was his usual cautious self. So Barbella went behind Cus's back and signed up with a manager named Irving Cohen, who was a front man for the mob. That infuriated Cus. Cus never forgave Barbella and when he went on to become a champion boxing under the name of Rocky Graziano, Cus would rail against him as a double-crossing coward. Cus really took his disloyalty personally, especially after Cus had done so much for the guy.

Cus was one of those Italian Americans who would rail against the mob, saying that if they did you a favor, then they'd sink their hooks into you for the rest of your life. It wasn't as if Cus didn't know any mobsters. He grew up with plenty of gangsters in his neighborhood. But even if he knew wiseguys, he didn't associate with them. Cus was a crusader. The idea of fixing a bout made him sick to his stomach. "I love boxing," he told *Life* in 1957. "I have a feeling for it as a force for good, and that's more than most other people have in this business. Maybe my reward is helping a boy do what I couldn't do—but just watching a fighter mature and find himself is reward enough."

When Cus would see that one of his young fighters was gravitating toward trouble and hanging out with the wrong crowd, he'd sit them down. "Listen, you've got to make sure you're not making bad choices. You have to stay away from the mob. They're going to tempt you in a lot of ways." A few times Cus had to teach this lesson by example. Cus told me that one time four wiseguys came up to the gym while about forty boys were training. Two guys stood by the door, another guy went over to the lockers, and the leader of the group went up to Cus and politely inquired if he could talk to him in private. Cus took him into his office. As soon as Cus walked in, the guy closed the door and stuck what appeared to be a gun under his coat into Cus's stomach. He mentioned one of Cus's fighters.

"We're in. I'm taking the fighter," he told Cus. "I'm just telling you. Even if you go to the law, it won't matter. We make our own laws."

As he was talking, Cus slowly turned around, inching his way toward the door. Then he threw the door open and stepped out into the gym, catching the wiseguy by surprise. Cus remembered his father's reaction years earlier when some tough guys with knives threatened to take over his ice business. "You could cut me up in little pieces and I wouldn't give in!"

Cus stuck out his hand. "You can start here," he said, hacking one hand at the fingers of the other, "and you can cut off my hand piece by piece but you're out! Get the hell out of here!"

The wiseguys retreated down the stairs and Cus went back into his office. He said his legs were shaking so much he had to lean back against his desk when all his fighters came in and congratulated him. "You showed those guys, telling them they don't belong here," they all said. "Way to go, Cus." That's what we all loved about him. If I ever showed any signs of doubt about a fight, he'd say, "Mike, are you scared? I'll fight him for you. I'm seventy-seven, but I'll fight him for you."

But the story didn't even end there. The wiseguys had let Cus know that Irving Cohen was going to take over his fighter. So Cus went to the Boxing Managers' Guild and filed a formal complaint. Cohen was one of the premier managers then, real tight with the guild, and Cus was an outsider. When Cus told them the story, they were amazed by Cus's courage.

"Suppose those guys come back?" one of the guild officers asked. Cus told them that he would tear those guys apart. And then he pointed at the officials at the table. "If those guys come around again, *you're* the guys I'm going to go after."

That wasn't the only time that the mob tried to strong-arm Cus. Another time two guys came up to inform him that they were going to take over one of Cus's fighters. After Cus threw one of the guys down the steep stairs, the other one left immediately. Paul Mangiamele said that Cus told him of an incident that happened in an alleyway near the gym. A guy came up to Cus and pulled out a gun and pointed it right between his eyes. "You gotta do it our way—" the guy started, but Cus cut him off.

"Pauly, the barrel looked like a cannon," Cus remembered. "I was scared to death but I looked that son of a bitch right in the eye and stared him down. 'Are you going to use that thing or just talk to me? Because you don't scare me.' I was shaking in my boots but I stared him down and he walked away."

Cus was fearless. "Believe me, I would not want to die," he told *Sports Illustrated*. "But I would not be afraid to die for a principle."

Sometimes Cus used humor to defuse a situation. One time two pretty benign-looking "tough guys" paid him a visit and suggested that they become partners. "If you're interested in this boxing business you'll have to work right along with me. Your day will start at five a.m. getting fighters ready to do their roadwork. Then you have to rub them down and later on during the day put them through their training paces." The two guys looked at each other in dismay. "You two can start by emptying out the spit buckets." They made a beeline for the door and never returned.

If they couldn't get to Cus, wiseguys would try to approach his fighters directly. Anthony Caruso remembers Cus warning him about being approached. "After Cus grooms you and you're ready for the championship, now they want you. Before, they didn't want nothing to do with you. That's what Cus told me too. 'Everybody is going to want you now. Get up there a little bit and see how many people come to you.' When I won the Golden Gloves, everybody was on the chairs standing up, clapping, screaming, and two guys came over to me. They wanted to give me twenty-five thousand dollars because I was knocking everybody out. That's seventy years ago, that was a fortune and I was dead broke. They said, 'Hey, come with us, we'll give you a car.' I said, 'Look, you've got to talk to my manager, Cus D'Amato.' So I went back and said, 'Cus, these guys want to give me twenty-five thousand dollars to leave you. But I told them to fuck themselves.' 'No kidding, you said that? That's my boy. That's what I want, loyal guys.' "

Eventually the wiseguys tried to negotiate with Cus to buy his fighters. One guy asked Cus if he would sell a certain boxer. "I don't sell fighters," Cus told him. "If they can't fight, I retire them. If they can fight, I keep them." Cus said that if the fighter wanted to leave him he could as long as he told him directly and paid Cus the money he'd laid out for the fighter's expenses. The kid came to Cus and told him he wanted to go and Cus cut him loose. But Cus got the last laugh. His new management knew nothing about boxing and they threw the kid into a main bout after a few four-round fights and the kid wilted. Cus would always say that he used to make guys look good, even if they weren't as good as they looked.

But all this intrigue only made Cus paranoid. A friend of Burt Young's told him to check out Cus's gym, so he went up there one day. Cus immediately asked Burt to empty his pockets. "I thought he was a deviant," Young told me. "But Cus explained that Tony Ducks [who ran the Lucchese crime family] was trying to take over his fighters and he wanted to make sure that I didn't have a plant on me."

Cus's former fighter Graziano was trying to poach some of Cus's guys for the mob. Cus told us a story of how he ran into Graziano on a street in Manhattan. "I was standing with a big plate-glass window behind me and Graziano walks by, comes from my blind side and all of a sudden he's standing right in front of me and he says, 'Cus, I hear you've got a beef with me. You got something to say?' " Cus can just tell by the look in Rocky's eye that he was thinking of doing something. "So I said, 'Rocky, if you do what you think you're thinking of doing, we're going to do it your way, but I promise you this. I'm going to come back and we're going to do it my way, and I'm going to finish it for good.' He saw in my eyes how serious I was and he said, 'Ah, Cus, I'm not going to deal with you,' and walked away. I just envisioned Rocky pushing me through this big plate-glass window, and glass falling on top of me, so I had to let him know that I would come back and finish it."

Cus was so fearful that he even threatened Rocky Marciano when the former heavyweight champ came up to the Gramercy one night. Marciano was hanging out with gangsters then and Cus was alarmed when he heard two sets of footsteps coming up the stairs to the gym.

"Who is it?" Cus yelled from behind the door.

"It's me, Cus. It's Rocky," Marciano said.

"Who's with you?" Cus asked.

"Nobody," Rocky said.

"Rocky, I don't want to see anybody. I've got a shotgun here and if you don't leave, I'm going to shoot right through this door. Do you understand that?"

Rocky turned around and left real fast.

MONEY MEANT NOTHING TO CUS. He had enough self-confidence that he felt that anytime he needed money, he could earn it. He tried to instill that attitude in his fighters. Over the years Cus was criticized for his cautious approach to managing his fighters, sometimes even turning down fights for big purses if he felt that his fighter wasn't ready. He defended his approach in an article in *Sport* magazine in 1957. "I've always felt that if I accomplish my objective, the money would be there, but the money had to be secondary. I often tell the boys that we're like runners in a close race for a hundred thousand dollars in gold, in which one boy is leading all the rest by a step. Just before he reaches the finish line, he sees a twenty-dollar gold piece, stoops to pick it up, and loses the hundred thousand. The same applies to certain big money fights, which I had been offered for my fighters. Had I accepted bouts with certain fighters at different stages, my fighters might never have gotten to be champions."

Cus used to love to say, "Money is something to throw off the back of trains." For years I wondered about that saying and then it hit me. He meant that money was something to give the people who are following the train. He loved that romantic urban hero Robin Hood stuff. "The truth was I wasn't careless with money," Cus said. "I gave money to people in trouble. I don't consider that wasting it." I got a lot of my attitude toward money from Cus. I've been criticized for going through millions of dollars and it's true. But I always broke off cash for people who needed it.

Cus was that way with all the fighters in his gym. Anthony Patti remembers Cus's generosity back in the fifties. "Cus always had something for the boys, whether he could afford it or not. I remember one day I'm at the gym and a fighter comes in and he goes, 'Hey, Cus, could you help me out with some money? I'm short.' Cus said, 'Sure.' He didn't hesitate, went through his pockets, he came out with, I think, four singles and a pocketful of change. He gave the fighter three singles, and he kept the dollar and the change. That's the way he was. He bought fighters trunks, he got others new punching bag gloves. Whatever money he had, it always went to his fighters. And he never asked for anything back from any of them. Just 'Be faithful to me.' He was like a father to everybody. Every fighter would go to him with their problems, and he'd take us into the office, close the door, and we'd have a talk."

Grey Gauvin was a homeless kid from the Gramercy neighborhood who was always getting in trouble. Cus took him on and taught him boxing in an attempt to steer him the right way. Gauvin was interviewed for that 1957 *Life* article about Cus: "Thank God for Cus is what I say. I was sleeping in the back seat of a car. He put me up in a hotel, got me a job. He's never asked me for a cent. If it hadn't been for Cus I'd probably be in jail today. He taught me to get over my hostile feelings to society."

Gauvin wasn't the only kid that Cus took off the streets. At one point he was paying the rent for up to seventy fighters to stay at an old hotel near the Gramercy. Plus he gave them sixty dollars a month spending money. On Sunday nights he'd take a few of his fighters to his brother Tony's house for dinner. Back then boxers were called prizefighters because they didn't necessarily get cash for a victory; they might get a prize. If one of his fighters won a watch in a competition, Cus would buy the watch from the kid for cash and then he'd either resell it or give the watch away. All Cus's nieces and nephews were taken care of. "We wore cardboard in our shoes because the soles had holes, but we always had nice wristwatches," his niece Betty remembers.

Cus expected that his fighters would follow his advice. Anthony Caruso remembers how Cus used to lecture him. "He didn't like no girlfriends. He didn't want me to hang out with nobody but fighters. He told me, 'After you become a champion you can do anything you want. Right now, you don't fool around with no girl, you don't drink, you don't smoke. You've got to put your mind on boxing. And you've got to listen to your father and your mother, they're your best friends.'"

Anthony Caruso was with Cus for fourteen years starting when he was fourteen. He had tremendous potential but he didn't have the motivation to become a champ. At one point, Cus told Anthony that he was going to put him on an undercard at Madison Square Garden so Caruso could get some exposure. Cus wanted him at training camp before the fight but Anthony never showed. The day of the fight, Caruso went to the gym.

"What are you doing here?" Cus growled.

"Well, the fight is tonight, right, Cus?"

"No, it ain't. I canceled the fight," Cus said. "What do you think? You're gonna knock everybody out in one round? Those kids are tough." Anthony left and never came back to Cus again. But he realizes now that Cus was right: you had to train or you couldn't go ten rounds.

After years of seeing young boys come up those foreboding stairs to enter the Gramercy Gym, one day in 1949 Cus finally found someone who could fulfill his dream of nurturing a champion. He was a fourteen-year-old black boy from Bedford-Stuyvesant in Brooklyn named Floyd Patterson. He came up alone, which impressed Cus. Floyd seemed content to watch the other boys hit the bag until Cus asked him if he wanted to work out. Floyd seemed very shy but he managed to grunt, "Yeah." Cus was even more impressed when Floyd came out of the dressing room wearing boxing trunks. Floyd was a boy but he had the body of a man. Cus felt his back and his muscles were hard and firm and lay close to his bone structure. Cus could sense that he might have a hard punch. I wonder what Cus thought when he saw me for the first time at thirteen. If he thought Patterson was like a grown man, I must have been a god in comparison!

Cus loved Floyd's motivation—he wanted to box and make money so that his father didn't have to work himself to death trying to feed his wife and eleven children. Bingo! Cus thought that being part of a big family was good for a fighter because it meant he had never been coddled or overprotected. After coming to the gym every day for a few weeks, Floyd brought his older brother Frank one day. Frank was an accomplished boxer who went on to win a Golden Gloves title, and when they sparred, Frank took Floyd to school and hurt him. Floyd retreated to the dressing room and started crying. Cus followed him back and consoled him.

Cus also must have made an impression on Floyd when he threw Frank out of the gym shortly after Floyd began training. Cus found out that Frank had thrown an amateur bout. Anthony Patti was in the gym that day and when Frank came in Cus charged him. "You get the hell out of the gym and don't you ever come back here again," he screamed.

Cus began to peel the layers off Floyd. What he found was enough to make Freud salivate. Floyd had incredibly low self-esteem. He had been bullied as a kid at school and he would cut classes, walk to the end of the High Street subway station, and climb down into the tunnel. Then he'd squeeze himself into a maintenance shed where the workers kept their tools and curl into a fetal position and go to sleep. He was nearly autistic, avoided all social contact, and sometimes was found by his neighbors sleepwalking in the street. As the youngest of the eleven kids he thought of himself as a drain on his family. "My mother told me I used to point to a photograph of myself hanging in the bedroom and say, 'I don't like that boy!'" Floyd told *The New York Times*. "One day my mother found three large X's scratched with a nail over that photograph of me. I don't remember doing it. But I do remember feeling like a parasite at home." When his father came home exhausted from his longshoreman job, Floyd took off his shoes and cleaned his feet. "And I felt so bad because here I was, not going to school, doing nothing. . . . Friday nights was even worse. He would come home with his pay, and he'd put every nickel of it on the table so my mother could buy food for all the children. I never wanted to be around to see that. I'd run and hide."

As he grew older Floyd started acting out and began stealing and bringing his spoils back to his mother. "All I wanted to do was help my parents and all I did was ending up in failure and making matters worse." Finally, a judge convinced his mom to send Floyd to the Wiltwyck School for Boys in upstate New York. Floyd loved getting out of the city and enjoying nature and he began to thrive and learned how to read. After two years he was sent back to the city and he enrolled in P.S. 614, a "600" school for problem kids. And then he wandered into the Gramercy.

Floyd was tailor-made for Cus's reclamation projects. When he saw that Floyd cried from being hit, he began to teach him the peekaboo technique and worked with him on the slip bag. And he worked on Floyd's psyche too. Cus realized how fragile Floyd was, so he would talk to other people in Floyd's presence so Floyd wouldn't feel he was being singled out for criticism. When Cus realized that Floyd had a hygiene problem, he made sure Floyd was within earshot when he lectured Anthony Patti on the importance of taking regular showers. Cus was a master psychologist.

Cus was convinced that Floyd was the fighter he could rely on in his quest for a world championship when he heard an anecdote about Floyd's time at Wiltwyck from one of his teachers. She was convinced that Floyd would someday be successful because one week he was named the most deserving student, which came with a reward of a bag of candy. Floyd was crazy about candy, but he refused his reward because his teacher told him that he could not share the candy and he had a previous agreement with another boy that they would share any prizes either boy won. His teacher kept pressing Floyd on why he wouldn't accept the candy, and when she found out about the agreement she gave him the candy anyway. Floyd's selfless act made a huge impression on Cus. "It told me that he had the character to stand up and do what he thought was right. Now this is a very important thing, because character is what makes a man predictable. It's very easy to fold up like an accordion. But a man who has character will stick with it and go along to what he has to accomplish and this is what this boy had. This told me that I could trust this boy and not be afraid that he'll go behind my back and allow someone with money or some other inducement to get him to turn against me so I'll be left holding the bag."

Cus launched Floyd's amateur career and he performed great, knocking almost everyone out. But Cus was concerned that Floyd wasn't psychologically ready to go pro. He needed to build up Floyd's confidence. Cus thought that Floyd hadn't developed an ego yet, that he was influenced by those people around him, from his teachers at Wiltwyck to Cus himself. So Cus became conscious that he had to be a role model for Floyd. He didn't smoke or drink in front of him. He began dressing up in a sharp coat topped with a homburg so he would look like a dignified guy, even if he wasn't. One day Floyd was being interviewed and Cus was over to the side and the journalist said to Floyd, "You know, you dress very well for a boy your age." Floyd said, "Oh, I watch my manager. I always watch my manager." That just confirmed Cus's behavior.

Cus always preached that you should act like a champ before you become one. So it was partly that and partly an attempt to keep the mob away from Floyd when Cus bought his young fighter a white-walled 1952 Cadillac Coupe de Ville. Floyd wasn't even a main-event fighter yet and Cus was broke at the time but one of his friends who Cus had helped back in the Bronx helped him with the payment.

Floyd urged Cus to take him pro at the end of 1951 but Cus had a different timetable. He wanted Floyd to fight in the 1952 Olympics in Helsinki. Cus knew that Floyd would win a gold medal in sensational fashion and the publicity would help Cus get Floyd attractive pro bouts. Plus a gold medal hanging from his neck would do wonders for Floyd's confidence. It took Floyd just four fights and eighteen minutes of work and he won the gold fighting as a middleweight.

Cus didn't go to Helsinki, but he was at the docks when a huge crowd of newspapermen met the boat carrying Floyd back to the United States. At an impromptu press conference, the reporters peppered Floyd with questions about when he would turn pro. "I kept my mouth shut," Floyd revealed in his autobiography. "My answer was that Cus answered the questions and it was to remain that way for many years. He not only provided all the answers, but I did what I was told to do by him."

Cus was more than happy to talk. "This young man is going to be the champion of the world and go down in history as the youngest heavyweight champion that ever lived. In addition, he will be the most promising fighter of this era."

Cus was confident that the publicity Floyd got from winning Olympic gold would help Cus in his fight outside the ring. It was to be the biggest fight of his life—a struggle between him and the mob and the International Boxing Club (IBC), which controlled virtually all the top boxers, venues, and promoters in the sport. But then Floyd did something that threw Cus for a loop and made him question his young boxer's character. It was behavior that in an instant could derail Floyd's pro career just as it was beginning. The incident involved a woman—and an allegation of statutory rape.

This story has never appeared in any biographies of Floyd or in Floyd's ghostwritten autobiography. But Ratso was able to find sections of an early draft of Floyd's autobiography, written by Cus's friend, the journalist Arthur Mann. These pages were uncovered among the thousands and thousands of pages of Mann's collected writings that he donated to the Library of Congress. So let's check out the sanitized Cus-tomized version of this story from the original manuscript of Floyd's autobiography.

"November of 1953 brought my worst defeat, though it's not in the record book. The guardian of a girl in Brooklyn appealed to a welfare agency with a claim that I was the father of his ward's baby, due to be born in three or four months. I knew the girl as a neighborhood friend. So did many other fellows. But I protested the charge and said I'd fight it in court as a trap. Cus D'Amato, my manager, thought otherwise.

" 'You have more chance of losing than any of her boyfriends,' he said. 'You're famous. You earn big money and will earn more. But a court fight without airtight proof would finish your career. The public would turn against you and end all your dreams of helping your family. The only answer, Floyd, is a quiet marriage. Then pay money to the guardian. It's only money, and you're going to earn far more than he will ever want.' " Floyd said that he only wanted to marry one girl, Sandra Hicks. He was worried about her reaction. Then they consulted Father McLees at Holy Rosary. Floyd was a new convert to Catholicism. "Naturally he objected to any marriage that wasn't holy. Cus argued that quiet marriage and payments was the only way I could avoid terrible headlines, public disgrace and the end of my career as a future great fighter. I was nearly nineteen. The girl was sixteen. So we went to New Jersey. There I submitted to a civil ceremony. After that, Cus took care of all monthly payments. I took care of opponents in the ring with greater determination than ever."

But there's a completely different account of what transpired between Floyd and the girl, whose name was Gloria Wanamaker. It appeared in the May 1957 issue of *Confidential* magazine, one of the first scandal magazines. We found the article in Cus's papers, stored in boxes at the Catskill home. The article was titled "I Had to *Force* FLOYD PATTERSON to Marry Me to Give Our Baby a Name," and bylined "Gloria Patterson Schmidt, Floyd Patterson's first wife." Gloria tells a radically different version in her account. She claimed that she was a virgin, not a friend "to many other fellows," as Floyd wrote. She said that she was only fifteen when she met Floyd in their neighborhood. It was a few weeks before he was to go to Helsinki for the Olympics and he wanted to date her before he left. She said her parents, not "a guardian," refused to allow her. Floyd then wrote her "many letters" from Finland, and when he returned a champ her father was wowed and invited him to the house for dinner. The night he came back from the Olympics he rushed right to her house and then he saw her every night for the next three months. Floyd then started pressuring her to have sex. She claimed that she told him that she was a virgin and that she wouldn't entertain the idea of having sex until she was married. "But Floyd kept insisting. He warned me that if I didn't go to bed with him, he would find himself a girl who would." She didn't want to stop seeing Floyd, because her parents had fallen in love with him, so she gave in. They had sex days after her sixteenth birthday for the first time. They repeated their tryst many times on the couch of her living room. In June of 1953 she discovered she was pregnant. Floyd promised to marry her, but the months passed and nothing happened. Her father pressured him, and when she did too, Floyd allegedly said, "I've thought it over and I've decided not to get married. I can see the fire, so why should I jump in and get burned?"

When she told her father what Floyd had said, he was furious and he marched down to the 81st Precinct and told them the story. Then the police called Floyd in and told him that he faced a sentence of eighteen months in jail for statutory rape if he didn't marry her, because she was still a minor. "Cus D'Amato, his manager, pleaded with my father not to make any trouble, because the bad publicity might ruin his fighter's career. We were offered money to forget the whole thing, but Pop said he didn't want money and neither did he want any bastards in the family. It was finally agreed that Floyd and I would get married immediately." Six weeks later, Floyd, Cus, and Gloria and her parents went to New Jersey for the ceremony. Floyd didn't give her a wedding ring and he grabbed the marriage certificate right out of her hand when she tried to take it. Arthur Mann had a copy of the marriage certificate in his files, and sure enough, the wedding was witnessed by "Custer D'Amato" of 116 East 14th Street, New York. Floyd stopped seeing Gloria after the wedding except for one time that her father had him summoned to Domestic Relations Court because he hadn't paid her any money for maternity clothes. Floyd "reluctantly" agreed to pay her $250 after each of his forthcoming fights.

But the story didn't end there. Floyd finally came to the hospital five days after their child, named Michael Constantine Patterson, was born. It took a couple of weeks but Floyd warmed up to the baby. Then he started visiting Gloria's house every day. "Three weeks after his first visit we had an affair and it wasn't long after that I discovered I was pregnant again." Then Gloria started getting hostile calls from Floyd's girlfriend, Sandra Hicks. She didn't believe that Floyd had gotten Gloria pregnant, because he told her he had been true to her. Gloria gave birth to a girl this time, Elizabeth Anne Patterson. Floyd came to the hospital every day and took Gloria and the baby home. Nobody knows what happened between Gloria and Sandra, but what we do know is that Floyd's career started taking off and Gloria didn't see him for many months. In March of 1956, Cus called her and suggested that she agree to a divorce. Since she wasn't seeing Floyd anymore she agreed. They agreed to a settlement of $13,000, $250 each month for the children's support until they were eighteen, and $10,000 in trust, payable at the rate of $1,000 after each fight. Gloria went to Mexico, and they were divorced in June of 1956. The money was paid when the papers came through. Five months after the divorce, Sandra, who married Floyd a month after the divorce, gave birth to a baby girl. And the press, thanks to Cus, celebrated the happy couple and welcomed Floyd's "first" child into the world.

In the years before Cus found Floyd, boxing was being run by two figures. One was Mike Jacobs, who worked his way up from being a ticket speculator on Broadway to being the number one boxing promoter in the world, thanks in part to his company, Twentieth Century Sports Club, holding the reigning heavyweight champ Joe Louis in "contractual bondage." Jacobs started his company with three partners who were journalists, including the world-famous columnist Damon Runyon, whose short story "The Idyll of Miss Sarah Brown" was turned into a portrait of colorful Broadway characters called *Guys and Dolls*. Using fundraising for a legitimate charity, the Free Milk Fund for Babies, as his cover, Jacobs took control of boxing at Madison Square Garden.

Jacobs had never promoted a fight in his life but he learned the ropes from Tex Rickard, a P. T. Barnumesque promoter who ran boxing at the Garden and controlled boxing in the 1920s through his promotions of Jack Dempsey's fights. In 1935 Jacobs got a tip about an up-and-coming fighter out of Detroit named Joe Louis. He immediately signed Louis to an exclusive promotional deal and then had the newspapers blow Louis up. It didn't take long for Louis to demolish James Braddock and become the heavyweight champ in 1937. Now Jacobs was in the catbird seat. From 1937 to 1947 he promoted over 1,500 boxing cards, including 61 world championships. His fights grossed over $30 million and he made extra pocket change by scalping press seats. He virtually controlled boxing. Along with another man they called "Mr. Gray."

Paul John Carbo, better known as Frankie Carbo, was born in 1904 on the Lower East Side of New York City. When he was eleven he was sent to a youth reformatory for stealing an apple. Instead of being rehabilitated he began a brazen life of crime. Cus knew Carbo all his life. "Carbo was a professional killer," Cus said years later. "I knew the man when he was a young fellow. I remember the first man he killed came from my neighborhood. It was up in a pool room. He was about eighteen. He had a piece in his belt and he was playing with a hat, the type the real tough guys wore in those days. So a fellow says, 'What the hell are you carrying that for? You haven't got the guts to use it.' 'I don't?' 'No.' Bam! Shot him just like that. That was the beginning of his career. After then, he became a professional killer for Murder Incorporated, an organization that did the killings for all the mob guys around the country. God knows how many guys he killed."

Working for Murder Inc. boss Louis "Lepke" Buchalter, Carbo was charged with murdering two bootleggers but released when the witnesses got cold feet and refused to testify. By the time he was in his late twenties, he had been arrested seventeen times and charged with five murders, including the murder of Harry Greenberg, who had worked for Lepke and Albert Anastasia, Lepke's partner, and was threatening to spill the beans on Murder Inc. unless he got five thousand dollars. Supposedly Bugsy Siegel drove the getaway car and Carbo put five bullets into Greenberg's head. That case disappeared when one of the prime prosecution witnesses, Abe "Kid Twister" Reles, conveniently fell out a window of a hotel room in Coney Island while under police protection.

Carbo got into boxing in 1936 when mobster Gabe Genovese took him in as a partner in managing the middleweight champion Babe Risko. Ten years later he was described as "the more or less benevolent despot of boxing's Invisible Empire," boxing's underworld commissioner, and openly written about by columnists. "Carbo had his fingers on the throat of boxing and could squeeze the air out of it any time he wanted to make a move," Teddy Brenner, who was a famous matchmaker and no stranger to the mob, wrote in his autobiography. "If he did not own a certain fighter, he 'owned' the manager."

Carbo operated out in the open from a dining room in a hotel around the corner from Madison Square Garden. He dressed impeccably and got his nickname from his gray hair. (He was also known as the Uncle, the Southern Salesman, the Traveling Salesman, Our Friend, the Ambassador, or just the Man, to keep police wiretappers confused.) But his piercing black eyes were the true window to his soul. Carbo, like Cus, fancied himself a Robin Hood and he was always a soft touch for a down-and-out fighter. Of course, most times the fighter might be down-and-out because of being ripped off by Carbo and his henchmen. The most prominent of these men was Frank "Blinky" Palermo. He was short with a peering stare that earned him his nickname. Carbo met Palermo through his book-making partner Nig Rosen and soon Palermo became the manager of record of such prominent fighters as Ike Williams, Billy Fox, and Carmen Basilio and, eventually, the undercover manager of Sonny Liston.

Carbo and Palermo regularly fixed fights, the most notorious among them being the Billy Fox–Jake LaMotta fight in 1947. But most times they didn't even have to put the muscle on boxers to throw fights because they'd have a controlling interest in both the fighters. And when they needed to, they'd use their connections with "certain members" of the New York State Athletic Commission and come up with close decisions for their fighters.

By the end of the forties, both Mike Jacobs and his cash cow Joe Louis were at the end of their ropes. Jacobs had suffered a debilitating stroke in 1947. Louis was reeling from assaults on him from both the IRS and his wife, who wanted a divorce and a big settlement. During the war, Louis had boxed some charity fights and the IRS claimed that he owed taxes on $90,000 worth of income from those fights, money that he had donated to the war effort! He was also in debt to Jacobs, who floated him money during his years of service. Louis turned to a black lawyer in Chicago named Truman Gibson. During the war, Gibson was a civilian aide to the secretary of war tasked with investigating racism in the military. He created a propaganda film, *The Negro Soldier*, directed by Stuart Heisler, that extolled the value of black soldiers. It became mandatory viewing for new recruits.

When Gibson returned to Chicago after the war, Louis sought his help and he created Joe Louis Enterprises. Joe was tired of fighting and he wanted to cash out on his heavyweight title, which he had held for ten years. It took a small, fat New Jersey–based press agent to come up with the idea that would change boxing forever. His name was Harry Mendel, and Joe Louis loved the dude.

Mendel's idea was for Joe Louis Enterprises to sign the four leading heavyweight contenders to contracts and then Joe would retire and assign the rights to the elimination tournament to a promoter. Gibson met with a Florida hotel owner named Harry Voiler, who offered to put $100,000 into a new promotional corporation and in return get 49 percent of the stock, leaving Louis in a majority position. Louis was desperate for cash so Voiler agreed to let him immediately withdraw $60,000.

The scheme fell through when Voiler decided that he would finance the corporation by putting up only the mortgages of his hotels, not cash. Then in a meeting in Miami with Mendel, Gibson, and Louis, Voiler's wife put the kibosh on mortgaging their hotels. But Mendel came through for Louis once again. He made a phone call and set up a three a.m. meeting with a millionaire who would change all their lives forever.

James Dougan Norris was the son of Canadian businessman James Norris Sr., who owned grain companies, mills, and a fleet of ships. His father's family had relocated to Chicago when his father was eighteen. The Norris family had amassed a tremendous amount of wealth since the 1800s, so James D. had no real incentive to do anything but spend his daddy's money. James Sr. had partnered up with a shrewd businessman in Chicago named Arthur Wirtz, and together they owned the Chicago Stadium, the Detroit Olympia, the St. Louis Arena, and a big chunk of Madison Square Garden. The senior Norris was a huge hockey fan so he bought the Detroit Red Wings. To keep his son happy, he bought him the Chicago Blackhawks.

Norris was sent to prep school, where he played football, but after only a semester at Colgate University he dropped out to pursue his real interest, racehorses. He was a gambler, betting as much as $6,000 a day on the ponies. In 1930, when he was twenty-four, he went to a Chicago racetrack and, as he was getting out of his car in front of his house at the end of the day, he was held up at gunpoint. The thieves stole $1,100 from his golf bag in the trunk but were kind enough to give him back a prize club he had won, along with

$10 cash. A few days later, he was approached by a stranger at the track who gave him his $1,100 back. He was "Golf Bag" Sam Hunt, a hit man for Al Capone who kept a machine gun in his golf bag and shouted "FORE" before pumping lead into his victims. Cus claimed that Norris would see important political people come up to his father's office and court him while Norris Sr. would sit at his desk like a reigning king. But when a wiseguy came in, his father would jump up and greet him like royalty. This made a big impression on Norris, who became a gangster groupie.

Norris met a lot of his wiseguy friends at the horse tracks. He kept a stable in New York called Spring Hill and met all the top bookies and utilized their services. It was at tracks in New York that Norris met Frankie Carbo and Albert Anastasia, the chief executioner for Murder Inc. Truman Gibson would soon learn just how much clout the young Norris had with the mob. A few years later, George Raft threw a party in one of the Havana casinos he fronted for. Tommy "Ducks" Lucchese, who ran the Lucchese crime family, approached Gibson and asked him how Norris was doing. At the time, Norris was banging down gin with Ernest Hemingway. "Give him my regards," Lucchese told Gibson. Then he pointed to a ragged scar on his face. "Tell him I carry the scar from the beer bottle he inflicted on me. It's lucky I didn't lose the sight of one eye."

The real brains behind the Norris dynasty was Wirtz, certainly not James Dougan. When the stock market crashed, Wirtz steered the Norrises into real estate that was selling at ten cents on the dollar. Wirtz also expanded their operations into lucrative cash-generating liquor distributorships. In fact, Wirtz once boasted that he supplied the booze for two of every four drinks poured in Las Vegas. Wirtz steered them into owning banks in Florida and Illinois, a good thing to own when you have cash businesses. Years later, when Castro booted the mob out of Havana, Wirtz and Norris put up stakes in the Bahamas. They used their $10 million yacht, named *Blackhawk*, and anchored it off a casino in Lucaya Beach. Not only could they make radio contact with their Miami bank to check gamblers' credit, but according to Truman Gibson, they used the boat as "the electronic nerve center for the world's biggest bookie operation."

As much as he loved horses, Norris was aching to be a player in the boxing business. Back in 1919, his father had taken him to the Dempsey–Willard fight where Dempsey knocked Willard out. From then on, his major ambition in life was to manage a heavyweight champion of the world. That pursuit would put him on a collision course with Cus.

Norris, naturally, was thrilled at the prospect of promoting the fights that would determine the next heavyweight champ. But Norris couldn't do anything without Wirtz so he suggested that Mendel and Gibson fly to Chicago the next day to meet with his partner. The negotiations started. Gibson asked for $250,000 for Louis to re-sign and 51 percent of the new promotional company. Wirtz was too good a negotiator and he ended the meeting. Four days later, Norris joined the group in Wirtz's office. Now Gibson went down to $150,000 and 20 percent of the stock along with an annual salary to Louis of $15,000. Agreed. The International Boxing Club was born in 1949. Word leaked out and Harry Markson, who ran the Garden for Jacobs, rushed to tell his boss that despite having a valid contract with Louis, the Brown Bomber was stiffing him. Jacobs couldn't believe it. But he managed to get $20,000 for ripping up their contract and then pulled down $10,000 a month as an honorary consultant until he hit $100,000. Poor Harry Mendel didn't do as well. He had been promised $4,000 for brokering the deal but he wound up getting hired to do PR for the IBC at $135 a week. When he complained, Louis blew him off, telling him that all he did was make a phone call.

Now Norris and Carbo solidified their relationship. Norris had all the arenas and the lucrative network TV fighting shows, so all he needed was a plentiful supply of fighters. Carbo had the fighters and their managers, like Hymie "The Mink" Wallman and Al "The Vest" Weill in his pocket. Together Norris and Carbo ruled boxing and in the process destroyed the smaller boxing clubs, which faded away without TV access.

But Carbo played both sides of the street. Through his influence with the Boxing Managers' Guild he ordered the managers' fighters to feign injuries and pull out of fights and threaten the TV revenue that the IBC depended on. The IBC was grossing about $24,000 a week from the broadcasts. A few weeks later, Norris caved in and offered the managers a bigger payday for their fighters that fought on TV. But when the managers sought to renegotiate their fighters' fees each year, Norris engineered a takeover of the Managers' Guild. He got Jack "Doc" Kearns, who had managed Dempsey and Mickey Walker, and now managed Joey Maxim and Archie Moore, who was then the light heavyweight champ, to work behind the scenes and infiltrate the guild with his guys. Kearns, who was seventy at the time, was broke and needed the money. He also hated Carbo, so this was a labor of love. Kearns and his men, who included the guild president Charley Johnson and William "Honest Bill" Daly, sowed dissension in the ranks, pitting the rich managers against the struggling ones. By 1952 the guild had split up its treasury, and Johnson organized a meeting in Chicago where he was voted president of a new national managers' guild called the International Boxing Guild. Norris won and never had to worry about managers asking for more TV money again. And just to be sure, he hired Carbo's girlfriend and paid her a nice salary to facilitate, according to Gibson, "the orderly presentation of unfixed fights on television," so as not to "antagonize or alienate" any of the fighters and managers with whom Carbo had "influence."

Two years into its existence, the IBC had a total monopoly over boxing. It had televised boxing shows three nights a week. There was no competition except for Emil Lence, who televised a show once a week from his Eastern Parkway Arena in Brooklyn. After four years, forty-four world championship fights were held in the United States and the IBC was involved in 80 percent of them, grossing over $7.5 million. By all rights, Joe Louis should have been a millionaire. But thanks to Arthur Wirtz he wasn't. Because of a complex web of interlocking corporations that was almost incomprehensible, the IBC showed losses or minimal profits each year and Louis's 20 percent wound up being worth bupkus. Gibson got ripped off too. For all his work, he pulled in a measly $7,200 a year, plus expenses.

In Seattle, Jack Hurley, considered by some to be the greatest trainer ever, loudly protested the IBC and told the press that his star light heavyweight prospect Harry "The Kid" Matthews would "never get a chance to win the title because Jim Norris and those people run a nice little store and monopolize everything." His statement began to reverberate and federal and state officials began to pay a little more attention to the IBC.

Norris was shrewd enough to curry favor with the boxing press. Some of them saw him as a "millionaire sportsman" who was working unselfishly to further boxing. Others were happy to get an envelope with a little bonus. Norris even gave one newspaperman a check for $10,000 when he learned the writer needed the money to buy a house. When the deal fell through Norris told him to keep the check and use the money when he found a house. He seemed like a nice guy—until he got drunk and did things like throw beer bottles at mafiosi.

All the good press couldn't help Norris when the Department of Justice filed a suit in U.S. District Court in New York City on March 17, 1952, charging the IBC and Madison Square Garden with "conspiring to restrain and monopolize the promotion and broadcasting of professional championship boxing in the U.S." Almost two years later, on February 4, 1954, a federal judge dismissed the government's case, citing that when the Supreme Court ruled the previous year that baseball didn't fall under the Sherman Antitrust Act, boxing should also fall under that ruling. Now Norris and his IBC had no obstacles in the way of their total domination of the sport. Except for a forty-six-year-old balding bulldog named Cus D'Amato.

SHORTLY AFTER PATTERSON RETURNED from the Olympics, Cus received a visit from Doc Kearns. Kearns was a slick hustler who got his start during the gold rush in the Klondike at the turn of the century. He went on to become a dognapper and a human trafficker smuggling Chinese laborers from Canada into the United States. Now he was working for Norris and came with an offer for Cus. The IBC was offering Cus $125,000 for Floyd's contract. "What are you going to do with him, Cus?" he said. "We control all the fighters."

Kearns was right. The IBC did control all the contenders, they controlled the commissions, and they even controlled Nat Fleischer and his *Ring* magazine, which was the bible of boxing's ranking system. If you didn't get work from Norris, your fighter didn't get any work. But Cus thought he had a secret weapon. "I said with this boy [Patterson] I can make the fight." Cus's first move was to seek out Emil Lence, the last important independent promoter left. One of the reasons that Lence wasn't put out of business by Norris was that Lence had a silent partner at his Brooklyn arena named James "Jimmy Doyle" Plumeri. He was a capo in the Lucchese crime family and he ran the garment center in Manhattan, where Lence owned a dress manufacturing company. He was also close to Carbo.

"I . . . made a deal with Emil Lence at a clambake over in Jersey," Cus told *Sports Illustrated*. "I told Emil I could make him the biggest man in boxing. I said Mike Jacobs got there because he had Joe Louis and he rose with the fighter. 'I have such a fighter,' I told him. Naturally he was interested. . . . So we got dates there and I got the right to pick the opponent. Even so I was careful, very careful. Some matchmakers, after a fighter has won four or five times, want to put him in against a fighter who will beat him. Destroy him! Not because the matchmaker is vicious, but because it is his business to make exciting fights. I turned down many opponents for Floyd when he was coming up; but I also had to pick some very tough opponents— tough for his stage of development at the time—that I believed he could beat. A fighter must surmount obstacles, he must reach peaks or he will never grow. I made some mistakes too—but Floyd saved me."

Patterson started his career in style, going 5–0, all knockouts or TKOs, but Cus was still concerned. He told a newspaperman friend of his, "Floyd lacks the killer instinct. He's too tame, too nice to his opponents. I've been trying all the psychology I can think of to anger his blood up, but he just doesn't have the zest for viciousness. I have a big job on my hands." So Cus began to work on Floyd's technical faults and made him even harder to hit. But working on his psyche was more of a challenge. Even though Floyd and I came from a similar background, I was just the opposite. I had that killer instinct. I wanted to hurt people because I knew it would make Cus happy. Cus must have been in heaven when he met me. Imagine if he had me back in the fifties? Oh man, they would have killed my black ass.

Sports Illustrated began to pay closer attention to Floyd after his sixth fight, a hard split decision over Dick Wagner. "A fighter like Patterson is enough to make boxing's gang-gray eminence, Frankie Carbo, lick his chops in anticipation," they wrote. " 'No tough guys have a piece of Floyd,' says D'Amato fiercely, 'and I'll carry a pistol before they do. I'm a free agent. . . . But I can't get fights in the Garden. We don't get on television. We fight out of town.' "

Cus got some sympathy from the press that wasn't in Norris's pocket. The April 1954 issue of *He* magazine had a bold headline: "IBC—Is It Killing Boxing? Patterson Passed Over." The article detailed the problematic nature of the monopoly and gave Cus credit for refusing "to play ball." Maybe it was articles like this that shamed the IBC into allowing Patterson to fight former light heavyweight champ Joey Maxim. Cus knew that Maxim had everything but a knockout punch so Floyd couldn't get hurt. It was an exciting fight and eleven out of the twelve sportswriters polled thought that Floyd had won. But they gave the split decision to Maxim. Cus was happy, though. Maxim didn't wear Floyd down. Now Cus knew he could fight good fighters. But Floyd didn't take his first defeat so well. He hid in his apartment for five days.

Now Madison Square Garden began to deal with Cus. Al Weill, who was the IBC's matchmaker (as well as Marciano's manager, which was illegal and would ultimately get him sacked from the Garden), approached Cus to get Floyd to fight Joe Gannon, who Weill was grooming as Marciano's successor. Cus let Weill "talk him into" the fight and Patterson won a tough eight-round decision. Then Weill "persuaded" Cus to let Floyd fight Jimmy Slade, who was a notorious spoiler. Another unanimous decision put Floyd's record at 18–1.

Floyd had fought three straight fights at the Garden and now Lence pleaded with Cus to bring Floyd back to the Eastern Parkway, where he'd put him on their televised show. Teddy Brenner, their matchmaker, proposed a fight with Don Grant, a sensational light heavyweight who fought out of L.A. Dan Florio, Cus's assistant trainer, begged Cus not to take the fight, saying Grant was a "second Floyd." "You're crazy, Cus," Florio said. "This guy Grant's murder. He fights like a miracle." "Dan, in my life God made only one miracle," Cus replied. "And his name is Floyd Patterson." Floyd stopped him in the fifth.

Cus was now convinced that Floyd could fight anyone. But Norris was freezing him out of good fights. So Cus took Floyd out to a secret training camp in Summit, New Jersey, and hired good heavyweights, paid them a hundred dollars a round, and arranged actual fights with no head guards, not just sparring sessions. One of the fighters was Harold Drucker, a big guy with fast hands. When Drucker used to spar with Floyd in the city, Cus would tell him to take it easy on Floyd. But in Jersey it was all-out war.

According to Cus, Floyd knocked out twenty-two opponents in a row "and most of them were one-punch knockouts." Cus then took Floyd out of town. He fought Yvon Durelle, "The Fighting Fisherman," in his hometown of New Brunswick, Canada. Durelle was a tough fighter and Patterson knocked him down in the first with a left hook to the hip. Durelle wanted to stay down but the crowd exploded, begging him to get up, chanting, "FOUL! FOUL! FOUL!" Then the crowd started rushing the stage. Cus told me that he looked at Floyd and he saw an aura around his whole body. He had achieved that Zen calmness and impersonality that Cus always talked about. Meanwhile, the crowd started trying to get in the ring and Cus jumped up on the apron and started kicking the rioters in the face to protect Floyd. It was almost a full-fledged riot when the timekeeper suddenly rang his bell to signal the end of round one. That calmed the place down. They carried Durelle to his corner and Cus read his trainer's lips. "You stay the distance and you'll win the decision." So Cus told Patterson not to hit him below the chin anymore, since Durelle was going to crouch to avoid body shots. Patterson kept bouncing punches off his arm and his head, and in the fourth round Durelle refused to come out of his corner.

When you think about it, it's amazing that Cus had the balls to go up against Norris. Norris had the money, he had the mob connections, he had the press in his pocket, plus he controlled all the venues and the fighters. Norris was so arrogant that he mocked the idea of controlling boxing through a monopoly by naming one of his Thoroughbreds Octopus. How could Cus go up against that? For Cus, fighting Norris took on all the aspects of a military campaign. He began with reconnaissance of the enemy. Cus relied on a large network of paid spies and informants who would pass along inside information to him. These were mostly other promoters or managers or even newspapermen who detested Norris and supported Cus's insurgency. Cus also cultivated the foot messengers of the IBC who had been neglected or treated rottenly by Norris. He'd routinely take ten thousand dollars' worth of tickets off his cut and give them to people who normally couldn't pay for the fights. These IBC gofers would be privy to sensitive conversations while delivering coffee and handling administration. Cus had a standing policy of accepting all collect calls at his office. So he cultivated loyalty among the very people in a position to know the IBC's moves. Finally, Cus also used his lines of communication with wiseguys to get information that was vital in his campaign. One of his closest friends was the bookie/manager Charlie Antonucci, a.k.a. Charlie Black, who had close ties to "Fat Tony" Salerno, a top capo in the Genovese family. Black had ties to Carbo too.

By the end of 1955, Floyd's record was 27–1 and he was in the conversation of challenging for the heavyweight title. Cus took the occasion to blast Norris and his lackeys for forcing Floyd into fighting in Canada and out west because they couldn't get fights with IBC-controlled fighters. "Patterson is available to the highest bidder—but such is the power of the IBC that other promoters . . . do not dare compete," he told *Sports Illustrated*. "People ask me how I can lick $200 million [a reference to the fortune Norris supposedly enjoys]. I say Floyd Patterson has to be licked in the ring and there's nobody in the world that can do that. I'll lick $200 million with Patterson. The public will demand him. If Marciano retires no one will recognize a champion unless he fights Patterson first. As for Marciano, I knew six months ago that Patterson was ready for him, and he's better now than he was then."

Cus knew he had something else going for him. At the beginning of 1955, three years after the district judge had thrown out the Department of Justice's monopoly suit against the IBC, the Supreme Court ruled by a 6–2 vote that the federal government *could* regulate boxing as interstate commerce. At the time, Norris joked, "At least it was a split decision," and thought little of it, but behind the scenes the Department of Justice began collecting evidence. By the end of April 1956 the trial against Norris and the IBC began in Judge Sylvester Ryan's court in New York. The prosecutions brought out tons of documents to prove their case that the IBC was a monopoly, but they also called witnesses who had been squashed like bugs by Norris. The surface facts alone suggested guilt. The IBC had promoted 80 percent of all the world championship bouts from June 1949 until May 1953. A local Cincinnati promoter, who had worked almost all of Ezzard Charles's bouts since he was fourteen, wanted to promote a fight between Charles and Jersey Joe Walcott after Joe Louis retired. He met with Norris, who told him he would allow him to go ahead with the fight as long as Norris was paid a $150,000 fee. "Charles belongs to me now. Mr. Walcott belongs to me. I just paid Louis $100,000 to retire," Norris said. Seven more witnesses testified for the government and then they rested. The defense made a motion to dismiss, which was denied.

Meanwhile, Cus was putting a brilliant plan into effect to force Norris's hand to get a title shot for Floyd. This is how Cus remembered it in 1985: "Rocky Marciano is about to retire, but nobody knew about it and Al Weill, his manager, was swindled out of ninety thousand dollars by Jim Norris, so when he discovered it, he tried to get the money back and he couldn't get it, so he turned against Norris. Now Weill and Carbo were partners, so Carbo gave him privileges that nobody else had. He could make his own decisions, believe it or not, but when I learned there was trouble, I went into the place where the mobsters were hanging out. They all said to me, 'Look, why don't you make up with the IBC, you can get a million bucks under the table, you're better off, you can't trust fighters.' So I said, 'What the hell is Norris going to do? Let me tell you. In order to defeat me, he needed a better fighter. He can't beat me with hundred-dollar bills, he needs a better fighter. Since he hasn't got one, he can't beat me. Furthermore, unless he makes the match that I want, which is a match he doesn't want to give and pays the money I want, unless he pays me the money I'm after, I'm going to fight Rocky Marciano for another promoter.' See, I gambled on the fact that this guy Weill, being angry with Mr. Norris and his people, wouldn't open his mouth to them if I said I wanted to fight Marciano. So when I said this they laughed, they said it's under Carbo's control. But I also knew that Weill had the privilege of doing his own business.

"So the moment I left, one guy ran across the street to the Garden and said to Norris, 'Do you know what's happening to Cus D'Amato and Weill?' [Norris], knowing it was a result of this quarrel, immediately made arrangements to meet with me to prevent me from fighting Marciano, which is all I wanted. If I fought his fighter, the number two contender, I knew who was going to win, see? And that's how I got to the championship."

That's pretty much close to the truth. Weill had been disenchanted with Norris for years, going back to when Norris screwed him out of profits from the IBC, the same way he had screwed Joe Louis. Weill was playing both sides—he was the matchmaker for the IBC and he was fronting his son as the manager of Marciano. But when he made a mistake and called Marciano "my fighter" at a weigh-in, the New York State Athletic Commission forced Norris to make him resign as the IBC matchmaker. So Norris brought in a guy named Billy Brown, who was totally in the pocket of Frankie Carbo. Norris screwing Weill out of his money wasn't a new development, but Weill still harbored resentment toward Norris. And don't forget that it was Weill who gave Floyd three fights at the Garden, so he was always willing to do business with Cus.

What Cus doesn't mention is that Marciano retired because he had been screwed by Weill when Truman Gibson told a promoter to skim ten grand off the top of the gross of a fight and Weill got it without Rocky knowing about it. But Cus had put the word out on the street that he would go around Norris and his fighters and fight Marciano for the title, knowing that Marciano was going to retire. At the same time, Cus went to the head of the NYSAC and got the commission to agree to recognize the winner of a match between Floyd Patterson and the IBC's Hurricane Jackson, the number two contender behind Archie Moore, as a challenger for the next heavyweight championship match after Marciano retired.

Eventually Norris negotiated with Cus, but first he had his lackeys try. Billy Brown offered Cus only $4,000 for Floyd to fight Jackson, the standard amount they paid for fights that were televised. Cus told him to shove it. He wanted $50,000 for Floyd, since it would be an elimination fight to see who would fight Moore for the vacated title. "If this is an elimination fight, it's an open air show," Cus told reporters. "This is a quarter million-dollar fight, not a $4,000 fight. Patterson should get at least $50,000." When the reporters noted that the IBC had to honor their television commitments, Cus was ready. "Okay, I'm a reasonable man. If Norris pays $50,000, I'll go on his weekly show." When the IBC was asked to comment, Harry Markson, Brown's boss at the Garden, said that $4,000 was the most that Brown was authorized to make and that any bigger guarantee had to come from Norris himself. Cus responded by turning his back on Markson when he encountered him on the street.

Rocky Marciano retired undefeated on April 27, 1956. When asked, he named three worthy contenders for his vacated throne: Archie Moore, who Marciano had come off the canvas to stop in his last fight, in September of 1955; Hurricane Jackson, managed by the fur mogul Lippy Breitbart, who had bought Jackson's contract for $10,000 (money that was loaned to him by Norris); and Patterson. Since Doc

Kearns, who had been on Norris's payroll, managed Moore, it was clear that Norris controlled two-thirds of the contenders. The only person between him and his long-desired heavyweight champion was Floyd—and Cus.

A week after Marciano retired, Norris opened negotiations with Cus for the elimination match with Jackson. Cus was sure he had Norris by the balls now. Instead of going to Norris's office, Cus rented a hotel room and made Norris come to him. Cus brought his pal Charlie Black along. Norris wasn't the only one who could brag of mob ties. When Norris arrived, he seemed a little awkward.

"People have told me that you said many bad things about me, but I never really believed them," Norris joked, trying to break the ice.

"Well, they were all true," Cus snarled.

Norris seemed taken aback and told Cus now that they'd become acquainted, they should meet another time, and he beat a hasty exit. Black thought that Norris's departure put the kibosh on the proposed fight, but Cus was confident and told Charlie that Norris would be back. Cus was right. When Charlie called Norris a few days later and told him that Cus wasn't interested in preliminary ice-breaking, only in results, Norris came back to the table. And now Cus pulled off one of his finest moves ever. He told Norris that before they could even talk about the Patterson–Jackson fight, Norris must compensate Cus for all the financial damage that Norris had rained upon Cus by blocking his fighter, disparaging him in public, even for hurting Cus's friends' fighters. For those damages he wanted $20,000 up front. Norris had no choice but to put in for a "loan" to Cus from the IBC, a practice that the IBC had done for years to keep managers and fighters indebted to them. But this was different. Cus had no intention of ever paying Norris back. And he never did. Cus thought this was the ultimate slick move. He was so proud of himself. "I made them pay me twenty thousand dollars before he even opened his mouth," Cus bragged to me. He didn't respect Norris at all.

When they got down to the nitty-gritty negotiations for the fight, Cus was adamant that both fighters, Floyd and Hurricane, get $50,000. Norris got Cus down to a $40,000 guarantee, but when the gate was factored in, both Hurricane and Floyd walked away with almost $50,000. A lot better than the $4,000 they were originally offered. Norris might have seen this as a one-time expense because he probably thought that Jackson would beat Floyd. But Cus had an ace up his sleeve. When he had conducted those secret fights in Jersey, Jackson came up and fought Floyd. They were close friends but Floyd beat the shit out of Hurricane.

Norris had to defend his practice of loaning money to fighters and managers, and now Cus, when he was called to testify before Judge Ryan in the IBC monopoly case. His defense attorney asked him why he lent large sums of money to fighters. "Oh, to help boxers and their managers when they are in trouble, when they need a little money. Rather than have them go to a loan shark or possibly sell part of the contract of their fighter to someone who might not be acceptable in boxing, I have advanced money at different times to fighters," Norris said, as if he were a boxing philanthropist. "To help them stay out of the clutches of those who might influence them, perhaps in throwing their fights, you give them money?" Judge Ryan said incredulously. "I wouldn't say that, Your Honor, but I think it helps them," was Norris's lame reply.

The fight was set for June 8 at Madison Square Garden. Jackson was a full-fledged flake. Anthony Patti once saw him fall asleep punching the heavy bag in the gym. Most sportswriters didn't think much of Hurricane. Arthur Daley of *The New York Times* wrote, "Hurricane can't fight worth a lick . . . akin to fighting a swarm of bees. He never stops throwing punches in tireless, windmill fashion. The sting in those punches is completely harmless." In *Sports Illustrated*, Martin Kane wrote, "Hurricane . . . is a mysteriously successful fighter who has pushed himself into the No. 2 contender's position (right behind Moore, no less) with a weird assortment of pawings and slappings. . . . [Hurricane will fight Patterson] with a strange assortment of double uppercuts (a Hurricane original), open-glove slaps on the flanks, downward chopping rights and upward flailing lefts, all delivered in a nonsensical sequence."

But where Kane saw Floyd as "perhaps as good as, perhaps better than the young Joe Louis," Daley joined the anti-Cus press, noting that Patterson "has been kept in cotton batting by his overcautious manager, Cus D'Amato, and has been knocking over a goshawful collection of stiffs." The truth was Hurricane was durable and he took a lot of punches. He was very perpetual motiony and didn't have a devastating punch, but he did wear a lot of guys down. But not on the night of the fight. Floyd fought him perfectly. Patterson didn't try to keep up with Jackson's crazy pace, and he defended Jackson's slaps well and then, in the last thirty seconds of each round, opened fire. While the ref gave the fight to Hurricane, Patterson had Jackson in trouble in eight of the rounds and won by a wide margin on both of the judges' cards. But it was a costly victory. Patterson fractured the fourth metacarpal bone in his right hand when he hit Jackson's hard head. "He didn't follow orders," complained Cus. "He tried to out-hurricane Hurricane."

While Cus was pleased that Floyd was now in line for a title shot, he was furious with Norris again. While they were negotiating the Jackson fight, Cus made Norris promise that, in the future, the IBC would use the best available fighters in their preliminary fights, whether they were IBC controlled or not. Also he vowed to help independent promoters and small clubs. After the Jackson fight, none of that transpired. Norris blamed it on his lackeys, Brown and Markson at Madison Square Garden, and Cus challenged him to fire them. When Norris didn't, Cus never forgave him.

But now Cus did have Norris where he wanted him. Floyd was one fight away from the title. How had Cus manipulated such a powerful empire? Here's where that black-magic stuff came in again. Cus would tell reporters over the years when he looked back on his fight with the IBC that there were strange forces allied against his enemy. Cus wasn't the typical fight manager. He didn't care about money, for one. Then he threw himself into this fight with insane passion. Sometimes he didn't sleep for days. He studied his enemy Norris constantly. He turned his strength, money, and power into his weakness. He made sure that Norris continually underestimated him. And as time went by, he played with Norris. He would visualize Norris sitting in a room that had twelve doors. Then he would see himself lock every door from the outside. When Norris decided to leave the room, he tried the first door but it was locked. Then he tried the second door—locked also. Now Norris was getting panicky. Seven, eight, nine, he's freaking out completely. Finally, he's down to one door. Cus unlocks it and Norris tries to open it, breathes a sigh of relief, and steps out. Except Cus is waiting there with an ax. He actually would tell this story to Tom Patti and me.

But how could he explain beating Norris at every turn? By the law of averages he had to be wrong some of the time, but he never was. One day Cus was thinking about this and it came to him in a flash. He knew their minds. And more than that, Cus would project the actions that he wanted Norris and his cronies to take through the air and they would comply! Just as he could see the wheels going around in the minds of his fighters, he could do that with his enemies too. Cus had such amazing powers of concentration that he would mobilize every cell in his body to impose his will on Norris and his gang. His logic told him that it was impossible but the evidence proved otherwise. Cus would go into a trancelike state, like a daydream, and he would visualize his enemies DOING WHAT HE WANTED THEM TO DO! He focused so intently on that picture in his head that suddenly it would disappear but he knew that what he pictured was going to happen. There was not an ounce of doubt in his mind.

Most people would probably say that it was all bullshit and Cus was crazy. But think about it. Was Cus irrational or was he practicing some dark arts? The idea of connecting your brain waves to another man's brain waves isn't that novel. You yourself can sometimes look at a guy and say, "I know what this nigga's thinking." And that's just little layman shit. Imagine somebody deep into that. That's all it is, a form of black art. Cus called it developing the mind and showing your essence, but it's a form of witchcraft. It all fits into that shit, so he takes pieces of everything and makes it a Cus D'Amatoism. Since I met Cus, I've been around the world and seen that a lot of what he was talking about is just dark art. This is what Cus believed in and I guess I did too. It worked for me, it made me somebody.

But Cus wasn't going up against just Norris. Don't forget that Frankie Carbo and his wiseguy friends controlled the boxers and managers that had to deal with Norris. Cus had a strategy for dealing with them too, one that took into account the importance of respect to these guys. In 1985, Cus gave a talk in Albany and he laid out what his plan had been for dealing with Carbo. "Carbo called me the Crazy Man, because nobody would ever do what I did. But you see everything I did was calculated. I knew this type of mentality, I grew up in the streets, I knew the thinking they lived by, so I knew exactly how far to go. But you had to be very careful, it was like walking a tightrope, just a little bit off and you'd be shot. I could never let on what I was doing to challenge them, because if I challenged them they were the kind of people who never dropped a challenge. Because anything that was a threat to their reputation, they couldn't afford to have anybody challenge that. So I did everything to accomplish what I was going to accomplish, just short of a challenge. And while I irritated and aggravated them, I never let them get to the point where they were going to do something about it."

Look, Cus was challenging the boxing establishment but he wasn't doing it for his own self-aggrandizement. He had an interesting article around that time called "The Boxing Monopoly Is Not Dead," ghostwritten by his friend Arthur Mann. In it Cus revealed his motivation for his fight against Norris. He noted that people called him a psychopath. "Perhaps. But if so, I'm a psychopath who believes sincerely in what he's doing. And the reason for my long fight against the most powerful and ruinous combination in this history of a great sport is the same as when I started. My only goal is to restore open and independent competition to boxing at all levels. I want to revive the small, neighborhood club that offers normal and necessary experience to the ex-amateur, and puts the rungs in the ladder to the top. I want to bring back the right of a fighter's manager to bargain on the basis of his boy's skill and crowd-appeal. In other words, free enterprise for boxing in a country that guarantees this priceless freedom as a constitutional right."

Now that goal was within his reach. But Norris had one last trick up his sleeve. Despite the commissions and the public naming Patterson as the man who should challenge Moore for the vacated heavyweight title, Norris tried to match his man Moore with another IBC-controlled fighter. So Cus used his friends in the TV and radio media. One of them was a young Howard Cosell. Cosell had developed an affection for Cus and for Floyd. He used to put Cus on his radio show so much that he seemed like a regular. Cus felt that the newspapers could lie to the public all they wanted, but if Cus could get his voice and his face out through radio and TV, then people would listen to his side of the story. And they did. "I became a bit of a hero," Cus said modestly.

So he went to Cosell and told him that Norris was trying to screw him out of the championship fight and Cosell put Cus on. Cus went right on the offensive, sparing little detail. When Cus got home that night, Norris called up and said, "Why, I had no such idea of alienating Floyd Patterson."

Norris had reason to be so magnanimous. He thought that Judge Ryan would rule in favor of the IBC. And both Archie Moore and his manager, Doc Kearns, assured Norris that Moore would knock Floyd out. So the match was set for November 30, 1956, at Chicago Stadium. Floyd had been so underestimated by guys like Nat Fleischer that he wasn't even listed in the top heavyweight rankings in *The Ring* magazine.

Norris wanted the fight in his hometown of Chicago and Cus was worried that he might get a "Chicago decision" but he was assured by people close to both the governor and Chicago mayor Richard Daley that the fight would be fair and square. Cus set up Floyd's camp at Sportsman's Park, an abandoned racetrack on the outskirts of Chicago. On seeing it Cosell wrote, "The place was so barren, so unattended, I left there feeling sorry for them."

Sports Illustrated saw some benefits to the old racetrack. "D'Amato, who reads Freud and wears a Homburg . . . has followed the Pavlov principle, long honored in the training of dog acts. Every time Floyd fights well Cus rewards him with a gift, thus setting up a conditioned reflex. One recent day, after watching his fighter ride a palomino lead pony around the race track, Cus decided to present him with a saddle horse should he win the championship. Since Patterson is fond of horses and rides well, this promise presumably will set him to drooling like a Pavlov puppy when the timekeeper sounds the opening bell."

Floyd did his roadwork on the racetrack and sparred in a ring set up in what was the VIP area of the grandstand. Floyd's sleeping quarters were in a jockey's room. Each night, Cus pulled out a cot and set it up outside the entrance to Floyd's room. Cus normally posted his brother Tony in front of a fighter's dressing room the night of a fight to keep wiseguys out but this was going a step further. He might have gotten that precaution from Al Capone, whose bodyguard Phil D'Andrea would sleep outside his door. Floyd wrote about the cot in his autobiography: "[Cus] was so frightened that somebody was going to try to do us in, that after I would go to sleep each night, he'd place a cot bed across the entrance to the room in which [sparring partner] Buster and I slept. . . . Half the time he wouldn't even bother to undress. He'd get on the cot still in his clothes. He was on guard. One day a reporter asked Cus if he wasn't overdramatizing things. 'I know I sound crazy guarding him like that but you hear all these stories and you never know.' "

Cus took pride in being a tough guy. He didn't take any shit from anyone. But why is he the one sleeping outside the door? *He's* the one they want to get. They don't want to hurt Patterson; they want Patterson to work for them. They want to break Cus's kneecaps and get him out of the way.

Cus had studied Archie Moore his whole career and he devised a way to break through Moore's famous defensive posture. It was hard to punch the body on Moore but he did expose his jaw. He told Floyd to crowd Moore in close and use his speed. The majority of sportswriters and boxing pundits thought that Cus had brought Floyd along too fast and that he wasn't even a legitimate heavyweight. They seemed to be rooting for Cus's comeuppance. But Cus would never have put Floyd in a situation where he thought he was overmatched.

At a press conference on the eve of the fight, Cus predicted not only a win for Floyd but the press's reaction after the fight. "All of you people have picked Archie Moore to win and your choice was based on your observation in these few weeks, prior to the fight. You watched both these men perform, but from what they showed you that they could do, you have chosen Archie Moore to win, most of you have chosen him to win by a knockout. . . . However, tomorrow night, after Floyd Patterson knocks out Archie Moore, all of you men will say, 'He beat an old man.'" Floyd had picked up on Cus's arrogance and when he was interviewed on a Chicago show and asked how a guy with only four years' experience could beat a guy with twenty, Floyd smiled. "Well, maybe I learned as much in four years as it took him to learn in twenty."

On the day of the weigh-in, a Chicago paper revealed that Norris had given Moore a secret guarantee of $200,000 regardless of the gate, which was not the contract with Moore that was filed with the Illinois State Athletic Commission. Cus was furious with another Norris betrayal. When the fight was announced, Moore was favored by 3–1 odds even though he was thirty-nine years old, eighteen years older than Floyd. Charlie Black and his friends in East Harlem put a lot of money on Floyd. By fight time the odds had dropped to 8–5, but that didn't worry Norris, who had bet a small fortune on Moore.

Floyd's wife was due to give birth at any minute the day of the fight. And sure enough, five hours before the fight, she delivered a daughter. But Cus forbade anyone from telling Floyd that he was a new daddy. "About two hours before [the fight], Cus whispered it to me because he knew that the news would add to my ability. And it did," Patterson would say later.

As the fighters made their way into the ring, Cus admitted that he was nervous. In the corner he whispered last-minute instructions. "I wasn't so much giving him advice as trying to make it seem as if this was just another fight. But it wasn't." Floyd looked at Cus and Cus knew what he was thinking. "He was thinking the same as I was: Would our program pay off? Would all our years of special preparation make our dream a reality? Or had I been too careful, giving

Floyd too much of the kid-gloves treatment like some of the news-papermen charged?" Cus had the same feelings that everybody has, but he hid those feelings well. He started doubting himself. But after one round, his confidence came back. "Don't do anything foolish and you're the new champ," he told Floyd. Patterson boxed masterfully for the next few rounds. Archie couldn't even touch him. Then Floyd knocked him down and that was the beginning of the end. The referee stopped the fight in the fifth round.

The crowd went wild but Cus was in control of his emotions, even then. He had visualized that scene. And his thoughts went to his father. "I remembered that he once said, after beating me, that the day would come when I would be glad to take a severe whipping, just to have him around. Right now I was willing to take the worst beating of my life so my father could see what his discipline did." Cus was such an awesome guy. Floyd made $114,257 that night and Cus and Floyd sent $3,000 of that to a priest they had met when Floyd was doing an exhibition who was trying to integrate his congregation near Little Rock.

Of course, the day after the fight, true to Cus's prediction, the Norris-backed press said that Floyd's victory was tainted because he had fought an "old man." But Floyd had a champion at *Sports Illustrated*, where Martin Kane gushed about him: "In one poisoned punch he displayed a power that would not have shamed a Louis or a Dempsey. In somewhat less than five rounds he showed the defensive skill and tactical assault genius of a Tunney. He did not fight in the style of any of these three—he fought like a Patterson—but he stepped grandly into their illustrious company. . . . When Floyd Patterson knocked out Archie Moore to become history's youngest heavyweight champion, it was more than a ring triumph, it was also a defeat of the boxing monopoly."

A few days after the fight, Howard Cosell was home in New York when his doorbell rang. It was an ebullient Cus. He brought Cosell a bottle of hundred-year-old Armagnac brandy as a gift. "Take it, you've been with us all the way," Cus said. They sat and talked for hours and Cus told Cosell that he was going to call a press conference and announce that the IBC would not be involved in any of Floyd's fights from then on. Cus held that press conference and it was a shot across the bow of Norris.

In the days that followed, Cus would call Cosell at all hours of the day and night. One time, Cus had his driver pull to the side of the Merritt Parkway and Cus whispered into the roadside pay phone that his life was in jeopardy. "If anything happens to me, you'll know who did it. Tell the truth," he begged Cosell.

7

Cus D'Amato took me in hand and started me on my way to the top. I'll never forget him. He's one of the greatest of all boxing managers and a decent, honest Christian human being in whom I have unlimited faith," Patterson told *Ebony* shortly after he won the crown. "Cus handles the business angle and always will, as far as I'm concerned. He insisted that I get a 30-30 split of the gross from the Moore fight, and my paycheck was $114,257."

Sugar Ray Robinson was also a big fan of Cus's. He loved Cus's credo, "My job is for my fighter to get the most amount of money with the least amount of risk." One of the reasons that Sugar Ray loved him for that was because all Robinson did was fight monsters. Even the guys he knocked out were monsters. Plus with Cus now getting more money for fighters, Ray was able to hit up Norris for 45 percent of the gate when he defended his middleweight title in September of 1957 against Carmen Basilio. Yet another reason for Norris to despise Cus.

Norris began a disinformation campaign that Moore was old and inept when Patterson beat him, just as Cus had predicted. But what really pissed Cus off was that the Norris-controlled boxing press didn't even name Cus manager of the year after they won the crown. Cus loved getting awards and recognition. Instead Norris sent his employee Joe Louis to meet with Floyd and beg him for a favor: Fight for the IBC. "As much as I respected Joe, I had a greater responsibility of loyalty to Cus and his cause," Floyd wrote in his autobiography. "When Joe made a suggestion that I see some of the IBC bigwigs about a match they had in mind, I couldn't say no to Joe, but I couldn't say yes, either. All I could tell him was that D'Amato arranged my fights. I gave him Cus's phone number. I knew what Cus's answer would be."

Of course, Cus anticipated attacks like this when he went into battle. "Now at the time I made my plans, I knew the people I was going to cope with. I knew they were tough guys and all that. I made my plans knowing at some point the pressure was gonna build up, and when it built up, and the threats were there, my reaction would be, Let me get the hell outa here, you know, because nobody likes to get hurt. . . . A man's gonna give himself an excuse to run. . . . I didn't give myself that chance, see. I said to myself, 'When I get to that point when the threats have built up, I must remember, I made my plan when I was cool, calm, and collected, when there were no threats. So therefore I must never change my plan unless some factor comes to my attention that I didn't consider in making the plan.' See, in that case, and only then, would I change it. Otherwise, I'd stick to it."

Cus knew how to control his feelings. He was no fool, he wasn't going to be in front of some killers and be disrespectful. But he wasn't going to crumble under pressure. He just knew how to read situations. Cus taught me that. I'm a great reader of situations. I know if I get too aggressive, I'm going to get shut down. And I know if I'm too docile, it's not going to turn out well, so I just know how to read the situation, when to be aggressive and when not to. He gave me the tools to analyze situations with no emotional attachment. Cus was so schooled in the art of deception. He told me that he "borrowed" that $20,000 from Norris before the first Jackson fight with no intention of ever paying it back. He wanted Norris to think that Cus was just another schmuck manager getting himself indebted to Norris.

Cus told me that he tried to get fights with all the top contenders in the heavyweight division then but they were IBC controlled and Norris didn't want to let them fight Floyd. Cus sent a letter out to the managers of the top ten challengers offering them a right to fight for the title. One of them, Willie Pastrano's manager, agreed to a fight and they began negotiations, but after hearing from Norris he withdrew Pastrano and claimed Cus had misunderstood him. Norris's strategy was to freeze Cus out and then try to buy him out again. He didn't know Cus. Then if that didn't work he'd try to put pressure on the sanctioning groups and the state commissions to get Floyd stripped of his title. And they could always threaten Cus too.

But Norris had other problems. On March 8, 1957, Judge Ryan ruled that Norris and his boys were guilty of a conspiracy to monopolize boxing in violation of the Sherman Act. Then three months later Ryan ruled that the IBC had to divest, dissolve, and divorce. He gave them five years to sell off their stock in Madison Square Garden. He limited the number of championship fights that they promoted to two per year. Both the IBC of Illinois and the IBC of New York had to be dissolved. And all exclusive service contracts with both fighters and stadiums were rendered null and void. But Judge Ryan allowed them to retain control of their two televised boxing shows. The IBC's reaction to all this? Gibson vowed to appeal the decision to the Supreme Court and Norris started working on Robinson's defense of his crown against Basilio.

While Ryan was deciding the appropriate punishment for the IBC, Cus, despite having an agreement for the IBC to promote Patterson's first title defense, went to the press in May and defied Norris. "The IBC is a detriment to boxing. I do not intend to let Patterson box for the IBC." Sensing that Norris was on the ropes, Sugar Ray Robinson and Archie Moore both tried to back out of their upcoming IBC fights. A week later Cus twisted the blade a bit. He announced that Emil Lence would promote the fight and that the most likely opponent was Hurricane Jackson, who was rated number one challenger. Jackson's manager demanded an outrageous guarantee of $250,000 but his wacky client only asked for "a new English bicycle."

By the end of the month Jackson had been signed. And *Sports Illustrated* heralded the changing of the guard. "The man who controls the heavyweight champ controls boxing. The man today is Cus

D'Amato, a party of passion and righteousness whose apocalyptic statements have earned him a reputation as an eccentric and windmill-tilter. . . . Just about everyone has now come to the conclusion that the white-haired, grim-jawed Cus is the smartest, toughest fight manager to come along in many a year. . . . D'Amato is certainly an individualist but just as surely no windmill-tilter. He can wheel and deal in the finest tradition and has done so. Otherwise he would not have been able to maneuver Patterson to the title against the fitful but formidable opposition of the International Boxing Club (James D. Norris, president), an achievement that demanded much more than fervor and rhetoric."

Cus claimed that Floyd would fight four or five times a year and that if any number one contender refused to fight, they would forfeit their right to go for the title. He also sketched out his ideal promoter. "I want a man who intends to stay in boxing, not a man looking for a lucrative one-shot. I want a man independently wealthy, so he can turn his boxing earnings back into boxing. I want a man with an aggressive spirit, someone who will take a stand, a man whose personal feeling has been hurt by the way boxing has been run. I want a man who will remain competitive and in constant opposition to the IBC; a man prepared, moreover, to take on one of the network TV shows if and when the IBC is forced to give one up—and this court trial will be a farce if they don't make them give one up. I also want a man who will promise to give a chance to those fighters and managers who haven't had the opportunity to get work because of the IBC and are deserving of it. Now, does that sound like I'm crazy, as they call me? After all, those that control the vehicle can drive it any way they wish."

That was the ideal promoter Cus wanted. Who he got was Emil Lence. But Cus was fond of Lence. Lence had given Floyd a chance when no one else would and Floyd fought a majority of his early fights at the Eastern Parkway, owned by Lence (and possibly his silent mob partner Jimmy Doyle). Cus had promised Lence Floyd's first defense and Lence was appreciative. "Cus is one of the few gentlemen in his business who keeps his word," he said. But despite his ties to Doyle,

Cus at fifteen with his best friend.

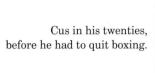

Cus in his twenties,
before he had to quit boxing.

Cus at the candy store outside the Gramercy Gym building.

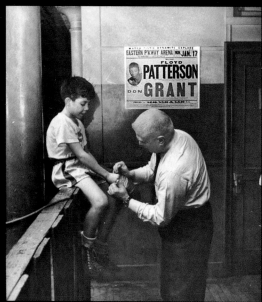

Cus puts the gloves on a young Willie Colón.

Holding the heavy bag for one of his students.

Cus shows a young student how to throw a left.

Cus poses with
Floyd Patterson
and trainer
Dan Florio.

Cus was at Patterson's
side at every press
conference.

Cus with independent
promoter Emil Lence.

Charlie Black was
small—but he was
an imposing figure.

Cus testifies before a
Senate subcommittee.

The staged demonstration of hypnosis before the first
Patterson–Liston fight.

Cus demonstrating his famous peekaboo defense.

A favorite pastime for Cus: talking on the phone.

D'Amato deep in thought.

Lence was no fan of Norris's. "I know Jackson will put up a real good fight—but not too good, I hope. If he wins, Norris and the IBC could get control of the heavyweight championship again," he told *Life*.

Cus also kept his word to his good friend Charlie Black. Black and Cus went way back to when they were young and Cus trained Charlie. But their relationship was cemented right before Christmas 1950. "In those days I was not only broke, but we were in pretty bad shape, most of us in boxing," Cus told a journalist. "At that particular time, just before Christmas, maybe a day or two before, we were crying on each other's shoulders. Between the two of us we might have had a twenty-cent piece. Every Christmas I gave a little party for the boys in my neighborhood and the boys that train in the gym, during which time I gave them things. It was the first time I had failed to get the money to have the party. We were standing on Broadway and while we were talking, a fellow walked along and said, 'Hello, Charlie. I've been looking for you.' He shook hands with him and asked, 'How are you? How's the family?' After he shook hands, he ran. Apparently he left a couple of bills in his hand. They were fifty-dollar bills but I didn't know it then. After Charlie got them, he looked at them and put one inside my suit pocket, said, 'Merry Christmas,' and left. When I got to my gym, I looked in there and I found a fifty-dollar bill. I got all excited because fifty dollars looked very big. I said, 'Charlie didn't realize how much he gave me,' so I called him. He said, 'I know how much it was. I said "Merry Christmas."' After that, I became very friendly with him. We didn't see too many fellows like that in the boxing business."

Charlie managed a few fighters, but his principal occupation was bookmaker. He was a close associate of "Trigger Mike" Coppola and Fat Tony Salerno, key members of the Genovese family. Charlie was also a Cus stalwart in Cus's fight with Norris, siding publicly with his friend. At one point, Cus gave Charlie his managerial rights to Frankie Ryff, a promising lightweight contender. But because of his opposition to Norris, he couldn't get any fights for Ryff and the fighter defected to the IBC. To support himself between fights, Ryff serviced elevators. In 1962, while training for a comeback, Ryff died after an eight-floor fall down an elevator shaft in a building under construction in Rockefeller Center.

Charlie was always around Cus's offices doing odd errands, and he'd come to Patterson's training camps too. He was also friendly with Lence, who loaned Black $3,200 in four installments that year.

Norris had to allow Jackson to fight because of the Ryan ruling but he tried to sabotage the fight by announcing the Robinson–Basilio fight on the same day that Lence announced Floyd's defense, even without having a specific date or locale. Norris's defiance of Ryan's ruling to refrain from championship fights while the IBC was being dissolved and his petty tactic to upstage Lence infuriated Eddie Borden, a boxing writer and handicapper who put out an influential tip sheet called *Weekly Boxing World*. "Whatever the fight game lacks in ethics, it certainly would never have reached the low level attained by Jim Norris, head of the IBC, in his insatiable desire to curb the aspirations of newly made promoter Emil Lence in his attempt to make a success of the Patterson–Jackson heavyweight title match. Mr. Norris is a college man, mingles with society, has a stable of horses and a multitude of other interests, but I think boxing is guided by an unwritten code of ethics which are far superior to those that he uses." Lence was a little more succinct: "Every time I say I don't want to hit Jim Norris, he hits me by stealing publicity. I'm getting a bit mad."

Patterson was favored by 5–1, but Jackson claimed to have come up with a secret weapon for this fight—a punch he called the Yagash, a right-hand body blow delivered downward, added to his unique two-fisted uppercut, which he had claimed to have learned from a kangaroo. While Floyd was his methodical, drab self in camp, Jackson had some unique diversions—he pretended to be a galley slave while rowing on the Delaware River, and he and three of his sparring partners formed a quartet and sang spirituals for hours, including his favorite, "Nero, My God, to Thee."

Nero didn't seem to have been listening. Floyd battered Hurricane around the ring for ten rounds and had him on the canvas three times. One writer even compared the fight to "a dark, uncomfortable dream out of Dostoevsky of a man beating a horse." Ruby Goldstein, the ref, stopped the fight in the tenth. Jackson was hospitalized overnight with a bruised kidney and Cus and Floyd and his wife visited him the next day.

Cus also helped Lence with his own wounds. Because of a threat of rain and because of a lackluster advance gate, Cus had agreed to waive Floyd's guarantee of $175,000 and accept 40 percent of the gate, which came out to only $123,859. His rationale was that he wanted to keep Lence in business as a promoter and work with him again down the line.

Cus could be that generous because he had gotten a call before the Jackson fight from Joe Gannon, a heavyweight who had fought and lost to Floyd in his eighteenth fight. Gannon had retired and now was an inspector for the D.C. boxing commission.

"I have something so fantastic I don't like to talk about it," Gannon told Cus.

"You're talking to a man who likes the fantastic," Cus replied.

The idea was concocted by Pete Rademacher, who was the reigning world Olympic heavyweight champ. He was the vice president of a company called Youth Unlimited that advocated for kids. He had reached out to some businessmen friends of his who would raise a $250,000 guarantee for Floyd. Cus claimed that he did his due diligence, met with Rademacher, and was convinced that Pete thought that he could win. Other people in the boxing community were indignant. The NYSAC commissioner Julius Helfand was against the fight. Some writers urged Congress to ban it.

But for Cus this fight was a lifesaver, coming just twenty-three days after the Jackson bout. The IBC was boycotting him, so having $250,000 dropped into his lap was like money from heaven. But he realized that for the fight to succeed he needed to bring in an old-school promoter who knew his way around ballyhoo. Jack Hurley was the man for the job. Hurley was one of the most colorful guys in the history of boxing. He was a trainer, manager, promoter, and matchmaker and regarded as a master in each. As manager and trainer he demanded 50 percent of his fighter's purses and most people thought that was a bargain.

Hurley was most famous for his gift of gab. His verbiage could hypnotize boxing writers. When he was promoting a fight between his mostly mediocre heavyweight Kid Matthews and Rocky Marciano, his savage lampooning of Marciano's talents moved the famous New York restaurateur Toots Shor to exclaim, "If I listened to Hurley for a week, I'd take off thirty pounds and fight Marciano myself." Hurley and Cus were both outsiders and they were united in their hatred for Norris.

The fight was scheduled to take place in Seattle, Washington, Rademacher's home state and Hurley's base of operations. Despite Hurley's best attempt at hype, and the pressroom where liquid refreshments were served every night, the press didn't fall for the fight. Arthur Daley writing in *The New York Times* was particularly sardonic in his criticism of the fight. "Nothing about [the fight] makes much sense. This is a fantasy which might have been lifted from *Alice in Wonderland*. . . . The Mad Hatter is Jack Hurley. . . . Trying to sort out the other characters is not easy. The drowsy-eyed Patterson may be the Dormouse who keeps falling asleep. Cus D'Amato, the champion's proprietor, may qualify as the White Rabbit, who is always in a hurry. . . . Rademacher has never fought more than three rounds! Mickey Walker said, 'Professionals should never fight civilians.' . . . Rademacher is a civilian."

Once again, a few days before the fight, the backers told Floyd that they could raise only $175,000 of the guarantee because a few of them had reneged on their pledges. Cus blamed it on the IBC, of course, and he paid Hurley $25,000 out of the new sum. The fight did well, drawing sixteen thousand fans despite all the freeloaders who camped out on Tightwad Hill (which overlooked the stadium) and watched the fight for free. Floyd went down from a right to the head in the second round but he rallied and knocked Rademacher down four times in the fifth and KO'd him in the next round. I talked to Mr. Rademacher about that fight. He was a real nice big guy. I remember him telling me, "I knocked Floyd on his ass."

The real winner of the fight was Rademacher, who was praised by the press for his courage and offered a contract for $20,000 to fight in an IBC promotion. Hurley, his promoter, was furious at the offer. "That 20K is an insult. Chicken feed! This is the new Masked Marvel! No one knows what he looks like, and everyone wants to see him. He would fill up the Garden, which is a haunted house, just fighting a street car conductor."

After Rademacher, Floyd was inactive for almost a year. The IBC refused to deal with Cus so Floyd kept busy fighting exhibitions in places like Joplin, Missouri; Wichita, Kansas; and Minneapolis. Lence offered Rocky Marciano a cool million to come out of retirement but Rocky was also being wooed by Frank Sinatra, who offered to promote the fight for nothing and give Marciano all the profits. Sinatra was fronting for Carbo, who was trying to take over ABC's *Wednesday Night Fights* from Norris. But Rocky stayed retired and Floyd remained inactive.

Now the Norris-controlled press ganged up on Cus. It was an open secret that many boxing reporters were on Norris's payroll. Robert Boyle, who covered Cus for *Sports Illustrated*, confirmed to us that reporters would get money from Norris or IBC-controlled promoters so they would slant their coverage in favor of the IBC. John Bonomi, an assistant district attorney in New York, described how the boxing-beat writers would line up at Madison Square Garden on Saturday mornings to pick up their weekly envelope, which was filled with cash. He said that at big events, like a championship fight, the press would be provided with hookers at no charge for the columnists and at a significant discount for the poorer reporters. Bonomi never went public with his findings because he was going after the big fish like Carbo and he needed the reporters on his side.

For a variety of reasons, little of the press were on Cus's side. Joe Williams wrote, "If Floyd Patterson isn't the worst managed heavyweight champion in history he'll have to do until someone can produce a more enigmatically bizarre character than Cus the Christian. . . . There is no market for a heavyweight champion who has been managed into obscurity." Wendell Smith, a Chicago columnist, urged Patterson to leave Cus and defect to the IBC, where he would do much better. Cartoonists drew Cus as Don Quixote riding a

horse holding a shield with Floyd's face on it, complete with wind-
mills in the far background.

Cus did have some journalists in his corner. Eddie Borden often
editorialized in the pages of his tip sheet and defended Cus. Under
the heading "Shakedown Continues," he wrote, "The merciless,
heartless crusade against Cus D'Amato continues in the New York
papers. Merely because the man has principle and steadfastness,
they are trying to create friction and bad feeling between Cus and
Floyd Patterson. If fight managers used these methods they would
probably be referred to as unprincipled, uncouth, and roguish. But as
long as the press can continue these shabby, cheap tactics it is merely
considered the work of a sports writer pursuing his line of work. God
help the writers if this is a sample of their ethics."

Sports Illustrated always gave Cus fair treatment. "To me, they
were always honest and supporting me because they knew that I was
fighting an organization which was detrimental to my business. The
IBC tried to belittle my efforts and called me Don Quixote and all
that sort of thing. . . . The truth was, I was nothing but a professional manager, trying to get the opportunity for a talented fighter
that I thought he deserved . . . but the IBC organization would not
allow him."

Arthur Mann, a respected journalist who mostly covered baseball,
was close to Cus and worked with him on a series of articles docu-
menting Cus's struggles with the IBC. In one he wrote, "The most
malevolent press in the history of sports writing has descended to all-
time lows to blacken [Cus's] name, character, integrity, and methods
by printing any and all rumors, distorted interviews in absentia, and
deliberate lies calculated to support the sustained attack."

Gene Kilroy told us that the IBC even started spreading rumors
about Cus's sexuality. "They started rumors he was gay, he was this,
he was that. They did everything to degrade the man. But you
couldn't degrade him to the real people in boxing, not the kiss-asses
in boxing, but the strong people." The attacks on Cus continued on
another front. Nat Fleischer, in *The Ring* magazine, blamed Cus for
the "deplorable conditions in boxing" then. Cus wrote a response de-

fending himself that was published in Eddie Borden's *Weekly Boxing World*. "I wonder whether it was sheer coincidence that *Ring* has consistently rapped Floyd Patterson and me while defending the actions of the IBC. . . . My position in regard to boxing has been to bring about competition on a proper competitive basis so that fight managers would have an opportunity to get the best prices for their fighters as a result of bidding instead of the promoter dictating the price. I believe that the fighter should get his fair share of the proceeds of his fights on television, theater-television, radio and movies." Cus went on to attack the ruling that allowed the IBC to control televised boxing. "Since the IBC controls the only two nationally televised shows they are in a position to exclude all of those who refuse to subject themselves to the terms and will of their monopoly. My effort to oppose and expose the IBC was done in the hope that some independent promoter would wind up with one of the television shows and thereby establish competition on a proper competitive basis. Once such competition would be established then the fight managers and their fighters would be unafraid to oppose the IBC." Gaining a televised boxing show was Cus's next plan, a plan that would put him in new, even more dangerous competition with the IBC.

A few issues later, Cus took out a full-page ad in Borden's weekly. The ad was titled "A Message from Cus D'Amato." It read: "Boxing like every other endeavor, whether it be war, industry or show business, must have replacements. Boxing is my profession and it is imperative that we have to have reinforcements. In addition to FLOYD PATTERSON, the World's Heavyweight Champion, here are the stars of tomorrow." Then Cus listed nine fighters he managed, including the most sensational rookie of the year, Gene "Ace" Armstrong, a middleweight with thirteen straight victories; Joe Shaw, an Olympic welterweight who had just turned pro; and José Torres. The ad ended, "We entertain every offer and would like to hear from promoters around the country." Cus didn't hear much and he was forced to pay his stable a weekly salary just to train.

Meanwhile, his prize, Patterson, lived a monastic life, spending all his time at his training camp, separated from his family, working out every day. Cus turned his attention to European fighters and began a relationship with Harry Levene, a British promoter who worked in the shadow of Jack Solomons, who was aligned with Norris. Levene came to the United States on February 3, 1958, and the two men discussed a fight with Joe Erskine, the British Empire champion.

While Cus was discussing fighting in Europe, Norris and Carbo and their minions were discussing Cus in private. On February 10, Norris and Carbo and Billy Brown, the Madison Square Garden matchmaker, met at manager Hymie Wallman's New York apartment. They were there ostensibly to discuss the welterweight crown that Basilio had vacated when he beat Sugar Ray Robinson for the middleweight championship. But their talk got around to the Zora Folley–Eddie Machen heavyweight fight that was to be held in California. Folley and Machen were Norris's best heavyweights. Even though he had refused to allow them to fight Floyd right after Floyd defeated Moore, now Norris was upset that Cus had refused to do any business with him.

"What are we going to do with the winner?" he asked Carbo. Carbo had no response. They went back to talking about the welterweight situation and they had many more cocktails. And Norris went back to a topic he was obsessed with—the heavyweight crown. "If only we could get Patterson to fight Machen," he said. Carbo finally responded. "You will never get the crazy man to fight you," he said dismissively. Norris didn't know it, but Carbo was protecting Cus. When Carbo would call Cus "the crazy man," it meant that he wasn't someone who would be swayed by intimidation or willing to negotiate.

Meanwhile, the press continued to attack Cus. "The heavyweight champion of the world sits like a brooding Buddha, knowing the peace that passeth understanding. The six-month period ordinarily allowed to a champion between title defenses expired on Washington's birthday with Patterson hermetically sealed in a cocoon of jeweler's cotton," Red Smith, a columnist for the *New York Herald Tribune*, wrote on March 20. "It is time for the Boxing Commissions to speak firmly to D'Amato. His social relations with promoters are no concern of theirs, but when he immobilizes the heavyweight division to press a private quarrel, the situation calls for official cognizance and action."

There was action the next day at Madison Square Garden but it didn't involve Cus directly. As one of the elimination fights for the welterweight championship ended, New York district attorney Frank Hogan had his detectives fan out around the ring and issue grand jury subpoenas to wiseguys and Carbo-controlled managers, including Hymie Wallman. Eventually it was Wallman's testimony that netted Hogan his big fish—Mr. Gray himself.

At the same time, Cus and Floyd were in England for an exhibition tour. At a press conference Cus took over the mike. "We must destroy the IBC," he said, getting right to the point. "We must destroy them and their activities and that is more important to the future of boxing than my future or Patterson's."

A few days later, on March 25, Sugar Ray regained his crown from Carmen Basilio in Chicago. Jack Leonard, a West Coast promoter, was at the fight and Norris told him that Frankie Carbo wanted to see him. Leonard was brought to Carbo's hotel room by Al Weill, the former manager of Rocky Marciano, where, according to Leonard, "they held trial for me more or less." Carbo felt that Leonard wasn't giving his friend Weill's fighters enough work in California. Leonard got the message. Two days before the fight, the Chicago Boxing Writers held their annual awards dinner. James Dougan Norris was awarded the Packey McFarland Award for his outstanding contributions to boxing. Among the attendees at the gala were three undercover detectives from D.A. Hogan's office.

Back in New York, all the talk in the boxing world was about Hogan's investigation. When word leaked that Wallman had testified to the grand jury about Norris and Carbo's meeting at his apartment, that was the final straw for Norris. Citing his doctor's concerns about his health after he had a heart attack a few months earlier, the IBC of New York announced Norris's resignation as president. Truman Gibson, his right-hand man, was elevated to the position. "We are continuing under our present setup until the Supreme Court makes its ruling," Gibson told the press. Cus responded immediately. "So long as they control televised boxing, they control boxing. So long as there's no competition, Patterson won't fight for the IBC."

Floyd was still inactive when his two main rivals, Folley and Machen, stunk up the joint at the Cow Palace in San Francisco on April 9. The National Boxing Association World Championship Committee wanted to force Patterson to fight the winner of this match but it was such a lousy fight that the arena was rocked with boos. The fight was judged a draw even though Folley seemed to be the clear winner. The columnist Dan Parker, who was an equal-opportunity critic of both Cus and Norris, wrote that "the bout reached its finest moment when an inspired TV program director switched on a deodorant commercial."

"What were they afraid of?" Cus chimed in. "That they'd have to fight Patterson?"

The boxing commissioners were getting restless with Floyd's inactivity, so on April 22, Cus said he was working on "five different deals." Now Julius Helfand got in the act. Helfand, the chairman of the NYSAC, was also the president of the World Boxing Committee. On June 2, Helfand ordered Patterson to fight "a recognized challenger" before September 30. "In case Patterson should refuse, the committee shall no longer recognize him as world champion." They named four challengers: Eddie Machen, Zora Folley, Willie Pastrano, and Roy Harris.

Cus fired back. "They won't push me. If the world committee tries to force Patterson to defend against one of four men who blacklisted him when we needed a challenger, I'll take that committee into court together and individually. . . . Floyd will defend this summer. In fact, he may defend three times this summer, but against fighters whose managers haven't tried to cut our throats."

Two weeks later, Cus announced that Roy Harris would fight for the title and that it would take place in Los Angeles. And the promoter who Cus picked was his close friend (and Frankie Carbo's) Al Weill. The thing that bonded Cus and Weill the most was their hate for Jim Norris. Cus's rationale for picking Harris was that he wasn't IBC connected, unlike the other three contenders Helfand

was shoving down his throat. Cus felt that Machen, Folley, and Pastrano were boring fighters who had been overexposed on TV. But a
relative unknown like Harris, promoted properly, could excite the
public. Plus he was rated number three by the National Boxing Association and he had a record of 22–0.

So Cus, with the assistance of Roy's manager Lou Viscusi (another Carbo associate), created an image for Harris. He was from a
small Texas town named Cut and Shoot, so they developed the ultimate good-old-boy persona for him. They claimed that he came from
a large family of coon hunters and he had a cousin named Armadillo,
after his local record for exterminating over five thousand of the
creatures. When *Sports Illustrated* came to shoot him for the cover,
Roy posed shirtless and barefoot on his porch. When the local media
had come around earlier, Roy and his brother killed some squirrels
and hung them on the front porch. By fight time, all the publicity had
worked. Roy was getting so much fan mail that the federal government had to open a post office in Cut and Shoot.

The first complication to the fight occurred when the California
State Athletic Commission refused to give Al Weill a promoter's license, citing his friendship with Carbo. Cus was in his home office in
New York when he got word that Weill was out. But a young, ambitious closed-circuit-TV executive named Bill Rosensohn happened to
be there. Rosensohn was born in New York City. His father was a
prominent obstetrician. After college, he moved to Los Angeles and
started a company that rented televisions to hospitals. After a few
years he moved to TelePrompTer Corporation, a company that got
rich selling the devices to TV networks for their broadcasts and now
was branching out to closed-circuit theatrical broadcasts of major
fights.

Rosensohn immediately said he'd like a crack at promoting the
fight. "You have that kind of cabbage?" Cus asked. He told Rosensohn
he'd need a hundred grand to start and Rosensohn said he could raise
that. Cus said if he passed the commission in California, then he'd
make Patterson available.

Cus had met Rosensohn while negotiating with Irving Kahn, who was Rosensohn's boss at TelePrompTer and had done the closed-circuit theater broadcast of the two Robinson–Basilio fights. In a memo to his boss on March 18, Rosensohn had suggested that the heavyweight division was where the real money was for closed circuit and that TelePrompTer should sign Patterson to a five-year exclusive contract, which would help them develop relationships with local closed-circuit promoters and make more money.

"In dealing with a man like D'Amato, I think it most important to establish a relationship of mutual trust. This could only be done by straight shooting and straight talking. This man is tremendously on the defensive. He is highly suspicious of everyone. If any negotiations are to be carried through to a successful conclusion, I feel the secret must lie in making this man a friend, therefore in all talks with him, let us do our utmost to be accurate even to the point of understatement. Certainly insofar as any discussions with the IBC are concerned, I would think that we would have to tell them, as we would tell D'Amato, that any conversations between us and either parties would be completely confidential and that we would never do anything more than acknowledge the fact that we were having such conversations. We would never, and in fact we should never, discuss with either group the subject matter of our conversations with the other," Rosensohn wrote.

After Rosensohn obtained his promoting license, he quit his TelePrompTer job. So a totally inexperienced promoter was about to handle a heavyweight championship fight. That didn't seem like something that Cautious Cus would sign on to. When he was asked a few years later, Cus disclosed why he'd agreed to use Rosensohn. "I was suddenly left in what I considered a very dangerous position in my fight against the IBC and its policies. I knew that if the fight didn't take place, no other independent promoter would try because they figured the IBC prevented the scheduled fight of Patterson. I was desperate."

So Cus then suggested that Rosensohn hire his old friend Jack Hurley as the associate promoter. Hurley was tremendously experienced and Rosensohn agreed to pay Hurley $25,000 for his services. But Cus wasn't finished. He wanted Charlie Black to play a role in the promotion. Rosensohn agreed to give Black 50 percent of the profits.

Before the contracts were signed, Cus and Black went to Texas to talk to Harris, his father, and his manager Viscusi. Cus wanted to talk to them because he "was constantly on the alert to see whether or not this man was being weakened so that he wouldn't fight." While they were in Texas, Cus discussed having a document drawn up where Charlie Black was to manage Harris for a rematch in case Patterson lost the fight. "I was always thinking in terms of somebody stealing a decision or a referee would stop the fight with a phony cut or something like that," Cus would say later. When Black was asked about this at a hearing a year later, Black described his prospective managerial duty as "a sort of escrow. I was insurance to Cus that I would give him the return match." If Harris won, Black alone, not his regular manager Viscusi, could sign the rematch contract. For that, Black was to get 10 percent of Harris's purse but "that was only in writing. I don't think I would have got anything."

Remember the movie *The Sting*? This is some *Sting* stuff. Cus is putting all these people in positions who are not who they're supposed to be. These people were all fakes. Cus pulled a sting. Cus was a big-time Machiavellian guy and he did this stuff at such a high level. The stakes were so high because his life was at stake.

When all the dust settled, the contracts were signed. Harris got a flat $100,000 guarantee to ensure that he didn't come down with a suspicious injury right before the fight and withdraw. The revolutionary part was that Patterson got 50 percent of the gate and a remarkable 60 percent of the closed-circuit theatrical rights (with $210,000 guaranteed), while TelePrompTer got 40 percent. That was unheard-of participation by Floyd in the ancillary rights. Previously the promoters got the lion's share of those rights. Norris had never allowed the fighters fighting for the IBC to get close to that amount of money for ancillary rights.

That wasn't the only challenge to Norris that Cus was making. Right before the fight, Cus had one of his attorneys contact Gillette, which sponsored one of the IBC weekly TV boxing shows, to discuss an independent weekly show that would feature Floyd and other fighters Cus controlled. Emil Lence was to promote the series and Irving Kahn and TelePrompTer would also be involved. Cus got no response except a "violent attack and a threat to sue" him from Ned Irish of the Madison Square Garden Corporation. Irish claimed that Cus was trying to break their contract with Gillette. "All I wanted was an opportunity to discuss the situation, to let Gillette know what was going on in the boxing picture. I wanted to tell them that there were worthy fighters around the country that were sensational and could rekindle an interest in boxing who couldn't get an opportunity to appear on television. In dealing with the people they were dealing with, they weren't giving these people an opportunity," Cus later said. More fuel was added to the fire of Cus's feud with Norris.

WHILE THE BOXERS set up camp in California for the August 18 fight, back in New York, in late July 1958, D.A. Hogan announced at a press conference that Frankie Carbo had been indicted on a ten-count bill charging him with conspiracy, undercover management of fighters, and conducting matchmaking in IBC fights without a license. The only problem was that Carbo, knowing that the indictment was coming down, went on the lam. The D.A. sent out a nationwide wanted bulletin for Mr. Gray. "Male, White, 54, Five Feet Eight Inches Tall, 180 Pounds with Brown Eyes, Gray Hair, Partly Bald, Sallow Complexion and a Neat Dresser." At the same press conference, Hogan said that Carbo had last been seen at a racetrack in Mexico. With him was his old friend Al Weill!

A WEEK BEFORE THE FIGHT, the press descended on the two training camps. What was shocking to them was that Patterson looked slower than Harris did. Floyd was even knocked down by a right hand thrown by José Torres, Cus's middleweight prospect. "I don't know what's wrong. My reflexes aren't working. I can't get off. I can't get started," Floyd told Martin Kane in *Sports Illustrated*. "I think he's bored," Cus said, putting his spin on it. "He's been in training for a year, almost steadily. All he does is play cards and watch television. He needs something to divert his mind." So Cus bought Floyd a couple of air rifles and Floyd did some shooting to break the monotony. Over at the Harris camp, the ballyhoo continued. His trainer said that Harris had courage because down in Cut and Shoot, Texas, "they drown cowards."

Harris proved that he wasn't a coward. Despite flooring Floyd in the second round, Harris took a horrible beating for twelve rounds. His face was a mask of blood when his corner threw in the towel before the thirteenth round. He had earned his $100,000. But Floyd went away with a lot more. The fight established a record gate for California, pulling in $234,183.25. And it also confirmed Cus's view that closed-circuit fights in theaters would revolutionize the boxing business. The TelePrompTer feed attracted almost two hundred thousand customers and grossed a million dollars. After paying Harris his fee, Floyd wound up with almost $300,000. Charlie Black did well too. Cus paid him $2,500 for his "spying" services at camp and he pulled in an additional $2,500 from Harris's manager Viscusi. Rosensohn didn't pay Black any of the 50 percent profits that Black was promised because he wound up losing $3,000 on the fight. Hurley also lost because Rosensohn initially stiffed him on his $25,000 fee.

Martin Kane filed a piece for *Sports Illustrated* that claimed the fight "changed the economic face of boxing." But he warned that Patterson needed stiffer and more frequent competition. "Lessons may be learned from the fight: Cus D'Amato . . . has won his war with the IBC. . . . The big fights for a long time hereafter will be dominated by theater television. . . . This alone is enough to put the IBC, tied so intimately to home television, in second place. TelePrompTer and Theater Network Television have the money and potential income to offer the fighters guarantees far beyond anything they would get from stadium promoters or free home television, or both."

Despite the success, the attacks on Cus continued, centering mainly on the quality of opponents Floyd was facing. In an article titled "The Big Mystery of Floyd Patterson," William McCormick noted the shoddy performances of Floyd in all three of his title defenses, including being knocked down by nonentities like Rademacher and Harris. "There is little doubt that Patterson today is a mediocrity, hardly more than a run-of-the-ring fighter. The big mystery is *whatever happened to the Floyd Patterson we saw, or thought we saw, in the beginning?* There are two possible answers. Either he has been mismanaged out of greatness or the 'great' Floyd Patterson never really existed." McCormick gave Cus kudos for steering Floyd to the crown against the opposition of the IBC. But then, when everyone was on Cus's side, he claimed Cus went too far. "Cus quickly converted the sublime to the ridiculous. He honestly believes the IBC has engineered an awesome, world-wide master plan to ruin him and his fighter. Those who do not agree implicitly with everything he says or does concerning boxing automatically become sinister representatives of the IBC carrying out their carefully conceived roles in the 'plot' to ruin him and his champion." He went on to document the top contenders that Cus ducked. But after dissecting each of Floyd's three defenses, he then made the case for Cus's brilliance as a manager.

"There is, of course, the possibility we have mentioned that Floyd never was the fighter we thought him to be. In that case, D'Amato is an even better manager than we credited him with being before he won the title with Patterson. He certainly has selected Floyd's opponents with consummate skill. Patterson fought only one ranking heavyweight, Jackson, on his way to the title and the blown-out Hurricane almost beat him in 12 rounds. Since winning the title, Floyd has fought only [nobodies], guys who probably couldn't even have made Joe Louis' 'Bum-of-the-Month' Club. It is possible that D'Amato, knowing his fighter better than anyone else, has always been aware that Floyd can't fight and never could fight. If that be the case, Cus deserves the highest praise for the way he has protected his pride and joy."

Whoa. This guy makes a lot of interesting points. There's no doubt that Norris had a lot of the press in his pocket, but I'm also sure that Cus antagonized a lot of the press who might have been his ally. Cus was the kind of guy who if you didn't agree with him, you were his enemy. It was his way or the highway. And if he'd run into you, he'd be on you, he'd just pound you. I've seen him do that with reporters. One guy was a nice guy and Cus would be nailing him so hard I wanted to get up and go in the other room.

But this writer goes beyond the accusations by most of the press that Floyd's skills had deteriorated under Cus's tutelage. This guy is saying that maybe Floyd wasn't that good at all and that Cus was a genius in navigating him to the crown. Cus was always worried that Floyd didn't have a killer instinct, that when guys like Rademacher and Harris could put him down, maybe he couldn't take a punch from a real heavyweight. Cus did tell me that he always protected Floyd.

After the Harris fight Floyd was idle again. Part of the reason was that one of the top contenders, Eddie Machen, got clocked by Ingemar Johansson in the first round of their fight in Sweden. Nino Valdes was proposed as a substitute and Emil Lence began a dialogue with Ned Irish at Madison Square Garden for a fight that would have been televised on NBC and sponsored by Gillette. Irish offered Lence the Garden for a fight in late October. On August 26, Lence reported that he was "optimistic" about the fight but a week later he called Irish to say he was "having trouble" with Cus. Irish offered a discount and said he'd charge only 20 percent of the gate to have the fight at MSG. On September 30, NBC wired a $300,000 offer for TV rights to Cus. It would have been the largest in history but Cus turned it down because "it's too good to be true."

Lence then made the mistake of going to NYSAC commissioner Helfand to get involved in the negotiations. The prospect of working with two of Cus's enemies, the IBC employee Irish and Helfand, who had threatened to strip Floyd of his crown if he didn't fight by a deadline, made Cus go ballistic. "Lence has absolutely no authority to make a match for the heavyweight champion. If there's a match to be made, I'll make it—and if it's for New York, I may let Lence promote it. That is—if he conducts himself properly."

Now Cus was pissing off his one ally, Lence! This intrigue and open warfare was too much even for Cus partisan Martin Kane at *Sports Illustrated*. "Today the champion is paying the price for D'Amato's bedevilment by the feuds and fussing of a sport that in recent years has taken on the aspects of a struggle for power in the Kremlin."

By now Cus had alienated some of the most prominent columnists, even ones who had his back in the past. Dan Parker was generally seen as impartial, putting down the IBC but calling Cus out too. But he had enough of Cus's long-winded harangues. "A strange quiet descended on the metropolis Wednesday night. Investigation revealed that a dirigible had taken off for St. Louis with Floyd Patterson. Everyone knows a dirigible is a big gas bag. This particular one is Constantine Windermore D'Amato, who had just finished a 24 hour talkathon that finally exhausted all his listeners, forcing him to head West in quest of new ears to bend."

Man, Mr. Parker is right! When Cus would talk he'd go on so long you could fall asleep on him. If you began to nod off, Cus would be all up in your face talking loud—"You seem as if you're not interested in what I'm saying. I'm wasting my time."

One of the greatest boxing columnists, Jimmy Cannon, was able to portray Cus in a balanced way. At the beginning of 1958, Cannon wrote a great piece about Cus titled "Cus Fights the Good Fight." "You just don't run into many people who turn down a fortune for principle. You don't find any at all in the fight racket. . . . Cus D'Amato will not be bulled or switched in his lonely fight with the IBC, James D. Norris, President. . . . You could offer a reward and never find another guy on Broadway with his sincerity." A few weeks later, he wrote this: "You're Cus D'Amato who must be judged by the enemies you have. You are angrily honest, obstinate, generous, unafraid, conceited, suspicious, idealistic, domineering and independent. You manage Floyd Patterson, the heavyweight champion of the world, in a lonely crusade against the IBC." Cannon dealt with Cus's charges that the IBC bribed some of the press. "But such tirades have alienated honest journalists. Some consider you an eccentric who can't be trusted. Others are bored by your wild monologues. There are those who see you as a clever con man who intends to have Patterson knocking off marks as long as boxing commissions will allow it. You may be wrong but you are dedicated. You are a guy who is not accustomed to wealth. You suffered in obscurity for most of your life. You handled amateurs. You ran a gym on 14th Street and slept on a cot. Your companion was a ferocious dog. And then you found Floyd Patterson. No pug ever got a more honorable deal from a manager. But your stubbornness has caused him such unpopularity. Yet, without you, Patterson would probably have never made it. Greed would have forced most managers to hustle him. Now it would compel them to take an immense sum from the IBC. You refuse it. You could fold up and get rich off the IBC but then Patterson would have to fight a contender. You're Cus D'Amato who must be judged by the enemies you have."

All the negative press against Cus prompted a man named Paul Kaufman to write a letter to Jimmy Cannon on October 21, 1958. Kaufman started out noting that 99 percent of the articles that the boxing press had written about Cus had been uncomplimentary. Then he said that he didn't want to debate Cus's feud with the IBC but he just wanted to give Cannon his view of Cus as a person. A year and a half prior to the letter, Paul brought his eight-year-old son to train at the Gramercy Gym. Paul was forty-six and a high school teacher, but both he and his son started taking boxing lessons there. "Cus once said to me, 'I have no children of my own. I look at these boys as my boys.' Sounds maudlin, doesn't it? But I know that he meant it. Stories of his kindness and generosity are numerous. The boys who come up to the gym are, as you can well imagine, from under-privileged homes and neighborhoods. Some of them cannot afford to get the equipment necessary for the gym. Cus provides it. By keeping some of these boys off the streets, he in no small way helps to curb juvenile delinquency. He paid the living expenses of one of the boys for 2 years. This was a boy with a prison record, thrown out of his home by his parents and on his way downhill. Today the boy is happily married, has a job and in addition a promising future as a boxer. Should a kid hurt himself as a result of boxing at the gym and need medical attention, Cus is there again. Should Cus hear that there is trouble at the home of any of the boys, he's there with a helping hand. This is not something new. It had been going on for many years, long before he became the manager of the world's heavyweight champion. Bread cast upon the waters. He does not take his share of the purses of any of his fighters until well after they attain main-event status.

"A great deal is heard these days about the role racketeers play in the fight business. Sporting writers allude to sinister influences, and the recent Carbo scandal as a case in point. Those writers who make snide references to 'Saint Cus' unwittingly never wrote a truer word. Can they point to any other manager who had done and is continuing to do as much as Cus has for boxers and boxing? He furnished a shining example for other managers to emulate."

Maybe this letter moved Cannon to write a column called "Cus" a few months later. He began by writing about other managers like Jack Kearns and Felix Bocchicchio and Joe Jacobs, who, he said, were "entertaining rogues." But then there was Cus. "The most peculiar of the species is Cus D'Amato, who is Floyd Patterson's custodian. The underworld doesn't influence him and this alone makes him unique because seldom has a modern heavyweight champion made it without being allied with important hoodlums. . . . There is no doubt that D'Amato is the most powerful man who ever controlled a heavyweight champion. The delegates of other champions were subservient to promoters and granted them a sort of partnership in their fighters. This guy is absolutely independent.

"He is a man of principle and his devotion to Patterson is unique in a racket notorious for brutal men who regard pugs as if they were cattle. But he is also devious and mysterious, suspicious and domineering, innocent in many instances and rigid in his frequently impractical beliefs. He is one of the great teachers of his business. He created Patterson's style and any kid who comes to him improves. . . .

"The crusade against the IBC has imposed a boycott on D'Amato's pugs. They train continually, and they have no income. But he supports them with the longest payroll in the ages of the fight racket. They draw salaries every week as they wait until the clubs open up for them again. He also has a troupe of old-timers who are liberally staked. He doesn't make stooges of them and gives them the dignity they once enjoyed when they functioned at their lost work. I have found D'Amato to be obstinate and unforgiving in trivial matters, but he is a sentimental man. It is a common trait of managers to despise even the fighters who make them rich. They consider pugs to be dumb ingrates who become pests when they cease to produce revenue by bleeding. But D'Amato is a man who worships good fighters after they are through with the racket and he treats them all as if they were still celebrities. Joe Louis is associated with the IBC. He is the only one connected with the firm that D'Amato doesn't hate. I have heard him make excuses for Louis when some of the fight mob singed him for being an errand-boy for the IBC.

" 'But Louis was once a champion,' D'Amato said, as if that explained it all and gave Louis immunity from all the flaws of mankind.

"His personality has alienated sports reporters and he has suffered for his evasion. He trusts few people and his secrecy in insignificant matters is infuriating to anyone who tries to get him to make a positive statement. . . . Cus D'Amato is dead square, but I pity him. The fight racket is a tough place for an honest man."

Reading that gives me chills. Cannon hit it on the nose. He got to the heart of Cus. Cus loved fighters. And he never forgot their sacrifices. When he was in Miami for a Patterson fight he ran into Beau Jack, who had been reduced to shining shoes in a hotel lobby. Beau Jack saw Cus and he asked to shine his shoes. "Me? The great Beau Jack shine my shoes? Are you crazy? I'm going to shine your shoes!" And he had Beau sit up on the chair while Cus was on his knees shining Beau's shoes. That image made the wire services and it was printed in papers all over the country.

Cus taught me to respect and worship all the old fighters. Every time he came across an old fighter, he'd literally take his hat off to them. So I'd go out of my way to find someone who was in the *Boxing*

Encyclopedia and I'd pepper them with questions about boxing when they were in the game, hoping that they'd reveal a trick to me. I was a desperate person.

And Cus defending Louis even when he was working for the IBC? That quote killed me. I remember that the morning after Larry Holmes fought Trevor Berbick, Cus found out that Joe Louis had died. Cus went up to his room and didn't come out until the next morning.

One of the charges against Cus was that he was paranoid. But if you go to the dictionary, one definition of "paranoia" is the "suspicion and mistrust of people or their actions without evidence or justification." By that definition Cus was definitely not paranoid. It took a tremendous amount of courage to go up against the financial interests of ruthless guys like Norris and Carbo. Cus knew what he was in for. He used to tell us that he prepared for his fight with Norris ten years before his moves against him. He began by isolating himself from his family. He used to have regular dinners at his brother Tony's home. But Cus used to tell me that people were too predictable. So Cus began to never do the same thing twice. He disappointed all his nieces and nephews who loved him and missed him.

All the newspaper articles about Cus talked about how he was a bachelor and he lived in his office/apartment first on 54th Street and then on 57th Street. That was just Cus protecting Camille from the mob. When we talked to his niece Betty, she told us that Cus had a love-nest apartment in Queens where he hid Camille. She also said that none of the kids knew anything about Camille. In fact, her mother, Tony's wife, didn't even know that Camille was a part of Cus's life. Betty said that it wasn't until they celebrated Father's Day sometime in the mid-1960s up at José Torres's training camp that her mother first met Camille. And she wasn't even introduced to her by Cus. She thought that Camille was one of the staff serving the lunch!

When Betty told Cus that she was getting married, Cus gave her a lecture. He said that marriage wasn't a fifty-fifty proposition; that each person had to give a hundred percent for it to work. That's probably one reason why he didn't marry Camille, because he was so involved with teaching his fighters and also navigating them through the minefields of the IBC.

Cus never tried to expose his friends to danger either. If he thought that you might be in danger because of his association with you, he'd wait until there was a group of people around you and then he'd get into a loud fight or argument with you so people would think that you weren't friends with him anymore.

Cus took great precautions for his own physical safety. Besides having a gun under his bed at home and the cot in his office, he had two doors that were close to each other that led to his bedroom and the room where he sometimes slept in the gym. So when you opened one door, there was another door a few feet from it. He did that so he'd have time to prepare if you were coming in with hostile intent. He was leery of saying anything over his home phone in case it was being tapped. Robert Boyle, a reporter from *Sports Illustrated* who got close to Cus, told us that one evening the two of them were walking down Broadway and Cus turned to him.

"I've got something to tell you," he said.

"What is it?" Boyle asked.

"I can't tell you. Someone might be listening," Cus said.

"But there's nobody here, just people walking by," Boyle said.

"Look over there," Cus said.

"What is it?"

Cus nodded toward two phone booths that were side by side across the street.

"Go to the one on the left," Cus instructed. They both walked across the street and Boyle went into his designated booth. Cus got into the booth next to it. Then Cus got out and went over to Boyle.

"What's your number there?" he asked. Boyle read off the number. Then Cus went back to his phone booth and put in some change and called Boyle.

"We're safe now," Cus said, and he proceeded to tell Boyle his big secret.

Cus never took the subway, so nobody would have a chance of pushing him in front of an oncoming train. He never cut open the pockets on his new suit jackets, so that nobody could put some dope in his pocket when he wasn't aware and then frame him in a drug bust, which would ruin his career. In fact, he even stopped going into bars because he thought that was the likeliest place for a drop like that to occur. He once told a reporter, "I am not a handsome man. So if a woman approaches me, I'm flattered. But I can't go out with her. I don't know who sent her." When he went into an apartment building he never took the elevator. One time he was with the writer Pete Hamill and they had to take the elevator to a high floor in an office building. As they were waiting for the elevator door to close and ascend, Cus turned to Pete. "If this thing goes down instead of up, we're in trouble."

A MONTH AFTER THE HARRIS FIGHT, Rosensohn started to bug Cus to let him promote another championship fight. Cus told him that he had a lot of obligations to other people but that maybe he could promote another fight in a year or two.

"Suppose I develop my own contender and bring him in? Would I then take precedence over some of those people you have obligations to?" he asked.

"If the contender is acceptable to me," Cus said.

"Well, let me try," said Rosensohn.

Rosensohn happened to be in Cus's office when a friend of Cus's who was a Swedish journalist was telling Cus how a Swedish heavyweight named Ingemar Johansson would demolish the number one challenger, Eddie Machen, when they faced off in Sweden on September 14, 1958. That was all he had to hear. Rosensohn, who was scheduled to take a vacation, decided to vacation ringside in Stockholm. Johansson knocked out Machen with a devastating right hand in the first round and, after determining that Ingemar had no ties to the IBC, Rosensohn paid him $10,000 for a forty-day option on a fight with Patterson.

When Rosensohn came back Cus was friendly but noncommittal to a fight with Johansson. He had been negotiating for a title defense against the Cuban Niño Valdés. As the days went by, Rosensohn saw his $10,000 deposit slipping away. With only days left on his option, he went to Cus's office to express his concern.

"Well, I didn't tell you to sign that option," Cus said. "That's your problem."

Discouraged, Rosensohn left the office and ran into Cus's close friend, Charlie Black. He told him his tale of woe.

"I have a friend who might be able to help you," Charlie told him. He said he'd bring him over to Rosensohn's apartment the next day. Sure enough, the next day Charlie showed up with his friend, Fat Tony Salerno, the star of the Genovese crime family. He was a protégé of Trigger Mike Coppola and ran a multimillion-dollar gambling and loansharking operation out of his social club in East Harlem. With the days ticking down, Salerno said he was interested in getting involved in the promotion, would put up all the money, and in return get a third of the profits.

"Will I get an agreement for the fight before the forty-day period expires?" Rosensohn asked Fat Tony.

"Don't worry," Tony said. On the way out, Salerno turned around and asked, "What are you going to do for my friend Charlie?"

Rosensohn thought that since Charlie was Tony's friend, Tony should take care of him.

"Oh no, you see Charlie is Cus's friend. I think you should take care of him. He ought to get the same as I have," Tony said.

Rosensohn was no stranger to Fat Tony. He had met him at a party earlier that year thrown by Gilbert Lee Beckley, one of the biggest bookmakers on the East Coast. As a gambler, Rosensohn was friendly with Beckley. In fact, Fat Tony had helped Rosensohn out of a jam very recently. He had gotten on the phone with Jack Hurley and gotten him to agree to half of his fee for the Harris fight, a fee that Rosensohn hadn't paid yet.

AROUND THE SAME TIME that Rosensohn was scrambling to save his $10,000 investment in the Patterson–Johansson fight, a promoter on the West Coast was beginning to have his own problems. Jackie Leonard was the matchmaker of the Hollywood Legion Stadium. He was the guy Frankie Carbo had pressured earlier in the year to get more West Coast fights for Al Weill's fighters. He was also, through the Hollywood Legion Stadium, a co-promoter of the Harris–Patterson fight. Leonard's boss was George Parnassus—along with Norris and Gibson, who had put up the money for the new company that was promoting fights at the stadium.

Leonard was close friends with an independent manager named Don Nesseth, a used-car dealer in L.A. who managed Don Jordan, a promising but wacky welterweight. Nesseth had trouble getting nationally televised matches for Jordan until Leonard called in a favor from his pal Gibson. After getting exposure on three TV matches, he got a title shot versus the champ Virgil Akins set for December 5. But on October 23, Gibson was in L.A. and he was discussing the Akins–Jordan fight when the phone rang. It was Blinky Palermo, Carbo's right-hand man, and he wanted to talk to Leonard.

"Hello, Jackie," Blinky said. "Do you know we're in for half?"

"Half of what?" Leonard said.

"Half of the fighter, or there won't be no fight on December fifth. Didn't Truman explain this to you?"

Leonard hung up and conferred with the others. He explained to Nesseth that if Jordan won the title, then Carbo and Palermo would own half of Jordan.

"The hell they will," Nesseth fumed.

Gibson suggested they all meet again later. "You know how Carbo and Blinky are. They want all of everything before you can get a welterweight title fight. You should go along with this thing, and I will straighten them out when I get back to Chicago tomorrow," Gibson said.

But Nesseth and Leonard didn't want to string along two dangerous, violent mobsters.

"We'll end up in the river," Leonard protested.

"They won't resort to violence," Gibson tried to reassure them. "That kind of stuff went out with high-button shoes. Go along with it.

This is the way that the welter- and light heavyweight title has worked since Carbo and Blinky got into the picture. When I get to Chicago I will straighten everything out so there won't be any problems. It won't cost you any money."

Leonard went to a pay phone and called Blinky. He told him that he thought things would be all right.

"What the hell do you mean 'think'?" Blinky screamed. "I don't want no thinks. Can you handle it? Otherwise there's no fight, we're pulling out. Unless we get half the fighter."

Leonard then said seven words that would prove very costly to him.

"All right, then, you have a deal."

"All right, then, you have a fight." Blinky beamed.

When Gibson got back to Chicago, he got a visit from Bernie Glickman, Akins's "manager," who was fronting for Carbo. He demanded a $40,000 guarantee for the fight instead of the agreed-upon percentage. So Carbo and Palermo were winners either way.

By the end of November, Cus invited seventy-five guests to his two-room apartment to introduce Ingemar Johansson to the New York press. But he double-talked his way around telling them when the fight would be held and then refused to pose with Ingemar and his adviser. "It would look like we've agreed to the fight," he reasoned. The truth was that Johansson and Edwin Ahlquist, his Swedish promoter, had spent a few days at a secret hideaway discussing a bout with Patterson.

A few days later the Jordan–Akins fight went off and Akins looked dismal losing a unanimous decision. After the win, Leonard got a series of calls from Palermo, urging him to fly down to Florida to see "Mr. Norris" because Leonard hadn't been able to get any good matches at Hollywood Legion Stadium. Blinky even made a reservation for Leonard and then picked him up at the airport. But instead of seeing Norris, he drove Leonard to a motel in Miami where Frankie Carbo was waiting for him. Palermo demanded their 50 percent of Jordan again. "Can you or can't you control Nesseth?" he asked. He wanted Jordan to fight Garnet "Sugar" Hart, the number one contender, who just happened to be controlled by Blinky. Leonard said that Nesseth wouldn't go for that fight.

"What's the difference? Our fighter wins the title and Nesseth gets half of Hart. That's the way it works," Blinky said. Carbo said he was just looking out for his pal Palermo. "As long as Blinky's making money I don't have to be doling out money to him." Leonard said that he wanted to take a walk but Carbo ordered him to stay put. He was never left alone the whole time he was in Miami. On the way to the airport, Carbo and Blinky told him to take care of "this thing." Leonard flew home shaken.

Nesseth told Leonard that Jordan was going to fight a nontitle bout with Alvaro Gutierrez on January 22, 1959. A few days before the fight, Blinky called Leonard and told him to send his share to his wife in Philadelphia. Leonard called Gibson and, frantic, got assurances that Gibson would send Blinky the cash. Jordan knocked out Gutierrez in three rounds and earned $12,500. After a few days Blinky called Leonard at home. He was irate. When he asked about his money, Leonard said that Gibson was going to send it. In the background Leonard heard, "Give me that phone." Carbo came on. "You son-of-a-bitching double-crosser," he shouted. "Your word is no good. Just because you're two thousand miles away don't mean I can't have you taken care of. I have got plenty of friends out there to take care of punks like you. The money had better be in."

Gibson hadn't paid anything by February 6 and Leonard was freaking out so he authorized a check for cash drawn from the Hollywood Boxing and Wrestling Club, which he and Norris co-owned. Leonard then wrote out a personal check to Blinky's wife and sent it east. A few days later, Blinky called Leonard and screamed at him for sending his wife a personal check. "Only money orders in the future." He was probably pissed because his wife had been charged for cashing the check!

Maybe the reason that Gibson took so long to pay off Leonard's obligation was that he had bigger things on his mind. Ten days before the Jordan fight, on January 12, 1959, the Supreme Court ruled on the IBC monopoly case. By a 5–3 decision, Judge Ryan's decree was upheld. In its decision the court held that the IBC "had exercised a stranglehold on the boxing industry for a long period . . . and still dominated the staging of championship bouts and completely controlled the filming and broadcasting of those contests" and that it amounted to "an odorous monopoly . . . still feared in the boxing world." Bye-bye, IBC. Within a week, Norris and Wirtz sold their 40 percent interest in Madison Square Garden for millions. Norris's men at the Garden, Ned Irish and Harry Markson, remained in their posts and continued their Friday-night fight card on NBC. While most of the sports press hailed this as the death knell for the IBC, the famous columnist Dorothy Kilgallen was a little more cynical. "Biggies in the IBCorp outlawed by a recent Supreme Court decision have completed plans to get around the legal blow. The same key men—Truman Gibson, Harry Markson and Jim Norris— will continue to exercise control, although in a slightly different manner," she wrote.

Cus was with Kilgallen. "The Supreme Court's recent order to dissolve the IBC as a monopoly was like cutting a rattlesnake in half," Cus proclaimed in his unpublished article "The Boxing Monopoly Is Not Dead." "Both ends continue to wriggle and the head, being full of deadly poison, is still dangerous. The divided reptile of big-business boxing remains a threat today because the high court said nothing about the sport's major evil: Direct or indirect control of fighters and managers, and the blacklisting of those who refuse to cooperate."

A few weeks after the Supreme Court decision, Rosensohn announced that Patterson had signed to fight Ingemar Johansson. The hoopla surrounding a big heavyweight championship fight was just beginning when there was some noise coming out of Chicago. "Norris and Wirtz Form Ring Group—National Boxing Enterprises Is Subsidiary of Chicago Stadium Corporation," the headline read. Norris and Wirtz were co-chairmen and good old Truman Gibson was named director and administrative head. "Our new organization has the know-how and the resources and we are going to continue in boxing on a major basis," Wirtz said. "The new N.B.E. has the full

backing of Jim Norris and my companies." They would operate on a
national basis and continue the presentation of Wednesday-night
televised fights from various cities in cooperation with local promoters. Cus was right, the rattlesnake was not dead. But he had to have
had a laugh when Norris's original name for his new company, the
National Boxing Club, had to be changed when writers began referring to it as NBC, whose executives were not pleased.

Cus always hated Harry Markson, who ran the boxing program at
the Garden, even after Norris and Wirtz sold out and the New York
branch of the IBC was defunct. I never could figure out his animosity
toward Markson until I came across a story about Markson and Joe
Louis. A few years before the Supreme Court decision dissolving the
IBC, Joe Louis was tired of getting screwed on the back end by Wirtz
and sold out his percentage in the IBC for a flat $20,000 a year paid
by the Chicago and New York IBCs. On March 20, 1959, Markson
sent Joe this letter: "Dear Joe: As you must know, the Supreme Court
decision in the government's antitrust case against the IBC, the Garden, etc. made it necessary to separate completely the operations of
MSG and the Chicago Stadium. We learn that you are to be associated with the National Boxing Enterprises. Our lawyers tell us that
we are not permitted to carry you on our payroll at the same time. We
are sorry that this is so, Joe, but maybe sometime in the future we
will be able to use your services again without breaking any of Uncle
Sam's laws. With kindest personal good wishes, Sincerely yours,
Harry Markson, Managing Director, Boxing."

Louis was screwed again.

With the title fight against Johansson announced, national magazines began writing stories about the reclusive heavyweight champ.
Ebony did a big story on Floyd titled "Boxing's Most Misunderstood
Champion." The writer spent some time with Floyd and reported
that Patterson has received unkind, often harsh treatment from the
press, and in the United States and abroad had been sneeringly and
patronizingly referred to as a "phantom champion," a "reluctant
champion," and "the forgotten man of boxing." "No man who ever
held boxing's most glittering crown has been more undeserving of

such criticism than the champion himself but it is a matter of cold, objective fact that the public image created of Floyd Patterson has been substantially shaped during the last two years by two factors: (1) Patterson's personality, and (2) the relentless one-man crusade by his manager Cus D'Amato against the IBC, which on January 12 was ruled a monopoly by the U.S. Supreme Court and ordered dissolved.

" '[Patterson's] a retiring boy,' Cus said. 'He's an introvert who doesn't particularly enjoy being interviewed. He avoids the limelight. That's because he has a shy, withdrawn personality and I wouldn't want to change that.'

" 'I don't want glory or publicity,' Floyd says. 'I just want to be like other people.'

"D'Amato is grateful to Patterson for his loyalty and his faith. 'I would be nothing without Patterson. Patterson doesn't need me. When in the history of boxing has there been a champion with his honesty, intelligence, and sportsmanship? There was never a champion like him before and there will never again be one like him. If I had a son, I'd be very proud if he could be like Floyd. In fact, I'd be proud if he were my son.' "

The Johansson fight was scheduled for Yankee Stadium on June 25, but Cus figured that Floyd could use a tune-up fight so he signed an English heavyweight named Brian London, who somehow was rated the number four contender. Cus wanted Floyd to fight the winner of the UK championship fight between London and Henry Cooper in January of 1959, but when Cooper won, he demanded twice the $75,000 that Cus was guaranteeing for the fight, so London was enlisted. "I'd be daft to turn it down," he told the press.

Things got stranger still. The fight was being promoted by a young Ivy Leaguer named Cecil Rhodes, who claimed that he had three degrees from Harvard. (He did have one, from Harvard Law School.) Rhodes told Cus that he wanted to leave his prosperous steel-fabricating business to get into boxing promotion to advance boxing and give fighters their fair share. He also claimed to have good contacts with Gillette. All this was music to Cus's ears. "The man doesn't care about making money. He wants to plow it back into the sport," Cus said proudly. The fight with London was set for May 1 in Vegas and NBC would broadcast it over home TV with Gillette sponsoring it. NBC put up a $250,000 guarantee. The first sign of trouble was when Rhodes held a press conference that Cus didn't attend and said that he was teaming up with the new chairman of Madison Square Garden to stage two future defenses of Patterson's title both to be broadcast by NBC.

On April 23, a week before the fight, Cus came up to Floyd's training camp. He asked Floyd to come outside and sit with him in the car. Cus was in the backseat in a state of tremendous agitation. "I'd seen Cus upset before. Usually there was no real reason to worry. He had a habit of making things more serious than they really were. Still, I went out," Floyd wrote in his autobiography. "He looked disturbed. I got in with him, and he told me that the papers were not what he had thought they were, so that I would be getting less to engage in the London fight and subsequent ones. It was quite a mess."

It seemed that Rhodes was a flimflam man. Cus believed he had gotten him and Floyd to sign a four-page contract, without initialing each page, and then he replaced the first page of the contract with completely new terms that screwed Patterson. Cus had been alerted by Day Mangus, a horse breeder, who had just filed a $48,000 lawsuit against Rhodes saying he had done just that in a transaction he handled for the sale of one of Mangus's horses. Now it was a week before the fight and there was no promoter, Cus had been forced to pay Rhodes $55,000 of the NBC advance to disappear, and Cus had decided to move the fight from Vegas to Indianapolis because he was convinced that Rhodes was being backed by mob money in Vegas, a move that pissed off NBC, which then reduced its guarantee to $200,000.

To further complicate matters, Cus had flown in Brian London and his family and then secreted them in a hotel so they couldn't spill any of these beans to the press. Cus had made a trainer friend of his, Nick Baffi, London's American manager because he was afraid that the IBC might try to kidnap London before the fight. Then Baffi began to train London at Cus's gym, using Cus's sparring partners! "I wasn't fit for that fight," London told the *New York Times* reporter Arthur Daley. "I'd just been beaten by Henry Cooper and wasn't certified for a title fight. In order to get it, Cus D'Amato demanded that I sign on his man, Nick Baffi, as my manager. He gave me one sparring partner, Dusty Rhodes, who had been discarded by Patterson. Before that he kept me locked in a lawyer's office for two days, somewhere in the old New York downtown where the big skyscrapers are. I lived on sandwiches and coffee for two days."

With no promoter and a week to go before the fight, Cus turned to Bill Rosensohn, who wasn't particularly thrilled about this tune-up fight because London did have some power and he didn't want anything to ruin his big Johansson production coming up in June. Arthur Daley knocked Cus's production. "If Jim Norris and his outlawed International Boxing Club had ever attempted to do even a fraction of the things that D'Amato has brazenly done the screams of outraged indignation would have sent Octopus Inc., cowering in terror. They might even have flushed Frankie Carbo out of hiding."

Cus was also attacked by one nemesis, the columnist Red Smith, who, on April 17, in a nationally syndicated column titled "Boxing Really Needs a Doctor," savaged Cus's handling of the London fight and called for the return of Frankie Carbo and Jim Norris to run boxing! "Boxing is sick, got to have the doctor, and not just any old doctor either. Boxing needs Dr. Gray, sometimes called Big Mr. C., known to the District Attorney as Frankie Carbo. . . . They do say Frankie Carbo is a man of questionable moral repute and they've been saying it for some little while. Back before boxing got scrubbed up, though, and all unsavory characters eliminated, it was not uncommon for fighters to pull on mittens and punch one another. Guys like Johnny Greco used to be around fighting all the time. Kid Gavilan was a busy welterweight champion. Johnny Saxton couldn't fight much, but he did win the welterweight title twice. There were ugly rumors about some of these guys. It used to be implied, broadly and rather unpleasantly, that Mr. C. took an interest in their activities. It was deplorable. It was wonderful. Frankie come back."

WHILE CUS WAS HAVING his troubles in New York, life wasn't exactly a bed of roses for Jackie Leonard and Don Nesseth out in L.A. On April 24, 1959, their fighter Don Jordan was set to defend his title in a rematch with Virgil Akins in St. Louis. Palermo had been harassing Leonard to set up a meeting with Nesseth so they could arrange for his boy Hart to fight Jordan for the title.

"I don't think Nesseth would go for that," Leonard told Blinky over the phone.

"Well, he is going to have to fight Hart," Blinky said matter-of-factly.

"What are you doing, taking over complete possession of Jordan?" Leonard protested.

"In a way, yes," Blinky said. "We want to know who he is fighting for, who he is fighting, and we have got to give the okay. Carbo told you that in Miami. If you're going to work with us, you have got to go all the way with us or you won't get any help out there."

Leonard was too spooked to fly out to the fight but Nesseth attended, accompanied by a sergeant of the St. Louis Police Department. During the fight, Nesseth saw Blinky talking to Bernie Glickman, Akins's manager of record, in Akins's corner. If they were talking strategy it did them no good. Jordan beat Akins decisively, winning another unanimous decision.

The next day Blinky, accompanied by Glickman, entered the office of the promoter of the fight and demanded his cut of Jordan's purse. When Glickman's lawyer, who had been consulted on the phone, told Blinky to get the hell out of the building, he went to Nesseth's hotel.

"You know why I'm here," he told Nesseth in his room. "I want my money."

"I don't owe you any money," Nesseth said.

"Well, you paid me last time," Blinky said.

"I never paid you a cent and I don't intend to," Nesseth said. He told the mobster that he couldn't care less if Gibson paid him $10,000 each time Jordan fought, but he was never going to pay him anything. Blinky then asked Nesseth to accompany him back to L.A.

"You don't understand English that well," Nesseth said. "I told you earlier that I was going to see you this once and not again."

"Well, the Man is not going to like this," he said, and left the room. In the lobby, he called Leonard in L.A.

"What the hell is going on?" he screamed, and recounted his conversation with Nesseth.

"I told you Don was his own man," Leonard said.

"Well, I'll be out to the coast to see you," Blinky said ominously.

What Blinky didn't know was that Nesseth was about to make his own trip the next day. He was flying to New York to meet with Cus.

Maybe one of the reasons that Cus had wanted to settle with Rhodes over the London fight contracts was that Cus had been working around the clock on a new plan to establish dominance over all of boxing! With the IBC in tatters and Norris and Gibson trying to regroup in Chicago, Cus was poised to deliver the knockout punch. He had been in secret negotiations with ABC to promote a series of six fights from October 7, 1959, to March 30, 1960. One was to be a heavyweight championship fight, one was to be a championship bout in another division, and the other four were to be from the heavyweight, light heavyweight, and middleweight divisions. ABC would pay Cus $65,000 for each program. And they would have an option to extend the contract for another six months. So now Cus would be directly in competition with Norris and Gibson, who still had their weekly *Wednesday Night Fights*, also broadcast by ABC!

Cus began putting together a lineup. His handwritten notes included heavyweights Johansson, London, and Henry Cooper, as well as Patterson. His middleweights were Gene Armstrong and José Torres—fighters he managed. Cus sent out a letter to sympathetic independent managers to sign and return to him. It read: "May I acknowledge to you that I am most concerned with boxing's present status and that I am in general sympathy with your efforts to reestablish the interest and confidence in boxing that is necessary to return it to its position of importance. I understand that you are hopeful of advancing boxing's interests by encouraging the introduction of a series of once-weekly television programs presenting boxing bouts that will conform with your standards for promotion and distribution of revenues. I assure you that fighters under my management will be available to participate in bouts to be televised as part of a television series that receives your support. Listed below are the fighters I am not managing, and I confirm to you that a fee of not less than Seven Thousand ($7,000) Dollars plus some reasonable expense allowances would be acceptable for each of them for their participation in a televised main event (except if my fighter is a world champion or participating in a championship bout)."

Cus had everything in place for the series except for ABC's second stipulation, a championship bout in another division other than heavyweight. This was why Don Nesseth and a fight promoter from Oakland, California, named Don Chargin had flown to New York to meet with Cus. They met on Monday, April 27. By the end of the day, they had reached an agreement and Nesseth and Chargin checked out of the Hotel Edison and flew back to Los Angeles. A few days later the news broke. The *New York Times* headline was "D'Amato Has a Partner—Report Says He Pools Stable with That of Jordan Pilot." "Cus D'Amato and Don Nesseth, managers of heavyweight champ Floyd Patterson and welterweight champion Don Jordan, signed an agreement today to pool their managerial interests in an undisclosed fashion, an authoritative source reported. This was the first agreement of its kind in boxing history. Neither pilot was available for immediate confirmation. However, close friends believed that they had teamed for mutual benefits in the new promotional era that followed the court ordered breakup of the IBC's monopoly. D'Amato has eight pro fighters, Nesseth has five or six in addition to their champions."

On the West Coast in Oakland, Don Chargin was talking to reporters. Described in a newspaper clip as "one of D'Amato's lieutenants," Chargin sounded the charge. "There's little doubt a new order is moving into power in boxing. . . . The new group will be composed of independent clubs, such as ours, and will have the services of at least two champions—Floyd Patterson and Don Jordan—at its command. . . . D'Amato and Nesseth hope their stand against the NBE will convince other managers and promoters that there is a way for all to advance in boxing."

Cus was attempting a hostile takeover of boxing, and Norris and Gibson, heads of the NBE, were watching intently.

While Nesseth and Chargin were discussing their new business with Cus, Gibson called Leonard at his office in Hollywood. He was very, very upset with Leonard and Nesseth. He said that he had heard that Nesseth was putting out a release that he was going with Cus D'Amato and forming a new organization. "Although I am upset with you, Nesseth, and everyone else, how much was the purse Jordan made?" He said that he was going to have to pay Palermo his cut because he had "agreed to pay them."

Nesseth arrived in L.A. the morning of April 28 and he went right to Leonard's office. Leonard got another phone call, this one not as cordial as Gibson's had been.

"Hello, hello, hello? You know who this is?" the voice said.

"Yeah, I know who this is," Leonard said. He had recognized Carbo's, or the Man's, or Mr. Gray's, voice. Carbo was still on the lam, evading the New York City arrest warrant.

"You're a no-good motherfucker. I am going to gouge your eyes out. You're gonna get hurt and when I say 'hurt,' I mean dead! You double-crossing, son-of-a-bitch bastard! We are going to meet at the crossroads. You are never going to get away with it. I have had that title for twenty-five years and no punk like you is going to take it away from me. When I say 'get you,' you are going to be dead. We will have someone out there take care of you."

Then he hung up. Leonard excused himself, ran across the hall to the bathroom, and vomited.

Five minutes later the phone rang again. It was Blinky. Leonard related to him the conversation he'd just had with Carbo.

"Well, Jesus, he was right, wasn't he? What do you think you got coming? You're nothing but a double-crosser. I'm coming to the coast and I'm going to see some people and they're going to pay a visit to you," Blinky said.

Leonard told him that it was no good to come, that he was very mad, and he hung up on Blinky.

Two days later, Gibson's associates at the Olympic Auditorium in L.A. who had put up a $20,000 surety bond guaranteeing the performance of Leonard and the Hollywood Boxing and Wrestling Club withdrew their bond. California would then have to close down Leonard's business. The next day Palermo checked into the Bismarck Hotel in Chicago and charged his room to the "IBC." It was okay—even though the IBC was no longer in existence, Norris owned the hotel. The next day, Gibson phoned Leonard in L.A. and told him that he would put up additional money for the surety bond if Leonard would convince Nesseth to fight Sugar Hart for the belt. They could even stage the fight at the Hollywood Legion Stadium. Later that day, Blinky met with Gibson and Marty Stein, Hart's manager of record, and then he rushed to the airport without even checking out of his room. He had to get to L.A. right away.

PATTERSON'S FIGHT WENT OFF without a hitch on May 1. He was a 10–1 favorite and was set to get 60 percent of the gate and all the NBC money. It took Floyd eleven rounds to knock London out. "I was not satisfied with my showing. I think I was sharper in my training sessions than I was in the fight," Floyd told the press. "He kept coming on and I couldn't seem to slow him up in the early rounds. He gave me a hard fight and I'm beginning to get the feel of fighting again."

Cus put his own spin on the fight. "The fellow was extraordinarily tough. How else could he have stayed in there that long? He just took too much in the body and it finally led to a collapse," he told the press. He said that he was trying to get lighter-weight sparring partners for Floyd to increase his hand speed but that it had proved difficult. "We have used a special chest and rib harness—similar to a baseball catcher's chest protector—for some of Floyd's heavyweight partners and still he hurt them."

Brian London had his own take. "They led me to believe that they'd let me go the distance," London told *The New York Times*. "When Patterson tried to knock me out in the first 40 seconds, I said to myself, 'You bloody bum. I won't let you knock me out.' By the 11th round, I was too tired to continue. I never got marked but he cut me up terrible in the kidneys and I couldn't breathe."

Eddie Borden covered the fight for *Monsieur* and after commenting on the strange events leading up to the fight, he gave Cus a backhanded compliment. "Legally, he was violating every law prescribed by the Boxing Commission rules. Cus defied the world in his campaign to secure the right kind of engagements for Floyd Patterson. It is difficult to analyze D'Amato properly. He is mysterious, stubborn and self-opinionated. He will not stand for any advice given him, and strangely enough he firmly believes that everything he does is correct. He emerges from the fight a virtual hero who defied the precepts and background of boxing. He did everything wrong and it turned out right."

BLINKY PALERMO ARRIVED in L.A. late on May 1 and checked into the Beverly Hilton hotel. The next night he called Leonard at his home and told him to come meet him at the hotel. Leonard said he had the "wife and kid" there and Blinky said to bring them, they could stay in the hotel lobby. Realizing how serious Palermo sounded, Leonard bundled up the wife and his son and had them sit in the car in the hotel parking lot as he went in to meet Palermo. But Blinky wasn't alone. He was accompanied by Joe Sica, a well-known local mobster and strong-arm man. Sica then lectured Leonard for getting himself into a jam with his good friend Mr. Gray. When Leonard kept saying that the whole issue was Gibson's fault, neither Joe nor Blinky wanted to hear about Gibson. For them it was all about Leonard controlling his pal Nesseth. Sica suggested they call Nesseth and get him to come over.

"I don't even have the number," Leonard said. "Can you see him tomorrow?"

"Drag him in. Go out and grab him by the neck and get him out of bed and shake him and get him in line," Sica said. "Can't you whip him?"

Leonard was flabbergasted. "I don't know if I can whip him or not, but I am going on doing business with him again," he said.

"Look, Jackie, you made a choice," Sica said. "It's a question of either you or Don Nesseth is going to get hurt. Wouldn't you rather go grab him by the neck and straighten him out than for me to go back and tell 'The Gray'? You're all right but it's Nesseth that's no good. If you have to, go out and beat the hell out of Nesseth. If you need any help we will go with you and help you and drag him out of bed."

Leonard said that he wouldn't assault his friend.

"Are you going to see this guy in the morning and straighten things out?" Sica said.

"I am going to try," Leonard said.

"Try, hell," Palermo said. "You are going to straighten it out. I can't go home like this. I am in a hell of a jam with the Gray."

Leonard left the room and then he got in his car and drove the family home.

The following afternoon, Nesseth met Leonard at his office and Leonard called Gibson's home in Chicago. Nesseth got on the line and told Gibson about all the threats that had been made to them in person by Palermo and Sica.

"Nesseth said, 'Blinky's in town yelling,'" Gibson wrote in his autobiography. "I said, 'Well, it's very hard for me to be sorry for you after what you've done to us in your Cus D'Amato announcements, but don't walk, you run to the chief of police or the nearest district attorney and tell him Blinky's in town yelling. I don't know what you want me to do about it. I can't feel sorry for you.'"

"Can't you call up your boss and have him call off the dogs?" Nesseth asked.

"When you say my boss, you mean Mr. Norris?" Gibson said.

"Of course I mean Mr. Norris. If you don't call Norris and get these people out of town and leave us alone, I'm going to call the sponsors of your television shows and tell them just what kind of people they are dealing with."

Then Gibson said he never threatened them but that "all the pressure could be relieved and you can do your own Jackie Leonard a favor by saving his club if you will just agree to fight Sugar Hart."

Nesseth told him that wasn't going to happen and then Gibson agreed to call Norris.

Monday wasn't any more pleasant for Leonard and Nesseth. They were in Jackie's office at the Hollywood Legion Stadium when Blinky Palermo walked in unannounced. He was accompanied by Louie Dragna, another well-known mob enforcer in L.A.

"I want to talk to you," Blinky told Nesseth.

"Well, I don't want to talk to you," Nesseth replied, and left. The next morning he didn't walk, he ran to the LAPD, where he was given police protection.

Meanwhile, Leonard was now a captive audience of one in his office. Blinky kept pressing him on a Hart fight and Leonard kept blaming Gibson for telling him to lie about giving up half of Jordan.

Blinky started screaming. "It's you we're looking to, we don't give a damn about Gibson."

"Hey, doesn't Don Nesseth live out my way?" Dragna said.

"I think he lives somewhere near San Bernardino," Leonard said.

"No, it's West Covina, isn't it?" Dragna said with a sardonic smile. "He has a wife and kid, doesn't he?"

Leonard nodded. Then Blinky started screaming again about Leonard having to grab Nesseth and shake him and get him in line. After Blinky and Dragna left, Leonard got an eviction notice—his lease on the stadium would be terminated in five days. It was another day in paradise.

Leonard also ran right to the police and an LAPD sergeant bugged his home phone and also his office.

Gibson had reached Norris, who reached out to Blinky and called the dog home to the East Coast. But Blinky couldn't resist one more shot at Nesseth and Leonard. On Wednesday morning, Sica was already waiting for Leonard when he arrived at his office. Then Nesseth came by and, shortly after, Palermo strolled in. Sica reminded Nesseth that he was "lucky" to have won the title and that certain commitments had to be fulfilled. Nesseth was hurt. He said that he had groomed his fighter for two years and he had gotten his fighter a shot at the title on his own. "You did like fun get it on your own," Blinky said. Nesseth changed the subject and objected to all the harassment he and Leonard were going through. "No, no, I don't agree with the harassment. You're right. That's out. There ain't going to be no harassment, that's out of the question." Sica had had enough. He and Blinky got up to leave and as they were about to exit the room, Blinky leaned over and whispered in Leonard's ear. "Jackie, you're it." But he didn't whisper so low that his words weren't picked up by the LAPD's sophisticated tape deck.

That night, Blinky flew home on Norris's orders. But he couldn't stop himself from stealing a few magazines and a pack of gum while he paid for a package of crackers at an airport shop. The cop that was tailing him arrested him for petty theft. They brought him downtown and he had to post $500 bail. While this was taking place, a captain from the force had a few questions for him about his visit to L.A. Blinky told the cop that he had never heard of any Louie Dragna and that he had not seen the "Sica boys" on this visit. After all, he hadn't been in L.A. on business; his had purely been a "social visit."

Truman Gibson was about to try another tack. Since the bad-guy routine hadn't worked, he brought in a "good guy" to talk some sense into Leonard. Bill Daly was a longtime well-respected manager who was close to both Carbo and Norris. He would be the voice of reason. But his conversations with Leonard revealed an incredible insight into the minds of Carbo and Palermo. Daly flew to L.A. with Gibson on May 11. They checked into the Ambassador Hotel and then Gibson called Leonard, who was in Mexico for a few days. He told him that he had to leave town the next day but he was leaving Daly there to "straighten all this mess out." On the 13th, Daly visited Leonard in his office.

"You're in a hell of a jam two ways," Daly told him. "You're in a jam with the club and you're in a jam because of what you and Nesseth had done in going with Cus D'Amato."

"I don't have anything to do with that," Leonard protested. "I never even discussed that with Nesseth."

"Well, I don't know what I can do for you. You have the whole East upset," Daly said. "Everyone's blaming everyone else. Norris is upset, Gibson is upset, Carbo is upset, and Palermo is upset."

Leonard told him that he was finished with boxing and that he had been talking to Nesseth and Don Chargin about taking the club over from him.

"What are you going to do about Nesseth?" Daly asked. "You should have come to me in the first place. If you hadn't went to that damn Blinky, I could have saved Nesseth a lot of money. I would have went to Carbo and you wouldn't have had to give any money unless it was a real big fight. I would have told them I was getting the 15 percent and let Nesseth keep it. But you went to Blinky. He will take anything to stay out of Carbo's pocket. Carbo had to throw him the chicken feed. Now you're in a hell of a mess."

They agreed to talk more the next day in Daly's hotel room. That morning, before he went to the hotel, Leonard stopped off at the LAPD Intelligence Division and he was fitted for a body wire. It worked.

Daly's conversation was like a master class in the mob control of boxing. He began by going after Nesseth. "This geezer, this Nesseth, he shot his mouth off. Instead of using the same diplomacy he handles when he sells automobiles, used the same bullshit with them, and went along with Truman to bullshit them, con them, and win them over to his side, he just challenged them and said, 'Go fuck yourself. You ain't gonna have no money.' He played possum until he got the title. They know he fucked them."

Now Leonard had to repeat some of the things that Daly said the day before so they could be caught on the wire.

"Like you said yesterday, Bill—they're not going to let anybody get away with this shit, because all the champs will be doing the same goddamn thing."

"That's right," Daly said. "Fuck him the same way. I know what their move will be. They won't hold you. They're trying to harass you in order to make him come in line. So if he don't come in line, they'll know at least, if I get the word to them, at least you'd have talked to the guy and he's just stubborn."

Then Daly told Leonard that Truman Gibson was "in the jackpot," which is slang for being in trouble. And he revealed that Gibson was most angry about the company that Nesseth and Cus were setting up in opposition to Norris's NBE. " 'I never thought the guy [Nesseth] would jump the fence and carry on this way,' " Daly said, quoting Gibson. " 'They're trying to destroy me. Fuck them, I'll have them destroyed.' He's fucking mad, Truman is."

Then Daly explained the way that Carbo and Palermo maintained control over boxing champs. "If I ever had two champions I'd be having fucking parties and laughing and clowning. I wouldn't want to hurt nobody. This cocksucker steps out and wants to hurt everybody. Sure they did wrong if they want to tell this fighter who to fight. But they're taking that attitude for a reason. They never told Viscusi who to fight and what to do. They couldn't tell Weill who to have Marciano fight. Weill pays off like a fucking slot machine. If he has a fighter, he gets a crack at the title right away. Frankie don't like Weill as a person because he's a greasy fucking pig. It's a business transaction. Carbo don't give a fuck as long as they keep their income up. That's how they live. And that's how they're going to live as long as they can get away with it."

What Daly said next blew me away.

"One thing," Daly told Leonard. "If you get the fucking title on your own, they don't interfere with you. You know, if you get through. If you bust through the barrier, they don't interfere with you. They're pretty much on the level that way."

That's exactly what Cus did. He outsmarted Norris and busted through the IBC barrier. But he never threatened or double-crossed Carbo in doing that. Cus never even attacked Carbo in print. He always went after Norris. Cus knew the wiseguys, and I think they each had a mutual respect for the other. Bernie Glickman was a mob-connected manager but he loved his boxers and he paid a lot of money out of his own pocket, just like Cus did, to keep them alive. Glickman ruined his legitimate business and wound up bankrupt because of his involvement in boxing. I think that Carbo respected Cus and didn't give a shit when Cus beat Norris's fighter for the heavyweight championship. Carbo never controlled the heavyweights and Archie Moore was managed by Doc Kearns and he and Carbo despised each other. So when Norris bitched about Cus to Carbo and Carbo dismissed Norris by saying Cus was "crazy," he was refusing to be sucked into Norris's war with Cus.

But the welterweight title was something else. Carbo had controlled it for over twenty-five years. So Gibson was "in the jackpot" for letting it slip away.

"He doesn't want to grab another Nesseth as long as he lives," Daly told Leonard. "Oh, Truman is all fucked-up."

Leonard said that Gibson had told him that he had met with Carbo. "Jesus, the man down there is giving me holy hell," Gibson told Leonard. "And on top of that Norris is mad."

"This is the first time that proves to Norris that Truman was wrong. He okayed the fight, but Don [Nesseth] was in the conspiracy to fuck them, you know."

Now here's where the "good cop" angle comes in. Daly went into what he thought Carbo and his boys might do to Nesseth and then he brought up another famous example of a guy who tried to double-cross Carbo and paid the price in 1953. Ray Arcel was a great trainer who got involved with a television promotion that was going up against Norris's *Friday Night Fights*. On top of that, Arcel started paying his cuts to a new guy who he assumed would break off to Carbo. But he didn't and Arcel got dealt with by two guys with lead pipes wrapped in newspaper on the streets of Boston. That scared Arcel out of boxing for eighteen years.

"They're up to something with Nesseth. They'll get—throw some fucking—"

"Bomb?" Leonard interrupted.

"Bomb his porch off or something."

"Arcel thought he was pretty smart too," Leonard said.

"Lucky thing Arcel didn't die," Daly said.

"He probably didn't even know what hit him," Leonard said.

"It's like you and I talking and somebody walking over," Daly said.

"Oh Jesus Christ! When Carbo called me—"

Daly interrupted him. "See what they do. They used a water pipe, see. They just get an ordinary piece of newspaper, see, that's all they ever use. And they try to give you two bats, and they kill you with two, if they can. But they whack you twice and fracture your skull and knock you unconscious. And they just drop it. There's no heat. You haven't got no weapon on you. You drop it in a crowd or out on the street. They drop it immediately. No witnesses."

"That's what Frankie told me," Leonard said. "He said, 'We got friends out there. I don't even need to leave here.' I don't know where he was at. I don't even know where he was calling from."

"Ray was lucky he lived," Daly said, not picking up the bait. "The poor son of a bitch. He just got fucking stupid. He had no fucking right doing this. He was with Carbo for years. Frankie gave him Teddy Yarosz, gave him this fighter and that fighter and he always worked with him. Son of a bitch had to be hurt. They used a couple of kids from Boston to do it."

"Like here if they wanted Don and I, they're not going to use somebody that we'd know around here," Leonard said.

"No. The Sicas would be home," Daly said. "Or in a public place."

"And the first thing you know—boom, I'll be laying out there and don't know what the hell hit me."

"I don't know what way they're going to handle that Nesseth but they're going to handle him some fucking way. Come to think of it, he's got a used-car lot yet?" Daly asked.

"Yeah, he works with his brother. His brother's running it," Leonard said.

"You know where the joint is?" Daly asked.

"It's advertised on TV," Leonard said.

Meanwhile, Leonard complained to Daly that he was being harassed. "For the last two days someone's been prowling around, just checking to see where I live, to talk to me. Making sure nobody's around. Last night the same car went around the block four or five times and kept slowing down by my car every time they went around. My wife noticed it. She was watering the lawn. It was just dark and then she called me and I watched the car and it came around again and never did stop."

The talk turned to Don Chargin, Nesseth's promoter friend from the Bay Area who had met with Cus in New York. Chargin was planning on moving into L.A. and taking over Jackie's club and retaining Leonard as matchmaker. None of those things were in Norris and Gibson's best interests.

"Chargin was supposed to come in last night. He didn't come. He's not coming till today. And now Joe Sica wants to see him. He's liable to screw it all up," Leonard said.

"Does Sica know Chargin?" Daly wondered.

"No. He just read about [his buying into the Club] in the paper yesterday. And right away he wanted to get a hold of Chargin. They've checked him already. They've sent some cars up north, trying to find out where they can locate him and who he is. Try to scare him away," Leonard said.

"Oh, they'll get somebody up around San Francisco to go see him and tell him to lay off you people. It'll make the guy think a little bit too. And the guy is going to say, 'Look, we don't want your money to be hurt, but we'll fuck up that club every way we can.' All over a fucking nitwit like Don Nesseth. You can't talk to Nesseth?" They had come full circle. The "good cop" routine didn't budge Leonard or Nesseth. That would prove very costly for Carbo, Palermo, and Gibson.

CUS'S MOVES TO EXPAND beyond the heavyweight title and control all of boxing started getting more and more play in the national press. On May 19, a few days after Daly left L.A., the *Los Angeles Times* ran a story titled "D'Amato Builds His Own Empire," using Rosensohn and Irving Kahn as his lieutenants. The same day, the *Los Angeles Mirror News* ran a larger piece, "Champion Patterson's

Manager Pictures Self as Boxing's Savior," the first of a two-part
series by Murray Olderman. Olderman spent some time around Cus
in New York and his reportage captures what Cus was like at this
crucial juncture of his life.

"Cus is 51, white all over, with a little paunch from nervous over-
eating, a rugged Neapolitan chin and a blink in his eyes. Until Patterson won the title in 1956, he never had a place to call home. Now
he's got a neat little two-room apartment overlooking Broadway, dec-
orated with a lavish bar and a vibrating chair. There is no bed. At 2
or 3 in the morning, if you've been out with Cus, you're ready to hit
the sack. Cus goes up to his apartment and starts telephoning the
world. His phone bill for one month has been $1500. He has gone ten
days by actual count without once getting into a bed. He simply showers and shaves and keeps going, dozing off occasionally in a chair.
Why this frantic schedule? Cus believes sincerely he alone can make
boxing respectable 'against the evil forces of Jim Norris and the IBC.'
The court decision dissolving the IBC doesn't count.

" 'Nothing's changed in boxing,' he says gloomily. 'Things will get
worse. This is a lone fight. I'm in training, like my fighters. As long
as this war lasts, I'm swearing off women and drinking because
they're tools of the enemy.' It's a real thing with D'Amato. One of his
inner council confirms that he's seen Cus come up the elevator at
night carrying papers over his arm—and concealed in his hand was
a knife. An intruder in the hallway outside his apartment once felt
the grip of D'Amato's fingers on his neck. Sometimes he goes out of
town to meet people 'because I've suspected a wiretap put on my
phone by the IBC. Secrets were getting out.' Cus sees enemies everywhere. When I asked him how he stays busy, he said, 'I'm trying to
grow a third eye in the back of my head to prevent 'them' from sneak-
ing up on me with a stiletto.'

"Yet, ironically, D'Amato's vendetta against evil has brought only
ridicule in the press, which objects to his secretiveness and double
talk. 'I am ridiculed,' shrugs Cus, 'because I oppose the IBC. Criticism
is unwarranted.' What has his crusade done for D'Amato? 'I used to
owe $30,000. Now I owe $50,000 to $60,000.' Is it worth it? 'Don't you

think I'd like to eat and sleep like normal people? At 51, I want to play games? Now I will be more cloak and dagger than I ever was.'"

ON MAY 20, the California State Athletic Commission held a public hearing about the conspiracy to horn in on Don Jordan. Leonard was scheduled to testify but he was completely freaked out. Carbo was still on the lam and Blinky had left town but Gibson, Sica, and Dragna would all be in the audience listening to his testimony. Leonard asked the guy who was going to question him not to make him appear to be a stool pigeon. He thought that if he made a full public disclosure at that time the defendants would "kill him." What he did tell the commission was that Palermo tried to muscle in on Jordan and enlisted the aid of Carbo. But he said that Jordan's manager, Nesseth, wouldn't go for it and "usual gangster threats followed."

Truman Gibson was sworn in and he claimed that he came to L.A. to persuade Palermo to refrain from any threats to Leonard and Nesseth. Gibson admitted that he called Norris to fill him in on what was going on and that shortly after that Palermo called him and Gibson told him "he was being very silly and very foolish. What the hell was he doing in Los Angeles?" He also told him to "cut out things that went out with high-button shoes."

After the testimonies finished, the commission voted to ask the LAPD chief of intelligence to investigate Carbo, Palermo, Sica, Dragna, and Gibson. The chief then gave all their evidence, including the wiretaps, to the FBI and the U.S. attorney in Los Angeles. A grand jury was empaneled.

Meanwhile, Cus was having his own problems in New York. Once again, he tried to make an opponent of Floyd's take on an American manager who had close ties to Cus. The first inklings of this came out when Ingemar Johansson published his memoir in Sweden. In the book, he recounted a visit he had gotten in Sweden from Bill Rosensohn and Cus's lawyer Edwin Schweig. "They offered me a contract that promised me a title fight against Patterson. I read it and said, 'No, thank you.' Nobody could persuade me to sign that contract to get a world championship bout. It was a slave contract. They wanted me to have an American manager who would take 33⅓ percent of my earnings. That 33⅓ percent was reduced to 10 percent. My American manager got partly the right of determination over one of my fights in America each year. But my word would always be decisive and I would decide entirely myself about all other fights but I am under obligation not to fight for the IBC or its successors."

The manager that Cus tried to foist on Ingo was Harry Davidow. Davidow had been a partner with Cus years earlier and ran the Gramercy Gym while Cus was in the Army. Davidow hadn't held a manager's license for ten years and he now owned a candy store–luncheonette in Brooklyn. The word on the street was you could get an egg cream and also play your numbers there. The papers picked up on the story, so when Davidow went before the NYSAC they were primed for him.

q: Is it not a fact, Mr. Davidow, that this contract between you and Johansson was signed only as a price for Johansson getting the right to fight for the championship? a: No sir. q: Isn't it a fact that you are only a stooge and a dummy for D'Amato in this thing? a: I don't think so.

Johansson was called to the stand. He testified that Cus told him that he couldn't have his father as his manager and that he didn't believe he would have gotten the fight if he didn't use Davidow.

The commission didn't even bother to deliberate. They immediately disapproved Davidow's managerial license. And Commissioner Helfand went even further. "This whole thing stinks to high heaven. It is obvious that Davidow is acting as a dummy for D'Amato to retain an interest in this man's career after this fight," he said.

"You are accusing me of acting as a stooge for someone," Davidow protested.

"If you don't like the description, it's too bad. This whole thing is reprehensible," Helfand sniffed.

Just a few days later the story broke that Cus and Rosensohn, his promoter, were feuding. Rosensohn went to Arthur Daley of the *Times*, who was no friend of Cus's but had been bamboozled by the smooth-talking Rosensohn. "As far as Cus D'Amato is concerned, I've had it. I'm fed up, right to here," Rosensohn told Daley. "For the better part of a year the overanxious Rosensohn yielded to the capricious, high-handed demands of the distrustful Cus. However, Bill has made his last backward step and has turned to challenge the knight whose armor has become tarnished of recent weeks. The attacks that D'Amato has made on the boxing commission and his veiled threats to take the fight out of NY have done more than alarm the Boy Promoter. They've driven him to cold anger. Yesterday he could contain himself no longer. He just spilled over.

" 'One man, D'Amato, has singlehandedly created all this doubt,' said Rosensohn, voice low but trembling with emotion. 'Since his denunciation of the commission, he's been quoted as saying that he's thinking of moving the fight and that he's suspicious of the commission and everyone connected with this situation, including me. But at this point I must take a firm stand. . . . I will not tolerate any interference with [the plans for the fight in New York] even if it comes from D'Amato. This may be the last fight I ever promote but I must stick to my principles. I take orders from no one and I refuse to be intimidated.' "

This was all bullshit. Cus never wanted to take the fight out of New York, even after the commissioners voted down Davidow. But Rosensohn used this article to claim that Cus strong-armed him into forgoing a cut of television, radio, and movie rights. He had never had those rights in any of the fights that he had promoted for Cus. Every ridiculous charge Rosensohn made against Cus, Daley swallowed whole. He gave over his column to Rosensohn. But the damage to Rosensohn had been done. "What's next? I don't know. Whatever D'Amato does hereafter indicates that he's afraid to have Patterson fight Johansson or that he's trying to destroy a promoter who refuses to knuckle under to his demands or that he's attempting to defy and overrule the commission or that he thinks he's more powerful than any figure or figures in boxing or civic life. D'Amato is now confronted by a real dilemma. Theoretically he might try to pull out by claiming an injury to Patterson. But Floyd is too honest to make such a pretense and too proud to be part of such chicanery. D'Amato's only alternative would be an out and out power play, refusal without reason. He'd find this lonely, expensive and disastrous."

ON MAY 29, 1959, two days after Daley's puff piece about Rosensohn, a combination of New York City detectives, D.A. Hogan's men, and New Jersey state troopers surrounded a nondescript house in Haddon Township, New Jersey. Inside, Frankie Carbo, who had crisscrossed the globe for fifteen months, wasn't going to go out gentle into the night. Or at least through the front door. The tough guy tried to sneak out through a back window and he fell right into the arms of two detectives. He surrendered without a fight. John Bonomi, the assistant district attorney in Hogan's office and the head of the Carbo investigation, breathed a sigh of relief. Hogan had put thirty-five detectives on this case. Now they had their man. And Bonomi wasn't the only one thrilled.

"The troopers were awestruck by Carbo. They asked if they could take him out to breakfast. I guess they thought they had this great celebrity on their hands. I had to tell them that not only would Carbo not be provided with full restaurant service, he would be handcuffed and kept under armed guard," Bonomi told David Remnick years later. "All I kept thinking about was the famous picture of John Dillinger, just before he escaped, standing with the smiling prosecutor. I didn't need that kind of publicity."

Carbo was cooling his heels in jail in Camden, New Jersey, his bail revoked, when things began to heat up on the West Coast. Just five days after Mr. Gray's arrest, Jackie Leonard was in his garage in his L.A. home when he was attacked from behind by a pipe-wielding brute. He was hit in the head twice, the same MO that Daly told him had been used with Arcel. He had a concussion and a week later he was still suffering from partial paralysis on one side of his face.

The day after Leonard's attack, Don Chargin, Cus's partner in Oakland, was about to fly down to L.A. to talk to Leonard about buying the Hollywood club, but he got a threatening phone call. "Stay out of Los Angeles. You saw what happened to your buddy Leonard." The caller even knew Chargin's flight number. Needless to say, he didn't board that flight.

Sports Illustrated covered the attack on Leonard and then, referring to that Red Smith column of the previous April when he sarcastically begged for the return of Carbo, blasted him without naming him. "This April one of the ablest of syndicated sportswriters, ridiculing the fears and the labyrinthine ways of Cus D'Amato, manager of Floyd Patterson, told his readers with cheery sarcasm that 'the fist fight industry needs a great big shot of Sinister influence, triple-strength, quick, before it wastes away and dies of Moral Uplift.' He called for the return of Carbo 'to restore the healthy glow of corruption.' 'Frankie, come back!' he cooed in conclusion. The era when such a line could be written, even in sarcasm, and read with enjoyment, has now come to an end."

The prevailing new tone may very well have been struck by sports editor Curley Grieve of the *San Francisco Examiner*, who wrote: "The brutal beating of Jackie Leonard is one of those things you wouldn't believe could happen. It is a throwback to the days of Capone. It strikes at the very core of justice. It is a slap in the face of all decent people."

But then a strange thing happened. L.A. police chief William H. Parker, who initially said the attack on Leonard was a "typical attack by mobsters," reversed himself a week later and issued the following statement: "We have carefully amassed and evaluated all known available facts. It is the considered and unanimous opinion of our investigating officers assigned to this case that the physical facts fail to support the probability that Mr. Leonard was subject to assault as originally reported. It now appears that Mr. Leonard suffered some acute physical incapacitation of a stunning nature that produced an illusion of assault."

Leonard's response was, "All I know is I have a headache." But the harassment didn't stop with the "illusion of assault." Leonard's house was later firebombed. He was tailed by menacing-looking strangers who taunted him with calls of "stool pigeon." It was even reported that Skid Row bums were offered $250 to beat him up. And his assault was confirmed by a friend of Joe Sica's who would later testify that Leonard was indeed beaten up.

WITH THE JOHANSSON FIGHT LOOMING, Cus tried to put on a PR offensive to offset the bad press he had been getting. He wrote a first-person article for *Look* magazine, published on June 5, that gave a detailed account of his battle with the IBC and pleaded with the American public to realize what a great fighter Patterson was. At the signing of the fight on June 10, he talked to Bill Rosensohn for the first time in weeks, and then he glad-handed all the sportswriters who had blasted him over the past year.

Meanwhile, Norris went on the offensive against Cus. Talking to Harry Grayson, a syndicated columnist whose work appeared in more than six hundred papers, he boasted, "Let's lay it on the table. Sonny Liston is my fighter. I believe he's the best of the lot. . . . I'll chase Patterson around the country until I corner him and find out if he can really fight." Norris took some flak for suggesting that Liston was "my fighter" since he wasn't a licensed manager. But it wasn't far from the truth. The largest portion of Liston was owned by Carbo and Palermo. Norris was basically telling Grayson that despite the courts dissolving the IBC, he was still controlling boxing. And he had some ominous words for Cus. "D'Amato could be hit by a streetcar, you know?"

Norris's people tried to get the Floyd–Ingo fight derailed when they sued because they claimed that Eddie Machen, who was obliterated by Ingo in the first round, had a return-match agreement. The defense argued that the agreement was invalid and obtained by "duress" and even if there was a contract, it wasn't with Machen but with the now dissolved IBC. The defense called Cus partisan Tommy Loughran, the former light heavyweight champ of the world, to testify that it was "extraordinary" for such a rematch clause to be signed for a nontitle fight. Eventually the judge refused to issue an injunction and the fight went on.

Floyd trained at his usual spot, Ehsan's, in New Jersey. It was a dump. The furniture was flimsy, the paint was peeling, the shades were in tatters. But he seemed ready. He had sparred more than five hundred rounds and was in great physical condition. Johansson was making headlines not for his prowess in the ring but for the opulence of his digs and his wild lifestyle. He was training in the luxe resort Grossinger's in the Borscht Belt of New York and living in an "architectural gem of a ranch house." He also was making frequent trips to the city to party. Nat Fleischer of *The Ring* magazine, no friend to Cus, told Swedish newspapermen covering the fight, "Ingemar has a weakness for night life and dancing. His training methods are contrary to all the rules. I am seriously worried about the title fight. I favored Johansson originally. I thought he would be the new world champion. Now I am beginning to doubt that he can make it. He is not preparing himself the way a challenger should."

Other reporters thought that Johansson's public sparring sessions were so unimpressive that he had to be hiding something. His fabled right hand, the "Hammer of Thor," the same one that destroyed Machen, was nowhere to be seen. Harry Grayson wrote, "His pawing left has looked as ineffectual as a Geneva conference. The right hand with which he is supposed to slay dragons is as invisible as Patterson between engagements."

So Patterson went off a 5–1 favorite and Rosensohn told the press that he was betting a half a million dollars on Ingo. "If Johansson wins, I've got a made-to-order return bout that ought to clear me $500,000."

Rosensohn's optimism was dulled a bit by the heavy rainstorms that forced him to postpone the bout until the following day and wound up putting a huge dent in the live gate, with only 21,961 people in the vast stadium, which was his only source of income from the fight.

When the fight finally started Ingo looked tentative. Floyd pressed him the whole first round. Then Ingo began using his trick. Years later, Cus explained it for a video that Jim Jacobs made. "The fight began with Johansson flicking a left jab, just flicking, without any apparent intention of hitting Patterson and the jab was awfully short by three or four inches. And I was struck, and as I watched I then realized what was happening. The methods that Johansson used were similar to that used by a three-card monte expert or a man who operated a shell game, wherein a three-card monte expert, by movement, draws your attention to that which is not going to happen in order to do what he wants to do, to cause that little card to disappear from your view in a split second.

"Patterson's eyes suddenly became focused on the left hand, because he flicked it without intention and continually repeated that, almost like having a hypnotic effect, of drawing attention to that left hand. As this continued, and when he thought that Patterson had now focused his full attention on the left hand, he threw a slow, lazy left hook and shot the right hand so fast that the right hand got there long before the left would have gotten there. And Patterson, having focused his attention on the left hand, was hit."

Floyd was knocked down seven times in the third round and referee Ruby Goldstein stopped the fight. It was a shocking upset. Howard Cosell jumped in the ring and was the first to reach Floyd and interview him for the radio.

"What happened Floyd?" Cosell asked.

"I got hit, Howard," Floyd said.

Then Cus grabbed the mike. "I will tell you right now that for the first time in the history of boxing, you will see a defeated heavyweight champion win his title back."

Meanwhile, Rosensohn sprang out of his seat with joy. "Let's arrange a party for Johansson," he crowed. Floyd's wife tried to rush up and battle the crowd pouring into the ring. "I've got to get to him. I've got to get to him," she kept repeating as a friend prevented her from the chaos ringside. It took an hour for Floyd to face the reporters after the fight. One reporter asked Floyd whether Johansson's right was the hardest punch he had ever taken. "Evidently so," Floyd said.

The next day everyone was stunned. Most experts had picked Floyd to win, including Jack Dempsey, who had made his prediction days earlier. "I really liked Johansson," he said, "but my ghostwriter wouldn't let me say so." Martin Kane from *Sports Illustrated* found Cus and Charlie Black commiserating in a deli near Broadway. Cus told him he wasn't hungry. When Kane asked him if he was the same man, Cus said, "I don't think I changed when Floyd became champion. I don't think I've changed now. I have no feeling myself. Whatever feeling I have is about Floyd personally. But he is an intelligent fellow who knows that things happened for specific reasons even if he does not know now how they happened. I am very detached. I was very detached at the end of the fight. The first thing I thought of was Charlie (who had a bad heart). The second thing I thought of was I wondered if I had enough money to pay off all my debts."

Charlie Black tried to put a nice spin on the loss. "When Schmeling knocked out Louis they said Louis walked from the ring," Charlie said. "He didn't walk. Twelve cops carried him. I know. I was there. Your fighter walked, Cus."

"Yes, I know," Cus said ruefully.

Meanwhile, Rosensohn was already counting his money the next day. "This is the best thing that has happened to boxing since Frankie Carbo went to jail. It makes it clear that you never can tell what will happen when two good fighters get into the ring. Hereafter no one will ever pay attention to 5-to-1 odds. They don't mean anything," he told the press. "On the rematch I'll get a good share of the supplementary fees. You can bet that I do, or there will be no return."

The boy promoter wound up losing about $40,000 on the fight. Patterson earned more than a half a million and Ingo got half that. But the money wasn't coming so fast. Truman Gibson and Eddie Machen got a judge to attach Ingo's purse as they pursued their lawsuit.

Of course, Patterson's loss gave Arthur Daley a chance to make the fight all about Cus and not Floyd. And to continue his fawning over Rosensohn. Three days later he wrote, "The dramatic dethronement of Floyd Patterson by Ingemar Johansson did more than rock the boxing world. It changes its geography and its entire pattern. . . . As the manager of Patterson, the cantankerous Cus not only was handpicking the champion's opponents, but he also was running each title defense as a behind-the-scenes promoter. What's more, he allied himself with Irving Kahn, the Aga of the theater-television trade who was to serve as an 'angel' with a limitless supply of money. The squeeze was put on Bill Rosensohn, the Boy Promoter whose resourcefulness and enterprise had made the bout possible in the first place. . . . Only one thing could save him, a dramatic knockout victory by the big, handsome Swede. Hence there will be no Octopus Jr. to replace the Norris monopoly. D'Amato and his allies are balked. The return match will be a million-dollar epic and Rosensohn will direct the orchestration from the podium, never permitting D'Amato to blow one sour note on his trusty kazoo."

Patterson took the loss hard. He withdrew to his home and shut all the blinds to keep the world out. For the first three weeks he left the house only twice, both times to check his punctured eardrum. Cus pleaded with Howard Cosell and Jackie Robinson to visit Floyd and try to cheer him up. Archie Moore sent him an upbeat letter telling him that he could regain his crown. He started to feel better but then he read a Jimmy Cannon column. "It should be clear to him now that [Patterson] isn't even a competent heavyweight but a toy man pretending to be a great champion. The first time he was hit by a right hand by a valid heavyweight he fell apart. It is too late for him to start all over again. The knowledge of his inadequacy had made a metropolitan hermit out of Patterson, who was a proud kid. The despair will do as much to him as Johansson's right hand the next time they fight. The longer they wait the more Patterson will be maimed," Cannon bellowed.

That sunk Floyd back into a depression. Now he might never go out again. Then his wife finally convinced him to go to a movie with her. Just when they got to the theater Floyd looked up at the marquee and saw that it said JOHANSSON–PATTERSON FIGHT FILMS. They rushed right home. It took a visit to a children's hospital where Floyd saw a young boy dying from leukemia to snap him out of his funk. "Who are you to feel sorry for yourself?" he thought. That day he called Cus and asked him to find him a training camp somewhere in the woods.

While Floyd was licking his wounds, Bill Rosensohn was planning how to take Cus down. He always had aspirations to become a major force in the boxing business and he was ready to stab Cus in the back to do so. In the months leading up to the fight, he had tried to form an alliance with the Zeckendorf family, rich developers in New York, and was ready to slash Fat Tony Salerno's and Charlie Black's participation in the profits in the process. Rosensohn had a five-year deal with the Zeckendorfs set to go, until they found out that Rosensohn wasn't going to participate in any of the ancillary revenue. Seeing their money going into a black hole, the savvy Zeckendorfs turned tail.

What happened next is pretty murky depending on who you believe gave the most truthful testimony before a Senate subcommittee looking into corruption in boxing a few years later. Rosensohn claimed that the day after Floyd lost his crown, a New York columnist named Joe Williams came to his office and told him that he was a good friend of Jim Norris's and that the Chicago tycoon wanted to meet him. They made an arrangement that if Rosensohn wasn't in his office Williams would leave a message for him in code stating that "the meeting with his son was on." Rosensohn didn't want anyone in his office to know he was meeting with Norris because he was paranoid that it might get back to Cus and Cus would pull the plug on the rematch.

Norris told a different story. He testified that Williams had called him to tell him that Bill Rosensohn wanted to meet with him. It probably doesn't matter who initiated the idea because both men had one common interest: screwing Cus. So on July 2, Rosensohn and Norris met at the home of Williams. According to Rosensohn, after a few minutes, Williams left the room and Norris "asked me if I would be interested in heading up a company which he was thinking of forming for the promotion of championship fights throughout the world." Norris said that he was merely interested in finding out what Rosensohn had in mind because he had an "in" with the new heavyweight champ. "I knew I had no chance of getting Patterson.

Now here is a new heavyweight champ. Possibly he would box for us once or something. Maybe he was not poisoned against me or my organization."

The rest of the meeting could not be recalled because of the vast amounts of alcohol both men consumed that night. The conversation "got somewhat incoherent," Rosensohn remembered, but they both agreed to discuss these ideas again.

The next day Rosensohn flew to L.A. for a vacation, excited that he was now in the orbit of a multimillionaire with common interests. While he was sitting by the pool in L.A., without a care in the world, Jackie Leonard was in the same city but in a different place. He had recovered from his beating but the Oakland promoter Don Chargin reportedly had been scared off and Jackie did not get the money he needed to keep his club afloat. Disgusted by the whole situation, Leonard quit boxing and got a job as a car salesman. We don't know whether he wound up selling cars for Don Nesseth.

While Rosensohn was in L.A., Truman Gibson, who was in town for an NBE fight, called him and they met and began to figure out the framework for a new worldwide boxing combine. Rosensohn was so jazzed that he came back to New York a week early so he could start making plans for the Patterson–Johansson rematch.

What Rosensohn didn't figure on was the extreme street savvy of Fat Tony Salerno and his attorney Vince Velella, who had fronted for Salerno during the promotion of the first Floyd–Ingo fight. The day after he got back from California, July 14, Bill got a telegram from Velella stating that Rosensohn was not to take any action on behalf of Rosensohn Enterprises, the corporation that was owned by Fat Tony, Charlie White, and Rosensohn—the corporation that held the rematch promotional rights.

Rosensohn told the Senate subcommittee that Salerno was upset that the fight lost money and there was no profit participation for him. Rosensohn blamed the losses on what he called "the D'Amato formula." "[D'Amato] had worked out a formula which meant that his fighter could make money and no promoter could, and this formula was to the effect that the promoter would keep 50 percent of the gate receipts, net. Paring up the other 50 percent would be turned over to the fighters, 30 percent to Patterson, 20 percent to Ingo."

What he left out was the part where Floyd and Irving Kahn split up all the ancillary rights.

Salerno and Velella were also upset about rumors that were coming out of California. Included in the telegram to Rosensohn was this sentence: "I am amazed at the lack of communications and advice from you particularly by published reports that you have granted an option for the next promotion to California interests." Rosensohn immediately called Velella and asked to speak to Tony. "I don't know any Tony," Velella said.

Rosensohn then called Gibson and told him that things were about to "explode." Gibson suggested that he should come to Chicago to meet with Norris. On July 20 they all met. When the issue of the telegram came up, Rosensohn said that Norris "indicated that he knew Salerno and that he could intercede." Norris was more interested in setting up the new company. Gibson proposed the idea that had been generated in California—a worldwide boxing combine that would include the three of them and Jack Solomons, the IBC-friendly leading boxing promoter in Europe, along with Ingo's adviser Edwin Ahlquist and Johansson himself. Rosensohn was ecstatic over Norris's proposal: $100,000 a year for five years, stock interest in the new company, a salary of $35,000 a year, and expenses that included a car and an apartment. The gambler had hit the jackpot instead of being in it! Now all that had to happen was for Johansson and Ahlquist to sign off on the deal and for Norris's lawyers to meet and try to figure out how to set up the company so it would not run counter to the antitrust decree against the IBC.

Rosensohn then got a little greedy. He figured that Rosensohn Enterprises, which was in the process of being taken over by Fat Tony and Vincent Velella, meant nothing to him anymore. So he offered to sell his one-third share in that company to Norris. Norris seemed excited and agreed to pay $25,000 for the stock.

The next day things started going south. Wirtz, the brains behind Norris, didn't like the idea of Jim "dignifying" Velella with his partnership. Now Rosensohn was pissed that Norris was reneging on the deal, so his lawyer suggested that Norris lend Bill the $25,000 with the stock being the sole security and when and if the stock was sold, Rosensohn would repay the cash to Norris and they would split any profits. Norris agreed to that.

What Rosensohn didn't know was that when Norris showed his lawyers the details of the new company, they thought "we were skirting dangerously close to maybe violating our decree," Norris would testify later. "And, naturally, when that came about, that certainly dampened any interest we had." Lying Jim is not being totally honest here, as we shall soon see.

Now Rosensohn made a very bad decision that pretty much sealed his fate as a boxing promoter. Back in New York, he got a phone call from a newspaperman who told him that Velella and Irving Kahn were in Sweden and they weren't saying nice things about him. He was skeptical, but then he got a call from a Swedish journalist who told him that Kahn said that he was "dishonest, incompetent," and the two of them were going to take over the promotion to protect Johansson.

Those were fighting words. So the next day, July 22, Rosensohn paid a secret visit to John Bonomi up in D.A. Hogan's office, where he blew the whistle on Fat Tony, Charlie Black, and Velella. The D.A.'s office was thrilled to hear all this and they immediately gave him police protection.

A week later, on July 31, Rosensohn Enterprises had a stockholders' meeting without Bill there. Irving Kahn, the owner of Tele-PrompTer and Rosensohn's old boss, was elected chairman of the board of directors. The prior contract that TelePrompTer had for the TV rights of the first Patterson–Johansson fight was renewed for the rematch. Somewhere Cus was smiling, especially when Rosensohn announced that he was quitting his own company and was willing to sell his one-third share to anyone, "even including the Madison Square Garden Corporation."

Despite Norris's asserting he lost interest in backing Rosensohn after the July 20 meeting, he and Gibson met with Rosensohn in Norris's apartment on August 3. Bill got his $25,000 loan and they decided that Gibson and Rosensohn would fly to Paris the next day to meet with Solomons and Ahlquist. Rosensohn neglected to mention that he had spilled the beans to the D.A. on July 22. When Norris was questioned about this meeting before the Senate subcommittee he had only a vague recollection of it. Senator Kefauver pressed Norris: "You had paid [Rosensohn's] expenses to go to Paris to talk about this international organization. Which must have been of importance to you?"

"Yes, sir. The heavyweight championship is very important," Norris responded.

It was a crazy scene in Paris the next day. Everyone checked into the same hotel and the wheeling and dealing began. First Rosensohn had to meet privately with Ahlquist and Ingo to explain why he had quit his own company. Then he, Gibson, Solomons, and Ahlquist met to discuss the new proposed company. Everyone seemed jazzed. Rosensohn was so pleased that he decided to go down to Cannes to gamble away some of that $25,000 Norris had loaned him.

The next day the announcement of D.A. Hogan's probe into the "promotional activities" behind the Patterson–Johansson fight made headlines. Hogan said that John Bonomi, his assistant D.A. who had collared Carbo, would be in charge of the investigation.

Sports Illustrated called Sweden to get a reaction from Ingo and his adviser. What they got was not music to the ears of Cus and Kahn and Velella. Johansson started griping about the Davidow situation again. "I tell you another thing. I will not fight again unless this Davidow thing is pushed aside finally. . . . I liked [D'Amato] and the way he talked the first few times we met. He say everything is for the boy. Everything is not for the boy. . . . [If] they think they can push me around, I warn them. . . . They cannot push Bill Rosensohn around any more, either. What he did before, I know it was because they pushed him. I want to give Floyd another chance and I want to fight him because it means a lot of money, but I don't fight for Kahn and D'Amato. They cannot make me."

Ahlquist said that he was happy that Hogan was going to

investigate the fight. "You know, I like D'Amato. I think he is being influenced by other people. I think it is that Schweig [D'Amato's lawyer]. . . . The first time that I met Schweig in his office, he boasted to me about how much money D'Amato owed him. . . . But I like [D'Amato] except the way he talks about the IBC. The first time I met him he took us to some hideaway in Long Island with dogs, and for six hours he told us about the IBC. . . . [Kahn and Velella] are greedy people. There is plenty of money for everybody but they're greedy."

Meanwhile, Rosensohn was putting his own spin on the story. He had invited *Sports Illustrated* writer Gil Rogin to talk to him in Sweden when he was there on July 24 and he promised to give him the exclusive behind-the-scenes story of the promotion of the fight. With Rogin ghostwriting it, Rosensohn fronted a long piece for the magazine where he said that Cus had cheated him out of the ancillary rights, that Cus had forced him to give Velella and Charlie Black one-third interest each in his company and Velella then ousted him from his own company, and that Irving Kahn and Velella had tried to sabotage him with Johansson but Ingo didn't go for it. What he didn't tell Rogin was that he had brought Fat Tony into the promotion because he had no money.

Sports Illustrated went for Rosensohn's account hook, line, and sinker. In an editorial accompanying the article, Martin Kane, one of Cus's few friends in the press corps, wrote, "If Floyd does not get his chance to regain the championship, it will be the fault of D'Amato's desire for power and his self-defeating urge to control every possible eventuality in a sport that, like all sports, lives by hazard or is not a sport at all."

Cus was furious with what he felt was a betrayal by his allies at *Sports Illustrated*. He confronted Rogin and told him, "I want to cut your legs off—below the knee." Cus stayed away from making public statements about the developments, but Velella was happy to talk to the press. When he was asked why Rosensohn quit his own company, Velella said, "He's a nice young boy trying to do a man's job. He quit because he can't take orders. He's made some wild statements that can't be documented and has spoken half-truths." When Rosensohn was asked by the press if he had been threatened he said that he "didn't know if any underworld boys are in the picture." Both Velella and Rosensohn denied Carbo had anything to do with the promotion. At last, they both said something that was true.

Hogan convened the same grand jury that had convicted Carbo and began hearing testimony from the principals in the case, including Velella and Charlie Black, whose lawyer said that he had no interest in Rosensohn Enterprises and that he "never was a front man for D'Amato."

Now the Cus combine counterattacked. Kahn talked to *The New York Times* and responded to Rosensohn's claim in his article that he was Rosensohn's nemesis. "This is the kind of nemesis I am. The guy came to me broke two and a half years ago. I took him in and made him vice president of the operation. I invested a quarter of a million dollars in equipment and I gave him a two-year contract . . . and a $15,000 loan he hasn't paid back yet. This was not TelePrompTer, this was me, his nemesis." Kahn also said he had total faith in Cus. "Cus supports an awful lot of boxers. He hasn't got a quarter and he owes I don't know how much, but it's in the middle to high five figures."

Hogan's probe and the huge publicity around it may have prodded New York State attorney general Louis Lefkowitz to open up his own investigation. His office issued a statement saying, "Preliminary discussions and inquiry indicate that the alleged tie-ins of the promoters of the fight with other individuals and firms concerned with broadcasting and the actual staging of championship fights may be in violation of the antitrust laws of this state."

It had come full circle. Now Cus was being investigated for the exact same violations that brought down Norris and his IBC.

The grand jury plowed on. They subpoenaed Frank Erickson, a bookie who ran a $10 million-a-year operation partnering with Frank Costello and Meyer Lansky. They also brought in Rosensohn's bookie Gilbert Beckley. After those sessions Hogan told the press, "We have not a scintilla of evidence that the fight was fixed or that any attempt was made to fix it." But he seemed troubled by the fact that Rosensohn met with Erickson twice before the fight and with Beckley too. "We believe the conversations at those meetings had to do with the promotional activity of Rosensohn and we think the discussions also concerned the arrangements for the fight, financial and otherwise."

On August 13, Cus spent a whole day up at D.A. Hogan's office and testified for half an hour before the grand jury. At the end of the day, Edwin Schweig, his lawyer, said Cus would have no comment. The same day Rosensohn, reached in Cannes while on his vacation, said he would rather not comment on Hogan's statement that he had met with "underworld characters" Erickson and Beckley. The next day, Hogan asked Rosensohn to cut his vacation short and come back for further questioning because new testimony had contradicted his earlier testimony.

The shine was beginning to come off the boy promoter. On August 17, the New York State Athletic Commission suspended the licenses of both Rosensohn and his company Rosensohn Enterprises. Martin Kane and *Sports Illustrated* began to hedge their bets on Rosensohn. "The disclosure that Rosensohn got financial backing from a mobster puts the novice promoter in a less pleasant light than has previously shone on him but it must be noted that he himself made the disclosure, thus opening the door for Hogan's clean-up drive." But more importantly Gibson sent Norris a telegram. "Rosensohn lost promoter's license today. Talked with Jack [Solomons]. Story has reached London. Eddie [Ahlquist] does not want Rosensohn in our meeting now set for Sunday per schedule. See you Saturday. Signed Truman." He also told Norris that Johansson and Ahlquist now wanted Rosensohn out but were open to talking about working with Norris!

The next week, Johansson delivered his "Hammer of Thor" to the chins of everyone involved in the fight. In an exclusive first-person article in *Life* titled "Ingemar Fingers the Mob," Johansson, who was pissed because his money had been frozen by the IBC's Machen suit, threatened to walk from the rematch and take his heavyweight crown with him.

"I can't fight Patterson and the fight mob too. Fighting the mob may take some time, but it comes first because I feel that I am being robbed. . . . The other day I got a cable from Floyd telling me to 'honor my obligation' over the return match. I like Floyd. He is a nice guy and he deserves a chance to try and regain his title. But Floyd's biggest trouble is Cus D'Amato, his manager. . . . Cus D'Amato is the Little Napoleon who runs Floyd Patterson and tries to run everything else. You know what happened to Napoleon. He was crazy for power and in the end he lost everything. In his way D'Amato tries just as hard. He tried to run me by insisting that one of his henchmen be my manager in America. Isn't that nice? Fortunately, the New York commission wouldn't stand for it. But D'Amato's attempt to manage me was only the beginning. Strange things began to happen as soon as I returned to Sweden after the fight. About the middle of July, I received a letter from my lawyer in New York saying he was having trouble getting information about money from radio, TV and movie rights. He had talked to Irving Kahn, the man who runs the TelePrompTer Company that bought those rights. When I read Kahn's name I recalled what I had heard in America: that D'Amato and Kahn were partners and because of this I probably would not receive as much money as I should."

Ingo wrote that his adviser Ahlquist got a call from Kahn, who said that Rosensohn had made mistakes and spent too much money and he shouldn't promote the next fight. Ahlquist said they wanted to stay with Rosensohn and give him a chance to make his money back. "He didn't lose a quarter," Kahn yelled. "Velella put up all the money." On July 20, Ingo and Ahlquist met Kahn and Velella in Sweden. Kahn did all the talking, for two hours. For the first time the Swedes learned that Rosensohn did not own Rosensohn Enterprises anymore. Two-thirds of Rosensohn Enterprises was owned by Velella, including Rosensohn's contract for the return fight. Rosensohn had been forced to sell out to Velella without telling the Swedes first. "We don't even have to discuss TV, radio, and movie rights," Velella told Eddie. Rosensohn had sold those rights away before the first fight. Of course, Kahn owned them. Then the Americans offered Eddie a job for their European promotions. "You cannot buy me," Eddie huffed.

The Swedes were also told that the second fight would be in Philly. Cus made that call. "I demand to be consulted about where I will fight," Ingo wrote. "Some of D'Amato's actions seem worse than those which he complained of in the IBC." Then Ingo researched and found out that Rosensohn could sell his share without consulting him. Who was responsible for this? "I think I know now. He is a man with bleak eyes, a cold smile and a big handshake. He is Edwin Schweig, Cus D'Amato's lawyer and the brain behind all the maneuvering. When Schweig was in [Sweden] last January before the first fight he told me, 'D'Amato is a neurotic. He has spent all his money fighting the IBC. He owes me $50,000.' At the time I thought 'Poor Napoleon.' Now it all began to fit." In August, Ingo got a statement from Schweig, the first accounting of ancillary rights. His share came to $1,050. Then he heard that if he didn't fight the rematch on September 22, Schweig, Kahn, and Velella would sue him for all the money he was supposed to have coming.

Now Rosensohn came to Sweden. He admitted he had made big mistakes but said he was forced into them. Ingo said he thought that Bill was lying but he still wanted to give him another chance. On August 6, Rosensohn met Ahlquist and Ingo in Paris. They were shocked to see that Rosensohn brought along the IBC's Truman Gibson. "We wanted nothing to do with the shady IBC," Johansson wrote. " 'I don't see how you could even think of talking to us,' I told Gibson, 'when you have a court case going against us—and you don't have to think of talking to us after it is over, either.'

"It was decided by all of us not to discuss the meeting. . . . Yet next day the newspapers had the story. Who am I to believe? Is Bill Rosensohn a chattering squaw? . . .

"Velella, Kahn, Schweig, and D'Amato—they make me want to be sick. But I am glad that someone will have the chance to stop them. . . . The crooks and the gangsters will have to go before I fight—no matter what kind of contract there is."

Johansson wrote that he would fight Floyd under three conditions: "1) I must have my money in a bank under my own name before I come to America to fight. 2) I must have a good explanation of who is promoting the next fight, who owns who, and who has lied to whom. Where does D'Amato come in and where does his backer Velella get his money? 'Don't worry about money,' Velella told my friend Eddie. 'There's no limit.' That is a funny statement and it should be cleared up. 3) I must wait until the investigations are over.

"I don't think I am asking too much after what the fight mob has done to me."

Now it looked like everyone was out—Cus, Velella, Rosensohn, Khan, Norris, and Gibson. But Cus came up with a brilliant Hail Mary of an idea. He knew that both Ingo and Ahlquist idolized Jack Dempsey. So in a few days it was announced that Dempsey had accepted a salaried position as promotional director and adviser to Rosensohn Enterprises. Dempsey was a man of undoubtable honesty. "I did not take the job until my legal advisers assured me that Vincent Velella and Irving Kahn were upright characters, men of integrity with whom I could be properly associated." LOL, as my daughter might text.

On August 20, Rosensohn met Norris in a hotel lobby in London. Norris basically gave him a cordial cold shoulder. He told the Senate subcommittee years later that he had soured on Rosensohn because he had "represented to us that he and Johansson and Ahlquist were very close and Ahlquist or Johansson would not make a move except if he OK'ed it." But Bonomi, Hogan's crack investigator who was on loan to the Senate subcommittee ascertained the real reason. He got Norris to admit that he blew off Rosensohn because Rosensohn's ties to Fat Tony had been revealed.

On August 23, Jack Dempsey, Vincent Velella, Irving Khan, and Cus's lawyer Schweig flew to London and then got seats on the same plane to Sweden that Ingo was on. Johansson had been in London meeting with Norris, Gibson, and Solomons. Dempsey told the press that he had no personal or financial agenda in the meetings. "My mission here is to clear up this mess and make the fight game an honest business." Vince Velella, Fat Tony Salerno's lawyer, stood there and smiled. And prepared to pay Dempsey $500 a week for his services.

On the same day, Rosensohn testified again before the New York grand jury. He met the press after his session and offered a mea culpa of sorts. "I knew there was something unsavory in the promotion but I never thought these things would be made public." He had seen the writing on the wall after he learned Dempsey was lobbying for Cus's guys, so he told the press that he had no intention of attempting to interfere with a rematch, because "I still hold a one-third interest in Rosensohn Enterprises."

Within days, Velella and his group had reached an agreement for the rematch with Ingo and Ahlquist. Velella would promote the fight. Davidow was out. Ingo was to get a full accounting. And Rosensohn could go back on vacation. "I know now that Bill Rosensohn was not the right man to arrange the bout," Ingo said diplomatically.

Back in New York it was finally revealed that the behind-the-scenes mobster involved in the promotion of the fight was Fat Tony Salerno. Rosensohn had finally come clean, at least a little. But despite all the testimony to the grand jury, the jurors came to the conclusion that no laws had been broken and refused to return any indictments. To save face, Hogan said that the info they had amassed from the witnesses pointed to two areas that the NYSAC might investigate further. "The first is the element of underworld participation in this promotion. The second is the curious role of D'Amato, who had such a powerful role as the man who controlled Patterson, the man who, through Davidow, attempted to control Johansson, and the man who, through Black, attempted to control the promotion itself."

Cus didn't know it at the time but that declaration from Hogan would come to haunt him for the rest of his life.

Of course the press had egg all over its face and had to find a way to spin their incompetence. The *Times'* Arthur Daley had been totally hoodwinked by the boy promoter, praising him lavishly as the next messiah of boxing, so he decided to go after his favorite punching bag, Cus. While he admitted that Rosensohn was "an ambitious young man who was in over his head" and grabbed for ready cash from Salerno, it was Cus who Daley savaged. "D'Amato, who had tilted at the windmill of Jim Norris' IBC and accused the IBC of being too close to Frankie Carbo, the undercover king of the ring, is now charged with having played footsie with Salerno, the mobster pal of such outstanding citizens as Trigger Mike Coppola, Joey Rao, Joe Adonis and the like." Daley quoted Hogan's call for a NYSAC investigation into Cus and then went into a self-righteous call to ban boxing. "Boxing is the slum area of sports. Maybe the time has come to destroy this slum. . . . The IBC at least ran things in a professional manner."

Over at *Sports Illustrated* they mocked Daley's purple prose and naive notion that Norris would ever have wanted to play saint and clean up boxing, noting that they were all over Norris's shit for years. But they, too, attacked Cus, saying he had a "curiously devious mind that claimed closer kinship to Napoleon and Machiavelli than to St. George. In the transition from outsider to man-in-the-saddle this potential St. George's attitude changed enough to give him a startlingly dragonlike appearance in subsequent dealings with a new promoter and a new potential champion." And they also went light on Rosensohn, cheering the "Ivy League enthusiasm" he brought to boxing. "But he lacked the experience, the acumen and, as it turned out, the basic courage to cope with the undercover crowd or to resist the blatant efforts of Cus D'Amato to keep himself on the gravy train regardless of who might unseat his champion."

The man who had revolutionized boxing by getting the most money for his fighters, who always put his fighters first, who supported scores of boxers, aspiring and retired, was now being portrayed as a schemer who was in the sport just for his own financial aggrandizement. Whoa.

Everybody jumped on the bandwagon. Governor Pat Brown of California said he would recommend abolishing boxing unless there were some national laws implemented. Senator Kefauver, who had hearings on boxing the year before, was poised to investigate boxing again. Jimmy Cannon, the dean of boxing writers, wrote, "Boxing is the garbage dump of sports." Even Truman Gibson got into the act.

While announcing that the NBE was forming a partnership with Jack Solomons, he declared that he and Norris would campaign for federal control over boxing.

On September 15, Rosensohn testified before the NYSAC, in their probe that they called the "Inquiry into Alleged Irregularities in the Conduct of the Promotion of the Patterson–Johansson World's HW Championship Contest." He continued to assert that Cus had forced him to make Charlie Black a partner in the promotion and that Cus had forced him to forgo his ancillary rights. The commissioners also suspended Cus's license because he had not answered a subpoena to testify and instead took a boat to Puerto Rico, where José Torres was scheduled to fight. In fact, Cus had not answered subpoenas from the D.A., the attorney general, and the NYSAC, all on the advice of his lawyer Julius November.

The next day Velella appeared and he denied that he was a front for Salerno, claiming that all the money invested in the fight was his own and that he was worth $250,000. Two days later Charlie Black testified. The commissioners tried to tie Cus into the promotion and Black claimed that Cus had no knowledge of Fat Tony's involvement. At times the proceedings were like something out of a Marx Brothers movie. Black's testimony began when his lawyer told the commission that Charlie suffered from "cardiac disturbance" and "Berger's disease," so he might get fatigued and need to relax. He told the group that he had been convicted of bookmaking in 1942 and again in 1943. He was a fight manager until 1958. When asked his present occupation he said, "Nothing." The talk turned to the subject of this investigation. When asked about meetings in 1958, Black said he didn't remember any meetings because "that's too far back. I can't say yes and I can't say no about meetings."

They asked Black about a late December meeting with him and Salerno and Rosensohn.

Q: Did you meet with Salerno late in December? A: I might have. Q: Did you talk about Rosensohn at that time? A: To Salerno? Q: Yes. A: Well, he knows Rosensohn. We might have spoken about him. Q: I am asking you if you talked to him. A: We might have. I don't know what we spoke about. Q: Did you talk to him in connection with the Patterson–Johansson fight? A: I don't remember what he talked about. Q: Did you talk about Velella at that time? A: We might have. He is Velella's friend too. Q: I know he is Velella's friend.

Black was driving the commission's attorney crazy with his vague answers.

Q: Did you advise D'Amato about the Patterson–Johansson fight? A: What do you mean advise? Q: Well, did you discuss it? A: He may say things to me about it. If I thought it was all right, I would answer. You can't tell Cus too much, you know. He is smarter than I am. Q: I'm not so sure about that. A: Well, I think so. Q: It is a known fact, is it not, Mr. Black, that you are a very close confidant of Cus D'Amato's? A: I am a good friend of Cus D'Amato, if that's what you call it. Otherwise, he wouldn't be giving me that little money that he gives me. ATLAS [BLACK'S ATTORNEY]: Don't volunteer Mr. Black. Just answer the questions. A: I am getting nervous.

Then Black denied that he ever held any share in either of the corporations, but it was established that Charlie had been put on the payroll by Rosensohn and been paid $150 a week.

Q: What did you do for $150 a week? A: I went down to Bill's office. I went up to Velella's office. Besides that, I have been up to the camp. Q: Were you running errands for D'Amato or Rosensohn? A: For Rosensohn. Q: Not for D'Amato? A: And Velella. Q: And not for D'Amato? A: Naturally, D'Amato too. I am his friend, ain't I? Q: Did he ask you for all these errands that you were running, who was paying you? A: I told him Rosensohn paid me. He said, "That's nice."

The questioning turned to a May 15 meeting between Beckley, Salerno, Velella, Rosensohn, Brocksie, and Black. Beckley and Brocksie were bookies. Charlie said the conversation was about everything, including horses. He also said that their main interest was in finding out how good Patterson looked. He was asked if he told Cus about the meeting.

A: I couldn't dare tell D'Amato anything that I knew these people. Q: You didn't? A: No sir. I wouldn't want him to know that I knew these people. He would have nothing to do with me. Q: Well, he knew you knew Beckley, didn't he? A: No, he didn't know no one, I wouldn't tell D'Amato, no matter what the circumstances were.

He was asked about a meeting with Cus, Rosensohn, and Velella at Velella's club in East Harlem. Black maintained that he heard very little of the meeting.

Q: That was another instance when you were out of earshot at these meetings? A: When they talk business, it wasn't my business to listen. Q: But you happened to be at all those meetings. A: That's right. Q: Did you go along for color or just to be around? A: To be Charlie, that's all.

James Fusscas, the committee lawyer, was about to tear his hair out. After getting nothing from Black about an important meeting at McCarthy's Steak House where Rosensohn had to sign a waiver, Black kept testifying that Fat Tony never said anything in these meetings. He'd just sit there and smoke a cigar.

HELFAND: At any of these meetings, [Salerno] never talked? A: He don't talk much. CHAIR: Did you hear him say anything at these meetings? A: He might say to me, "How are you, kid? How's everything?" He ain't got no business to talk to me about. He has his own business. Q: Is that how he referred to you, "How are you, kid?" A: Yes, or "How are you, pop?" More likely it was "pop."

When Black was asked about a meeting after the fight, Black interrupted.

A: I think it was before the fight. After the fight, I was too sick to go anywhere. Q: You mean you were sick because Patterson lost? A: In one way, yes.

The last line of questioning revolved around the last time Black had seen Cus.

Q: Tell me, have you spent much time at D'Amato's country place? A: I don't even know where it is. I never was in it. I don't know what kind of a place. He said a log cabin to me. I never seen it and never have been there. I think that's where he hides himself. Q: Well, I have been trying to get him and so have the state troopers been trying to get him. He has done well hiding. A: I never been there. Q: Has he called you from Puerto Rico? A: No sir. Q: And what happened to

Mr. Salerno? Have you seen him lately? A: No. Q: When did you last talk to Salerno? A: Before this trouble happened. Q: Did he tell you he was going to take a powder? A: No sir. Q: He never said a word to you? A: He never spoke to me. Q: Do you know where he is now? A: No sir. Q: Mr. Black, I am sorry I had to ask you these questions. I hope it hasn't affected your health? A: Well, I am pretty sick, sicker than you people think. ATLAS: I thank you, Mr. Chairman, for the courteous treatment of me and my client.

ON SEPTEMBER 22, 1959, police in four different cities made coordinated sweeps and arrested five men. In Chicago, Truman Gibson was at a friend's house watching his beloved Chicago White Sox on their way to winning the American League pennant, when they saw flashing lights outside. The FBI barged in the house, cuffed the lawyer, and brought him to jail, allowing a line of photographers to catch him in a perp walk. "It was as though Dillinger were reincarnated," he said. Carbo had finally been released on $100,000 bail from his New York arrest, but his chronic kidney disease had sent him to Johns Hopkins in Baltimore, which was where he was arrested again. Palermo was arrested in Philadelphia, and Joe Sica and Louie Dragna were nabbed in L.A.

The police were sent out after the L.A. federal grand jury had returned a ten-count indictment charging the five with crimes ranging from violating the federal antiracketeering act to extortion. Gibson got off the lightest, as he faced only a conspiracy rap. Bill Daly was named as an unindicted coconspirator. The indictment said that Nesseth and Leonard had been "subject to mental torment and abuse resulting from repeated economic and physical threats" from October 23, 1958, through September 22, 1959.

Carbo was immediately held on $100,000 bail, while Blinky pulled down bail of only $25,000. Gibson was a whole different story. Some calls were made and his friend Michael Igoe, who was a judge in the U.S. District Court for the Northern District of Illinois, ordered the FBI to deliver Gibson to Igoe's own house. The cuffs were taken off, and the two of them watched the remainder of the ball game waiting for a bail bondsman. Gibson's pal had ordered him freed on $5,000 bail.

Blinky had tried to avert the indictments and arrests back in August. He had called Leonard one night and wanted to know if Leonard "still felt the same." Leonard said that he did. "Well, if you should change your mind, you can get all the money you want, if you just act right and be right with the right people." Leonard told Blinky that it was too late, he had already given his testimony.

ON THE SAME DAY, Cus was threatened with losing his license unless he testified two days later. Schweig made a plea for a delay, since Cus was still in Puerto Rico, but the commission was adamant. Cus never made that Thursday's hearing and the commission ended its inquiry. On October 13, the NYSAC called a press conference and gave out a two-page summary of their investigation. They directed their counsel to prepare charges against Rosensohn, his company, and Cus and to revoke their licenses. Cus was cited for the monopolistic practice of foisting a manager on opponents. Rosensohn was criticized for not informing the commission of Velella's role in the promotion as well as for dealing with a "shady character" like Salerno. Velella was judged to be less than candid when he claimed that Salerno was just an "innocent bystander" when he attended meetings in Velella's office. Finally, they banned Charlie Black for life as a licensee of the commission and as a participant or spectator, whether paid or otherwise, in any sporting event over which the commission had jurisdiction.

The reactions to the hearings were swift. Rosensohn immediately asked for another. "I'll fight the action. I want to keep my license and remain in the boxing business." Velella changed the name of Rosensohn Enterprises to Feature Sports Inc. "I think the commission is trying to kill boxing in New York. Also I think the report is a left-handed whitewash of Rosensohn." In Sweden, Ahlquist made his most vicious attack yet on Cus. "It's time for Floyd Patterson to start thinking now. It is possible we will choose a new contender for Ingemar if Floyd refuses to get rid of his underworld controllers. I think Cus D'Amato is the greatest gangster of them all. He is a coward who refuses to show up before the commission. I hope he will get a permanent suspension. But that will probably not change things. He will keep control over Patterson through another Davidow." Julius November, Cus's lawyer, was the most restrained. "We'll wait until we see the charges before we ask for a hearing." When asked if he knew where his client was, he answered, "No, I don't know where D'Amato is right now."

Well, Cus wasn't that hard to track down. Gay Talese, the *New York Times* sportswriter, found him at La Ronda in Newton, Connecticut, an abandoned restaurant that had once belonged to Enric Madriguera, a bandleader. Cus had found Floyd a place near Westport, but when Fat Tony's name surfaced in the papers Floyd was horrified. One day he went to the gym and saw the headline on a local newspaper: "Boxing Gangsters Invade Westport." That same day Floyd had Cus find a new, more remote location. Talese discovered Cus in a contemplative mood. He asked him if he was after money. "No." "Power?" "Not even that. I've only had one ambition. I wanted to have three champions simultaneously, all of whom I started myself. I thought Patterson would keep the title long enough for me to develop José Torres as a middleweight and Joey Shaw as the welterweight." "Do you think you'll lose your license?" "I don't know." "What does the NYSAC have against you?" "They say I deliberately stayed away from their hearings. I didn't. I was in Puerto Rico for the Torres fight, and was trying to get a place for Patterson to train too." "If you lose your NY license will there be no fight in NY against Johansson?" "I don't want to get into that. They are trying to get me into a mess before the next fight." " 'They'?" "Yeah, the IBC." "What are they doing?" "They are trying to destroy me." "Why you?" "Because I exposed their monopoly." "Why do you say that?" "They have a monopoly on the Wednesday-night TV fights. Anybody that controls that TV fight controls boxing." "If you had your way what would you do?" "I'd put another TV boxing show on and give the IBC show some competition."

"Are you worried about Patterson losing again?" "No, my mind doesn't think that way." "Without Patterson what would you be?" "I'd still be what I am—a fight manager who thinks of his fighters first." "Do you think getting rid of Carbo will end the mess in boxing?" "No. Getting rid of Carbo and people like him won't solve the problem. We have to get rid of the monopoly." "What about Charlie Black?" "Charlie Black is an old friend whom I can trust. The trouble I have had these last few years have been with a new type of person, the Ivy League boys. Guys like Rosensohn and Cecil Rhodes. They're a Williams boy and a Harvard boy. Clean-cut, well-dressed guys. They are the guys I look out for. The boxing people speak a language I can understand." "You seem harassed, Cus. Why didn't you get married so you'd have somebody to tell your problems to?" "I was always running. My life was always with fighters. And then one day before I realized it, I was 51."

Robert Boyle, a top writer at *Sports Illustrated*, spent time with Cus in upstate New York during this period. Julius November had told Cus, "Go up to the Catskills, Cus, it's no problem. I'll handle these subpoenas." Well, he didn't, and the storyline of Cus on the run from the authorities, whereabouts unknown, or on a boat to Puerto Rico, was devastating to Cus's image. All Cus did when he was holed up in his log cabin upstate was to go fishing. Boyle told us it was like going fishing with Mr. Magoo, Cus was so blind. One time they were on a lake in the Catskills. Cus got all excited. "I got one," he yelled. What he had done was when he cast back he hooked the back of Boyle's jacket. "Ooh, ooh," Cus yelped. "Quiet," Boyle said. "You got one too?" Cus asked. "No, you got me," Boyle said. Cus looked confused. "Look, your hook is in the back of my jacket."

ON OCTOBER 27, John Bonomi's big fish finally went to trial in New York. Assistant D.A. Alfred Scotti told Judge Mullen that he would prove with "devastating clarity" that Carbo was "the underworld commissioner of boxing." The prosecution put on its case, which included wiretapped conversations and the reports of undercover detectives who had infiltrated some of Carbo's men. It also included a shocking account of a meeting between Carbo and Jim Norris just eight days after Carbo had been arrested on the federal extortion charges in the Leonard case. Scotti described the meeting. "On October 1, 1959, Carbo was observed riding in a white Cadillac, bearing Florida license plates, in front of the air terminal in Newark. Also seen was James D. Norris riding in a blue Cadillac, bearing Illinois license plates. Carbo was seen leaving the white car and entering the blue Cadillac with Norris in it. This took place at about 1PM. Carbo left the blue car at about 4:25 PM. While we do not know what these two discussed, this lengthy meeting certainly removes any doubt, if there should be any, as to the extent of Carbo's influence among those connected with the professional sport of boxing, including, particularly, James D. Norris."

After three days of damaging testimony, Carbo changed his plea to guilty on three of the counts. On November 30 he stood in front of Judge Mullen for sentencing. His hair was white by now but he was still dapper in his dark suit and black elevator shoes. Judge Mullen accepted the guilty plea and then addressed Carbo. "You had a long and merry dance in pursuit of power in the boxing game but the time has now come when the piper must be paid. You began at the age of eleven to throw your weight around in an improper fashion in school and in your neighborhood. You continued this way in the greater part of your early life till you developed a reputation that caused people to have a concern for not doing what you suggested. In boxing your wish was tantamount to a command performance. You had terrific, improper, and illegal influence in the fight game. You enriched yourself to a degree I can't contemplate." Mullen could have sentenced Carbo to three years but he took his health into consideration and handed down a two-year term in Rikers. Carbo thanked the judge.

ON NOVEMBER 5, the NYSAC scheduled a hearing where Rosensohn and Cus were asked to show cause why their licenses should not be revoked. The commission had revoked Cus's licenses because he had failed to respond to a letter mailed to him on September 2. He was due to appear while he was in Puerto Rico for the Torres fight. His lawyer Julius November then asked for an adjournment and promised that Cus would appear in October but his request was denied and the commission issued its final report, charging Cus in absentia and revoking his license. Now Cus would finally get a chance to tell his side of the story.

He was charged with five offenses: refusing to attend a hearing on September 14 dealing with irregularities of the Floyd–Ingo fight; associating with Charlie Black, "a convicted gambler"; acting as a matchmaker and promoter for the Johansson fight; "foisting" Davidow on Ingo as his manager; and failing to file his manager's report within five days after the fight.

The commission argued that "it appears that the petitioner, like the IBC, engaged substantially in a course of conduct condemned and enjoined by the U.S. Supreme Court as a violation of the Sherman Act."

There was so much legal back-and-forth the first day that Cus didn't get a chance to testify. Schweig, one of Cus's lawyers, asked Commissioner Helfand to recuse himself because of his "intemperate" comment at the earlier hearing where he said that the naming of Davidow as Ingo's manager "stunk to high heaven." Helfand refused.

Rosensohn testified first and he finally came clean about his relationship with Fat Tony Salerno. He admitted that Salerno was instrumental in creating All-Star Sports (the successor to Rosensohn Enterprises) and that he introduced Rosensohn to Velella, who "formed the company." He also admitted that Salerno's name was never mentioned in Cus's presence, saying, "Many times the conversation was in hieroglyphics."

After questioning Rosensohn about many meetings where Cus was not even involved, Schweig had enough.

CHAIR: Is it an objection? SCHWEIG: It is in the form of a plea. You people sit here as the party complainant. You originate the complaint. You sit as a judge. You sit as a prosecutor and what's more, you make the rules, so you sit as a legislature here. You don't give us a bill of particulars. What are we supposed to do?

Finally, after almost two hours of testimony, Cus's lawyer November got a chance to cross-examine Rosensohn. And he caught him out many times. He got Rosensohn to admit that he had introduced Velella to Cus as his lawyer. "But not in fact," Rosensohn said. "I had to introduce him as something." In discussing how Rosensohn obtained his promoter's license from the California commission for the Harris fight, November caught him in two lies. He lied when he stated that he was the only one who had an interest in the promotion, neglecting to mention the Hollywood Legion Stadium's interest. Then November pressed Rosensohn about Black's 50 percent participation. Rosensohn claimed these were errors of omission.

"I didn't lie. I didn't tell them."

November exposed how Rosensohn had hidden his relationship with Fat Tony.

Q: Then, by the same token, when Rosensohn Enterprises applied for a license before this very body, putting it your way, you forgot to tell them that you had sought out Salerno, is that right? A: I didn't forget to tell them. Q: Did you tell them? A: No. Q: Did you tell them that Salerno was going to lend you a sum of money? A: No, I did not. Q: Did you tell them that Salerno had loaned you a sum of money? A: I did not. Q: Did you tell them that, in your opinion, the man that you introduced as your attorney, Mr. Velella, was in fact, in your opinion, the nominee for Salerno? Did you tell them that? A: I did not. Q: When the stock interest changed in All Star Sports and Rosensohn Enterprises, or in both of them, did you tell the Commission of that?

Rosensohn balked at answering.

CHAIR: That is an easy question to answer. A: The answer is no.

But the most convincing testimony was to come. Now Schweig took over the cross-examination and he discussed the topic of the ancillary rights participation. Cus had always maintained Rosensohn's deal was that he had no interest in the ancillary rights and he was given 50 percent of the live gate, the same arrangement as in the Harris fight. He claimed that he had signed a waiver to that effect under duress. But Schweig found a TV interview where Rosensohn said that he brought in Fat Tony in an attempt to help him with persuading Cus to give him the ancillary rights, just as Fat Tony had assisted Rosensohn in getting Hurley to agree to cut his fee for the Harris fight.

Cus finally got his chance to face the commission the next day. He seemed nervous on the stand. The commissioners began by asking Cus about his background and if he had ever been convicted of any crimes. "Just traffic violations," he said.

q: I'm talking about misdemeanors or felonies. a: I don't know the distinction.

Then November asked Cus about his leaving for Puerto Rico on September 11. The commission seemed to suggest that Cus was fleeing his subpoena. But Cus explained his actions:

a: During that period, as everybody knows, my fighter had lost the championship. I had returned from the DA's office. The following day I was banged very badly in the press. I was very disgusted and very much upset. I wanted to get away from everything and everybody. During this period, I had neglected all my other fighters. The most important one was José Torres. In Torres' case, there was a great deal of difference of opinion as to his abilities and who he should be fighting. Since the responsibility lay with me, I felt it was not my job to take any match where I might be overmatching him, considering the limited experience and the number of limited rounds that he fought. He couldn't get fights over here or in this general area, opponents that I felt were proper. He, through his father, arranged for a fight in Puerto Rico, scheduled for the 19th I think. Arrangements were made which were not in the best interests of my fighter. I had planned to go to Puerto Rico. I never flew. Everybody in boxing knows that I never flew. The only way I could get there is by boat. q: After you were in Puerto Rico, did you read in the newspapers concerning your non-appearance. a: I did. q: Did you then contact our office? a: Yes, I did.

Then Cus was grilled by Fusscas about a possible relationship with Fat Tony: Black testified that he knew Salerno and Trigger Mike from growing up in East Harlem.

Q: Did you know these gentlemen? A: No sir. Q: Did he ever tell you he was acquainted with them or other notorious hoodlums? A: No sir.

Cus then started into another description of Charlie Black's help in fighting the IBC and the chair cut him off. That set Cus off.

A: I asked you, when I came here, if I would be permitted to say my piece, to tell everything about my actions, my motivation and the reasons. Otherwise, I said I wouldn't care to testify voluntarily. I came here in order to clear myself. The only way I can do that is by telling everybody why I did or did not do certain things. That is the only way I can do it.

Cus seemed to be losing it. Schweig took the mike.

SCHWEIG: This man is a witness. He is not experienced. He is under terrific tension. He has his own way of expressing himself. If he is going to be stymied, he is going to lose his train of thought. He will not only be a bad witness for himself, but he is going to make a bad record for the Commission. I suggest to you that you let him talk as he wants to talk.

They gave in.

CHAIR: Ask a question. NOVEMBER: Did you become more friendly with Charles Black as a result of any incident relating to the IBC? A: Yes. During my fight, very few people had the nerve to oppose the IBC and support me morally. He was the only one who stood up and remained in complete public support of my position in opposition to the IBC. I felt that this was a man who had integrity. That is why I continued the friendship. That is why the IBC disliked him too. Q: What happened to Mr. Black as a result of his friendship with you in connection with this incident? A: He couldn't get any more fights.

Now November asked how Rosensohn came to be the promoter of the Harris fight but Cus used his answer to explain why he was always concerned with keeping ancillary rights out of the hands of the promoter so that the fighters would get more than just a share of 25 percent of the gross.

A: I thought this was unfair because the fighter was entitled to the full percentage of every dollar which came in as a result of his performance in the ring. I felt that I as a manager to carry out my obligation to my fighter and in the process of doing the right thing for all the fighters, once it was established, had a right to negotiate for my fighter with the closed circuit people because I felt that these people were not promoters, they were agents. I made an approach as to close circuit, with the intention of getting a just and fair sum of money for my fighter, which was my obligation as a manager. As a result of this, I came in to contact with TelePrompTer Corporation. I spent about five or six hours the first day I arrived there. I went through the whole boxing picture and they in turn said they were perfectly willing to do business and give the fighters a larger percentage of the money. I wanted to establish, as a matter of principle, that this was going to be the future operation as far as the fighters in the heavyweight division were concerned. As a result of this, TelePrompTer agreed for the first time, at least to my knowledge, to put up a guarantee for the fighters.

Cus then described how he met Rosensohn and detailed examples of Rosensohn's attempts to change the terms of the promotion to give himself a piece of the ancillary rights. Then November addressed the charge that Cus was an unlicensed promoter of the fight.

Q: You are charged with being an unlicensed promoter. I would like to put the following questions to you: Did you arrange for the Yankee Stadium to be the site of the fight? A: Of course not. Q: Did you arrange for the printing of the tickets? A: No sir. Q: Did you arrange for the locations? A: No sir. Q: Did you arrange for the working press? A: No sir. Q: Did you arrange for who would be admitted gratuitously, who wouldn't pay. Did you arrange anything like that? A: No. Q: Did you arrange publicity? A: No sir. Q: You had nothing to do with any of these things? A: No sir.

Now the charge of Cus having foisted Davidow as Ingo's American manager was addressed by November. Cus basically repeated his contention that since Johansson had no manager, it was important that a manager be brought in "who would not be bought or bribed or in any way affected by anything the IBC may do."

Q: And you deemed Davidow an honest man? A: Definitely.

At this point that day's hearing adjourned.

The next day Cus took a shellacking. The *New York Times* account of his testimony was dripping with sarcasm. "D'Amato's testimony was a long rehash of his feud with the IBC, a newsworthy subject to few in the room." What was worse, that week's *Newsweek* ran an article about Carbo's guilty plea, and directly underneath, the magazine interviewed Patterson to see if he still supported his "manipulating manager." The magazine asked: "Why does Patterson, a clean-cut and seemingly sincere man of 24, still work with so questionable a character?" A young reporter named Dick Schaap was sent to Floyd's training camp in the abandoned restaurant. " 'A rift with Cus?' Patterson said, sitting up in his chair. 'There's no rift. The other day some of [Sugar Ray] Robinson's men went looking for me. They want me to leave Cus and go with them.' Patterson shook his head. 'I'll stick with Cus,' he said. Why? 'Cus did a lot for me,' Patterson said. 'He taught me how to fight when I was 15. He taught me how to speak right, how to dress. He was honest with me. He gave me a square count on my money when I wouldn't have known if he hadn't.' Patterson paused, and then he said, 'Cus got me the title.' " Schaap then repeated the litany of charges against Cus. He had helped himself as much as he had helped Patterson, used him as a pawn in his fight with the IBC, deteriorating his skills in the process. He mentioned that he foisted Davidow on Ingo and forced Rosensohn to turn over two-thirds of his company to Velella, who "allegedly" was a front for Fat Tony. "Finally, when the NYSAC first asked him to testify, D'Amato caught a slow boat to Puerto Rico."

"I know it all sounds funny," Patterson said, "and there are some things I still don't understand. But I got to trust Cus. He told me he didn't know Velella had friends like Salerno. I believe him. I don't blame other people for being suspicious. I can't figure the whole thing out myself. But I still trust Cus." Schaap wrote that Floyd went to the window and watched the torrid rain that was preventing him from running. Then the tension seemed to drain out of him and he changed from being intense and earnest to becoming "arch and droll." Floyd's

sparring mate asked him, "Why didn't Cus hang around today?"
"Maybe he had to meet Salerno," Patterson deadpanned.

It was no laughing matter two weeks later when Cus was brought
before the NYSAC again to finish testifying. This time he was inter-
rogated by James Fusscas, the commission's lawyer. He began by
probing into Cus's secret upstate hideaway. It must have killed Cus to
talk about it.

Q: Do you have a home in Beacon, New York? A: No place there.
Q: Where do you have it? A: A place in Fishkill. It is a summer place. I
bought this place for the purpose of sending some of the boys in my
gymnasium who can't afford to go away in the summertime, to spend a
week or more there until I learned that in the papers they give you
there was a clause prohibiting other than Caucasian people to be there.

Cus said he had a phone there but he didn't remember the number. He had three phones in his New York apartment. "All of them are
unlisted but everybody knows the number." He told them that he had
been suspended by the NYSAC two times in the early 1950s, having
to do with Managers' Guild business. He rehashed his long history
with Charlie Black, then Fusscas asked him about his relationship
with Emil Lence. And Cus began to get agitated.

Q: Before the fight was signed up, did you discuss this fight with
Emil Lence? A: I discussed this fight with everybody. Q: I am asking
you about Emil Lence, not everybody. NOVEMBER: Don't get so excited
please. Don't browbeat the witness. Q: In signing that contract, did
Lence agree to cut you in on the profits of that fight? A: Of course
not. Q: At the time when you were discussing the promotion of that
fight, did you tell Lence that he was to cut in Black as a partner.
A: Absolutely not. Q: Did you have any conversation with Lence with
reference to taking Black in on the promotion? A: No sir. Q: Black testified here that he received $3200 from Lence. Did Black tell you about
that? A: No sir. Q: You know nothing about it? A: No sir. I don't discuss
his affairs with Black. Q: He never discussed the fact that he had gotten $3200 from him? A: Not that I recall. I don't recall any such thing.
Q: Did he tell you that he borrowed $3200 from him? A: I don't even
recall that.

Cus kept repeating that he had no recollections of any such conversations. November objected. Fusscas argued that when Cus said "recollection," it left the door open that it might have been discussed.

A: You are asking me questions about things that happened years ago. I have been through all kinds of hell and you are asking me questions about this. I have no recollection. Q: Mr. D'Amato, you have a pretty keen recollection from the testimony that you have given here about the IBC. That goes back a few years. NOVEMBER: I object to that. A: This has been consistent and I lived with it up to the present day.

November then told Cus to "sit back and take it easy." Fusscas then asked what Black's job would have been if he did work in Patterson's camp.

A: He worked in the camp to see if anything went wrong that I should know about. This is a very responsible thing. In a training camp, especially when you are surrounded by enemies, you have to watch every possible thing that could happen that may be detrimental to your fighter. The person who does the watching must be a person of integrity, a man that you can trust, that they can't buy. This is what I wanted. I wanted a man who would observe anything that looked a little funny or queer or might give the impression that anything except the best interests of my fighter is going on, water, food, anything. Just a man who would be looking out for my interests in case anything went wrong. That's the only reason I had him there.

The questioning turned to the Harris fight. Cus went into a long explanation of how a guarantee was necessary to ensure that Harris would not pull out of the fight due to pressures from the IBC. When the original promoter Weill refused to guarantee the money, Cus came up with the novel idea that he would take the responsibility of guaranteeing Harris "who was close to the IBC and advised by a man who was close to the IBC. I felt that a guarantee of such a size, which would be far greater than anything he could earn with the IBC in more than four years, would insure his presence in that ring."

Fusscas then asked Cus about Charlie Black being named Harris's manager of a rematch in case Patterson lost.

Q: Who suggested Black? **A:** I don't remember now. It might have been them. **Q:** Did they suggest Black at your recommendation? **A:** No sir. **Q:** You didn't recommend Black for that? **A:** I don't think I did, but I wouldn't have hesitated to do so. **Q:** Well did you? **A:** I don't recall that I did. **Q:** Harris just named Black as the man? **A:** Not Harris. There were a group of people. Viscusi was there. He had his father there. **Q:** And you say under oath that you did not suggest Black? **A:** That is not my recollection. **Q:** Did you tell Harris that unless he took Black, he couldn't have the fight? **A:** I did not tell him that. **Q:** Did you tell that to Viscusi? **A:** I didn't tell Viscusi that. **Q:** Did you tell Rosensohn that? **A:** I didn't tell Rosensohn that. All I said to Harris and the group that was there was that in case anything happened, because I was always thinking in terms of somebody stealing a decision or a referee would stop the fight with a phony cut or something like that— **Q:** Mr. D'Amato, I asked you a question. I don't want you to wander all over the lot. **A:** I want the people to know why I said these things.

They moved on to the London fight, which was not Cus's finest moment. Fusscas asked Cus who London's manager was.

A: Nick Baffi. **Q:** Did you suggest Baffi to London? **A:** I believe I recommended him. **Q:** Did you ask Mr. Schweig to meet London at the airport? **A:** I did. I was afraid they were going to snatch the fighter. I have to tell you the reason why I sent him there and that's the truth so help me God. **NOVEMBER:** You have answered the question. Please don't make a speech.

At last the talk turned to the fight under investigation. Cus reiterated that the terms should be the same as for the Harris fight, that the promoter would get 50 percent of the gate and no participation in the ancillary rights. He denied that he told Rosensohn to give Johansson 20 percent of everything; he was under the impression that Johansson would be given a guarantee. Then Fusscas asked if Cus called his Swedish newspaperman friend Einer Thulin and had him sit in on any conversations between Rosensohn and Johansson.

A: I told him to look over the situation regarding Johansson and any attempt on the part of Johansson to negotiate because I trusted Mr. Thulin implicitly and I felt that any information I would get from him would give me an idea of what was going on. I told him that in view of the entirely intimate relationship between Mr. Ahlquist and Mr. Jack Solomons, an associate of Mr. Norris in the IBC, I want him to pay close attention and observe everything in regard to anything that was said there because I wanted to be sure that nobody would get a sore back a week before any promotion, if one were to take place.

Cus testified that he was "very anxious" when he met Rosensohn at the airport when he returned from Sweden. And when he saw that Rosensohn had a document that gave Johansson 20 percent across the board, he "didn't want to know anything about this document anymore."

Fusscas then questioned Cus about his meeting in Long Island with Johansson and Ahlquist. Cus then denied telling Ahlquist or Rosensohn that he wouldn't sign Ingo to a fight unless he took an American manager.

A: Must I answer this? Q: I just want you to limit yourself. I don't want to listen to that IBC thing. A: I'm sorry if you don't want to listen to it. All my actions, all my activities are motivated by this very thing. I would have money today if it weren't for this. . . . I gave them the picture. Then I said, "Gentlemen, this is the way I feel. I want fellows who are not connected with the IBC to be in a position to negotiate with an independent promoter." Somewhere along the line, I mentioned Davidow's name. He is an experienced manager. There aren't many better managers than Harry Davidow in the boxing business. Q: That is your opinion. A: That is my opinion. I qualify to a greater extent, perhaps a little better than some of the people here. Q: Why did you pick Davidow? A: Because he is an honest man, a man who I thought was capable. He was a man that the IBC couldn't bribe or anything else to do the wrong thing. Q: It wasn't because you could control him? A: Never. Anybody who knows Harry Davidow knows that nobody controls him. He is a thoroughly honest man.

The commission called a recess and after lunch, they started the afternoon session. Fat Tony was the topic of inquiry now. Cus denied ever meeting or even discussing Salerno with Charlie Black. He said he was not aware that Black had met with the gangster and that he didn't know that Salerno had a one-third interest in the fight.

Fusscas wasn't getting anywhere with his questioning so he decided to press Cus on why he had ignored their subpoena.

Q: A week after the fight, were you in New York? A: I think I was. I no doubt was in New York. I was a very disturbed man during that time.

Cus then said he was in and out of New York in July and August looking for a training camp for Floyd. He was in Connecticut in the early part of September.

Q: How long does it take to drive from New York to Westport? A: I don't know. Q: Is it an hour? A: I don't know. Q: An hour and a half? A: I couldn't say. Q: Is it fifty miles? A: I don't know. Q: Forty miles? You made the trip. Don't you know how long it takes you? A: No. My mind is constantly occupied with my problems and they are many.

Cus went on to say that his attorney Schweig never told him that he was wanted to testify before the NYSAC.

A: He never had a chance to tell me that. I was in that [Westport] camp—the local papers printed I was in that camp. I never knew anything. I was over there publicly and openly and everybody knew it. Q: Did you listen to radio or read papers in September? A: Practically none. I give you my word I didn't want to hear anything about boxing. I was sick in the stomach by what was going on. I was sick by the way I was handled after I was asked to appear downtown. I was sick about everything, sick about my fighter losing. I didn't want to hear about boxing.

Now Fusscas raised the issue of Cus's telephone records that showed that calls were made from his numbers in his New York apartment to Fat Tony Salerno. Cus categorically denied that any calls made from or to his office with Salerno had been made by him.

Q: How were these calls made, if you know? A: I absolutely don't know. Q: Does it surprise you to see these calls? A: I am amazed, except when I started to think that Mr. Rosensohn has often asked me for the use of my phone. I don't look over the bills; I just pay them. Q: June 28 there was a personal call to Salerno at home up in Red Hook, NY. A: I made no calls to these people at any time, at any time in my life. I have never spoken to them people. I tell you time and time again. Q: How were these calls made? A: I am telling you I had nothing to do with any of these people.

Then Fusscas asked about one last call, a call from Salerno to Cus's number on July 9, 1959.

Q: Did you receive such a call? A: Absolutely not. Q: Was Rosensohn in your office on July 9, 10 or 11? A: I couldn't say that he was. I don't know that he was. Q: Did you see him in your office after the fight? A: I don't remember. I saw this man pretty regularly. I was frankly in a position where I had to cater to his whims, and by this time I was convinced the man was ill. CHAIRMAN: The witness said he doesn't recall that particular date. FUSSCAS: The witness doesn't recall a great many things. NOVEMBER: I don't want your statement, Mr. Fusscas. FUSSCAS: You have to listen to them. NOVEMBER: No, I don't have to listen to them.

On redirect, November clarified a lot of Cus's answers. He had Cus explain Emil Lence's great help in promoting independent clubs and in giving Patterson a chance in his formative years. He established that both Harris and London were paid for television rights as part of their large guaranteed fees. Then November moved for a dismissal of the five charges, but needless to say, the commission refused to dismiss any of the charges.

Instead more trouble was ahead for Cus. On November 20, Detective Nat Laurendi went to the offices of Schweig and November, where Cus D'Amato was waiting for him. Cus surrendered himself to the cop and the two of them then took a short ride to a police station on Elizabeth Street in downtown New York, where Cus was booked on charges of failing to answer a subpoena from New York State attorney general Louis Lefkowitz, who was probing the Patterson–Johansson fight for possible violations of antimonopoly laws in the granting of radio, TV, and movie rights. They left the police station

and headed to Special Sessions Court, where Judge Joseph Loscalzo
freed him on $2,500 bail.

Of course, at both places there were tons of photographers and
reporters who had been tipped off that Cus was coming. The back
page of the next day's *New York Mirror* had a full-page picture of
a scowling Cus, with detectives flanking him as he was being
booked at a police station. Man, that coverage crushed him. Cus pictured as a common criminal. He always looked down on them. I would
look at a picture of Billy the Kid and say, "He looks cool!" and Cus
would go, "What? He's a bum, Mike. Look how he dresses. He shoots
people in the back. He's a bum. Unlike Wyatt Earp. He dressed
immaculate."

And it got worse. Three days later, the NYSAC called a press conference and announced that all the charges against Cus were sustained, except for charge two. I guess it was hard to make the case
that Cus was hanging out with disreputable people like Charlie Black
when the commission licensed him as a manager. The charges against
Rosensohn were also sustained. But while Rosensohn had his promoter's license suspended for three years, Cus's licenses as a manager and a second were revoked for life.

Newsweek's coverage of this was typical of the spin that the press
was putting on Cus's problems. After lauding Cus for developing
Floyd and breaking the monopoly of the IBC, they claimed that Cus
had changed. "He had won his war and now he could accomplish
what he had set out to do: Clean up boxing. But D'Amato had fought
corruption so long that he himself had become corrupted. He managed the champ, he tried to manage the challengers, and he wanted
to promote the bouts too. D'Amato had replaced group tyranny with
his own individual tyranny. Then, last June, Ingemar Johansson
knocked out Patterson and took away the title. The tight little world
of Cus D'Amato began to crumble. Last week it disintegrated. On
four charges (primarily that D'Amato had acted as an undercover
promoter), the New York State Athletic Commission revoked his license to manage fighters.

" 'I'll sign to fight Johansson without Cus,' Patterson said. 'I'll fight without a manager.' "

In three short months, Cus's "tight little world" *had* crumbled. He lost the title, he lost his license, and now he was on the verge of losing his "boy," Floyd.

8

At the end of our sessions in the gym, the other fighters would pack up and say, "See you, Cus," and then they'd go out and live their lives, go out with their girlfriends, go to the movies, go eat, whatever. But not me. I'd stay to clean the gym. I did this every night, and then me and Cus would go back to the house and devise our scheme for me to become the best fighter on the planet. On the way home, I might stop off to get a bag of potato chips and then I'd get back in the car. I'd be sitting in the backseat and Cus would be up front with whoever was driving him that day. We'd drive by the nicest mansion in Catskill, and Cus would point to it.

"You see that house there, Mike? That probably cost around three hundred thousand dollars. Five, ten years from now, if you listen to me, buying that house will be just like buying that bag of potato chips for you."

We'd talk about having houses in all different parts of the world. If he saw somebody driving a BMW or a Mercedes, he'd say, "You could get that, that's not the hardest thing in the world to do, getting wealthy. You're so superior to these people. They can never do what you are capable of doing."

Man, did we dream. We had dreams and ambition. I didn't know what ambition was before I met Cus. Cus always told me that I would be able to wear the most expensive clothes, I'd have to get a chauffeur to drive my Rolls-Royce. He knew how to stoke my engine and feed my ego. I'm not even sixteen, never got laid, and I'd ask Cus, "Do you ever think I'm going to get a girl?" My son says the same bullshit to me these days. Cus got so mad. "Forget about girls, Mike," he said. "Tomorrow I'm going to buy you a big stick. You hold on to that stick and I'll probably be dead by then, but you hold on to that stick because you're going to have to beat the girls off you one day."

Houses, nice cars, all the girls I could want—those were great dreams to me. Cus had already experienced that level of success but he didn't do it right. He had that fame but by the time that he got through giving his money away, helping boxers out, he never got a chance to enjoy what he was. He was instilling these dreams in me but he wanted another time around. This time he would be running the show. And he deserved it. He would have been cursing people out right and left. He's not shy. If he calls you a yellow dog, he'll call you a yellow dog in a conference room full of people. He'd tell you how he feels about you.

One thing that Cus never taught me was humility. He wasn't that kind of guy. In my mind, I would think he was a humble guy. Now that I think about it, there wasn't a humble bone in his body. He was extremely proud, and bitter and angry. He had a shitty life before he made it in boxing. He'd tell me all those stories about his mother dying and his brother getting shot and how he never forgot the piercing scream when his father found out about his brother Gerry. He would talk to me as if I wasn't even there. I didn't say a word; I was just there. And he'd go on and on and then, out of nowhere, he'd say, "Can you imagine how that would be? Huh?" I'd say "No" or I'd say nothing. I was there for him to lay all this stuff on.

Cus was just a bunch of rage. You would never think he was a ferocious old man, but he was. He'd talk to me about getting threats and guys putting guns to his head and he was big on being tough and hard, unafraid of confronting death. He'd say, "I don't care, I'm an animal. They had to kill me to stop me." Cus fueled my "I don't give a fuck" attitude.

Cus was the proudest and greatest boaster I've known. If Cus was around he'd love that I was writing about him. He could have a melt-down in front of a million people without batting an eye. I'd be the one who was embarrassed. Every now and then he might look back on something he did and say, "I'm embarrassed about that." I just wanted to say, "You don't have an embarrassed bone in your body. You have nothing but pride." But I'd never say that to him.

It killed him when he got banned for life. He was always plotting revenge. That's what I was all about, getting him back on top. All of it came out of vindictiveness and bitterness, that's what I came out of. And people expect me to be a rational guy? I wanted to help him, I wanted to be involved with that so badly. I was too young at that time; I didn't understand the nuances. But now I know what was going on. Cus wanted to show off, to front and floss. That's what the boxing game is all about—getting revenge. He just wanted to say, "Look at me now." And if he could get into any kind of position with leverage, he'd like to hurt his enemies or stop them from earning money. Cus was very vindictive. He couldn't live without enemies. If he didn't have enemies, he would make one.

Cus was also grandiose. He wouldn't handle people unless he thought they could be a world champion. Your purpose for being there was to be a champion. So when I got there Cus was training a heavy-weight named Greg Walsh. He was about ten years older than I was. Cus told him that his vision was that Gerry Cooney would win the title and that Greg could beat him and become the heavyweight champ. Then I would slide in right after him. Cus was talking about a dynasty!

Cus always used to say that we were in the hurt business. When I was getting ready the night before a fight, Cus would be reading the paper and I'd walk into the living room and he'd put his paper down and say, "The guy you're going to fight, I want you to break this guy's ribs, all right? He fights like this, I want you to do this and that, I want you to break his ribs." Every fight I had, Cus would be talking about breaking ribs, exploding livers, pushing a guy's nose into his brain. "Hit him behind his ear, explode his eardrum or give him a cauliflower ear that stops the fight automatically." He wouldn't be shouting it like "BREAK HIS RIBS!" He delivered the message coolly and calmly. He talked about hurting people with no feeling. But then he'd say, "The way you punch, even if you miss he should go down from the magnificent wind behind it."

If you could have heard Cus talking to me, it was scary what he wanted me to do to somebody else. It felt wrong, but it was legal. And it excited me. "You've got to tell them how you feel. Show them your pain. Show them your mother's pain." We wanted to leave a resounding message that he was back—a message to the other fighters, to the trainers, to the whole boxing establishment. I wasn't oblivious to what I was there for, what our pact was, what we were going to do to these guys besides just win. We weren't going to ever give them a chance to think they could beat us by giving us a tough fight, we were going to break their will, break their spirit, so they know they could never challenge us again. A tough fight might give them hope, inspiration, more strength. We had to make it so there was no doubt in an opponent's mind that he could never even compete with us.

One night I was fighting Kilbert Pierce up in Boston. He was handled by the Petronelli brothers, rival trainers to Cus. They trained Marvelous Marvin Hagler. Pierce was a regional champion. We drove up to Boston and Cus was with us. One of the Petronellis said to Cus that I was going to fight a big, strong, scary guy that night, and Cus immediately said, "My boy's job is to put big, scary guys in their place." I got so pumped, I turned into hot blue fire. Cus could do that to me, turn me into a bloodthirsty hound. As soon as he said it, I just knew: "Come on, motherfucker, I'm going to fucking start digging in your face right now." I wanted to fight this guy outside the ring. I was looking at the Petronelli family like "What the fuck you say, huh? You want some too, huh?"

We'd even talk about hurting people in the gym. The gym was supposed to be about learning but we learned through hurting people. Cus would laugh when he heard people screaming in the gym. And I loved him for that. I wasn't the only one he was training like that. Greg Walsh was sparring with a three-hundred-pound guy one day. It was the guy's first day, and that morning he was in the kitchen of the house, eating cereal and drinking out of a half gallon of orange juice. This was an hour before they were scheduled to spar. Cus happened to walk into the kitchen and he exploded. "What are you doing?" he said to the guy. "You can't eat and drink all that before you're going to go box." The guy goes, "Ah, I'll be fine." Cus pulled Walsh aside. "I want you to go after this guy with nothing but body punches." Before the end of the bell for the first round, the guy was in the ring throwing up on his hands and knees. And Cus was standing there going, "What did I tell you? What did I tell you?" Cus fired him that day.

Another time Walsh was sparring with a big black dude. He was getting into the ring and Cus saw that he didn't have his mouthpiece in. The guy said he forgot it and Cus said, "Well, you can't box." So the guy went into the bathroom and he took paper towels and wet them in the sink and rolled them up and put them in his mouth. "You can't use that for a mouthpiece!" Cus said. "I'll be fine," the guy said, and shrugged. Then Cus went over to Walsh and goes, "I want you to hit this guy with nothing but uppercuts." The guy lasted a round and a half before he was on his knees, spitting blood all over the place. Cus was going, "What did I tell you? You gotta listen to me!"

Cus would tell me to break people's ribs even when I was just sparring! Then he'd tell the sparring partners, "Don't think that just because he's a boy you have to go easy on him. You do your best." Cus loved the sparring partners who pushed me and kicked my ass. He stayed close to them and treated them special, because he knew that they gave me good work. He would try to make sure they wouldn't go anywhere else.

Cus was a vicious, cantankerous beast. He wanted the meanest fighter God ever created, someone who scared the life out of people before they even entered the ring. Every day Cus would tell me I'm the most fierce, ferocious fighter the world has known. Ferocious, invincible—God, those words turned me on, struck me to the core. He would talk about other fighters like Henry Armstrong and Beau

Jack and tell me how those guys fought like animals. They were mad dogs, they had to hold them back like dogs, and then, boom, they went at each other and clashed nonstop.

This stuff I'm talking about between me and Cus, this shit wasn't for everybody. Cus broke people down, so I know this was not for normal people training to be a fighter. Everything Cus said was law to me: if he told me to attack somebody, I would attack them. I was always in attack mode, since I was fourteen. Cus would start talking and wake me in the middle of the night, this motherfucker was so dead serious. When he would wake me up, I could feel him thinking, I could feel that shit coming through my mind telepathically. He wanted me to be where I was so confident, I could do this stuff in my sleep. Cus loved when I was arrogant, when I looked at these other fighters and snorted and looked like I was saying, "How dare you challenge me?"

We were sitting at the dinner table one night and Cus was talking, as usual. "Mike will go as far as the occasion requires him to go, because he has all the qualities that will make this possible." I interrupted him and said, "The young kids and the amateurs fighting now are good." And Cus said, "They lack ferocity. You are ferocious. At least your actions are ferocious. You may not be ferocious, but you appear ferocious." That was him goading me on. And when people began to describe me as savage, I'd get an erection. I loved it. Fifty years earlier people called Cus's heroes ferocious and savage.

Cus was so much more than a boxing trainer. He instilled so many values in me. Over the years I learned how to act politically and give everybody the same respect that I wanted from people. But Cus believed certain people didn't deserve respect. If he thought you didn't deserve respect, he would treat you accordingly. But if Cus dug you, he'd be there for you. He told me that a lot of his troubles came from standing up for underdogs who didn't deserve his support. "The people I invested the most time in disappointed me the most." In my experience, I agree with that a hundred percent.

Even though he could be cold and ruthless when it came to the boxing ring, outside the ring Cus was a compassionate guy. He understood discrimination and he was courageous in his civil rights activism. Blacks and Puerto Ricans loved Cus, along with poor whites. He thought money was a tool, and when he had it, he put it to good purposes, helping out poor boxers, both current ones and retired ones. There were papers in Cus's archives that showed he bought food for the old manager Bobby Melnick, who had managed his brother Gerry at one point.

Cus always told me that money could give you a false sense of security, and to him, security was death. He never wanted to relax and take it easy. Everything was conflict. Cus had no money when I met him but he was being supported by his friend Jimmy Jacobs, who saw Cus as a real mentor. I think those Union Square riots when Cus was growing up led him to identify with the Communists in the United States. He was a Socialist, for sure. He was in love with Che and Fidel.

We'd have political discussions, especially about Julius and Ethel Rosenberg, American citizens who were charged with spying for the Soviet Union and who were convicted and given the chair. Cus was obsessed with that trial, saying they were innocent. At that time, I wasn't politically sophisticated at all, so I just went along with a lot of stuff that he said. But one time when he was ranting about the Rosenbergs, just to mess with him, I said, "C'mon, Cus, you know they were guilty." Man, he almost busted a gut.

"Oh, yeah? You're talking big now but when they bring slavery back you're not going to be saying who was guilty or not," he said. "Because that's what they're planning to do."

A chill went up my spine. He was dead fucking serious. Then I regretted joking with him. He would get too outraged.

That was nothing compared to when Reagan came on the TV screen. Cus got apoplectic. "LIAR!" he'd scream at the TV. "LIAR! LIAR! LIAR! LIAR!" Camille would say, "Cus, calm down. You're going to get a heart attack!" I was too young, but when Reagan was running for president against Carter, Cus made sure that all the guys he was training voted for Carter.

Even though Cus lived almost like a hermit up in Catskill, he had all these great minds coming to visit and almost pay homage to him. Budd Schulberg, Norman Mailer, Pete Hamill, Dr. Robert Gross. These guys were radicals. And I'm sitting around and listening to every word they're saying. They always talked about the old times, never about anything current or topical. I don't know what's going on, but all this stuff is sinking in somehow. I couldn't add two plus two, but Cus had me reading Hemingway and Dostoevsky and Tolstoy.

Cus never treated me like a kid. When he's got Mailer or Schulberg there, I'd be sitting there and Cus would be talking about me like I was invisible. "That's the next champ of the world. He's a little rough around the edges, he comes from a real bad neighborhood, Brownsville." They would say, "That's where Bummy Davis came from." He was a Jewish fighter who got killed during a holdup in a bar. I'm right there, I'm cleaning up the garbage, and he's talking about me like I'm not there. "He's going to be the next heavyweight champion of the world." "You think so, Cus? He looks small." "Hey, that don't mean nothing. He's a giant killer, you listen to my words, he intimidates people."

Cus might have been visited by literary giants, but every Friday one of us had to take him to the supermarket so he could pick up the *National Enquirer*, *Star*, all the tabloids. Camille read them too. Cus always claimed he was picking them up for Camille, but I caught him reading them. He loved to read the stories about UFOs and aliens. But most of all Cus loved to read books, mostly nonfiction ones. He would read a book and argue with the author. Mario Costa salvaged a lot of Cus's books, and you can see how wide-ranging his interests were. Check out this list: *Marx and the Marxists* by Sidney Hook; *How to Develop a Better Speaking Voice* by Marjorie Hellier; *Karate-Dō: My Way of Life* by Gichin Funakoshi; *Mohammed Ali and His House—An Historical Romance*, from 1907; *Anatomy of an Illness: As Perceived by the Patient*—"How One Man Proved Your Mind Can Cure Your Body"—by Norman Cousins; *The Creation of the Universe* by George Gamow; *Moscow War Diary* by Alexander Werth; *Your Personality: Introvert or Extravert?* by Virginia Case; *ESP and You* by Hans Holzer; *The Catcher in the Rye* by J. D. Salinger; *The Note-*

books of Leonardo da Vinci; Anne Frank: The Diary of a Young Girl; and *The True Believer* by Eric Hoffer (which has a great blurb on the back cover: "Who is the True Believer? How can you recognize him? He's a guilt-ridden hitchhiker who thumbs a ride on every cause from Christianity to Communism. He's a fanatic needing a Stalin or a Christ to worship or die for. He's the mortal enemy of things as they are and he insists on sacrificing himself for a dream that's impossible to attain. He is today everywhere on the march. This explosive report on the psychology behind mass movements analyzes and dissects the motives, responses, potential and power of the True Believer. Here's a frightening and fascinating study of the mind of a fanatic. The man who is anxious to join a cause, any cause, and, if necessary, to sacrifice lives for that cause. His life or your life, if you let him.")

Cus always read like a fiend. Jimmy Glenn, who was a sparring partner and cornerman for Floyd Patterson, told me that even back in the fifties Cus "used to read all night. If you came in at twelve o'clock, he would be up reading." Cus didn't listen to music much. He liked Al Jolson but that was about it. Other than the news, he never watched TV. But he read every boxing magazine from every country religiously. Jacobs would send them up to him. Cus was too fixated on boxing to bother with TV shows.

Burt Young, the ex-boxer who went on to stardom in the *Rocky* movies, likes to tell a story that illustrates how tunnel-visioned Cus was. Burt would take the train from New York to California when he was going to do a film. He'd bring along his scripts, some books, and a bottle of Scotch. He was sitting on the train once and an old guy came up to him.

"Burt, is that you?" the guy said.

"Yes."

"You don't know me. It's Cus, Cus D'Amato."

Burt said, "Holy shit!" and asked Cus to sit with him. Cus sat down and for the next five hours he started in on Burt.

"At your level of development, you shouldn't have been able to do what you could do in the ring. But you were a bad boy, you go steal, you go rob, you were a bad boy. You know, I'm not into astrology but there are more middleweight champions who are Taurus than any other sign."

Burt couldn't believe that Cus remembered his birthday. But what was most amazing was Cus's total ignorance of Burt's Hollywood stardom. "He kept telling me I missed my life's calling," Burt told us. "I kept telling him, 'But Cus, I'm in good shape, everything is nice,' and he's reprimanding me like I could have been somebody special, you know? In the meantime, I'm an Academy Award actor, doing well."

People ask me if Cus had a good sense of humor but I really can't answer that because when he laughed, everybody else had to laugh too. If you didn't laugh at something he said, he'd go, "Hey, you don't think that's funny? I think you should have laughed." You can't win with him.

But there's one great story that shows Cus's quick wit. He was sitting at the dais at a boxing function in New York City in the mid-1960s and the writers were interviewing him and asking about him one of his old IBC enemies, maybe Harry Markson or Teddy Brenner. And one reporter said, "Forget it, Cus, everyone knows that he's his own worst enemy." Cus didn't miss a beat and said, "Not while I'm alive."

I'm not really into astrology either, but Cus is a classic Capricorn. It's the most egotistical sign. He liked to be on the stage, just like me. Capricorns know how to push us. They hit our sensitivity, they make us feel good and make us feel bad. Take a Leo, man, Capricorns eat those guys up and spit them out, and he has them working for him and turning against their own families.

It was always Cus's way or no way. He'd be willing to give you a hearing but then he'd go ahead and do what he wanted to do in the beginning. Cus wanted everyone to think like he thought. I guess it boils down to him being a glory hound. He was into fighting and he wanted to be successful. And if things didn't go his way, he'd feel sorry for himself. "Everybody is always leaving me. I did all that for that guy and then they leave me." Cus did do a lot for people but I could see that he wanted so much in return.

Cus was such a control freak. It went way beyond his insistence on unpacking the groceries. When the phone rang he had to answer it or he'd throw a fit. He was like a teenager with the phone. He was addicted to it because he wasn't in the city and he wasn't in the action, so he had to find out what was going on from his "spies." The house rule was I had only five minutes at a time on the phone, because Cus thought that whatever I was talking about wasn't that important anyway. I might be talking to a girl on the phone and he'd listen to my side of the conversation to get me to free up the phone so he wouldn't miss an incoming call. I might be listening to the girl talk and he'd go, "You're not saying anything. What are you saying? I don't hear five words out of your mouth. All I hear is you going, 'Mmmmm hmmmm.' You aren't saying anything. You're wasting precious time. I'm waiting on an important phone call."

When I'd go out with friends it was always a whole scene. One day when I was about seventeen, I was hanging out with my friends and we were drinking and partying. They dropped me off and I looked in the window and there was Cus sleeping at the table in the living room, waiting for me. I just said, "Come on, man, turn around, take me to your house. I don't want to even go here." He would rip me a new asshole every time I'd come in late. I'd try to hide, go up the stairs, the stairs would creak, and I'd go, "Fuck, I'm busted."

A lot of times when I'd come home late, and Cus had fallen asleep waiting for me to come home, I'd wind up sleeping on the front porch in one of the rocking chairs. In the morning Cus would wake me up. "What the hell are you doing out there? Why didn't you wake me up?" I'd say, "You were sleeping, Cus." I think that Cus was just happy that he knew I was at the house, even if I was sleeping outside.

But even when I stayed home, he'd be on my case. Me and Frankie would stay in the room and smoke some weed and talk about fighting or some girls, whatever, and we'd be laughing and all of a sudden we'd hear the steps going "creak" and that meant Cus was coming up and then it was like hell. When he'd come to the door, we'd be all quiet. Cus would say, "Oh, oh, oh, before I came upstairs it was like there's two of you guys just looking at the walls? What are you talking about? Cat got your tongue?"

Cus didn't drive but he'd sit in the front seat and give you instructions the whole way. "We've got to watch this turn up here, slow down." He'd fall asleep, and then he'd suddenly wake up and look at the speedometer, he'd look at his watch, he'd look at the mile marker, and he'd go, "You must have been flying! You'll break the sound barrier, for Christ's sake!" Meanwhile, because nobody could go over the speed limit with Cus in the car, the other cars would be zipping right past us. "The laws are there for a reason. We'll see those people up ahead, wrapped around a tree," he'd say.

One way to get at Cus was to show him visible signs of affection. Cus was never affectionate with people. He used to rationalize it by saying things to reporters like "I made it a point never to show affection with the tough boys, no matter how much I liked them or helped them, because I knew that affection meant a sign of weakness to them." I'd give him a big hug and he'd freak out, "Hey, stop! What's wrong with you?" At first I felt unlovable, but as time went on and I got to know him, I realized that he just didn't know how to show affection. So I'd just hug him to fuck with him and he'd go, "Hey, knock that stuff off."

Cus controlled the mood of the house. If he was happy, the whole house was happy. But if he's not feeling good, nobody else is, either. If he got bored or he hadn't been out, watch out! You're getting the third degree. I never heard anyone say the word "WHAT" nastier than Cus did. "What was that? WHAT??" Whoa, you'd be so intimidated you'd forget what you had to say. Most of the time Camille would ignore him but sometimes she'd laugh at him. "It's funny, huh? Everything is funny, huh, Camille?" he'd say.

Cus dominated the talk at the dinner table. He wanted to take over the conversation even if it was a subject that he knew nothing about. All the action in the house happened at the dinner table. And it wasn't always pleasant. Cus could make you feel like shit. He'd give

you that look that would go right through you. He'd bring up things
he'd been holding in, or if he couldn't get my attention, this is where
it went down. On everybody, not just me. Anything that he felt needed
to be addressed, boom, be ready. "And you, by the way. Don't think
you're off the hook. You think I didn't know about that, huh?"

Cus wouldn't just react to things that were happening in the
house or in town. If something anywhere in the world was not going
the way Cus wanted it to go, man, it was on and you were going to
hear about it. And if you tried to put in your two cents, he was all over
your shit. "Listen to me, these people are starving over there, and
we're not doing anything. They're getting murdered and raped
and we're not doing anything. We're in a room talking to their leaders and going to fancy state dinners and their people are suffering
and dying. These people are suffering and dying while their president
is getting laid with a whooooore."

He was always in a state of confrontation. Most of the day he
walked around going, "That son of a bitch. I can't believe what that
guy did." Camille would go, "Cus, Cus, calm down. Your blood pressure is going to spike." You know what I found out? It's easier to try
to have a rational conversation with a guy who was born a billionaire
than a guy who was a self-made man. You can't tell them shit. Cus
was one of those guys. You've got a better chance of talking to Prince
Charles. God forbid someone would try to give me boxing advice. Cus
would say, "What the hell do you know about what he can do or who
he can't beat? Who did you fight? Who did you ever beat?"

One day we were sitting around and I said, "How would I have to
fight to beat Dempsey? How could I beat Jeffries? How could I beat
Louis?" And we'd watch the tapes. But I couldn't figure out anything myself, that would have been disrespecting him. If I had to use
my brain to think, that was bad; he had to do the thinking for me. I'd
go, "I got an idea." "Where did you get an idea from?" If I showed
mercy to a guy in the ring, he'd be, "Where did you learn those feelings? Where'd you learn compassion? Who taught you that? I didn't
teach you that. Who have you been around in school? Some girls
have been telling you things, whispering in your ear? Oh, you've got

compassion now, huh? If that's your mother, your brother, me, anybody, you do what I've taught you to do to people. There's no feelings in here." I never forgot that phrase. "There's no feelings in here." Cold, so cold.

Cus understood drama. He was a good salesman; he was another P. T. Barnum. He knew what people wanted and he knew how to get you excited. After hearing all of Cus's stories about his battle with Norris and the IBC, I wouldn't exactly call Cus paranoid. Let's just say he was extra suspicious. He wouldn't give any of the guys in the house keys because they could be lost and then duplicated. So that led to situations where a guy might go out to town and then come back late and be locked out of the house. One time Oscar Holman, one of the new sparring partners, went out and closed the bars and came back to the house about five-thirty in the morning. When Tom Patti came down the stairs to do his morning run, he saw Cus lying on the living room floor doing his Army shuffle on his elbows and knees with his old Army rifle. I guess Cus had heard Oscar trying to jar the door open and Cus thought it might be a hit. Tom just stepped over his body, walked around to the back door, and let the guy in.

Cus actually had a few guns in the house. If anybody asked him why he was so paranoid, he'd say, "I'd rather be a little bit paranoid than a little bit dead." When Cus would answer the phone, he'd put on a fake voice. "Helloooooo," almost like a woman. And whatever you did, you never made any quick movements around Cus. He'd have his hands up so fast, ready to throw down. He'd throw punches in his sleep. And if we were on the road for a fight, he'd sleep with a knife by his side. He always jumped around and growled *grrrrrr*, like an animal charging, when someone knocked on the door. In the house, Cus's bedroom was off-limits. He had it rigged up with a matchbox that would fall on the floor if someone opened the door. Everybody wondered what Cus kept in his room and we'd all try to sneak a glimpse when he came out, but he'd always close the door behind him real quick.

It was no better when we were out of the house. Cus was from the old school of trainers where nobody was allowed to speak to their fighters. Back in the day, people would try to steal the fighter all the time in public gyms. If Cus saw you speaking to anyone he'd go crazy. I couldn't even talk to the guys I'd just fought. One of the trainers would come over to congratulate me and I'd shake his hand and then Cus would come over to me. "Do you know this man? What are you talking to him for?" I said, "Well, no, he just seemed like a nice guy." "What do you mean 'nice'?" Cus said. "Do you like him? You want to go on a date with him? You want to give him flowers? Explain that 'nice guy' thing to me." So the guys had to go through Cus first to even congratulate me.

After I was living with Cus for a few years, I learned that even though Cus could make me feel so good, like I could conquer the world, he had the same ability to make me feel like shit. Just with little comments like "You allow your mind to get the better of you." To me that was code for "You're a weak piece of shit. You don't have enough discipline to be one of the greats." Cus taught me that even if someone kidnapped their son or killed their mother, the greats can go out and fight the best fight of their life. The greats are totally emotionally independent.

He didn't use examples just from boxing. Take Judy Garland. She could be high on liquor, drugs, barbiturates, whatever. She could look incoherent but she kept making it through by the skin of her teeth. Some of these great performers like her would go to the arena from the hospital. What determination. I wanted to be one of those kinds of fighters and performers. A guy could be on his deathbed and still perform, fight for his life.

The worst was when he called me a tomato can. That's an old fight expression for a guy who's a such perpetual loser that beating him is as easy as kicking a can down the street. And they use a "tomato can" because he'd probably bleed like a stuck pig too. Hearing those words would make me cry. That was Cus saying I was a bum, someone who could be pushed over.

After a while, Cus wanted to break me down. Every day he would try to pick at me to find a weak moment so he could get into my head. "Come on, I didn't do that, that's not true." He was the hand that crushed you. I think it started when he saw that the confidence that he had built up in me was getting out of control. He would say things like "You're not mentally tough enough to fight their fighter," and I would be crushed.

If I ever tried to strut, he would check me like no one could. "Who do you think you are? Oh, you think you're going to be a big-time pro. If you don't listen to me now, you ain't going to listen to me when you're big-time." I said, "I'm listening to everything you say, Cus. What do you mean? What did I do?" "I saw you walking around with your tight clothes and your balls and your ass showing. Who do you think you are?" I'm thinking "What? My balls and my ass?"

Sometimes Cus's venom seemed random, like he was taking things out on me. I'd be downstairs eating breakfast and he'd come downstairs and start a fight with me and call me a traitor. I think Cus liked doing this to me, especially when I started cleaning up my act and not getting in trouble around the house. He accused me of things I didn't do and then apologized to me later. Probably to see how I responded to the aggravation.

Cus always used to give interviews where he said that he knew when to apply pressure to his boxers and when to lay off. Cus was always hard. Cus's idea of laying off is when he's not saying anything but giving you a look that could kill. And then he'd growl at you, *arggggg*. One day I was reading a boxing magazine and Cus was reading a newspaper and we started talking about fighters and out of the blue, Cus said, "I can see you're going to have to be hurt to learn." And then he went right back to reading his paper. "What do you mean? What did I do?" He liked to fuck with people.

He wanted to make you better, but in order to make you better, he had to break you. That's a bad process. Sometimes you break people and you can't put them back together. Some people are made out of emotional glass. Teddy Atlas was training one guy who had a lot of emotional problems and was in and out of jail. Cus was hard on the guy one day and kicked him out of the house. A few months later the guy committed suicide. Cus's action had nothing to do with the sui-cide but Teddy was upset about it and he was discussing the guy with

Cus. Cus said, "What? The guy was a prick all his life and now he dies and all of a sudden he's a great guy?" That's Cus.

Mixed messages. Cus would be mad at me for some shit I did and he'd say, "What are you going to do with your life?" But then I'd hear him physically threatening a guy for bad-mouthing me. That's what messed me up, because they caused me so many different highs, boom, from here to here. He's angry, then he's defending me—it's crazy.

Cus would always tell me, "Don't thank me. This is who you are. I'm just bringing it out of you. I've done nothing." And then he'd turn around and say, "There's no way to accomplish this without my direction. You have to listen to me."

When I'd get too enthusiastic about our dreams and our goals, Cus had a way of bringing me down to earth. I'd say something like "I'm going to do anything I can to win. I want to be champion so bad I'd give my life to be champion, Cus, I'd give my life." Cus would tell me, "You just be careful what you ask for, okay. You might get it." He always stepped in my face when I wanted him to say, "You'll get it, Mike," but he didn't say that shit, he didn't give me what I wanted. Cus used to quote Nietzsche to me. One of his favorite quotes was "Whoever fights monsters should see to it that in the process he does not become a monster. And if you gaze long enough into an abyss, the abyss will gaze back into you." That was a hard lesson that would take me years to learn. Ironically, that's what happened to Cus in the boxing biz. His downfall came because he fought the monster, only to become it.

Teddy Atlas instigated the idea that Cus was giving me special treatment. That was bullshit. Cus always treated me like a prima donna in front of people, but behind closed doors he wasn't that way. I was petrified when I was alone with him. If he called me—"Mike, I need to talk to you"—I didn't feel good going over to him. That's when he'd start giving me his detailed criticisms of my fights. People see the public celebrations of my sensational knockouts but they don't hear Cus talking to me alone after the fight. "If that guy was a little more relaxed and calm, he would have hit you with that punch." Now he's making me feel like shit. He's playing with my emotions. He didn't say I would get knocked out, he just said that he would have hit me—it was just the fact that the guy would have hit me. He would put things in your head, all day, talking about that punch. Then when you think he's finished talking about it, after a couple of days, he'd say it again. "Remember at the fight, I told you that guy would have hit you." They don't see that side, the side of habitual mindfuck.

They were never around when Cus made me feel two inches tall, when he asked me, "Am I wasting my time with you? I'm an old man. You're a phony." Today I'm messed up because he told me I'm a phony. He's telling me to act a certain way. I was a scared kid and he was saying, "Forget your emotions. You've got to control them. You've got to project an aura of calm and confidence." The man I worshipped was telling me I was a phony. It was crushing.

I soon learned to walk on eggshells when I was around Cus. When he would be happy, talking, laughing with the press, I knew that at any moment shit could happen and I knew I could get embarrassed in front of everybody if I spoke out of line. So I learned rather fast not to say anything while he was talking unless he invited me into the conversation. At home, I would never ask Cus anything when he went into those moods. But it worked both ways. The human mind can hear one good word and it can ignite a tiger.

All that extreme praise, building me up, was gone. Cus would rarely give me praise again, at least directly. From then on I was naturally insecure about what Cus truly thought about my fighting. One Saturday morning, Tom Patti, me, and Cus were leaving the gym. I pulled Tom aside and said, "Tom, when we ride back, I'm going to hide in the back of the car and I want you to ask Cus some questions about me," because I wanted to hear what Cus really thought. So we got in the car and Cus, who had been delayed in the gym, came out and said, "What about Mike?" Tom told him that I had walked into town. So Cus got in and Tom started driving home. I was lying down in the wheel well, behind in the backseat, and I whispered, "Tommy, ask Cus if he thinks I'm a good fighter." Tommy said, "So, Cus, do you think Mike is a good fighter?" "Good? Of course he's good, why would you ask something ridiculous like that? Not only is he good, but if he stays focused like he is and doing as well as he is, they're going to talk about Mike in terms of greatness, not just being good. Not only is he good, but he has the potential to be great, maybe the greatest ever." That was a pretty good answer.

So then I went, "Tommy, ask Cus if he thinks I punch hard." "Do you think Mike punches hard?" "Punches hard? Not only does he punch hard—the hardest punches I've ever seen—but he's got speed, and in addition to that he's got intelligence. When you've got speed, power, and intelligence, you've got the makings of a real fighter. Not only is he a hard puncher, but he's a smart puncher, and when Mike fights, people may not realize it but he's a smart puncher, because he knows how to hit and not get hit." Right about then we pulled up outside the house, Tom got out, Cus got out, and then I sat up in the backseat. Cus saw me and said to Tommy, "What the hell are you and the phony back there pulling? Don't give me that crap around here." Then he said, "Everything I said about you was true. If only you'd believe it." Before proceeding into the house he turned around and said, "You guys think you're a bunch of wiseguys, huh?"

I loved hearing Cus say that stuff. It validated who I thought I was. All that ride home I was thinking about how that championship belt would fit on my waist. Hearing him say that stuff made me feel like a million bucks. Before a fight, all day long I would haunt Cus. "Do you think I'm really good, Cus? Do you think I can beat him?"

"Keep your mind on the fight, you can beat him," he said. "I'm a hundred percent sure you could beat him."

Cus always praised Brownsville. "Tough guys come out of there, good fighters. They were just never taught right. If I could've taught those guys, they would be champions." He always put that in my head. So I know what it feels like for a boy who lives in a house with an overbearing father he has to live up to. But Camille balanced Cus out. Everything was beautiful to her, a perpetual party. She was such a nice lady. It would be freezing outside and she would put her coat on, her earmuffs, her shades, and then lie on a lawn chair and get some sun rays on her face.

Camille was a Ukrainian who came here by way of Canada. She

had three sisters and they were all stunning women. I saw pictures of them from the 1920s at Coney Island, they had the whole flapper thing going on. She and her sisters were the toasts of the town. She told me, "We would go out all night and come home at four in the morning and then cook food and just hang out until daylight."

As I grew older, I realized that Camille was carrying Cus. She handled everything. She ran the house while Cus handled the fighters and conducted the business. And the house ran like clockwork. Everyone had to wash their own dishes. Everyone had chores to do. No girls were allowed in the house. No cursing was allowed. Camille would get up early and set the table, sometimes she'd make me breakfast. Then she'd sit down and we'd talk. Cus would come down and say, "Good morning, Camillee! Thank you for the coffee, Camillee." Then he'd say, "Look at our champion, Camillee, the champion of the whole country. He knocked everybody out. He's the next heavyweight champ of the world."

Everyone wondered about Cus and Camille's relationship because they had separate bedrooms but I've watched them hugging and kissing and seen pictures of them lying on a bed. They'd been a couple since the 1950s so they must have some deep connection. Cus used to kid Camille a lot. One time there was a film crew filming a dinner at the house and one of the guests complimented Camille's cooking. "When's the last time you ate today?" Cus asked him. "Don't answer him," Camille said. "Food tastes best when you're hungry. If you haven't eaten for a long time, the food is delicious," Cus kidded. The truth was that Camille was a world-class cook and everyone always looked forward to her meals. It was like Thanksgiving every night.

I didn't like doing chores. Camille wound up doing my laundry for me so I had to take care of the lawn and sweep the house and take out the garbage. I did it reluctantly for years but I learned what discipline was—to do what you hate like you love it. So I learned to love doing my chores. Cus himself would get out of doing any work around the house. I can't recall him doing any manual labor, with the exception of taking the trash out or setting the table on a rare occasion or making me breakfast.

Whenever I'd get pissed off at Cus playing mind games with me, Camille would console me. I think she felt sorry for me. Whenever she sensed I was upset she would sit behind me and rub my head and I'd get a big grin on my face. We got really close, Camille and I. Cus would say, "What are you talking about? Stop talking about women's stuff. What are you telling him, Camille?" Sometimes Cus and Camille would disagree on stuff and I'd make the mistake of getting in between them. One time I told Cus that he was wrong and Camille was right. He exploded. "You're betraying me. You're doing it now, what are you going to do when you become a big fighter? You're going to leave me like everybody else. She didn't want you to stay here when you first got here, remember that? She wanted to kick you out because you weren't taking baths. You don't remember that, do you? I got you here."

But don't get me wrong. I'm not complaining about Cus. Nobody in the world could reach me in my soul like Cus did. Whenever I finished talking with him, I had to go and work out and burn energy. I was so pumped up. I'd be crying when I was running, because I wanted to make him happy. I wanted to prove that what he was saying about me was right. Everybody else was saying I was too small.

Peeling off the layers and getting to the core of a person is a painful process. And when Cus is building this ego back up, so much of that ego comes from the power he has over you. Cus always said that he feels like he hasn't done his job until he makes his pupil independent of him. But I was never independent of him. Every time I had a problem, I went to Cus. Cus was so charismatic. He used the English language like his slave, he was so articulate. Cus had a rare talent. He had so many different personalities to deal with and he knew how to deal with every one of them. He had the art of intimidation down to a science. Cus was like a Greek philosopher with his disciples around him, expounding on everything and everyone was listening raptly.

I was his ideal pupil. I hung on every word he said. When Cus was at the table, sometimes he'd forget a name or a date and I'd remind him. I knew everything in his mind, every story he ever told people.

Before he finished it, I'd finish it for him. He knew I knew the answer to anything he wanted to know. Teddy Atlas wrote a book where he said Cus was so desperate for a champ that he let me spit on him. That's far from the truth. I would never spit on Cus. I held Cus in such high esteem, like a god, and I was like his slave. If he told me to kill somebody, I would kill them. I'm serious. Cus doesn't turn the other cheek, he isn't that kind of guy. Everybody thinks I'm up there with this old, sweet, white Italian guy. I'm up there with an old warrior, that's what it was. Cus was all about disabling and dismantling opponents in an exciting manner. Everything had to be exciting. The knockout had to be done with charisma. If somebody got out of line, Cus checked them right away. He'd start punching right away too, no talking.

And I loved every minute of being with Cus. He gave me a purpose in life. All that hard work. After training, I got home and I had to crawl up the stairs. I sacrificed my soul to be the best—to be the champ of the world. I gave it everything I had. People say, "He got it too quick." That might be true because I overworked myself, I never took the time off. Even when I was sore and I could barely make it up those stairs, I'd force myself and sit in the little porcelain tub on the third floor, put Epsom salts in and run the water as hot as I could take it. I'd get burned up, but by the next morning my body would feel so much better and I could go work out again. Even after I fractured my wrists roller skating, I'd still go to the gym and train with casts on both my wrists. Incidentally, after that, Cus barred me from any physical activity outside the ring. I was truly a young man on a tunnel-vision mission. I never felt such a glorious feeling. You can't even explain that feeling to somebody. I don't know if I made Cus feel that good, but he made me feel good. He made me feel like I was somebody, that I mattered. He gave me a voice. I was only fifteen years old and my reputation was so widespread. I would go to Chicago, Boston, Rhode Island, anywhere. People would say, "That's Tyson. He's going for his second straight Junior Olympics."

Sometimes Cus's bragging embarrassed me. Cus was telling everyone that I'm the next heavyweight champ of the world, pushing it in their face, and I'm only fifteen. I could see the doubt in people's eyes. They'd say, "Well, Cus, he's kind of short." I could see that they didn't believe him but they were too polite or afraid to tell him to his face.

IN JUNE 1982, I defended my Junior Olympics heavyweight title. I won my first bout with a KO in the second round over Jonathon Littles and then went on to fight Don Cozad in the semis. Just eight seconds into the first round, I knocked him cold with a right hand. It took him about a minute to come to his senses and I went over to console him. But when I got back to my corner, the amateur officials were there. One of them said to me, "I'm going to have to ask you to come to a private room. We've received a formal complaint from the other corner and we're going to have to check your gloves for foreign substances." They couldn't believe someone could be knocked out cold with a punch like that. Of course, there was nothing in my glove but my fist.

Then it was time for the finals against a big white kid named Kelton Brown. There's famous footage of me and Teddy before the fight and me breaking down and crying. I just broke. It was the first time that I felt pressure like that, defending my championship and me still fifteen years old. Now there were all these cameras and I hear all that clicking and the flashbulbs going off. I was just fighting my insecurities. Here were all these educated white people saying these wonderful things about me. And fuck, I had lived in such a den of iniquity my whole life. I said to myself, "This is so wonderful, but it's going to end because I'm filthy, I'm dirty." I've got that shit still in me from the streets, but then I used it as motivation. My pride for Brownsville is keeping me ready, I'm not letting Brownsville down. Cus had instilled that in me. Cus is a cold piece of work. He said, "If you listen to me, when your mother walks the street, people will carry her groceries."

I thought if I didn't perform well, then nobody would ever like me again. But I didn't have to worry. The guy wasn't much of a fighter and his corner threw in the towel in the first round. The whole town of Catskill celebrated my victory. But it wasn't enough for Cus. He wanted the world to celebrate. "The public don't realize his accomplishments," he told the press. "Someday in the future, the town of Catskill will be put on the map."

Cus gave me rewards when I won something significant, and this time I got the best one yet. All my old boxing heroes like Armstrong had a wave in their hair so I did the same, applying a shitload of Murray's hair grease to get the wave effect while brushing my hair down. And they all had gold teeth in their mouths. Plus my mother had a gold tooth. So Cus got me two gold teeth, even though most people who weren't from my neighborhood wouldn't understand why someone would want gold teeth. But Cus encouraged me. "When the big fighters achieved success, they showed off that they had money by getting teeth made out of gold," Cus said. "Having gold teeth meant you were somebody."

Cus was so happy that I won that second Junior Olympics title. He was optimistic about my prospects for being a professional fighter, that I'd go on to win the Olympics and then the heavyweight crown, all according to his plan. Cus used to say to me, "I can't wait until they see you and you become champ. I used to have to protect Patterson, but I wouldn't have to protect you. You could fight anybody. There's no one that could beat you." He told me that, but he didn't say it like he was complimenting me. It was like he was talking right through me. I'm not smiling, I'm just looking at him with a blank face. It's only me and him there, no one else is in the vicinity, but he's not talking to me.

Cus's happiness was shattered when I got caught with some weed shortly after the Junior Olympics. I was so stupid to keep the pot in my room. Ruth, the German cleaning lady, found it and brought it to Cus. When I got home that day, the weed was on the dining room table. Cus couldn't wait to hold it over my head. "This must be some really good stuff, Mike," he said. "It must be really, really good for you to let down four hundred years of slaves and peasants for it." Whoa. Just writing about this gives me chills down my spine now.

He knew how to bring me to my nadir. I felt like a real Uncle Tom. Cus hated Uncle Toms too. I just went upstairs and locked myself in my room.

Even though I was settling into my middle-class white life in Catskill, I'd still go back to Brownsville, to my roots. I went down there after I won my second title and I brought a picture of me that was on the cover of a boxing magazine. When I got to my mother's house, my mother made me some crappy food. We're sitting in her dilapidated apartment—the walls were leaking, and it reeked of foul odors—and I started in again, telling her I'm the greatest fighter God ever created. I was so Custitized. I was talking nonstop. "I'm the best fighter in the world, Ma, ain't nobody going to beat me. I'm going to be heavyweight champion of the world. I'm going to win the Olympics . . ." "You've got to be humble, son," she kept repeating. She still wasn't feeling me at all.

Looking back at it now, being a parent myself, I just didn't understand how much my mother loved me, the same way my kids feel about me. I didn't know my mother felt it because I didn't feel that way about me, I couldn't believe somebody could care about me. I feel bad now, because I know how much my mother loved me and I didn't respect that, I didn't understand love then.

When I went to see my friends the next day they all went, "Wow, Mike, you talk different. Why are you talking like this?" I was emulating Cus's diction and vocabulary. "Whoa, you sound smart, man. Where did you learn that from?" And it was strange but everybody was telling me to get out of the neighborhood and go back to Catskill. Cus was well-known in Brownsville, he had trained kids from the neighborhood in the Gramercy Gym and most people knew him from when he managed Patterson. Strangers who saw me win the Junior Olympics would come up to me on the street. "Hey, you're Tyson. Congratulations, Mike. I saw you on TV. You're with that white man Gus. He loves you, man." A lot of people called him Gus.

It wasn't too long after that visit that I had to go back to Brooklyn. Cus told me that my mom had been diagnosed with cancer. That hit me hard. My mother, she didn't understand my drive. She never saw me intoxicated with the idea that I was somebody and it was totally against who she believed she was and I was. I don't know, I was just a dickhead all my life, robbing and stealing from her friends and from her.

I got to Brooklyn and I couldn't handle my mom being sick. I was going out to clubs, seeing my friends, and my sister kept telling me, "You're playing. Go see Mommy, that's what you came here for." So after a week I went to the hospital to see my mother. She was in horrible shape, so skinny she looked like a skeleton. I gave her a kiss and put the cover over her, because her chest was showing, and I left and never came back. Every day my sister would say, "Did you go and see Mommy?" I said, "Yeah, I saw Mommy, she's doing good, she's doing good." I'm a fucking liar. I didn't want to face going to see my mother. But it was my turn because my sister had been going to the hospital for a long time. One day, I was hanging out on the couch and there was a knock on the door. It was my sister and my cousin. I opened the door and my sister clocked me in the face.

"Why are you lying? Why didn't you tell me Mommy died?" I didn't know she had died. But I had to cover my lies. "I didn't want to hurt you," I told her.

We had the funeral a week later. My father, who was absent from our lives most of the time, decided to show up. He got in the limo and said, "I heard my boy is going to be a prizefighter." Then he laughed at me, like it was a joke. I didn't say anything to him, but I didn't like the fact he had smiled when he said it, like, "Yeah, right, you're going to be a fighter."

I went back to the apartment after the funeral and I began a robbing spree. That was the way I handled my pain. I hooked up with an old friend of mine and we started robbing houses using master keys that we had. We did that for a few days and then my friend confronted me.

"Give me the fucking keys, Mike. Get the fuck out of here and go back upstate with the white people. You don't need this, this shit is for me. I'm out here in these streets, man. You go back upstate with the white people who love you."

Everywhere I went, my friends would say, "Mike, yo, are you crazy? What the fuck are you doing out here, man?" They did not want me in Brooklyn. And all the guys who did that, they're all dead now, they all got killed. I said, "I came to see you!" "No, man, not here. We ain't doing shit out here."

I don't know what was going through my head then. I guess I got caught up in my robbing ways, caught up with that easy money. It had been a long time since I had a couple thousand bucks in my hand. We were all piss-poor up at Cus's house. Cus kept calling me, asking me when I was coming back. I'd say, "I'll be back soon but I have to do one more thing." And it really wasn't that.

Then I got a visit from my upstate social worker. I don't know whether Cus put her up to it or she did it out of the goodness of her heart. Or maybe Cus was putting the word out through some boxing buddies down there. The thing you have to understand is that I didn't even understand how I got on this ride with this guy but he wouldn't let me get off. People make a big thing about Mike Tyson, he did this and that. Look, I'm a product of somebody who was on my ass, that's what I'm a product of. Somebody who was on my ass so much that his way became my way of life, and now he's dead and this is still my way of life.

I went back up to Catskill. Cus saw how shook up I was and he sat me down and told me how he had felt when his father died. He told me that he was left alone in the house and his father was suffering and screaming all night long and Cus couldn't do anything about it. He couldn't call a doctor because back then the only house calls Italians could get were some Italian guy who came on a donkey and brought a box that had something like castor oil in it. Cus couldn't leave the house because his father was in such agony, screaming, so he was tormented but he stayed by his side the whole night and then his father died in his arms.

Cus was a great storyteller and I was caught up, crying my eyes out. Then he said, "I talked to your mother before she died. She told me, 'I love my son, please take care of my son,' and I told her, 'I'm going to take care of your son, your son is the best fighter in the world.'"

A few years ago I saw a movie called *The Great Ziegfeld*. At one point Ziegfeld, this great theater impresario, is talking to a female performer who is distraught because someone close to her has died. "What do I do, what do I do, what do I do?" she cries. And Ziegfeld says, "Sing, sing!" Then he puts her out on the stage. I thought to myself, was Cus giving me a snow job when I got back from my mother's funeral? Did he really talk to my mom and tell her all that stuff? Or was Cus acting? He was a master of illusion. Everybody said I was Cus's shining light and Cus was my savior. I couldn't let this guy down; I couldn't have him think I'm a fucking tomato can.

Cus had shown me a tender side when he shared the story about his dying father, but right after that he goes, "It takes your strongest form of discipline to overcome such adversity, and once you overcome this adversity, everything else is smooth sailing."

Cus was in the process of getting guardianship over me when my mother got sick. I didn't know until recently that Cus had reached out to Bobby Stewart and asked him for his permission to adopt me. "What are you asking me for?" Stewart told Cus. He said, "You started this thing, I want your okay." Bobby thought it was a good idea so he gave Cus his blessing. Then Cus rushed over to the Town and Country Restaurant in Catskill, where the Greene County administrator, William Hagan, was eating dinner with some friends in an upstairs room. Hagan reluctantly went down to see Cus. He told Cus to sit down but Cus was too agitated to sit. "Bill, the wiseguys are talking telephone numbers to this kid Tyson. I've got to get guardianship." "Cus, relax, go home. I'll call you in twenty minutes." Hagan went back up to his table and his dinner companions asked him what was up. "It was Cus. He's worried about Tyson and he wants guardianship." Hagan's attorney told him to call Cus and have him come up to his office first thing in the morning. The next day Judge James Battisti pounded his gavel and Cus became my guardian.

Now that Cus was adopting me, I asked Camille if it would be all right if I started calling her "Mother." Cus was saying, "We're your family now, okay? And you're our boy now." I'd be sitting in the living room, reading, and Cus would call out to Camille. "Look at your black son, Camillee. He's going to bring pride and glory to this family."

This was the first time that I really had a father-son relationship. And, like most kids, I wanted to make my father happy. I noticed that when I won my fights with a spectacular knockout Cus was so happy he'd act like a little child. He'd call all his old friends, they're seventy, eighty years old, and he'd say, "Hey, I got this new kid, he's going to be champion. He's only sixteen now, but he'll be champ of the world." He would light up like a lightbulb. I enjoyed making him happy.

Now that I was reenergized to our mission, I really began to resent having to waste time in school. Every time I'd get in trouble, Cus would go to the school and talk to my high school principal, Mr. Stickler, and get me reinstated. One time one of my teachers, who was a real ignorant redneck, threw a book at me and called me intolerable. So I smacked the shit out the teacher in front of the whole class. Now they had to throw me out of school for good, I thought. But no. Cus grabbed me and we marched into the principal's office and we had a conference with the teacher. Cus thought he was F. Lee Fucking Bailey in that room. He paced up and down dramatically. He grabbed the book that was thrown at me.

"You maintain that you merely dropped the book and it hit Mike by accident," Cus said. "But a simple demonstration will show the falsehood behind your testimony." He dramatically dropped the book to the ground. "Gravity teaches us that the book falls harmlessly to the floor. The only way that the book could have hit Mr. Tyson was if it was intentionally propelled into the air and it violated Mr. Tyson's physical person."

I'm thinking to myself, "Shit, I can't even get myself kicked out of school." Cus sat down and smiled at me with total satisfaction. Mr. Stickler revoked the suspension and I was back in school.

Not for long, though. Two of the so-called Five Percenters among the black kids at school were taunting me one day, following me around and calling me "Mighty Joe Young." I tried to ignore them but these ignorant fools kept at it a little too long. I started chasing them and they ran into Assistant Principal Turek's office, thinking that it would be a sanctuary for them. "You ain't gonna do nothing," one of the guys said. *Smash.* I beat the living shit out of him while Turek was trying to hold me back, and then when I went after the other guy I tripped and Turek grabbed me. They had another meeting and this time everyone agreed that my time in high school had come to an end.

Once again, Cus called Bobby Stewart. "I know you're going to get mad, but I got to do something, with your permission. You've got to let Mike quit school because the only problems he has are in school. But I'm getting him a tutor so he'll get his degree." Stewart agreed. But Cus was disappointed. That was a bad day. My graduation from high school was going to be one of Cus's big accomplishments.

Cus's friend Joe Colangelo told me that he went over to the house the next day and Cus looked totally down. "What's the matter, what's going on?" Joe asked. "You might as well hear it from me because you'll find out anyhow," Cus said. "Mike quit school. I wanted him to finish high school and go on to college, Columbia-Greene or something. Look, Joe, I'm not going to be around forever. I want to make sure this guy is on a solid foundation so he can move along with his life."

Cus wanted to have a big party when I graduated. But I wanted to be famous. Cus gave me that bug. I don't think Cus knew the extent to which I had this obsessive personality. We had goals to accomplish, we had some revenge to go take care of, so we didn't have time for school. This was the real deal. But Cus was so sad when I dropped out. I recently told Joe Colangelo that the one thing I would change if I could do things over was that I would never have quit high school. I think about that all the time. It broke Cus's heart. Me getting a degree was so big for him. But it also was still all about Cus, because he couldn't throw his party and brag about me. That's all he wanted to do, brag about me.

Cus got me a tutor for a little while, one of my friends' mothers, but that didn't last long. I was just so tunnel-visioned. I wanted to fight. I could be training or sparring and instead I'm in here with this woman, doing *a, b, c, d* shit. Cus let me blow off the tutor because I was improving fast by then. Say today is the tenth. I'm fighting a tournament on the tenth, I'm fighting three fights. I might fight two fights today, but I'm fighting three fights that week. I finish that tournament, two days later I've got to go to Denver, I've got to fight in the tournament and I'm beating everybody. My whole life was fighting then, I didn't have time for school. None of those kids in the tournaments went to school either. I was interested in sparring the best fighters they could get, pro fighters, top fighters, I just wanted to fight everybody, box and box. That's how I was going to get better, by boxing these top guys and one day my day would come.

Even though I was the two-time national junior champ, Cus still had me fighting smokers all over the place. And when you went to these places, you had to be on top of your game. No one knows who your opponents are, you don't know how many fights they've had. You see fighters there you've never seen fight before. When you're watching them in the dressing room or watching them shadowbox, you don't say nothing, you just go, "Wow, he looks good." But when you see him fight, boom, he's a brilliant fighter. You say, "Wow, I know what I've got to do." I'd see two guys out there fighting to the death and in my sick, egotistical mind, I'd think, "I'm going to be the fight of the night." I won all the rest of the smokers I fought in, all by knockouts.

After the fight, Teddy would call Cus and then he'd get on the phone with me. "I heard you were spectacular out there, you were exciting, and people loved you." I said, "Yes, yes, I was. Everybody was applauding me, they gave me standing ovations." And he said, "See, I told you if you listened to me you would get that. Didn't I tell you that?" I'd be saying, "Yes, you did. Thank you, Cus, I love you, thank you." "You ain't seen nothing yet. You'll have people at your feet, just to be in your presence." He was talking crazy shit. I fed into it and believed it.

But we had a little bump in the road when Teddy and Cus started fighting.

While Cus was attending a fight in New Orleans, Atlas left town quietly. With Teddy gone, everyone in the house—me, Cus, Camille, and Jay Bright, a friend of Jim Jacobs who'd lived with them for years—all bonded. We had each other's back. To replace Atlas, Cus turned to Teddy's good friend Kevin Rooney. Rooney was still fighting but Cus had Kevin work with me, carrying out Cus's orders like Atlas had done. Kevin was a real disciple of Cus's. Kevin was a soldier, a simple guy, real opinionated but not a coward. Kevin's an awesome person and we got along great.

Teddy had left around November of 1982, so my next big test was a fight on December 10 in my first Seniors competition, the Amateur Boxing Championship. I had a tough, experienced opponent, Al "Chico" Evans, who was from Chicago. I was fighting splendidly and I won the first two rounds but in the third he tagged me as I was coming in and I went down. I got up again and I rushed at him, and he threw a right hand and I slipped, but they stopped the fight because of the two-knockdown rule. I was crushed. That was my first loss in a regulation fight. I stayed in my dressing room for a long time, just sobbing. I didn't understand the dynamics of the fight world back then. I was too selfish. "More, more, more, gimme, gimme, gimme championships." I liked the way the champion was treated after he won. So I wanted that feeling, I was addicted to that feeling of winning championships.

Cus wasn't concerned with the loss. He sat me down and went to the *Boxing Encyclopedia* and he showed me that Henry Armstrong got knocked out in his second pro fight. Harry Greb got knocked out in his first pro fight. "You know what happened?" Cus said to me. "These guys got knocked out, but they didn't quit. Nobody is ever going to be better than these fighters, so look what happened to them, they learned from experience."

While Cus could be supportive like this, most of the time he still drove me crazy. He let me get away with some stuff but then he'd give it to me out of the blue. Cus would rip into me, talking about my character. "You have no discipline. You could never reach the apex of what we're aiming for with this infantile behavior and conduct."

One time, he pushed my buttons a little too far and I started screaming, "I HATE THIS HOUSE! I WANT TO GET OUT OF HERE!" I don't even remember what Cus was complaining about. I'm thinking, "I didn't do shit. I'm doing everything right, and Cus just won't let up." But then Cus made a major mistake. I was still screaming, but I heard Cus talking to Jay.

"I got him," Cus gloated.

That was it. It was like I had peered behind the curtain and seen the Wizard of Oz for what he was. From then on, I just played along. I wouldn't let him get me upset. I knew that was the purpose. I knew he was fucking with me for no reason. I was hip to his game now.

9

I f 1959 was a horrible year for Cus—Floyd losing his crown, Cus losing his manager's license and being forced into a perp walk—1960 was starting out just as bad. Early in January his attorneys appealed the order to revoke his license. Besides arguing that Cus was now deprived of his "sole means of livelihood," Julius November and Edwin Schweig painted a saintly picture of Cus. "Your petitioner has consistently aided young and deserving fighters by furnishing them with money, shelter, and the other necessities of life, all at his own cost and expense, and without reimbursement."

They also argued that Cus "was harassed on all sides, was before the District Attorney's Office of New York County on various occasions, and . . . that there was never any question of the honesty and integrity of the fight itself and . . . no evidence of any crime in connection thereof." Finally, they blamed the press. "Many articles were written in the daily press to incite this Commission against your petitioner."

On January 26, Justice Aron Steuer issued his determination. He wrote that since Charlie Black was a licensee of the commission, they could not ban Cus from consorting with one of their own licensees. He threw out the charge of failure to file a manager's report, but he upheld the three most serious charges, including the determination that Cus "deliberately failed to attend at the investigation and defied the mandate of the commission to do so." Cus was sunk.

Two weeks later, Cus was rocked when New York State attorney general Louis Lefkowitz brought an action to dissolve Floyd Patterson Enterprises, a corporation in which Floyd was two-thirds owner and Cus one-third. The attorney general went after Cus on the same charges that had brought down Norris's empire. "Acting principally through D'Amato, Patterson Enterprises became party to a continuing conspiracy and arrangement to gain and maintain a monopolistic grip on the World's Heavyweight Boxing Championship." In detailing Cus's arrangement with TelePrompTer, Lefkowitz revealed that Patterson and D'Amato were both voted a place on the TelePrompTer payroll, along with Sugar Ray Robinson. Lefkowitz cited all the attempts that Cus had made to foist his friends as managers for Floyd's opponents and noted Charlie Black's move to bring Fat Tony Salerno into the Johansson fight's promotion. Certainly Black, at least, was nothing more than a conduit for the D'Amato/Patterson interests. In its decision dated October 13, 1959, rendered in connection with its inquiry into the conduct of the first Johansson fight, the NYSAC said of Black: "Charlie Black is D'Amato's trusted adviser and go-between. Whenever there is a Patterson fight, Black appears on the scene either with a part in the promotion or in the boxer management. Black apparently has no occupation. He is friendly with Tony Salerno and has known him for 25 years; has known Trigger Mike Coppola for 25 years, and Velella for a good many years."

These arguments were compelling enough to have a judge order the dissolution of Floyd Patterson Enterprises. All these legal battles were having an adverse effect on the rematch between Floyd and Ingo. Johansson began to tell the press that he was about to defend his title with other opponents. Cus was worried that he had become a distraction, so he signed a consent decree with the NYSAC that he would never apply for a manager's license again.

Meanwhile, the situation surrounding the promotion of the rematch was getting more and more bizarre. Remember that Vince Velella, who was the lawyer and front man for Fat Tony, controlled

Rosensohn Enterprises, whose only asset was the contract to promote the rematch. Bill Rosensohn, the disgraced promoter of the first fight, was holding on to his one-third interest, which had a $25,000 lien on it from Jim Norris, for the loan he had fronted young Bill when they were plotting to take over the boxing business. Velella had been indicted for perjury when he testified in front of D.A. Hogan's grand jury, so he decided to cash in on the stock of Rosensohn Enterprises. At the beginning of December 1959, a group of very prominent New York businessmen, including Angier Biddle Duke, who was an heir to the vast American Tobacco fortune and a distinguished diplomat for President Truman, expressed interest in buying out Rosensohn Enterprises. When Velella asked for $325,000 for "his" two-thirds share, the businessmen walked away.

But three weeks later, the stock was sold at a considerably lower price to a most disreputable group headed by the controversial lawyer Roy Cohn. Here's where it gets interesting. Cohn first came to prominence when he was on the prosecution team in the famous espionage trial of Ethel and Julius Rosenberg, the case that Cus was obsessed with. It was Cohn's direct examination of David Greenglass, Ethel's brother, that was instrumental in convicting and executing the married couple. Years later, Greenglass claimed that he was encouraged to lie on the stand by the prosecution to protect his family.

One of the people who took notice of the young Cohn was J. Edgar Hoover, the director of the FBI, who convinced Senator Joseph McCarthy to hire him as his chief counsel in McCarthy's congressional witch hunts against Communists in the United States. He went from going after Commies to hunting homosexuals with crazy claims that the Communists abroad had been obtaining U.S. government secrets from closeted homosexuals in exchange for not outing them. Cohn and Hoover even convinced President Eisenhower to sign an executive order in 1953 that banned homosexuals from being employed by the federal government. The irony of all this was that both Cohn and J. Edgar were closeted homosexuals themselves!

So Cohn's group, Feature Sports, went about buying up the

Rosensohn Enterprises stock. They paid Rosensohn $78,000 for his one-third share. Rosensohn was supposed to split the $53,000 profit from the sale with Norris but the multimillionaire never asked for his share once his $25,000 was paid back. Rosensohn took his presumed windfall and, after testifying before a Senate subcommittee, faded into obscurity selling dry-cleaning equipment and hooking up some Chicago hospitals with rental TVs for their patients. The last we heard from Rosensohn, speaking of Cohn, was, "I have not yet been paid in full, but I hope to be."

When it came to buying "Velella's" two-thirds share of the company, Cohn paid less for the two-thirds than he did for Rosensohn's one-third. Cohn, it turned out, had a relationship with Fat Tony and would go on to represent him for the next twenty years. In his biography of Cohn, the journalist Nicholas von Hoffman speculated that Cohn was fronting for Fat Tony. "The in-the-know sporting bloods of the time suspected that the reason for this transfer of the ownership of the contract was because Fat Tony, who had promoted the first of the Patterson–Johansson fights, was fast developing a reputation which made it impossible for him to continue to have such a conspicuous position in an activity licensed and supervised by various government bodies. The Roy-Tony relationship was to last many years, and it may be that this transaction was a paper-only deal to accommodate a friend, although Bill Fugazy says they were ordinary business ventures." Maybe they were both. What wasn't up for dispute was the hatred that Cus had for Cohn. He despised him for his work against the Rosenbergs and his Commie witch hunts, and soon Cohn would give him more reasons.

Meanwhile, Cus and Floyd's relationship was deteriorating. The main reason for that was the underhanded behavior of their lawyer, Julius November. November's advice to Cus that he didn't have to answer the subpoenas of the attorney general and the NYSAC made Cus look terrible, and it led to both his arrest and the suspension of his manager's license. Robert Boyle told us that November "drove the wedge" between Cus and Floyd and then "wormed his way into Patterson."

One of the things November did was to fire Floyd's ghostwriter, Arthur Mann, who was among Cus's champions in the press. Floyd got his book deal before the loss to Ingo, and when Mann handed in his manuscript, an associate of November's shared portions of the book with Patterson, who suggested that it be retitled *Cus D'Amato's War Against the IBC*. November immediately fired Mann and hired *New York Post* writer Milton Gross, who was not a fan of Cus's. November even tried to remove Floyd's account of his relationship with Cus but Patterson overruled him.

So we can get a good fix on their relationship at the time by looking at Patterson's book *Victory over Myself*: "As much as I dislike thinking it or even discussing it, my manager has been a suspicious man. Undoubtedly he had some reason to be, but over the years Cus allowed his suspicions about the IBC and his fight against its president, Jim Norris, to warp his thinking. Without question, it also warped my career." Floyd claimed that his loss to Ingo made him furious and convinced him to take control of his life. "Nobody went down with me those seven times that I went down to the canvas. A fighter walks alone and fights alone. If I could be successful the next time, I promised myself I'd be my own man. The mistakes would be mine, the decisions mine. I had to be defeated to learn that. Ingemar made me think for myself. That's an awfully painful thing, especially for somebody who always had somebody else to do his thinking for him.

"Until Ingemar knocked me out, Cus was my mind, more or less. I had no reason to doubt anything he did or said, because every minute of my relationship with him I was like a son being guided by his father. Eventually, the son grows up. Inevitably he begins to think more and more for himself. Occasionally something happens that makes the boy become a man before it was intended. It is always a shock to the father, but after a while the father becomes resigned that that, too, is the way of life. It seems to me that's about the most accurate way to sum up what has happened in my relationship with my manager. Nominally, at least, Cus continued to be what he always was, but I tried to show him that too many things had happened for me to allow myself ever to be completely in anyone's control again. I was Cus's boy but in defeat and confusion I became my own man. This is a difficult thing to discuss, because I never want to make it appear that I'm deliberately trying to hurt Cus. I was hurt very badly and maybe inadvertently by him. But whatever he did, I know he thought he was doing it solely for my benefit."

Then he expressed misgivings about how the London fight was handled, horror at Cus's attempt to make Ingo use his friend Davidow as manager, and disbelief when Fat Tony's name cropped up. "Salerno was a gangster, Velella was his lawyer, Erickson and Beckley were gamblers with police records. I kept asking myself; what could they have had to do with the fight or the promotional with me or my manager? I began to ask Cus questions, 'Is all of this true?' 'I was only trying to protect your interests,' he'd tell me. 'I had nothing to do with Salerno, Erickson and Beckley.' . . . I began to see that maybe Cus had been taken by his friends. I didn't mistrust Cus then, but I did begin to develop a mistrust in the people around him, for whom Cus always did favors. The thing that bothered me most, of course, was that some of the dirt which had been uncovered about the promotion had to rub off on me.

"These were the things I kicked around in my mind in all those black months between the first and second Ingemar fights. In the meantime, I wasn't seeing Cus as often as I did before I lost the title. Maybe Cus understood that for a lot of that time I wanted to be alone. Much of the time too, Cus was away for one reason or another. Maybe he had a lot to think about too. Certainly I gave him a few things to think about when I began to assert myself more and more. In the beginning he found it difficult to accept my new attitude. We argued a bit, but I explained to him that certain things were inevitable. Little by little I had to begin depending more upon my own decisions and it just happened that the jolt of the Johansson defeat hastened the process. Let me say here too, so that nobody gets any other ideas, that as long as I keep fighting, Cus will continue to be my manager. I listen to any suggestions he makes and if they are good, I accept them, just as I accepted advice from my attorney, Julius November."

Look, it's not surprising that Patterson rebelled against Cus. Cus was an intimidating figure. And overbearing. Me and Floyd have two very different personalities. Cus can easily scare a person away.

Even though Cus wasn't in constant contact with Floyd, he was still functioning as his de facto manager behind the scenes. So he began butting heads with Cohn almost from the start. Cus always screwed the promoters on the ancillary rights. Floyd made over $600,000 from those rights for the first fight with Ingo, and the contract for the second fight had Ingo getting 20 percent of them and Floyd netting 50 percent after he paid TelePrompTer 30 percent of his share.

Roy Cohn didn't like getting shut out of the ancillary rights so he and his partner Bill Fugazy met with Cus in Cus's office before the rematch was signed. As much as Cus hated Cohn, he might have hated Fugazy equally. Fugazy was an arrogant Ivy League brat who became wealthy when he inherited the family travel business that his grandfather founded. He was married with five children but there were rumors going around that Cohn and Fugazy were lovers. Fugazy was a bit of a dandy. He wore custom-made Italian suits, got daily rubdowns at the segregated New York Athletic Club, and wore pink dinner jackets and white ruffled shirts to the fights he promoted. He also bragged about playing golf at restricted country clubs.

Fugazy started the meeting by requesting 15 percent of Patterson's earnings before they would give Floyd the chance to win back his crown. If Cus didn't relent to their demands, they planned to match Johansson with Archie Moore for the crown and freeze Patterson out. Cus was so infuriated that he threw the two promoters out of his office. Then Fugazy and Cohn went behind Cus's back to Patterson with a contract that called for 10 percent of Floyd's earnings. "I have had so much trouble with the bad elements in boxing and never gave up a piece," Cus told a reporter. "Do you think I'm going to change my mind now?"

Another time Cus had a lunch meeting with Cohn and Fugazy. The only reason Cus was even dealing with these snakes was that they had hired Fugazy's uncle, Jack Fugazy, who was a stand-up old-school boxing guy Cus liked, to run their promotional company. Jack was late for the meeting. When the waiter put a cup of coffee in front of him, Cus refused to touch it. And when Jack finally arrived and was served his own coffee, Cus said, "Jack, is that your coffee? I'll drink it. Jim Norris isn't trying to poison you."

On February 9, Cus found himself on trial in Special Sessions Court in New York City for failing to answer the attorney general's subpoena. Cus took the stand and testified that he didn't appear in Lefkowitz's office on the date he was subpoenaed because November had told him that he need not do so. He also claimed that he had never been physically served with the subpoena by an assistant attorney general because when he saw the man he "instinctively stepped aside" and never touched the document. His story didn't exactly resonate with the three-judge panel and he was found guilty two days later. On April 18, Cus was sentenced to a suspended thirty-day sentence and ordered to fork over $250 for his crime. Plus he was threatened with jail time if he took up association with the rematch.

Meanwhile, Floyd was in serious training at that old abandoned nightclub in Connecticut with only his trainer Danny Florio and his sparring partner and the rats to keep him company. "His controversial and de-licensed manager, Cus D'Amato, never comes near the inn and seldom calls on the phone," one newspaperman wrote. Floyd concurred. "Cus would call the camp at Newtown once or twice a week and I would speak to him if there was anything I had to tell him, but most of the time he'd be satisfied to talk to Danny. Toward the end of the training period he came up to camp and spent a few days, but it was not like it once had been between us," he wrote.

In June, a week before the fight, Cus broke his silence. He invited a *New York Times* reporter up to his apartment office. Cus explained that he had shunned interviews because "it might hurt the promotion." But he didn't see himself as a pathetic figure shunned by boxing. " 'I'm still keeping in touch with things in boxing,' he said, leaning against one of the two couches in his combination apartment and office just off Broadway in the Fifties. 'I don't have to be up there or talk to Floyd every day. I know what he's trying to do and he's making progress. That's enough for me. . . . After the fight, I'll climb into the ring as the crowd acclaims Floyd Patterson as the first heavyweight champion to regain his title.'"

Cus even had a good spin on his legal troubles. "I think it will make Floyd rise to the occasion and will help him. The trouble we've had could serve as an inspiration." Cus told the reporter that he would have to give up his goal of having three champions at once. "Still, he feels like a general who has lost a battle, but has a good chance of winning a war. 'I have a definite feeling for the military. Everything I've done has been based on military strategy. I've gone over all my plans in advance so that pressure would not alter a decision I had arrived at beforehand. Of course, in war, as in chess, you have to give up a piece or yield on some points to gain an objective.' Cus didn't have much to say about his war with the IBC except to note ironically, 'I was fighting the mob and I turned out to be the villain,' D'Amato said with a whimsical smile. Perhaps the whimsy comes from reading Confucius, which D'Amato uses to fill the many hours he is alone. He also likes to read factual war books, including the memoirs of Field Marshal Bernard Montgomery, another blunt-speaking individualist. Detective stories help D'Amato to unwind. His apartment office contains a bar, fight posters, portraits of fighters, a sink, faded tan wall-to-wall carpeting and a television set. D'Amato watches news programs and fights and perhaps an occasional cowboy picture on television. He stays with friends frequently and makes trips to the country on the average of three times a week. 'I don't like to be too predictable in my movements,' he says. Once his phone bills used to top $1500 a month as he kept track of developments in boxing in this country and abroad. The bills are still high as a result of collect calls from promoters or boxing figures seeking money. D'Amato tries to arrange help for those 'on his side' although he owes $100,000 including $47,000 in legal fees."

Two days later and a state away, Floyd was talking about Cus to a different *Times* reporter. "Since Cus D'Amato, Patterson's unfrocked manager, no longer was at hand to shatter the silences with his brainwashing chatter, training had to be quieter this time. 'Yes,' said Floyd, loyalty to Cus surging quickly to the surface. 'It's quieter without him. But a man can't have everything he wants. He has to sacrifice one thing to get another. Once he gets the other, he can call the turn just as he wants it.' His meaning was unmistakable. If he regains the heavyweight championship from the Smorgasbord Smasher, Patterson clearly intends to fight only in places where D'Amato will be acceptable as his manager."

WITH ALL THE ADVERSE PUBLICITY about boxing corruption peaking with the three separate New York investigations after the first Johansson fight, the federal government got in on the action. Estes Kefauver, a senator from Tennessee, was propelled to national fame when he went after the Mafia in televised hearings in the early 1950s. Now he convened his Senate Subcommittee on Antitrust and Monopoly and began what would be a four-year investigation of the influence that organized crime had on the sport. Kefauver didn't know much about boxing so he reached out to John Bonomi, Hogan's assistant district attorney in New York and the man who finally brought down Frankie Carbo. Bonomi became Kefauver's chief examiner and special counsel.

On the eve of the June 1960 hearings, Bonomi warned the public that Carbo still controlled boxing from behind bars. "Carbo boasts that he has friends in many high places and I know that many prominent people—including millionaire businessmen—have benefitted financially from Frank Carbo's control of boxing. Reports of payoffs of boxing writers have reached the subcommittee and they obviously deserve full and further investigation," he told a *Cavalier* magazine writer who profiled him.

"Bonomi won't reveal his strategy to anyone but Kefauver. 'I don't want to sound paranoid,' he told a friend, 'but you never know who you can't trust.' Then he stared out at the Capitol dome for a long moment thoughtfully. 'When you're dealing with such influential racketeers and immoral tycoons, sometimes it's a damn good idea to be a little paranoid.' He stood up and carefully locked his files for the night. 'Just a little paranoid,' he concluded with a good-humored smile." Influential racketeers and immoral tycoons—sounds like he was fighting the same two guys Cus was.

On June 14, six days before the rematch, Kefauver opened his hearings with a mission statement. "In recent years criminal investigations in New York have led to the conviction of Frank Carbo and Gabriel Genovese for undercover boxing activities and the exposure of Anthony (Tony Fats) Salerno, as the financier of the first Johansson vs. Patterson heavyweight championship match. A west coast probe resulted in the indictment of Carbo, Frank (Blinky) Palermo, and others for an allegedly extortive attempt to control the welterweight title. These investigations indicated that many boxing promoters and managers were in league with the underworld figures I have mentioned. I directed the subcommittee staff to determine if the underworld, together with certain powerful figures in professional boxing, were engaged in a continuing conspiracy to monopolize professional boxing."

The opening testimony centered on rigged matches and bribes that Jake LaMotta received so he could get a shot at the middleweight title. But later that year Kefauver was going to go mano a mano against both Frankie Carbo and Jim Norris.

THREE DAYS BEFORE THE REMATCH, Cus showed up at Floyd's open sparring session at his camp and took questions from the press. He did it openly because Connecticut was outside New York's jurisdiction. He claimed that he still spoke frequently to Floyd and that he was convinced Floyd would regain his crown, because Johansson was "afraid of him." But after the workout ended and Floyd took reporters' questions, Cus lurked in the background. "Cus is my manager," Floyd said. "He handles business matters. But in all my fights I have never once looked to my corner for advice."

Howard Cosell interviewed Floyd the day before the fight and saw "rage" in Floyd's eyes. This time it was personal for Patterson. He had stewed for months watching Ingo do all the talk shows and act arrogantly, displaying his Hammer of Thor right hand. Ingo was like the Swedish Joe Namath, and he was preening on TV and enjoying the spoils of the crown with an outgoing personality that Floyd didn't possess. Floyd wanted to train like a monk, and for years he had retreated to his camp for months on end, even when he wasn't fighting. But now he was summoning up the rage that he didn't realize he possessed.

Ingo was an 8–5 favorite. Many reporters including *Sports Illustrated*'s Martin Kane picked Johansson to retain his crown. The fight was held at the Polo Grounds, a huge baseball stadium where the New York Giants played. Cohn and his boys put on a totally amateurish production. Thousands of people smashed down gates and rushed past the inadequate security force to get in for free. There were fistfights all over the place.

Cus was sitting six rows from ringside nervously fingering his black homburg hat in his hands. In the second round when Ingo landed a right hand to Floyd's noggin, Cus winced and bit his lip. Thirty seconds before the round ended, Cus grabbed his neck as if he was choking. Then over the next two rounds, Cus's body moved with each punch, as if to project his elusiveness up to Floyd in the ring, and his feet, under his seat, were doing a version of the Ali shuffle.

It was a pretty uneventful fight until the fifth round. Early in the round, Floyd snuck in a left hook that put Johansson down. He was up by eight but pretty disoriented. Floyd stalked him and set him up with a few body blows. When his guard came down, Floyd delivered a picture-perfect left hook that sent Ingo to sleep. During the entire ten count his left leg was shaking violently. As soon as Johansson went down, Cus sprang from his seat. He crawled over the press seats, calling out, "Floyd, Floyd, I'm over here!" Patterson didn't hear him because of the bedlam in the ring. Cus waited until the rush of photographers finished their shots and their eyes met. Then Cus went back to his friends in the sixth row. "I told you he can punch," he crowed. "Now they all know he can punch."

Meanwhile, Cosell was in the ring, doing radio interviews. He wanted to talk to Ingo but he was still on queer street. He grabbed

Whitey Bimstein, Johansson's trainer. "For God's sake, Whitey, is he dead?" "The son of a bitch should be," Bimstein said. "I told him to look out for the left hook."

The next day, Floyd met the press at the Hotel Commodore. Floyd was seated, with Cus standing right behind him, his hands on Floyd's shoulders. Floyd said he fought with "detached viciousness," which must have pleased Cus. When he was asked if he considered this the high point of his life, he smiled smugly. "Of course I do. Do you want to know why? I'll tell you. Nothing you fellas can write about me from now on will be accepted by the public. . . . I'm the champ again. A real champ this time." Then a reporter set Floyd up with a softball question. "Floyd, was that punch you knocked out Ingemar with the hardest punch you ever hit someone with?" "I can't answer that one because I'd have to go around and ask the others guys that I hit." Cus went wild with glee and grabbed Floyd from behind and shook him triumphantly. Then another writer asked Floyd who had been the greater influence in his recapturing the title: Joe Louis, who had given him some advice on fighting Ingo, or his manager, Cus. As the question was asked, Cus leaned over and whispered in Floyd's ear. And Floyd dutifully repeated those words. "Floyd Patterson."

Floyd's performance made a lot of the hostile press eat some major crow. Dan Parker wrote, "There is no explanation of Patterson's strange showing in the first fight or of Manager Cus D'Amato's remarkable statement on TV while his warrior was still semi-conscious from the knockout, that Floyd would be the first heavyweight ever to regain the title in the return bout. This calm prediction isn't exactly what one would expect from a manager whose heavyweight champion has just lost the title. But whatever it seemed like then, it turned out to be much better prophesying than your deflated Daniel has ever been guilty of." Even Jimmy Cannon gave Floyd his due.

The Cus haters took Floyd's victory as an excuse to bash Cus again. Arthur Daley, from *The New York Times*, opened his column, "Sometime in the distant future, when Floyd Patterson joins Joe Louis as one of boxing's elder statesmen, he is likely to pause long enough to think back to the turning point in his career. When cantankerous Cus was refused a managerial license in New York, Patterson had to go it alone. It was exactly what he needed. Suddenly he discovered that he didn't need all that over-protection, all that mama-knows-best direction and all that brainwashing. Floyd struck off for himself and gained his manhood."

But Roger Kahn, writing in *The Nation*, savaged Cus and worried that he was back now that Floyd had regained his crown. "[D'Amato] has plans on exacting vengeance on his oppressors, real and imagined, which presumably will include more contracts under duress. He no longer talks of establishing a utopia for fighters and fight managers. His campaign now seems designed solely to restore the power and the glory of D'Amato."

But Cus was working behind the scenes to restore the power and the glory of Patterson. He convinced Jackie Robinson and TV superstar Ed Sullivan to cochair a testimonial dinner for Floyd on July 21 with all proceeds going to the Wiltwyck School for Boys, Floyd's alma mater. It was a lavish affair in the grand ballroom of the Hotel Commodore. Cus packed the dais with celebrities including Rocky Marciano, Jersey Joe Walcott, Barney Ross, New York mayor Robert Wagner, and Branch Rickey. When you look at the seating chart, it is like analyzing the secret power struggles in the Kremlin. Floyd, Cus, and Howard Cosell sat on the dais, along with Roy Cohn, who claimed to have sold one-third of the seats that night. Teddy Brenner, Ned Irish, and the rest of the surviving IBC crew at Madison Square Garden were exiled to table 36. Yet sitting prominently at table 3 were Mr. and Mrs. Charlie Black. Cus would hold grudges for years over the minutest slight and yet Charlie Black was somehow still golden in his eyes.

Cus had a bigger surprise than Black's attendance. At the dinner, he presented Floyd with a crown. A literal crown. He had asked jewelers to submit designs. "It's going to be solid gold," D'Amato told *Sports Illustrated*. "And it will have genuine jewels in it. I don't know what it will cost—maybe $20,000 maybe even $35,000. I have no idea and I don't care. Floyd gave me the greatest night of my life." Cus settled on a 14-karat gold crown studded with 174 diamonds,

248 rubies and sapphires, and 250 pearls. It had nine crests, and on the highest one was a golden globe to signify Floyd's domination across the planet. There were also a couple of jewel-studded boxing gloves. Floyd's initials, in diamond letters, were set into the front of the crown. There was even a band made out of ermine trim to assure a proper fit. "When the crown is presented I want to hear loud oohs and ahhs," Cus said. Cus was so proud of that crown. He showed me the picture many, many times. And he told me that it had cost him $250,000. I guess he was adjusting for inflation.

Only one other present meant as much, if not more, to Floyd. It was a cablegram of blessing from Pope John XXIII. To the Catholic convert, that meant the world.

A week after the dinner, Cus, or, as the mortgage showed, Camille, went on a slightly smaller spending spree. On July 27, 1960, there was a transfer of property between Creste Sicignano (a.k.a. Oreste Suignano), a Catskill resident, and Camille Ewald, shown residing at 50-05 43rd Avenue in Woodside, Queens—Cus's love nest. In consideration of one dollar ($1), Camille obtained the old Thorpe estate on the Hudson in Catskill, which included a huge Victorian manor and a carriage house. Now, this is some Mafia comrade stuff right there. You know that, right? That dollar signifies their friendship. That's what you say so you can get a hit, you say, "I'll sell you my house for a dollar."

Camille was probably used as a front. That secret little log cabin in Fishkill that was revealed in the NYSAC hearings—that house was in Cus's brother Tony's name. I think that buying that house in Catskill and putting it in Camille's name was all about eventually getting fighters in there. Everything was about fighting for Cus.

The shine wasn't even off Floyd's crown before Cohn pissed off both Floyd and Cus. Cohn and his crew announced that the third Floyd–Ingo fight would go off in L.A. on November 1, 1960. Only problem was they told everybody except Floyd and Cus. Floyd heard it announced on TV and he vowed not to fight on that date. "You'd think that since I'm the champion that the promoters, Feature Sports Inc., would be polite enough to please ask me—that's all. The guy who is behind all this, I think, is Roy Cohn. He thinks I'm an insolent dumb backwoodsman. Before the last fight, my lawyer, Julius November, asked Cohn if I shouldn't see the fight contract. And Cohn said, 'Floyd? Can he read?' You think I'm going to let those people come to me and tell me I'm going to fight November 1?" Cohn claimed that Floyd's statement was "ridiculous" and that he had the highest regard for him. But Floyd wasn't through. "In New York Cus is my 'adviser,'" Patterson said. "I'm doing the talking. My eyes were opened after my defeat by Johansson. I watched the changed attitude of people toward me. When I lost they dragged out everything against me and Cus—gangsterism, hoodlumism, everything. Even though my name wasn't associated with all that bad publicity, the public might have put me with some of it. Therefore, I decided if I ever won the title back, I'd make the decisions. I'd see that it doesn't happen again. . . . Cus had faith and trust in the human race. Not that I haven't, but we have to be cautious nowadays. There are hoods in every walk of life. And we have been fooled many times in the past."

Now Cohn went out of his way to woo Patterson. The rumor was that Roy Cohn flipped November for a substantial cash payment and then November, who seemed to have his own designs on Floyd going back years, joined in the snow job and they both began to feed Floyd disinformation about Cus and his business dealings. Floyd and Cus never had a face-to-face argument but the stories began to make Floyd pull away from Cus. Then Cohn came up with the most Machiavellian scheme to befriend Floyd.

Cohn was very close to the Cardinal Spellman, the longtime cardinal of the Catholic Church in New York City. Spellman, like Cohn, was a closeted gay. His biographer, John Cooney, wrote that "in New York's clerical circles, Spellman's sex life was a source of profound embarrassment. There were stories about his seducing altar boys and choir boys. He had his favorites among handsome young priests and was known to have lovers outside the clergy." One of those lovers was a chorus boy in the 1942 Broadway show *One Touch of Venus* and the boy bragged about the affair to Dr. Alfred Kinsey's researcher C. A. Tripp. The chorus boy told Tripp that he had once asked Spellman how he could get away with such blatant acts as sending his limousine several times a week to pick up the boy and bring him to his apartment. Spellman replied, "Who would believe that?" Roy and Spellman were never lovers, though. When Spellman vacationed on Cohn's yacht he was accompanied by an escort he called Uncle Frank.

So Cohn enlisted Spellman in a religious seduction of Floyd. Cohn set up a dinner at the Stork Club, an exclusive club that was owned by Sherman Billingsley, a good friend of J. Edgar Hoover's and a rabid anti-Communist. Cohn invited his partner Bill Fugazy, J. Edgar Hoover, Cardinal Spellman, and a few other friends. He sat Floyd directly across the table from him, but he ignored Floyd all night and spent all his time joking and laughing with the cardinal. The next day Floyd saw Cus and he said, "Gee, I guess that Cohn's a good guy." "What do you mean?" Cus said. "Well, he was with the cardinal at this dinner and him and the cardinal were best friends." That dinner opened the door for Cohn to begin to wean Floyd away from Cus.

On December 5, 1960, Senator Kefauver gaveled the second round of his investigation into the underworld dominance of boxing. Three months before that, he had charged Jim Norris with "evasion and delay" in dealing with the commission. In September, Kefauver's office got an "anonymous" letter from a boxing insider. "Be assured that Jim Norris should not try and kid you that he is not connected with hoods. He has admitted that many times in N.Y., proudly. Blink [sic] Palermo and nobody else manages Sonny Liston. Barone [Liston's "manager"] is only a stooge and cover up. The haven for the boys has been in Chicago where they meet and get all the Wed. TV dates. It has been the [Apalachin] for them with Gibson and Norris head of it. They cornered the fight game and kept it among them. Their hope is for Liston to get title shot and win it then they have control again. . . . Keep punching, Anonymous."

This session's star witness was to be Frankie Carbo. Kefauver began with questioning the IBC's front man, Truman Gibson. Gibson was under indictment in the Jackie Leonard case and he must have thought that his fortunes would be enhanced if he lied his ass off and distanced himself from his co-defendants Carbo and Palermo.

From the minute he was called, he minimized Carbo's influence on the IBC. "Time and again, I told the panel Carbo had not been allowed to influence the IBC decisions and contests. . . . Nobody has ever told us, 'Pay a fighter x number of dollars' or a cheap or bargain price." "The only times the Carbo influence became an issue we discontinued our activity with the individuals." "We never cooperated with the more unseemly elements, although we did have to live with them."

But when Gibson was asked whether Carbo "controlled" or merely "influenced" most of boxing's managers and promoters he had to be candid. Palermo, Wallman, and Glickman were deemed "exceedingly friendly with and close to Carbo." When Lou Viscusi's name came up, Gibson had to qualify if he was Carbo-controlled. "The word 'controlled' in connection with Viscusi raises certain problems. Viscusi is certainly and has been friendly with Carbo over the years, and yet Viscusi perhaps typifies the way in which these managers operate. When it is to his advantage to make a fight with us, he will do so; and when it is to his advantage to go elsewhere, he will do that. For example, we had the Roy Harris fight in California with our arch enemy and arch foe, Cus D'Amato, the Floyd Patterson fight. At the time of the London–Patterson fight in Indianapolis, Viscusi was one of the representatives at the promoter's meeting that Cus D'Amato and Irving Kahn called in order to get a new promoting combine."

BONOMI: Are you not saying, Mr. Gibson, that even though he might have been Carbo controlled, he worked both sides of the fence?
GIBSON: Undoubtedly worked both sides of the fence.

And on the other side of that fence was Cus. Gibson brought up Cus when he cited managers who were "hostile" to Carbo. "It is not the numbers that are important, but the persons whom the manager or managers manage. The manager of a heavyweight champion, for example, would be worth 80 percent of all of the other managers in terms of importance to boxing. . . . The heavyweight division has been dominated by Floyd Patterson, Cus D'Amato. So that the majority of the money is in the heavier weight category."

Bonomi then probed Norris's decision to pay Kearns, Dempsey's former manager and Moore's manager, and Viola Masters, Carbo's girlfriend, goodwill salaries to keep a steady flow of boxers for their TV shows. Kearns, who hated Carbo, wound up getting $115,000 in payments, while Masters pulled in $45,000 to "counterbalance" the payments to Kearns. She got a few perks too. "At one fight in Chicago Norris gave Masters a mink stole as a token of his affection for Carbo," Gibson testified. Asked why Carbo's girlfriend had been hired instead of Carbo himself, Gibson said, "It looked a little bit better on our records, not ever considering the possibility of being called before a Senate investigative committee, to have Viola Masters down instead of Mr. Frank Carbo."

Rosensohn was called to testify and gave a mostly self-serving account of his short tenure as a boy promoter. He said that Fat Tony and Charlie Black were both close to Cus and that Salerno, Black, Cus, and Kahn pushed him out of his own company. Then he took one parting shot at the NYSAC, which had revoked his license. "I spent many hours before the commission and tried in every way to help them when it came to their rendering a final judgment which I had hoped would exonerate me for what I had tried to do. Instead, the State Athletic Commission, for reasons which are not entirely clear to me, suspended my matchmaker's license for 3 years. That is the end of the story." Then Senator Dirksen asked, "You have no dreams at the present time?" "I have dreams," Rosensohn replied. "But they are nightmares."

Gibson was called back to the stand to testify about the rising new star heavyweight Sonny Liston. He couldn't remember whether Palermo told him that he owned a piece of Liston but he did remember Palermo complaining that "his fighter Liston" never got plum TV fights and that was immediately rectified. Then chief investigator Bonomi raised an interesting connection.

BONOMI: Do you recall being present on September 27, 1960, when I interviewed Mr. Norris? And at that time do you recall that Mr. Norris said, in substance, that he was pushing Liston's career out of animosity toward Cus D'Amato? GIBSON: Well, I think too he said that and I think there are other factors. I think certainly at that time he would have liked to have had a championship or championship fights in Chicago. BONOMI: But about that time there was this rather bitter feud between the Chicago Stadium interests and Mr. D'Amato, was there not? GIBSON: Yes. That had lasted for quite a considerable time. BONOMI: And Mr. D'Amato, as Floyd Patterson's manager, was refusing to let Patterson fight for the IBC?

Gibson agreed that Norris was pushing Liston as a challenger to Floyd and Cus.

The talk turned to dollars. Gibson testified that in a good year, the IBC would gross $7 million and make $300,000 profit.

KEFAUVER: What kind of salaries do you fellows draw? GIBSON: Wholly inadequate, senator.

Gibson testified that Norris and Wirtz didn't take a salary. They made all their money from the huge gross of the company, not the paltry $300,000 net. "They had so many interlocking companies it would be almost impossible to ascertain net worth. One company would own another, it would own something else, so that by the time you end up you would be in the Bismarck Hotel after having started from the Chicago Stadium and you would never really know what company owns what, except that all the stock is owned by Mr. Wirtz and Mr. Norris. They had 16 companies just in the boxing business!" Of course, Gibson owned no stock.

A little over a year after these hearings Gibson decided to move on and meet with Wirtz to work out a compensation package. Before the meeting, Wirtz sent Gibson a letter claiming that Gibson owed the Chicago Stadium Corporation $6,000. That was too much, even for Gibson. He had spent years hiding Norris's criminal activity and wound up being indicted in L.A. and had nothing to show for his participation in the creation of the IBC. "My glory days as the nation's top boxing promoter were over. [Norris and Wirtz] hadn't made me, or Joe Louis for that matter, rich. Norris and Wirtz funneled profits in their stadium holdings, bypassing the IBC. I was paid less than ten thousand dollars a year, the deal I struck with Wirtz in 1949 setting my pay at $7200," he wrote in his memoir.

So he wrote Wirtz an amazing letter. "You refer to the $6,000. What about the balance which was due me but unresolved at the time of payment of the $6,000? . . . So, at our meeting, add all of this and not just the $6,000 to the agenda. You measure everything in money. You are probably correct since you have been so successful. What measure do you put on a man's life? Was your shrewd bargain, when we last met, your determination? I could not help but think then and now that I never knew Carbo before the organization of the IBC. I never cleared championships with him. I talked with him most infrequently. I certainly did not clear the Akins–Jordan fight with him. Someone did, and the fact that I didn't indicates who put me in the soup. While you are remembering things in the past, please also recollect that I didn't collect any of the profits (nor did Joe Louis, despite his agreement) from the split up of IBC operations from behind a nice insulated shield. I thought of all these things in your office. I would not have said or written them except for your last letter. So, at our meeting, let us include everything on the agenda."

Norris got a carbon copy of Gibson's letter at his home in Coral Gables, Florida. Gibson never heard from either of them again.

The committee went into closed, private session when Norris came in to testify. His attorney had previously told the committee that Norris was suffering from a very severe heart condition and that the strain of testifying might give him another heart attack. So they compromised by letting him take questions in executive session.

He began by answering some background questions. He was fifty-four, his parents were Canadians, and his greatest love was hockey. Then Senator Dirksen, from Illinois and no stranger to the Norris dynasty, began a series of puff questions designed to put Norris in the most favorable light. The good senator pontificated that talk of Blinky and Carbo being "associates" of this great business leader was flat-out wrong. Wasn't their association merely "nothing more than people with whom in that line of business you feel that you have to deal"? Norris took the line. "I never had a cup of coffee with Frank Carbo until I went to New York to try and run boxing. I am out of boxing now, so I have no intention of ever having another cup of coffee with Frank Carbo. It has embarrassed my family tremendously. It has embarrassed me with my horses, which I think, after hockey, is my second love. . . . I am not a hero-worshipper of hoodlums. I do not care any more for hoodlums than I am sure you do, Senator, and that is my position." One statement in that harangue that was probably true. Norris would have no intention of having a cup of coffee with Carbo in the future. They always drank whiskey.

Following up on Norris's claim that he despised hoodlums, Bonomi brought up Capone's main executioner, Sam "Golf Bag" Hunt. Norris admitted to a long-standing friendship. But he "was reputed to be, what you would say, a hoodlum. That was his reputation. . . . To me he was not that type or individual that he had been portrayed, and it was hard for me to believe that he did the things that he had been charged with."

Then Norris went into a bizarre characterization of Carbo. He painted the former hit man as an altruist to "fallen managers."

NORRIS: Different managers over the years have told me it is a well-known fact that a broken manager would go to Carbo and say, "I do not have room rent" or "I do not have any money to eat with" and Carbo might have $30 or $40 and would pull it out and say "Well, take some of it," and give them $10 or $20. **KEFAUVER:** You are not defending Carbo, are you? **NORRIS:** No, I am not, but I do not think that he has anywhere near the control that I have read in some of these witness' statements.

Bonomi then asked Norris about a bookie named Max Courtney, who had been hired by Norris at a salary of $2,000 a month, and paid a total of $76,000 to sell fight movies from the IBC library to TV stations. Did he sell any? "I think he sold a few, not very many," Norris answered. Bonomi noted that Gibson testified that he had no idea what Courtney did for the company. Norris replied that it was up to his partner Wirtz to know what Max did. There were too many interlocking companies for even Norris to "comprehend."

KEFAUVER: It is just a little strange that you would pay somebody $76,000 and nobody seemed to know what he was doing. **NORRIS:** I knew what he was doing, Senator, and that was selling fight pictures, which, I think, will be very valuable someday. I think we are just a little bit ahead of that market. **KEFAUVER:** What made you think he could sell fight pictures? He is a bookmaker. **NORRIS:** Well, I know Mr. Courtney quite well. He is very personable, very affable. He makes a very nice appearance.

Norris then revealed that he never placed a bet with Courtney and that Courtney still worked for Norris in their St. Louis corporation.

Bonomi then asked Norris to explain his quote in Grayson's column that Liston "is my fighter." He said that he told Grayson that he thought Liston could beat both Patterson and Ingo in the same ring on the same night. "And I said, 'He's my fighter,' meaning, and I have tried to explain it time and time again, meaning he was my candidate, the person I thought in my own mind, from just watching fighters and so forth, that might possibly be the heavyweight champion if he ever had the opportunity. And I was doing everything in my power publicity wise, talking to newspapermen, talking to the public, telling them what a great fighter I thought Liston was. Now that is exactly what I mean."

SENATOR LEVIN: You didn't mean to imply you owned him? **NORRIS:** I don't have 5 cents. I have never met Liston. I have never said hello to Liston. I have never shaken hands with him. **BONOMI:** You have met "Blinky" Palermo, haven't you? **NORRIS:** Very well, very well.

Then Bonomi went for the kill.

BONOMI: Do you recall that on September 27, when you were interviewed by me and Mr. Williams, you stated, in substance, that you were "hustling" Sonny Liston out of animosity toward Cus D'Amato, the manager of Floyd Patterson? **NORRIS:** That was one of my reasons. **BONOMI:** So, in other words, you were building up Sonny Liston as a heavyweight contender, through the IBC, is that right? **NORRIS:** I was trying to build Sonny Liston up because I thought he could box. I thought he had great possibilities. **BONOMI:** But you were pushing him? **NORRIS:** Yes. I mean legitimately. If I sat down with a newspaperman, and he would say, "How does the heavyweight situation look to you, there is nobody coming up, is there?" I would say, "The heck there isn't. There is a Sonny Liston that I think will be one of the greatest we have ever had." I mean in that type of way, any way I could do it, to help the fighter, publicity wise, or any other way, I was happy to do.

BONOMI: During that period, you could not get Patterson to fight for the IBC, could you? NORRIS: Could not get Patterson at all once I promoted the fight where he won the heavyweight championship. BONOMI: You wanted to build up Liston so that he might get a chance at the heavyweight championship and perhaps win it; is that right? NORRIS: Yes, that is correct.

BONOMI: He was an IBC fighter, of course? NORRIS: IBC fighter— BONOMI: He never appeared in any televised bouts for any other organization, did he, from 1958 to the present? NORRIS: There were no other organizations televising. PETER CHUMBRIS [SUBCOMMITTEE COUNSEL]: In other words, you had exclusive contracts with them? NORRIS: No, sir. Where was he going to box on television, if he did not box for our organization? We had the only two. BONOMI: But it was your understanding that Liston was "your fighter" in the sense that you were building him up through the IBC, is that right? NORRIS: Well, I had no agreement with anybody on that. I mean that I did it on my own.

BONOMI: Do you recall that on June 26 of 1959, Johansson won the world's heavyweight championship? NORRIS: Yes, sir. BONOMI: At that time, you were still engaged in this feud with Cus D'Amato, the manager of Floyd Patterson, were you not? NORRIS: No, I would not consider it a feud. BONOMI: Let us call it a disagreement. NORRIS: No. BONOMI: You could not secure Patterson for IBC bouts? NORRIS: I did not try. Once he showed no gratitude, every promise he made to me when I broke my neck to get Archie Moore for him, and where he won the heavyweight championship, he just walked away from me, turned his back on me. He made a lot of statements: I was a monopolist, I was this, I was that. He did not believe in television. And he did everything that he could to try and hurt me with the newspapermen. I just washed my hands of him. I had no contacts. I never asked him to box again for me. BONOMI: But anyway as of June 1959, Patterson was not fighting for the IBC, was he? NORRIS: Oh, no. He did not box for the IBC from the time he won the heavyweight championship.

Bonomi then began a line of questioning that got Norris to admit that he paid for the flight and expenses for NYSAC commissioner Helfand to go to Cuba to attend an IBC fight. Helfand was the same man who had actively pushed for Cus's licenses to be revoked.

BONOMI: Do you feel if the IBC paid considerable expenses for these State athletic commissioners, they would be indebted to the IBC? NORRIS: I certainly do not.

Finally, Bonomi had one last line of questioning for Norris. He asked the entrepreneur if he owned a racehorse named Mr. Gray. Norris said yes. "Frankie Carbo was known as Mr. Gray in boxing, was he not?" Bonomi asked. "Yes, sir. Some people called him that," Norris admitted. "Was he partly in your mind when you named the horse?" "Possibly facetiously," Norris said. "Was he a good horse?" Bonomi asked. "He wasn't worth a nickel," Norris responded.

Norris's testimony made all the sports pages but it took the *New York Mirror* columnist Dan Parker to point out an inconsistency. He noted that Norris testified that Carbo was merely an acquaintance but that in an Eddie Borden column from 1953, Norris was quoted as saying, "Frankie [Carbo] is a friend of mine. If I have to give up his friendship for the sake of promoting boxing, I would just as well as give up boxing."

The hearings brought out some fascinating tidbits that tied up some loose ends. Detective Bernhard, an undercover officer from New York who was working on Bonomi's task force to arrest Carbo, testified that while he and his partner were in a restaurant in D.C. watching a fight with Carbo, Palermo, and Billy Brown, Carbo said that Norris was upset and told him that Liston was his fighter. Then Carbo told the group that he had a fight in New Orleans between Frankie Ryff and Ralph Dupas. Carbo said, "[Willie] Ketchum [a prominent manager] got greedy and took $1,000. I called Charlie Black and got that thing straightened out." So Charlie Black was close to Carbo as well as Fat Tony.

The same undercover cop was in Chicago for the testimonial dinner honoring Jim Norris on March 23, 1958. He reported that Carbo was in room 1150 of the Palmer House, registered under Blinky's name. Right down the hall was a room occupied by none other than Fat Tony Salerno. "There was constant contact between Carbo's room and Salerno's room," Detective Bernhard testified. The plot thickens.

The hearings wound down with the appearance of organized-crime members. Blinky feigned illness and missed the proceedings but John Vitale, who allegedly had a piece of Liston, was called. He had over twenty arrests on his record, including two on suspicion of murder. But after every question, he refused to answer on the grounds that it might incriminate him. Finally, one of the senators posed a question.

KITTRE: Mr. Vitale, you have refused to answer the questions asked of you up until now. Apparently you feel they would involve you in some of these situations described here. Would you care, on the basis of your general knowledge of boxing, to give the subcommittee some of your own thoughts as to how to eliminate underworld racketeering and monopoly in the field of boxing? VITALE: I take the fifth amendment. What a question!

Now it was time for the headliner. Mr. Gray. The Uncle. The Ambassador himself. Frankie Carbo, looking dapper but a little wan, strode into the room. Kefauver began by telling Carbo's lawyer, Abraham Brodsky, that Carbo would qualify as an "expert witness" on the sport of boxing.

Carbo began by answering some personal questions. He said that he was fifty-six and that he lived in Miami. Then it was, "I respectfully decline to answer the question on the grounds that I cannot be compelled to be a witness against myself." They asked him about his associations, if he had threatened any witness before the commission, on and on, and his answer was always the same. The Fifth. Then Kefauver gave him one last chance to answer anything and he conferred with Brodsky.

CARBO: There is only one thing I want to say, Mr. Senator.

KEFAUVER: Yes. CARBO: I congratulate you on your reelection. KEFAU-VER: That is very nice of you. I appreciate that, Mr. Carbo.

Carbo then asked for an orange juice because he was diabetic. CARBO: I had no breakfast. KEFAUVER: All right. We are about to excuse you, Mr. Carbo. CARBO: I mean I am trying to hold on as long as I can. BRODSKY: He's a pretty sick man, as Mr. Bonomi knows. KEFAU-VER: Very well. You look like a pleasant man, Mr. Carbo. CARBO: Thank you. BRODSKY: He is.

And the multiple-time murderer got up and walked out the door.

The reaction to the hearings was predictable. There was lots of moral indignation about how the sport had been infested by these mobsters. But only Murray Robinson, in the *New York Journal-American*, took a more cynical view of the hearings. In an article headlined "NOW Ex-Champs Tell Us!" he put these latest hearings into perspective.

"At the hearings Tunney, Dempsey, Louis, and Marciano apparently went along with the widespread and erroneous belief that hoodlum control of boxing is a fearful new development, like intercontinental missiles, or something. They should know better than that. The mobbies got into boxing in the early 1920's and they've been in it ever since. 'Mr. Gray' didn't get his manicured mitts into the middleweight title until 1935 when Eddie (Babe) Risko won it.

"Only Cus D'Amato, to give the Svengali his due and not examining his motives too closely, spoke out against the mobsters while managing a heavyweight champion. And Floyd Patterson still sounds off against Sonny Liston's hoodlum connections, even though it may be because he just doesn't fancy fighting that behemoth."

A few weeks after Kefauver finished his hearings, the real action shifted to L.A. when the trial of Carbo, Palermo, Gibson, Sica, and Dragna began in January 1961. Jackie Leonard, who was the target of Carbo and his henchmen, was so afraid of testifying in open court against these defendants that in November 1959 he tried to take Blinky up on his bribe offer from August of that year. He was ready to cash in for his silence. Leonard sent his wife, who had relatives in

Pennsylvania, to meet with Palermo. A deal seemed to have been struck—Leonard and his wife would leave the country in return for $25,000 in cash. But the deal was never consummated and the trial began.

Carbo found himself in the courtroom of Judge Ernest Tolin, who, unlike Kefauver, didn't characterize Carbo as "a pleasant man." Carbo was the only defendant who didn't testify. Leonard and Nesseth withstood hostile cross-examinations. An interesting sidelight was that both Gibson and Daly flew to New York during recesses in the trial to confer with Harry Markson at Madison Square Garden. MSG had said it had scrubbed out all vestiges of IBC corruption, so why were they meeting with Markson? Cus thought that he had the answer.

One of the highlights of the trial was the testimony of Don Jordan, the boxer who everyone wanted a piece of. He proved that he wasn't working with a full deck when he testified on Blinky's behalf. When he was asked to recall the specifics of a conversation he'd had with the defendant Louie Dragna, Jordan said, "Roses are red, violets are blue, besamany kulo y alva fong ku." Or that's how it was transcribed. But he might have actually said, *"Bésame el culo y vaffanculo,"* Spanish and Italian for "Kiss my ass and fuck off." That was most likely lost on all who heard it, and the rest of his testimony proved to be the exact opposite of his previous testimony before the grand jury. It didn't matter, though. On May 30, 1961, the jury brought in a verdict of guilty all around.

But then on June 11, Judge Tolin died unexpectedly. The defendants moved for a new trial but it was denied. On December 2, 1961, the replacement judge, George Boldt, announced the sentences: Mr. Gray got twenty-five years in prison and a $10,000 fine. Blinky got fifteen years and had to pay a $10,000 fine. Poor Truman Gibson got a five-year sentence that was suspended but he had to pay $10,000 also. Sica got twenty years in prison and a $10,000 fine, and Dragna got five in the slammer with no fine. Everyone posted bail except for Carbo, who was immediately sent to Alcatraz. Norris, at home in Coral Gables, ponied up most of Gibson's legal fees, including most of the $60,000 that was paid to an extorter, who had posed as a government agent and told Gibson's team that he had documents showing that the Department of Justice wanted to dismiss the indictment against Gibson. The exchange was made and Gibson's lawyers introduced the documents in evidence, only to learn that they were forged. The extorter wound up in a federal penitentiary. Norris did not pay his legal bills.

There was some fallout from the trial. After Carbo and Palermo's ruse of turning Liston over to Pep Barone while they were on trial backfired, they then coerced Liston to announce that he would persuade Barone to release him from his contract just out of friendship. "This would be no more improbable than if Dan Topping, co-owner of the Yankees, gave Mickey Mantle his freedom without a cent of recompense for the investment Mickey represents to the club," Dan Parker wrote. "The Liston case presents a powerful argument in favor of Federal control of boxing. If State Commissions can't recognize the danger to the sport involved in letting the undercover criminal element dictate proceedings, it is time their power was limited to licensing ring personnel and weighing the fighters."

THE THIRD FLOYD–INGO SHOWDOWN was set for Miami Beach on March 31, 1961. Floyd agreed to fight there only if the Cohn group would post $10,000 to guarantee unrestricted seating at the arena. At that time much of Florida was still segregated. Meanwhile, the tensions between Cus and Cohn's group began to boil over. Cohn and Fugazy forced old man Jack Fugazy out of the promotion, which infuriated Cus, since Jack was the only person he trusted at Feature Sports Inc. Eddie Borden described the treachery of the two young upstarts in his broadsheet. "Young Fugazy and Cohn are acting and performing in methods contrary to the accepted forms of boxing etiquette. One practice that is of paramount importance, 'Never talk to the fighter about business when he has a manager.' No matter how you feel about Cus D'Amato and his contrary actions you must realize one thing: boxing would never have heard of Floyd Patterson if it weren't for this same D'Amato. Luckily, Floyd has common sense, far above the average. He is well aware of the pitfalls that face him and sensibly ignores the [counsel] of people who are trying to discredit Cus. He is well aware of the mischief makers who are trying to create dissension between him and his mentor and sagely he listens and says very little. He realizes that Cus has done a superb job. They have gone through too much together to be separated at this stage of the proceedings by meddling interlopers." Little did he know.

In January of 1961, Gil Rogin of *Sports Illustrated* went down to spend some time with Floyd and Cus at Floyd's training camp at Ehsan's. Both men were in a pensive mood. Floyd looked back at the night before he lost his title to Ingo. He had been driven into the city from camp in a Cadillac accompanied by two off-duty Mount Vernon detective bodyguards because Cus thought that IBC goons might attack him. Once in his room at the New York City hotel, Cus set up a secret knock so Floyd would know it was him. They ate meals together in the room just as they had when they were doing a training exhibition years earlier in Kansas City because all the restaurants there were segregated. Rogin said that Floyd had few friends because he was afraid of "parasitic hangers-on." So he withdrew into himself.

"God created only one Floyd Patterson," Cus crowed. Floyd rolled his eyes. "Cus thinks I'm Superman," Floyd said. "Sometimes I have to run away and shut the door."

Cus was lying on his bed wearing gold pajamas and black velvet slippers. He was talking to Rogin while he held the real estate section of *The New York Times* over his head. "I turn around and I find that I am an old man. I want to accomplish something before I die," Cus said.

"You have," Rogin assured him.

"No," Cus sighed. "I'm just trying. I want to leave a scratch on this old stone before I leave it, like the soldiers in a war. They didn't know what to do, so they left their names all over the place. It all must end, the good and the bad. *Così è guerra.*" He told Rogin that meant "This is war" or "This is life." He said it was the same thing.

"Everything will be different in the morning," Rogin said, trying to cheer him up.

"Everything's exactly the same in the morning," said Cus.

Cus's pessimism was probably due to the fact that he saw Floyd slipping away from him. Both Cohn and November were chipping away at Floyd's connection with Cus. On February 8, Jackie Robinson wrote a letter to Cus in an attempt to cheer him up. "Floyd's next fight is so very important that I hope he responds in the same manner as he did last year. I am almost as proud of him as you are, and I sometimes worry about the direction he will take. However, lately, I know I need not worry. His stand on integration at the fight was especially pleasing. Keep him on this path. He is doing a great service. I keep wishing things would straighten themselves out as far as your relationship goes, but as I read the press, I can't help but wonder how things are going. While the press seems to be down on you, I feel what you have done for Floyd has helped him and his future though the press seems to be taking their gripes out on him because they apparently resent what you have done. Keep up your courage. I am certain the truth will come out. Sincerely yours, Jackie."

Before Floyd and his increasingly larger entourage departed for Florida, Cus got a very unusual phone call. He had gone on a television show recently where he was talking about his favorite new enemies, the Cohn gang. His host mentioned that they must remind him of James Norris. "Some of the peculiar antics of Feature Sports Inc. make Jim Norris stand out like a diamond in a coal pile," Cus said. A few days later Cus got a call from a Norris associate. He said that Norris wanted to extend an offer for Floyd to train for free at his racetrack near Miami. "Go look at the facility. It's got a kitchen and everything. And Mr. Norris would even supply the cook and the food." Of course, Cus never took Norris up on the offer. Food cooked by Norris's chef?

Robert Boyle had a field day describing, for *Sports Illustrated*, the zoo behind the scenes of the fight in Miami. For him it was the "most bizarre cast of characters to hit the road since Jack Kerouac and his buddies careened across the country. . . . D'Amato detests Cohn and loathes Fugazy, Fugazy regards D'Amato as 'mentally ill' and is often irked by Kahn, who, in turn, is suspicious of almost everyone. He tapes phone calls and visits in his office. Cohn thinks he hides a microphone on his body, 'He's so fat no one could find it.'

"The sole tragic figure in the lot is Cus D'Amato, entangled in all sorts of legal snares. The press often reviles him as a crook. A crook he is not; a kook he may be. He fought the gangster dominated IBC alone for such a long spell that he wound up with a deep and permanent persecution complex. For D'Amato, every night has a full moon. The sad thing about it is he has good reason to feel persecuted. D'Amato attributes his difficulties to Bill Rosensohn, the onetime promoter who accused him of all sorts of shenanigans a year and a half ago. On the face of it, D'Amato, who can be devious in his own fashion, looked completely guilty. His enemies—and he had made many crusading against the IBC—pounced. 'I was a person on the dirt surrounded by a pack of wolves trying to tear me apart,' he says. The NYSAC, which rarely said boo to the IBC, revoked his manager's license. The revocation was upset in court, where it developed that the commission had nothing to revoke because the license had previously expired. Now and then D'Amato toys with the idea of applying for a new license, but he is afraid that if he got it the commission would then 'frame me for good this time' and make the revocation stick. 'That would put me out of business all over the world,' he says.

"Nowadays, what with having to avoid a managerial association with Patterson in New York, D'Amato leads a lonely life. He spends most of his time in his cluttered two-room apartment at Broadway and 53rd Street, his main companion a boxer dog with a black eye. The dog is named Cus because he looks as though he's been kicked around, too.

" 'Most of the time I just lay around,' D'Amato says. 'I read. I play with the dog. Anything to avoid boredom. Sometimes I just walk around the streets.' He stays out of bars for fear an enemy agent might stuff marijuana cigarettes into his pockets, then whistle for the police. He avoids the press. 'I can't afford to make any mistakes or have what I say misconstrued,' he says. Although he has a bed in the apartment, he never sleeps there. He stays with friends, and he rarely spends two nights in the same place. 'I don't like my comings and go-ings to be predictable,' he says. He is wary of what he says over the phone because he says it may be being tapped. Sometimes, though, D'Amato will get carried away and talk about anything on the phone. Reminded of a possible tap, he'll shout, 'I don't care! I tell the truth!'

"At present most of D'Amato's fire is directed at Fugazy and Cohn. They are 'depraved' and they make him long for the old days when he was battling Jim Norris. 'I never had so much fun in my whole life,' he says. 'I would create illusions to have the IBC think one thing and then do something unexpected. I played with Norris and his henchmen. I'd lock all the doors except one, and at that one I'd be waiting with an ax!'

"Fugazy, D'Amato says, tried to shake him down for a 15 percent cut of Patterson's closed circuit money. 'Compared to Fugazy, Norris is like a diamond in a coal pile. Fugazy has definite psychopathic leanings. The man has no principles! This man lies to your face, and he believes his own lies. A respectable racketeer!' "

When Gil Rogin visited the house where Cus and Floyd were stay-ing in Miami he found a much different vibe than he had a few months earlier at the training camp. November was constantly around "sweet and submissive, hovering like some huge, pale butterfly in Floyd's company." But Cus was being frozen out. "As for Cus D'Amato, whose shadow, like the moon, used to eclipse Floyd's sun—he lives in the same house as Patterson but Floyd neither knows what he does nor seems to care. Not that the old bindings of love and loyalty have been totally broken, but the roles of father and son appear to have been subtly reversed. 'I tell Cus,' Floyd says patiently, 'that some of the people he knows have been using him and taking advantage of him, but he doesn't listen to me. My eyes have been opened.' . . . D'Amato comes frequently to training and then sits in the back and does not visit Floyd. November, however, comes lordly to training. 'I'm happy to present to you the attorney for Champion Patterson,' is the aston-ishing announcement."

Cus had obtained a license from the Miami Beach Commission, so he was working Patterson's corner the night of the fight. Floyd looked tentative from the start and he got knocked down twice in the first round. He rallied a bit and knocked Ingo down near the end of the round. But he was befuddled when he came back to his corner. "Cus, I can't find it. The style. I can't find the style to fight him." Talking to a reporter later, Floyd described his mind-set. "When I got in the ring my mind was very blank. I'd backpedal. I did that several times. I'd go back awhile. I thought it would help me find myself and that then I'd tear in there, the Floyd Patterson I know I am. But I wasn't accomplishing anything. Good thing I got knocked down. It woke me up."

There was confusion in his corner. Florio and Cus were giving Floyd contradictory advice. By the sixth round Floyd felt he was weakening and he knew he'd have to gamble and try for a knockout. For the first time all fight Johansson started stalking Floyd, who began retreating. But near the end of the round, Floyd threw his leaping left-hand lead and landed it square on Johansson's temple. Ingo was staggered and Floyd finished him off with two clubbing rights to the head. Johansson crumbled to the canvas and the fight was over.

Everyone agreed that the fight hadn't added to the reputation of either man. Howard Cosell wrote that it was a revelation to him. "I realized that Patterson was not an outstanding fighter. Johansson was overweight, out of shape, bloated, had virtually no movement in the ring. Yet Patterson was defenseless against Ingo's right. . . . The more I listened to Floyd talk after that fight, the more I began to wonder about him. On the surface he was still the same—diffident, almost timid. But things were happening. He had broken with Cus D'Amato, the very man who had made him, who had carefully selected his opponents and who, even though D'Amato would never admit it, knew Patterson's limitations as a fighter."

Now the drumbeat for a Patterson–Liston fight intensified. Liston went on the offensive. "I won't get a chance because of Cus D'Amato," he told one reporter. Patterson seemed to respond by echoing Cus's argument—when Liston got rid of his mobbed-up managers, they could fight. "I know who those men are and they'll have to take a backseat." When Floyd was asked to name the men in question, he just chuckled. "I'm not looking to get bumped off." Liston responded in Jimmy Cannon's column. Cannon asked Liston what he thought of Floyd Patterson. "I think he's a great champion," he said. "You don't mean that?" Cannon said. "No. He's afraid of me. I view it this way. He's just using any excuse so that he don't have to fight me. He's worrying about who manages me. I ain't worrying about who's managing him. Patterson's got a contract with Cus D'Amato. Cus's name on it. I'm quite sure he don't sit up all night and watch Cus. He don't sleep with Cus all night to see what he's doing every minute."

"Would you sell the contract if you had a good offer?" Cannon asked Liston's "manager" Barone. "I'm no piece of furniture," said Liston, suddenly angry. "I'm no hog or dog to auction off. You want Cus to be my manager?"

By now, the columnist Red Smith had shifted his attacks from Cus to Floyd himself. "Floyd Patterson has made it abundantly clear that he means to have no part of the No. 1 contender. The champion says he is making his own decisions now but he speaks with the voice of his sometime proprietor, Cus D'Amato. He has arrogated to himself the license formerly exercised by Cus to dictate the professional and social existence of challengers, including the right to choose their business associates. The invertebrates in nominal command of boxing have made it equally clear that they have no intention of speaking up for the rights of any contender, no matter how deserving. They may lift the title of a Ray Robinson or harass an Archie Moore but they are meekly subservient to the whim of the heavyweight champion. They approved amateur Pete Rademacher as a bona fide challenger. They sanctioned a title defense against Roy Harris, a comic strip character conceived by Al Capp. They accepted peace-loving Brian London as a werewolf after his own countrymen had rejected him for the role. They will not boggle at Henry Cooper. Taking up where he says D'Amato has left off, Patterson speaks and acts as though the heavyweight championship—indeed, the heavyweight division—were his private property and not merely a bauble which he holds in trust."

Floyd took the train back to New York from Miami and he was met at the station by reporters. A title defense was planned for the fall, but Liston's backers had not approached Floyd's people, they were told. What was interesting about all this was that the person talking to the press on behalf of Floyd was not Cus but Roy Cohn. Presumably Cus was on a different train headed north.

Cohn returned to New York to a lawsuit against him, Bill Fugazy, Tom Bolan, and Feature Sports Inc., filed by Humbert "Jack" Fugazy. Jack was supposed to get one-fourth of the promoter's share but they froze him out of the company and then refused to pay him. So he sued for $130,000. Speaking of his nephew Bill and partner Cohn, Jack said, "You never met two people who, according to their talk, control the universe. They know who to put their hands on. But when they need something, they come crawling. It makes me sick when I talk about them. Not one of them knows a thing about boxing. They have done more to kill boxing than all the mobsters put together."

Cus was Jack's main witness in the case but Roy Cohn had made a career out of delaying cases and he did that here too, getting five postponements. "Cohn is hoping to delay this trial long enough for me to die," said Jack. "Well, I won't. I'm in much better health than they think. I'm willing to take all three in the ring and beat their heads off. I will live long enough to see my nephew and Roy Cohn get what they deserve." He barely did. He was a beaten-down man, near death, when he finally got a judgment from the judge. Now the problem was to collect it. Cohn was also notoriously cheap and notorious for ignoring judgments. But Uncle Jack had the last laugh—one of the court bailiffs seized one of Cohn's cars, which was parked in front of the Essex Hotel overlooking Central Park, where Cohn was attending a board meeting of Lionel, the toy train manufacturing company that he had taken over from his grand-uncle and eventually ran into the ground. Cus was disgusted by both Cohn and Fugazy and he accused them of killing his friend Jack. "These people were terrible," Cus said. "They brought Wall Street into boxing."

In April of 1963, Bill Fugazy wrote a long article in *The Saturday Evening Post*. It was his farewell to boxing. He and Roy Cohn were stepping down from active involvement in Feature Sports but they were retaining their shares. Cohn had put his law partner Tom Bolan in charge of the day-to-day operations. The piece was a self-serving account of his attempt to "clean up" boxing from mobster influence, which, considering Cohn's representation of Fat Tony and other Mafia bosses, was laughable. He wrote that "living in boxing was like growing up with a pack of wolves. Let me introduce you to the wolf pack," and then went into thumbnail sketches of the participants, including Cus, "Patterson's manager in theory, not in practice"; Norris, "very rich and very powerful but not very good at remembering faces," specifically Carbo's when it came to testifying at Senate hearings; and Irving Kahn, the president of TelePrompTer, who "still owes Johansson money from the first fight, owes Feature Sports money from the second and third fights, and *he* doesn't trust anyone else." He even had harsh words for his partner Cohn, saying he had "the greatest ability to alienate and antagonize people of anyone."

There were a couple of nuggets in the article that blew my mind. Fugazy confirmed that November was moving in on Floyd. He wrote that Floyd was a decent person who was "influenced too much by the people around him. I'm certain he would not deliberately do anything wrong but he sometimes suffers from poor advice. . . . Like his lawyer Julius November, Floyd is overly suspicious. When November barks, 'Did you hear what he said, Floyd?' Patterson listens."

Fugazy traced his involvement with Feature Sports. He was the one who, on the recommendation of his uncle Jack, contacted Rosensohn and Velella, who both had their promoter's licenses revoked by the NYSAC. They wanted $247,000 for the contract for the return match, two-thirds to Velella and one-third to Rosensohn. He implied that they paid the money and then the two Fugazys went to Sweden in December of 1959 to talk to the new champ Ingo, who told them that he would never fight for the mob. "I don't want to get involved with Jim Norris," Ingo said. "He came over here and tried to tell me that I could never fight again unless he tied me up. He wanted to own me. No one's going to own me."

So when they came back to New York they applied for a promoter's license, but NYSAC chairman Melvin Krulewitch's two fellow commissioners—"young Jim Farley and Julie Helfand, who was obligated to Norris"—blocked their application. Krulewitch then called for a public hearing on the application. But a few weeks later, Fugazy heard that Jim Norris had been bragging at a cocktail party in Palm Beach that " 'these guys think they're going to get their license. They don't know that my boy is going to stop them.' His boy was Jules Helfand. It is a matter of public record that when Helfand was chairman of the athletic commission before Krulewitch, Norris paid his traveling expenses at least once." Interesting. We just read that testimony before the Kefauver Commission. And Helfand was the driving force to get Cus's license suspended by the NYSAC, which gave Norris a wide opening to get control of the heavyweight division with Patterson at home in Rockville Center, licking his wounds. Back to Fugazy's account.

"A few weeks later, Norris told Denniston Slater, who was then president of Feature Sports and had known the Norris family from Palm Beach society, 'Get your money back, you'll never put on this fight. You bought your stock from Bill Rosensohn, but you never got his stock certificate. You never got it because I have it.' It was the truth. Rosensohn had told them that he had lost his certificate but in fact he had borrowed money from a Norris company and when he couldn't pay it back, forfeited the certificate as collateral." According to Fugazy, Cohn then called Wirtz and said, " 'Look, this is really going to get Norris in trouble. If he owns stock in a corporation that promoted the last heavyweight championship fight, he's guilty of undercover promoting.' So Wirtz gave them the certificate." Hmm. So, knowing Cohn, maybe Rosensohn never collected *any* of the money Cohn offered him for his share of Rosensohn Enterprises, and Norris did retain the stock certificate.

Young Bill then complained that they should have had the rematch at Yankee Stadium but the stadium wanted a higher rental fee and "D'Amato claimed that the Stadium was controlled by Jim Norris. Sometimes I suspect that D'Amato feels Jim Norris controls

Khrushchev. As preparations proceeded, D'Amato kept telling us that the fight would never take place. He said that Norris would have somebody killed or somebody drugged. He once said that Norris was going to plant narcotics in his coat pocket and have him arrested as a dope peddler. No one was killed, no one was drugged and D'Amato has never been arrested as a dope peddler." Does sound like Cus.

Fugazy had one funny anecdote from the Miami Beach fight. He met Sonny Liston at the fight and he told Sonny that he had persuaded his pal Bob Hope to buy out Sonny's contract from Barone and to donate his part of the purse to charity. "Who's Bob Hope?" Sonny asked. "He's a comedian," Fugazy told him. "I don't need no comedian as my manager," Sonny snorted.

Cus stood to make some good green off the Miami Beach fight and he didn't have to shell out for another crown, so he could go on a shopping spree. One of the things he was looking to buy was his own private island in upstate New York. In Cus's files there is a letter dated March 29, 1961, from a real estate company called Meola and Meola—Specialist in Orange County Property. Harry Meola had written Cus that "we want to let you know that you can now buy the island for $25,000. We are sure that you will never find a more unusual and desirable retreat in New York State."

But Cus's desire for the ultimate hideaway got derailed when he received a letter from the IRS on April 12. He was being audited for income from the year 1959. As he would soon find out when the "books and financial records for the year in question" were delivered, November, who was not only an attorney but a CPA too, made some fundamental errors with Cus's tax payments and that was the last time in his life that Cus would be able to even entertain the idea of buying something grand—an island or a jewel-encrusted crown.

Meanwhile, the boys behind Liston were desperately trying to clean up his management situation. The ruse of Barone "surrendering" his contract with Sonny that had two more years to run didn't fly, so on April 20, Sonny agreed to pay $75,000 to Barone for his contract. Cus was dubious. "Where did Liston get the $75,000?" he told a reporter. "The plans for Floyd Patterson have already been made. Liston does not figure in those plans now. I am not interested in Liston at present."

Neither was Kefauver. But Patterson seemed to be. Or at least the Patterson that Roy Cohn and Julius November were talking to. On April 24, an ex-politician from Philadelphia named George Katz was introduced to the boxing world as Sonny's new manager. Dan Parker was a little skeptical of the arrangement. "George (Pussy) Katz 'bought' Sonny Liston's contract from his alleged owner Pep Barone. The deal was closed in the office of one of Blinky Palermo's regiment of lawyers the other day. The odor of stale codfish still permeates the vicinity."

But Floyd was quoted in the papers asking that Kefauver's subcommittee approve Liston's new choice. The next day, Kefauver sent out a press release in which he addressed Patterson. "I understand from newspaper reports that you have asked the U.S. Senate Subcommittee on Antitrust and Monopoly to approve the new managerial arrangement of Charles 'Sonny' Liston." He went on to explain that his committee didn't have that authority but that if his anti-racketeering bill was passed that authority would be given to a national boxing commissioner. "I would think that the Commissioner's first order of business would be to examine Mr. Liston's new management with a fine-tooth comb."

A few days later Kefauver went even further. His office released a new statement: "*The Washington Post* of March 15 carried a U.P.I. dispatch stating that the heavyweight boxing champion, Floyd Patterson, may defend his title against the No. 1 contender, Sonny Liston, in September of this year. If this match is held, and Liston wins, we face the ugly prospect of having the heavyweight championship revert to mob control." He then went on to introduce his legislation to clean up boxing.

On March 31, Kefauver convened follow-up hearings on the need for federal regulation of boxing. Marciano testified that the new boxing czar should be John Bonomi. Gene Fullmer, Tommy Loughran, and others supported the legislation but didn't nominate anyone. But Jack Hurley, the great Seattle promoter and trainer, testified and agreed that there was a need for a national boxing commissioner. Hurley nominated his old pal Cus D'Amato. "He's dead on the level, he's honest, he's qualified, he's fearless. Everything he has done has been done for Patterson. Today Patterson is a wealthy fighter, and Cus doesn't have change for a quarter."

Kefauver and his aide Bonomi went on a public relations spree the next few months to stir up public sentiment for their boxing legislation. Bonomi kept making the case that even with the convictions of Carbo and Palermo, it wouldn't end the mob's domination of the sport. "At this very moment Carbo associates are standing by to gather up the pieces of his crumbling empire," Bonomi told the National Boxing Association annual convention. He said that enactment of Kefauver's legislation would finally "boot" the gangsters out of boxing. The legislation never even made it to a vote. And Bonomi was right. Years later a boxing official told Nick Tosches, who was researching a book on Sonny Liston, that "Frankie Carbo and Palermo were running the fight game out of their cells. They were in jail, and they had a phone service at their disposal, and they made matches. They were running the Garden out of jail." No wonder Cus avoided the place.

Despite all the infighting in Floyd's camp, Cus still had enough juice to avoid Liston and have Patterson fight Tom McNeeley, a journeyman from Boston, over the objections of Cohn's group. Cus arranged for Floyd to get 40 percent of the gate and 50 percent of the ancillary rights. Then he made McNeeley's manager put $1 million in escrow as a guarantee for a return bout if Floyd lost. But Cus cut into Floyd's purse when he got into a fight with the Massachusetts State Boxing Commission. The only way that Floyd could make money on this fight was for a huge hometown crowd to come out and root for McNeely, who was undefeated in twenty-three fights. But when the local commission refused to allow Cus to bring in an out-of-state referee, the fight was moved to Toronto, where Cus again got into a shouting match with the chairman of the Ontario Athletic Commission over its policy that judges had to be residents of Ontario. The dispute got so heated that people there thought the fight might be in jeopardy. Then Cus complained that McNeely did little to promote the fight, since he had stayed back in Boston to train, which didn't help the gate.

No one thought much of this fight. Arthur Daley wrote that McNeeley "has a chance all right. So has Outer Mongolia of becoming the first nation to send a man to the moon." Jimmy Cannon was more sardonic. "There is no need for Frankie Carbo, the underworld commissioner of boxing, anymore. If he wasn't in jail, the old gunman probably would be drawing unemployment insurance. No champion has to fix fights anymore. You don't have to give a murderer a piece of your fighter to muscle the other guy into submission. You just find a place like Toronto and put your guy in with a clown like McNeeley. You can't lose and you won't be arrested, either."

The fight went off on December 4, 1961. Once again, Patterson looked bad despite flooring McNeeley eight times in four rounds. Each time he was on the canvas McNeeley got up with tremendous determination and even rocked Patterson in the fourth round before he hit the floor four times and the fight was finally stopped by ref Jersey Joe Walcott. Afterward Floyd rated himself "a 55" for the fight. Cus disagreed, saying, "It was a lot less." Afraid that the Patterson fight alone would tank on closed-circuit theater grosses, the promoters added a preliminary fight—Sonny Liston against Albert Westphal, a two-time German heavyweight champ. It took Sonny less than a round to knock Westphal down, face-first into the canvas, with a tremendous right hand. It was the first time that Westphal had ever been floored. Arthur Daley noted that Liston had belted Westphal "as enthusiastically as if the German had been a policeman."

By the beginning of 1962, November and Cohn were making the case for the Sonny fight to Floyd. Cus was being frozen out more and more. At the thirty-sixth annual Boxing Writers Association dinner, on January 14, 1962, Cus wasn't even sitting at Floyd's table 5. But November was. Cus was exiled to table 22, where he sat with his assistant George Lattimore, Howard Cosell, and a young man named Jimmy Jacobs, who would become one of Cus's closest friends and my manager.

Jacobs was the greatest handball player who ever lived and, some say, the greatest overall athlete. He also had a wicked sense of humor. Based out of L.A., he lived around the corner from a memory-training school. He researched the name of the school's director and waited for him to leave school one day. "George, how are you?" he said jovially. George strained to remember who he was. "George! Don't tell me you've forgotten me?" he said, and walked away. Jacobs was an avid collector of many things, including comic books and old fight films. In fact, after he won his handball tournaments, he would typically accept his trophy and then announce to the crowd, "I collect old boxing films and if you know of any old boxing films, please let me know." Robert Boyle was covering a championship in San Francisco when he met Jacobs. They chatted and Jacobs told him that he thought many of the old-time fighters were vastly overrated. Boyle told him, "You remind me of a friend of mine, Cus D'Amato. He says the same thing." About six months later Boyle was back in New York and hanging out with Cus and he told him about Jimmy. Cus said he'd love to talk to the guy and Boyle called Jimmy on the spot and made the introduction.

Cus met up with Jacobs at a handball classic and their relationship was cemented when Cus came up with an ingenious idea after Jacobs developed a big blister on his palm. At that time you were allowed to wrap your hands, so Cus got a silver dollar and placed it over the blister and then wrapped Jim's hand. Jacobs went on to win the match and he was convinced that Cus was a genius. But they bonded over their long talks about the role of emotion and fear in sports.

Boyle did an article on Jimmy in 1966, and when Jacobs talks about the role of emotion in sports it's as if he's channeling Cus. His favorite superhero was Robin. "Being Robin the Boy Wonder was a tremendous help to me in sports. All of us are susceptible to our emotions when under stress, and when I was younger I would think: What would Robin do? Instead of succumbing to nervous apprehension, I would transform myself into this other character who was emotionally unaffected. . . . Contests are won or lost by mental effort. . . . When I go to play in a championship match I meet an old friend I call Mr. Emotion. He is very predictable. When I want to win very badly he comes right into my body. But so that he doesn't interfere with what I'm trying to accomplish I have to take more time in the service box. I have to make more conscious efforts to give my arms clear instructions. The way I react to Mr. Emotion is not to get apprehensive. He is nothing but a feeling and he is there to let me know how important this match is to me. He acts as a reminder to me that the application of the physical talent that I have is under the complete dominance of what I call my control system, my brain, and that the orders that come out of this control system have to be very clear and explicit, just as if I were addressing some small child."

Cus was similarly impressed with Jacobs. "The more I studied this guy, the more impressed I became. He is extraordinary. He not only has an excellent mind, but a tremendous physique and stamina. I have never met an athlete like him," he told Boyle. Cus said he had only met two people who had the aura of a champion like Jim did: Joe Louis and Sugar Ray Robinson.

Around 1958 Jim began corresponding with Bill Cayton, an advertising executive who owned a fight-film library that he licensed for television use. Jim had in his possession many of the films that Cayton had the rights to but not the actual physical films themselves. Cayton then offered to buy Jacobs's films and bring him to New York and make him a partner in the fight-film business. Jacobs moved to New York around 1960 and moved in with Cus, who by then was living on 57th Street. Nick Beck, a childhood friend of Jacobs's, visited them there and he got the impression that Cus was not a great housekeeper. The place was a little "run down" and he felt that Jim seemed a little embarrassed by the boxes strewn around the apartment. "I don't know if Cus was a hoarder but he had a lot of stuff there that I don't think Jim had any interest in. And so Jim said, 'We're thinking about something else and trying to get something better.'" Cus was the same when we were living in the house in Catskill. If you peeked into his room the rare times the door was open, you'd see boxes and boxes of books and clippings lying around.

At the time of that boxing writers' dinner in 1962, Jim and Cus were working on a documentary about Floyd that was going to be syndicated to TV stations. Floyd agreed to do the interviews for a nominal fee (one dollar) and participate in a percentage of the profits. The film opened with Floyd's visit to the White House, where he met with JFK, and then became a retrospective of Floyd's career. Unfortunately, there was little interest from the networks and the film lost money. Years later, it would become a bone of contention between Floyd and Cus.

THE IDEA OF A PATTERSON–LISTON FIGHT took on a life way beyond the confines of the boxing game. Old-school civil rights groups such as the NAACP feared that Liston's thug image would set black rights back years. "Hell, let's stop kidding," the civil rights leader Percy Sutton admitted. "I'm for Patterson because he represents us better than Liston ever could." But Liston had a supporter in the radical comedian and civil rights leader Dick Gregory, who said, "It certainly isn't up to Patterson's manager to determine whether Liston should or shouldn't be allowed to fight."

Liston decided to take things into his own hands. Before he got rid of Barone, he went to see José Torres and asked Torres to take him to see Cus. Cus told me that Sonny thought that Cus was intimidated by him. José told him that Cus feared no one and the two of them barged in on Cus in his office, unannounced. José's such a political animal. He always wanted to be on the right side of everybody. Cus was startled to see Liston but he kept his composure.

"Cus, why ain't you gonna gimme a fight with Patterson?" Liston seemed pissed. Cus went into his usual rap about cleaning up his management but Sonny cut him off. "You pick my manager, then!" Cus politely said he wasn't in that business and didn't want any more discussion about the issue. By then Liston had calmed down and the two of them left.

On May 10, 1961, Liston announced that his new manager was George Katz, who had been investigated by a member of the

Pennsylvania State Athletic Commission, found to be an upstanding citizen, and approved for a license. Seven days later, Liston was told to move along by a cop. "Why don't you arrest me?" Sonny said, mocking him. So the cop did, and charged him with disorderly conduct and resisting arrest. But when he was booked, the charges were reduced to loitering. Sonny was very familiar with the inside of police stations. Back in Missouri he had served a sentence for five armed robberies. Talking back to the cop on May 17 was his eighteenth arrest. His nineteenth came on June 12, when he and a buddy stopped a woman's vehicle in predawn darkness and then tried to pass themselves off as cops. They took off when a park guard drove up but the guard went on an eighty-mile-per-hour chase and shot at Sonny's car before they finally stopped. After this arrest, the Pennsylvania SAC finally suspended him from July 14 until October.

Man, people thought I was a bad motherfucker? Sonny Liston made me look like a Boy Scout. My friend Mac, who's a barber in Vegas, knew Sonny very well. I would tell Mac how I worshipped Liston, and Mac would yell at me and tell me stories about Sonny going into bars, taking a guy's drink, and then smacking him around. He'd park his car in the middle of the street in Vegas because the cops were too scared to tell him not to. It was so bad that when the cops in a certain town heard that Liston was on the way there they would wait for him at the train or bus station or wait for his car and they'd tell him that he couldn't stay there. He was actually barred from cities!

He had broken a cop's jaw! I saw a documentary on Sonny. I'm watching this guy and this is back in the 1960s, when a black man's life wasn't worth much, and Sonny was up in a cop's face talking to him like he was a boy, pointing at him and cursing him. George Foreman told me Sonny was the only guy who could stand up to his punches. He was an animal. He was the quintessential hard, uneducated southern country Negro. He never lifted weights but he looked like he was born in a weight forest. Mofo looked like a human dumbbell.

When I was fighting I identified with Sonny a hundred percent. I don't know how to explain it, but he was just a freak. Liston didn't have an emotion in his whole soul. Maybe he smiled three times his entire life. Liston was a force of nature. I identified with him as a person too, because he was misunderstood. But the real thing that separated me from those other Neanderthal guys was that I had been around educated and sophisticated people and I emulated them. I listened to how they talked and comported themselves. I tried to change the image of myself because I wanted to improve myself. Those guys never wanted to or didn't have the ability or the knack to improve. I was around guys like Cus and Mailer and Pete Hamill, and Sonny was around guys like Blinky Palermo and low-level Vegas mobsters. Those guys couldn't read or write either.

Look, Cus never wanted Floyd to fight Sonny. First he said that Sonny was the last big fighter who was still mob-controlled. Then a few years later when he was interviewed by Jim Jacobs for a documentary they were making, Cus had a different reason—Cohn and November were messing with Floyd's mind:

cus: The Liston fight was made without my knowledge or without my consent. And the reason why I wouldn't consent to the fight was because Floyd Patterson had been involved with people whose sole objective appeared to be to separate him from his money. Having this objective, which they couldn't accomplish it with my presence; they took steps to remove me from the scene so that they could accomplish their objective. See, when Floyd spoke with me about this match, I said, "No, this man is a good fighter and he's a winning fighter and you can beat this fellow, but you have to be at your best to beat him," meaning his interest was now divided. He did not have the dedicated attitude that brought him to the top and made him the great fighter he was up to that point. jacobs: You didn't think he could beat Sonny Liston? cus: At that time, no. I did not think he could beat Liston at that time. I did believe and I told him that "if you get rid of these distracting influences and get back to training and applying yourself, as you did previously, if and when, at a period of time I feel that you're now capable of doing what I know you're capable of, then you will fight Sonny Liston, but not before."

But years later, Cus told me the truth. "I don't think he could have beat Liston on the best day of his life," he said.

Floyd made up his mind to fight Liston after his visit with JFK. President Kennedy told him, "You're great, stay focused, you've got to beat this guy." That fucked up Floyd's head. He told David Remnick, who was writing a book about Ali, "I felt all alone in there, completely terrified. You've got to remember how young I was, what my background was, and now I was getting advice in the Oval Office. What was I supposed to do? Disagree? I had to take the challenge. I was always afraid of letting people down and now I was in a position where I had to worry about letting down the president."

And JFK's telling that to a guy who was completely afraid of the limelight. Just think about the pressure that was on him. Patterson had so many opportunities to grab history, you know what I mean? A guy like me, with my ego and my vanity, I would say, "I'm a dreamer, I'm Achilles."

On January 10, Sonny supposedly changed managers again and this time he named Jack Nilon, who had a food concession company in Philadelphia. By the end of January, a deal was struck, with Cus involved in the negotiations. Even though the fight had been announced, the contracts hadn't been signed yet, and on February 12, 1962, Cus's friend Robert Boyle reported on the split in Floyd's camp over the fight. "The Patterson camp is a triumvirate: the champion, Lawyer Julius November and Manager Cus D'Amato. Up until Patterson's defeat in the first Johansson fight, D'Amato was the kingpin, but since then the three have been wrangling among themselves in semisecrecy, much like Russia, Red China and Albania. . . . D'Amato wants nothing to do with Sonny. November would like to see Patterson fight Liston next—at least that is what Liston says November told him—and Patterson, at present anyway, agrees with November. . . .

"All this drives D'Amato to desperation. An intense man, he has become even more wound up. The eyeballs roll more furiously, the black Homburg is clamped more tightly on his head and the mouth stretches even more to the side in conspiratorial grimace. He is a voice whispering in the wilderness. . . .

"At this writing, D'Amato is traveling around the country on mysterious errands doing what he can to prevent a Liston–Patterson fight. 'When I want to go from A to B, I go to Z first,' he says cryptically."

Cus did something else that was very cryptic. On March 12, he sent a letter to his lawyers Schweig and November. "This is to confirm the understanding I had with your firm for some two years, wherein I advised you that although you represent both Floyd Patterson and myself, it is my wish, intention and express desire that if there be any conflict of interest between Mr. Patterson and myself, that Mr. Patterson's interests are to be considered paramount." Was this Cus throwing in the towel?

Five days later, November made it official. Floyd–Sonny was on. Patterson got 45 percent of the gate and 55 percent of ancillary rights. Liston got 12.5 percent of each. If Liston won, Patterson's side could choose the place, date, and promoter of the rematch and Liston would get 30 percent of the gate and ancillary rights. Cus had one thing to say: "My position on his fight hasn't changed. The only reason that this fight will take place is that Patterson wants to fight Liston."

Cus was running on fumes. On April 5, he wrote a letter to his roommate Jim Jacobs, addressed to him at the Big Fights office on 40th Street. "Dear Jim, In consideration of your loan to me, I herewith hand you my promissory note as of even date in the equal amount of $10,000 received. This promissory note has a maturity date of September 25, 1962. . . . I agree to make prompt re-payment to you of your loan to me from the first proceeds that I may receive or be entitled to receive from the pending bout between Patterson and Liston. . . . I want to thank you most sincerely for the courtesies being extended to me in this connection. With kindest personal regards, I am Sincerely yours, Constantine D'Amato."

Meantime Sonny couldn't stay out of trouble. On April 27, after he had his driver's license suspended for doing more than seventy

miles an hour on the Jersey Turnpike, the NYSAC denied Sonny a
license to fight in New York because—as a *New York Times* article
quoted—his past "provided a pattern of suspicion" that could be "detrimental to the best interests of pro boxing and to the public interest
as well." Floyd was irate. "He has already served his time," Floyd
said. "What if they did that to me? You know how many times I went
to the police station when I was 9 years old? About a dozen. I used to
steal from stores and what not, but they've forgotten about all that. I
feel sorry for him. People keep pointing to Liston and saying, 'There
goes the ex-con, the criminal.' "

In the same *Times* article, Floyd told Gay Talese why he took the
fight. "One night in bed, I made up my mind. I knew if I'd want to
sleep comfortably, I'd have to take on Liston even though the NAACP
and the Kefauver committee didn't want me to take on the fight.
Some people said: What if you lose and he wins? Then the colored
people will suffer. But maybe if Liston wins, he'll live up to the title.
He may make people look up to him."

As the fight got closer Cus began to try to influence the outcome
of the event. Cus gave an interview where he complained in advance
about Liston's illegal tactics. "If anybody wins the title I want them
to win under the Marquess of Queensbury rules and under the rules
of the Athletic Commission, not under barroom rules. If the title is
won, I don't want Mr. Liston to be the Barroom Rules champion or a
brawling champion. I want him to be the Marquess of Queensbury
champion. All the rules must be enforced and carried out."

Then he tried another tack. It was one of the most bizarre events
in the annals of heavyweight championship fight history. According
to the hypnotist Marshall Brodien, some people from Floyd's camp
had seen his act one night at the Cairo Supper Club in Chicago, where
the fight was to be staged on September 25. The next day Cus called
Marshall and invited him to an office he was using on Michigan Avenue. Cus told the hypnotist that he had been granted a formal hearing before the Illinois State Athletic Commission and he needed his
help.

On September 10, Cus, Brodien, and a few others trekked up to the Illinois State Athletic Commission offices. Before a crush of reporters, photographers, and TV crews, Cus was given the floor. In his hand he had a letter that had been written to Sonny Liston but that had been mistakenly sent to Patterson's camp.

"Thank you for giving me this opportunity to present evidence in regards to a matter which came to my attention. I will indicate clearly that a proposal was made to Sonny Liston to hypnotize him and I wish to demonstrate to the satisfaction of the commission and everyone present, the effects of hypnotism on a subject. Under hypnosis it is possible to hypnotize a man wherein he becomes immune to pain, so that a fast, hard-hitting, accurate puncher such as Patterson, if he was rushing up to strike his opponent a blow which broke a bone or jaw or something, with repeated blows on the area affected there would be no sign on the part of the opponent that he's being hurt or that the injury exists. And I felt that repeated blows on the injured area might cause serious and permanent damage. I was very fortunate in being able to secure the services of one of the best-known hypnotists in the country. Marshall Brodien, who has brought with him subjects, who by demonstration would make very clear the point and the charges that I have made."

Then a member of the commission read from the letter to Liston.

" 'Sonny, you have plenty of ability, but at times we can all use a little help, especially when there is pressure. I suggest you invite me to your training camp, for two or three weeks before the fight. The atmosphere which I will create will be harmonious. Winning thoughts will dominate the mind. The vibrations and thought waves suggested by me, all around, would make you invincible on a particular night. Send for me, Sonny, I have power you've never dreamed of, no fighter has ever lost a contest that followed my suggestion. Sincerely, Jimmy Grippo.' "

Cus continued: "Now to those not acquainted with Jimmy Grippo, he was a former professional fight manager well known in the boxing fraternity. He's a sleight-of-hand magician and a hypnotist of national reputation. I have with me here now Marshall Brodien, one of the top hypnotists of the country, who will give a demonstration."

What Cus was saying in a roundabout manner was that if Liston was hypnotized by Grippo and he would be truly impervious to pain, then he would have an unfair psychological advantage over Floyd. And at the same time, Floyd might cause permanent damage to a Liston who felt no pain after absorbing power punches from Floyd. This was either a publicity stunt worthy of P. T. Barnum or an attempt to throw a monkey wrench into a fight that Cus never wanted Floyd to accept.

Brodien called upon a volunteer named John Lane. Marshall put him under and then slapped him across the face and he didn't even wince. Cus then addressed the room. "To the commission, I think it's a very good idea to have a member of the press strike a blow." Cus then laced a boxing glove onto the left hand of Frankie Mastro, a former professional boxer who had become a boxing writer. Mastro threw two hooks into the hypnotized subject's stomach.

"Now mind you, the blow is struck in an area, a liver punch, which can cause the most excruciating pain. If the first blow caused a fracture and the second blow in the same area would only compound this fracture and additional blows, well I can leave it to your imagination," Cus said.

Then Brodien brought up a woman named Brenda Green, a twenty-two-year-old receptionist. She was seated next to Lane and hypnotized, and then Marshall had them hold their arms out horizontally and he proceeded to hold a torch under their outstretched palms, to no effect. Then Marshall suspended the petite Brenda across the backs of two chairs and stood atop her body. She had no reaction at all.

"Now Cus, just what does this prove?" one of the commissioners asked.

"It proves that under hypnosis, a man may be hypnotized to an extent and to a degree where he is immune to pain. So that if he suffered an injury, no matter how serious, he may carry on whatever he is doing, without being aware of the injury," Cus said.

"And you, as the hypnotist, Marshall, believe this can be done?" the commissioner asked.

"Definitely."

"It was demonstrated to the satisfaction of everyone here," Cus chimed in.

"Are you afraid that your fighter or Sonny will be hypnotized?" the commissioner asked.

"Sonny is the man to whom the letter was addressed. I am the one who exposed this letter," Cus said.

It was a compelling demonstration, but the commission didn't see fit to interfere with the proposed fight. But what the demonstration proved was that Cus was a reluctant showman. It was interesting to find a letter in Cus's archives dated about a year a half before this demonstration from Jimmy Grippo. Floyd was preparing to fight Ingo in Miami and Grippo offered his services to the promotion. "I am familiar with every phase and angle in boxing and have kept my nose clean. You as manager of the champion, McDonald [the local promoter] and myself with your approval as adviser, or whatever capacity you see fit, can elevate boxing to the seat which it rightfully belongs. May I add my relations with the press have always been good. Best wishes, Jimmy Grippo." Cus may have finally found a position for Grippo a few fights later.

It wasn't until almost a year later that Harold Conrad, the legendary press agent who had been hired by Cohn to handle the Liston fight, revealed the whole story behind this scam. "Cus D'Amato is one of the real characters," he told Robert Boyle. "Of course, maybe D'Amato is for real. He's a method actor. He can register any emotion, and you believe it. Anger! He's angry. Amazement! He's amazed. He's better than Brando. Before the Liston–Patterson fight in Chicago, Jimmy Grippo, the hypnotist, writes a letter to each fighter offering to hypnotize him so he can't feel the punches. Grippo is trying to work it so neither fighter knows about his offer to the other fighter. But he scrambles up the letters in the envelopes so Liston gets the letter to Patterson and Patterson gets the letter to Liston.

"This is a natural! I put D'Amato on the Jack Eigen radio show, and he really shouts about how Liston is trying to pull something with a hypnotist. The next morning Cus is with the reporters and I say to him, like I'm disgusted, 'These guys need copy and you drop a story like that on radio.' Immediately all the writers get excited and yell, 'What? What?' They're hooked. This is great psychology. Now they're begging Cus to tell them. If he had told them straight out, they would have said, 'What are you trying to sell us?' Now they're asking for the story. So D'Amato announces he's going to the commission with a hypnotist. Everyone was all primed. Newsreels, television, everyone! Cus gets a hypnotist and this hypnotist hypnotizes a dame, touched her with a torch, belted her, and Cus says that this conclusively proves his argument that a hypnotized boxer does not feel pain. Boy, we got a lot of space on that. This is what hooks people who are not fight fans alone. You have to get the public aroused."

A surprising number of reporters and experts picked Patterson to beat Liston. While Joe Louis gave a strong vote to Sonny, Jack Dempsey gave a not-as-strong vote to Floyd, as did Jimmy Cannon. A survey in *The Ring* magazine favored Patterson. The fighters themselves showed stark differences when they opened camp in Chicago. Patterson was conciliatory toward Sonny. "I have met Sonny Liston several times and I believe there is much good in him. Should he be fortunate enough to win the heavyweight championship, I ask that you give him a chance to bring out the good that is in him." Sonny didn't demonstrate the same sportsmanship. "I'll kill him. I'd like to run over him in a car."

Floyd's comments scared his old friend Howard Cosell. He wrote in his autobiography that Patterson seemed "helpless" without Cus and that Floyd seemed to have a "preacceptance of defeat" in Chicago. Cosell's affection for Patterson was getting tested. "There was no profession of strength, no expression of confidence. . . . Our tie was growing weaker because of his constant excuses, constant escapes from society."

Harold Conrad realized that Cohn and Bolan knew nothing about the fight business, so he decided to make this fight an "event." He invited legendary novelists like Norman Mailer, Nelson Algren, and James Baldwin to cover the fight. He set up a debate a few days before the fight between Mailer and William F. Buckley, Jr. At one point while Buckley went into a meandering poetic flight of prose, Mailer interrupted him. "Mr. Buckley, you want me to lie down on the railroad tracks, tie my hands to the rails, and wait until the engine of your logic gets around to riding over me?"

Mailer was in Chicago writing an epic piece for *Esquire* called "Ten Thousand Words a Minute." Mailer was already friendly with Cus and he spent a lot of time with him in Chicago. His description of Cus might be the best ever written and I can read it again and again.

"Next morning I spent more time with D'Amato. . . . D'Amato talked only about his own fighters. How he talked! He had stopped drinking years ago and so had enormous pent-up vitality. As a talker, he was one of the world's great weight lifters, not brilliant, but powerful, nonstop, and very solid. Talk was muscle. If you wanted to interrupt, you had to bend his arm off.

"Under the force, however, he had a funny simple quality, something of that passionate dogmatism which some men develop when they have been, by their own count, true to their principles. He had the enthusiastic manner of a saint who is all works and no contemplation. His body was short and strong, his head was round, and his silver-white hair was cut in a short brush. He seemed to bounce as he talked. He reminded me of a certain sort of very tough Italian kid one used to find in Brooklyn. They were sweet kids, and rarely mean, and they were fearless, at least by the measure of their actions they were fearless. They would fight anybody. Size, age, reputation did not make them hesitate. . . .

"The likelihood . . . is that for a period D'Amato was one of the bravest men in America. He was a fanatic about boxing, and cared little about money. He hated the Mob. He stood up to them. A prizefight manager running a small gym with broken mirrors on East Fourteenth Street does not usually stand up to the Mob, any more than a chambermaid would tell the Duchess of Windsor to wipe her shoes before she enters her suite at the Waldorf. D'Amato was the exception, however. The Mob ended by using two words to describe him: 'He's crazy.' The term is given to men who must be killed. Nobody

killed D'Amato. For years, like a monk, he slept in the back room of
his gym with a police dog for a roommate. The legend is that he kept
a gun under his pillow."

Beautiful, just beautiful. But Mailer got it wrong about the mob
calling Cus "crazy." When we put Carbo's words in context, when he
was responding to Norris's insisting that Carbo get Cus to have Patterson fight for the IBC, Carbo was protecting Cus. That's why nobody killed D'Amato, as Mailer noted. But Mailer was right when he
described Cus's feelings of alienation from his prize pupil:

"Patterson had put his faith in D'Amato. . . . The aftermath of the
first Johansson fight, however, blew out the set. It was discovered
that D'Amato directly or indirectly had gotten money for the promotion through a man named 'Fat Tony' Salerno. D'Amato claimed to
have been innocent of the connection, and indeed it was a most aesthetic way for the Mob to get him. It's equally possible that after
years of fighting every windmill in town, D'Amato had come down to
the hard Bolshevistic decision that you don't make an omelet without
breaking eggs. Whatever the fact, D'Amato had his license suspended
in New York. He was not allowed to work in Floyd's corner the night
of the second Johansson fight. And thereafter Patterson kept him
away. He gave D'Amato his managerial third of the money, but he
didn't let him get too close to training. . . .

"The last sad item was the Liston fight. Patterson had delegated
D'Amato to make some of the arrangements. According to the newspapers, Patterson then discovered that D'Amato was trying to delay
the negotiations. Now D'Amato was accepted in camp only as a kind
of royal jester who could entertain reporters with printable stories.
He seemed to be kept in the cabin where I met him at the foot of the
hill, forbidden access to the gymnasium the way a drunk is eighty-
sixed from his favorite bar. It must have been a particularly Italian
humiliation for a man like D'Amato to sit in that cabin and talk to
journalists. . . . He could speak, but he could not act.

"Speak he did. If you listened to D'Amato talk, and knew nothing
other, you would not get the impression D'Amato was no longer the
center of Patterson's camp. He seemed to give off no sense whatever

of having lost his liaison to Floyd. When he talked of making the Liston fight, one would never have judged he had tried to prevent it. 'I didn't,' he swore to me. 'I wanted the fight. Floyd came up to me, and said, "Cus, you got to make this fight. Liston's going around saying I'm too yellow to fight him. I don't care if a fighter says he can beat me, but no man can say I'm yellow."' D'Amato bobbed his head. 'Then Floyd said, "Cus, if this fight isn't made, I'll be scared to go out. I'll be afraid to walk into a restaurant and see Liston eating. Because if I see him, I'll have a fight with him right there in the restaurant, and I'll kill him." I wouldn't try to keep Floyd from having a fight after he says something like that!' said D'Amato."

Yeah, right.

A week before the fight, Liston had been an 8–5 favorite but at fight time the odds had narrowed to 7.5–5. The fight lasted only 126 seconds after a minute and a half of tentative feeling out. Mailer nailed the end of the fight perfectly: "Then occurred what may have been the most extraordinary moment ever seen in a championship fight. . . . Patterson, abruptly, without having been hurt in any visible way, stood up suddenly out of his crouch, his back a foot from the ropes, and seemed to look half up into the sky as if he had seen something there or had been struck by something from there, by some transcendent bolt, and then he staggered like a man caught in machine-gun fire, and his legs went, and he fell back into the ropes. . . . Patterson looked at Liston with one lost look . . . the look of a man saying, 'Don't kill me,' and then Liston hit him two or three ill-timed punches, banging a sloppy stake into the ground, and Patterson went down. And he was out. He was not faking. He had started to pass out at the moment he stood straight on his feet and was struck by that psychic bolt which had come from wherever it had come.

"Patterson rolled over, he started to make an attempt to get to his feet, and [James] Baldwin and I were each shouting, 'Get up, get up!' But one's voice had no force in it, one's will had no life.

"Patterson got up somewhere between a quarter and a half second too late. . . . The fight was over: 2:06 of the First. . . . Liston looked like he couldn't believe what had happened. He was blank for

two or three long seconds, and then he gave a whoop. It was an arti-
ficial, tentative whoop, but it seemed to encourage him because he
gave another which sounded somewhat better, and then he began to
whoop and whoop and laugh and shout because his handlers had
come into the ring and were hugging him and telling him he was the
greatest fighter that ever lived. And Patterson, covered quickly
with his bathrobe, still stunned, turned and buried his head in Cus
D'Amato's shoulder.

"From the stands behind us came one vast wave of silence. . . .
'What happened?' said Baldwin.

"What did happen? Everybody was to ask that question later. But
in private.

"The descriptions of the fight [the next morning] showed no un-
certainty. They spoke of critical uppercuts and powerful left hooks
and pulverizing rights. Liston talked of dominating Patterson with
left hands, Patterson's people said it was a big right which did the job,
some reporters called the punches crunching, others said they were
menacing, brutal, demolishing. One did not read a description of the
fight which was not authoritative. The only contradiction, a most minor contradiction, is that with one exception, a wire-service photograph used everywhere of a right hand by Liston which has apparently
just left Patterson's chin, there were no pictures—and a point was
made of looking at a good many—which show Liston putting a winning glove into Patterson's stomach, solar plexus, temple, nose, or
jaw. In fact there is not a single picture of Liston's glove striking Patterson at all."

Mailer got it! Floyd died of fear. He was frozen. He had his glove
up when Liston hit him. Liston hit him on his glove, he didn't hit him
on his face. Later, in his dressing room, Patterson told the reporters
that he had seen all the punches except for the last one. When he said
that he'd like to fight Liston again, one reporter spit out, "Fight him
again? Why didn't you fight him tonight?"

Gil Rogin was in that dressing room, covering the fight for *Sports
Illustrated*, the one outlet that Cus trusted to tell the truth about him
and Floyd over the years. He wrote that Floyd was destroyed so

completely that he didn't even recall how he wound up on the ropes. " 'Did I come off the ropes like I was going to throw a punch?' he asked pathetically. He was astounded to learn he embraced Manager Cus D'Amato a minute after he had shakily regained his feet. 'I must have still been groggy because I have no knowledge of it. It couldn't have been me. It must have been somebody who looked like me, possibly my brother. You're sure I was hit? I thought I might have blacked out. Gosh, one of these days I'm going to start taking off my boxing trunks right there in the ring in front of all those people, thinking I'm in my dressing room already. Boy that was a terrible performance! My mind just wasn't on the fight. It was what I call a lingering mind. Instead of forgetting everything but my opponent, my mind lingered from here to there to the other place. The fact that my mind lingers is something that I cannot control. I fooled him, though. He said it would go five rounds.' "

Rogin then editorialized and wrote some very true words about Floyd. "What a strange champion Patterson was. What a suffering, bewildered and confused man. He fought superbly only twice in recent years against Archie Moore and against Ingo the second time. The rest of his fights ranged from bad to mediocre. . . . Patterson is a good fighter with a weak chin and—even more costly—serious mental problems that prevent him from fully applying his considerable skills."

As soon as his meeting with the press in his dressing room was over, Floyd got ready to leave. He had two cars waiting for him outside the stadium. One faced the highway that would take him back to New York. The other faced the direction where his hotel was and where a victory celebration had been planned. Floyd said good-bye to his wife and kids, and then he got his disguise out. Before his first fight with Ingo, Floyd had hired an expert to create a beard and a mustache if he lost. He even had a disguise ready if he had lost to McNeeley in Toronto. For this fight Cus had bought a beatnik-style goatee and mustache for $65. Floyd put it on, and he and his friend Mickey Alan got in the car that was pointed toward New York and drove straight through the night all the way to his training camp back on the East Coast.

Mailer took Floyd's loss so hard he stayed up all night drinking. He was still drunk when he went to the new champion's press conference the next morning. He was there on a mission. He knew how to make the rematch the largest fight in the history of boxing.

"The idea I wanted to present at the press conference was demented—namely, that the psychic forces that had surrounded Floyd Patterson had made it impossible for him to fight against Liston because he had been knocked out by a psychic vortex. The Mafia had so surrounded the ring, so surrounded Liston, who was their candidate, that they had established the evil eye, and in his vanity Patterson had separated himself from Cus D'Amato, who knew more about warding off the evil eye than anyone alive, and so it was the evil eye that got Floyd, not Liston. Liston was the most amazed man in the house when Patterson went down. My idea was to publicize all this. I was still thinking in terms of movie scenarios, and the notion was to bring back Cus D'Amato, with Patterson winning the rematch. That's why I said it was demented. As far as I was concerned, I had seen it all—it was absolutely true, there was no question in my mind. . . . I had picked Patterson to win by a knockout in the sixth round and I was still right. You see, it was just that the true scenario hadn't had a chance to enact itself, because Patterson was knocked down in the first round. And nobody ever was quite certain what knocked him out, so at the press conference I was going to attribute it to witchcraft, which in my grand and demented theory was going to build the greatest gate in history."

Liston was running late so Norman decided to sit down on a chair on the dais. Some of the newspapermen started complaining, and Harold Conrad made a snap decision and had a few security guards pick up the chair with Mailer still in it and remove it and him from the room. But Norman snuck back in later. By now Sonny was up on-stage answering a question about Floyd's punching power. "He hits harder than I thought he would," said Liston. "But he never landed a punch," the reporter followed. "That's true," said Liston, "but he banged me on the arm. I could feel it there."

Then Liston said something derogatory about reporters and

Mailer jumped to his feet from his chair in the back. "Well, I'm not a reporter," he shouted, "but I'd like to say—" Sonny cut him off. "You're worse than a reporter," he sneered. There was a chorus of "Shut the bum up" from scattered reporters. "No," said Liston. "Let the bum speak." Mailer tried to compose himself. "I picked Floyd Patterson to win by a one-punch knockout in the sixth round, and I still think I was right," he shouted. "You're still drunk," Sonny said. There were more shouts to shut Mailer up and another reporter asked a question and his moment had been lost.

But Mailer didn't give up. When the press conference started petering out, he approached Liston. "What did you do, go out and get another drink?" Sonny snorted. "Liston," Mailer replied, "I still say Floyd Patterson can beat you." Sonny actually smiled! "Aw, why don't you stop being a sore loser?" "You called me a bum," Mailer protested. "Well, you *are* a bum," Liston said. "Everybody is a bum. I'm a bum, too. It's just that I'm a bigger bum than you are." Liston stood and extended his hand to Mailer. "Shake, bum," he said. Then Mailer decided to let Sonny into his grand plan. He took his hand and drew Sonny to within a foot. "Listen, I'm pulling this caper for a reason. I know a way to build the next fight from a $200,000 dog in Miami to a $2,000,000 gate in New York." "Say, that last drink really set you up. Why don't you go and get *me* a drink, you bum?" Sonny suggested. As Mailer recounted: " 'I'm not your flunky,' I said. It was the first jab I'd slipped, it was the first punch I'd sent home. He loved me for it. The hint of a chuckle of corny old darky laughter, cottonfield giggles, peeped out a moment from his throat. 'Oh, sheeet, man!' said the wit in his eyes. And for the crowd who was watching, he turned and announced at large, 'I like this guy.'

"So I left that conference a modest man. Because now I knew that when it came to debate I had met our Zen master."

Liston was on a high from winning the championship and Mailer's admiration, but when he flew back to his hometown of Philadelphia, no one was waiting at the airport to greet him. In fact, no public figures even congratulated him. He got bitter and told his sparring partner, "I didn't expect the president to invite me into the

White House and let me sit next to Jackie and wrestle with those nice Kennedy kids, but I sure didn't expect to be treated like no sewer rat."

But Liston's manager Nilon put a great spin on Sonny's victory. He predicted that Sonny would demolish Floyd again and then destroy Johansson. Then he had high praise for Cus. "Nilon has little respect for any of Patterson's advisers," Boyle wrote, "except, oddly enough, his manager Cus D'Amato, who did all he could to stop Patterson from fighting Liston. 'Doesn't a mother protect her children?' Nilon asked. 'There isn't a man in the United States who knows more about the fight game. But it looks as if he's out. In my opinion, there are certain people who are misleading Floyd.' "

Cus began to get some sympathy from the press too. Dick Young, a columnist for the New York *Daily News*, wrote an impassioned defense of Cus a few days after the fight. "If your son comes to you and says he wants to be a fighter, the first thing you do is hit him on the head; if he persists, the second thing you do is send him to Cus D'Amato.

"The only thing bad that could happen to the kid would be that he began to take himself seriously, the way Floyd Patterson did, and that would be regrettable, because you don't get that big unless you want to find out what you really are.

"So, Floyd Patterson outgrew Cus D'Amato. He made new friends, who convinced him D'Amato was creating for him a craven image, and that he could do better without the old man. And Floyd Patterson listened. He drifted away from the man who had suckled him, and had made him, and had secured his family. . . . D'Amato will be around the fight business long after Floyd Patterson is gone. D'Amato will have other fighters, and he will do for them what he has done for Floyd Patterson."

The fight did very well, grossing more than $4 million. But that didn't do any of the fighters or their managers or the promoters any good. Roy Cohn had pissed off JFK's brother, Robert Kennedy, who was the U.S. attorney general at the time. Kennedy had given an associate of his a ten-man staff of IRS agents to take down Cohn. They even called it "The Cohn Squad." Its first move was to seize the proceeds of the Liston–Patterson fight minutes after the fight was over. They used a ruling called a "jeopardy assessment" and claimed that the precedent for doing this was when Johansson left the country after his third fight without paying his taxes.

One of the people involved in the seizure was a young lawyer named Robert Arum, who thought the move was justified by existing tax law. Years later he said, "As the head of the tax section of the U.S. Attorney's office, I was delegated to that case, and in connection with handling that case I met Roy Cohn who was the principal of Championship Sports. I took testimony of all the players involved, including Mr. Cohn, who I realized had a pretty good grasp of the business. . . . After that, years later, when I became a boxing promoter, he always told people that he was the one who taught me the business, and, in a way, that was true." This is obviously why Cus came to hate Arum so much.

Meanwhile, Floyd, Sonny, Nilon, Cus, and Harold Conrad, they all got swept up into this and all their money was put in escrow by the IRS. And they were pretty pissed, especially Sonny and Nilon. Nilon was the go-between between Liston and Carbo and Palermo. In the good old days, mobsters would just reach into their pockets and pay the fighters off. Those days were over, for the most part. On February 13, 1963, Carbo's and Palermo's and Gibson's appeals were denied, although Dragna's conviction was reversed. But that meant that Palermo and Sica had to go straight to jail. Carbo was already residing at a federal penitentiary in Washington State. Though Carbo and Palermo still owned a majority share of Liston, they wouldn't ever be able to attend one of his fights again. Carbo's ailments would catch up with him and he'd get a compassionate discharge so he could go home to Miami and die, which he would do on November 9, 1976. Blinky would do his time and be released in 1971, about a year after his fighter Liston would die of a heroin overdose under suspicious circumstances. Once Palermo got out, he would have the balls to apply for a manager's license. He would die in his hometown of Philadelphia at age ninety-one in 1996.

THE REMATCH WITH LISTON was scheduled for April 10, 1963, in Miami Beach, but in late March, Sonny strained some ligaments in his left knee as he was swinging a golf club. The doctors told him to take time off and rest but Sonny was itching to fight. "With my leg cut off, they might say it's a close fight." The fight was postponed until July 22 and moved to Las Vegas.

Cus then took off for London with one of his other fighters. The British press peppered him with questions about his relationship with Floyd and he was brutally honest about the intrigue surrounding Patterson. "I resent the people around Patterson who have distracted him. . . . I'm completely confident that without distractions Floyd would have proved himself superior to Sonny Liston. To see a man beaten, not by a better opponent but by himself, is a disturbing thing to witness. It is a tragedy."

Floyd probably didn't appreciate those honest sentiments. He opened up to Robert Boyle of *Sports Illustrated*, who was close to Cus. Floyd claimed that Cus had abandoned him in his camp leading up to the Liston rematch. "I don't think my manager wants to be my manager," Floyd said. "What's the expression about leaving a sinking ship? Cus made it seem like I was ducking Liston because I was afraid of him, and after the match was made he acted around the camp as if I were a kid going against my father. He never did warm up. When I needed him most he was very cool."

Despite Floyd's laments about Cus deserting him, the reality was that Cus was effectively frozen out of the Patterson camp before the rematch. November and Cohn had won. Cus was like a ghost in Vegas, so he began pursuing his new obsession—fishing. When we talked to Robert Boyle, he told us that Floyd "would have nothing to do with Cus," so Boyle and Cus would go fishing in the Colorado River. "Floyd struck me as a very flaky kid. He should have had trust in Cus, but you know Cus's behavior at times was so bizarre that

José Torres (center) with some of Cus's other fighters.

Ali versus D'Amato. Cus opened a cut over Ali's eye soon
after this moment.

Me and Cus hanging on the back porch of Camille's house.

Cus got me a pigeon coop so I could stay out of trouble.

Posing with my Rolls-Royce in Catskill. Our dreams of grandeur were beginning to come true.

It was always a feast when Camille cooked dinner.

Cus was so proud of his boys. That's Tom Patti to my left.

Cus's three champions!

The original Team Tyson: Cus, Kevin Rooney,
me, Bill Cayton, and Jimmy Jacobs.

Cus working me out. Man, was I in shape then!

This was taken right before my first pro fight.

Another shot before my first fight. I'd soon get that steely handshake from Cus and be ready to destroy anyone in front of me.

Me with two of Cus's brothers, Tony and Rocco, at Cus's memorial.

Norman Mailer (with Torres behind him) speaking at Cus's memorial.

Two men
about to take
on the world.
We're ready!

The press
conference after
I won my first
heavyweight
title. That's my
brother Rodney
behind me.

unless you could understand what he was up to, you'd think he was crazy." Whoa. My wife thinks the same thing about me.

Boyle wrote an amusing piece about fishing with Cus, both in Vegas and upstate, which ran months later in *Sports Illustrated*. Quoting Cus that he was a fishing "fanatic," Boyle described Cus's strategy for going up against the fish. "Never has there been such an angler as he is. He plots against the bass in much the same way he used to hatch schemes to foil Jim Norris. He talks to the fish. He shouts at the fish. He buys lures by the ton. He dreams about fish. He lives to fish. Fishing is all he cares for. 'It's a good thing I didn't fish when I was a kid. I never would have done anything else.' "

Boyle reported that Cus didn't begin fishing until he went upstate during the outcry over the Rosensohn scandal. Boyle suggested they fish together. Cus didn't catch anything that first day but on the second day he nabbed a smallmouth bass. "Catching a bass is like getting bit by a mosquito with malaria. You get a disease," Cus said. The next day Boyle couldn't fish but he did drive Cus to a creek. "I was all alone and then in a while it began to get dark. I thought I was gonna get caught in a thunderstorm. I began to get the gear together and then suddenly it dawned on me. It was getting darker and darker. It wasn't a thunderstorm. It was nighttime. The whole day gone! I lost a whole day in my life without realizing it. I wondered whether this is an illness. A particular type of illness where you get pleasure not pain, where you get reinfected each time. Where you want to get reinfected!"

Now Cus started wearing a fishing jacket, creel, hat, all the accoutrements. "If I look like a nonfisherman, the fish won't want to be caught. They have pride. So I remove this possible area of resistance. The fish look up, and they say, 'Ah, there's a real fisherman.' " If the fish balk, Cus pleads with them. "I sort of talk it up. I invent stories for them. I think all the adult fish are telling all the others not to bite. Somebody must be instructing them! If you go out there with confidence and proceed with enthusiasm, you'll get better results. When I'm there, it seems normal."

This is the shit I grew up with, right? I love this guy. When Boyle picked up Cus to go fishing in Vegas he saw that Cus was reading *Walden* by Henry David Thoreau. "I said, 'Thoreau,'" Boyle told us, "and with that, Cus said, 'You know the guy?' as though he was alive." Boyle told him that Thoreau had died a hundred years ago but that he would have loved Cus.

The thing that struck Boyle the most on that Nevada fishing trip happened back in Cus's hotel room. Boyle arrived at Cus's room at five in the morning to wake him up for the fishing outing. Cus started getting dressed. He sat down on the edge of his bed and then he carefully spread his trousers out on the floor. Then "with a joyous whoop, he quickly pulled both trouser legs toward him and in an instant was on his feet with his pants on." Boyle asked him what that ritual was all about. "I've always had a reason for doing that," Cus said. "You know when one of the mustache guys [he always called the Mafia the mustache guys] come to me and try to put the bull on me, I tell him, 'Get out of here.' He'll say, 'I'm going to take care of you, D'Amato; you're just like everyone else—when you get dressed in the morning, you put your pants on one leg at a time.' He said I'm going to say to him, 'I've got news for you.'"

Boyle told us about one other interesting event that occurred before the second Liston fight. "While I was away [on leave from *Sports Illustrated*] for a few years, that's when the uproar started about the first Johansson fight that Patterson lost, and *S.I.* went off the wall and almost portrayed Cus as a crook with Fat Tony Salerno, with this guy and that guy. That was all bullshit! That was Bill Rosensohn putting out a lot of lies. Cus had been a very wronged guy by the magazine. I mean that was obvious. They didn't understand him and they believed Rosensohn's bullshit. Rosensohn confessed to me that he lied and I brought Gil Rogin over to see Rosensohn because he was in Vegas to cover the fight if Patterson won. Rosensohn said, 'I lied; I made that stuff up.' I was glad to clear Cus's name."

A week before the fight, nobody knew which Patterson would show up to fight. Peter Wilson, the legendary British sports reporter, joked, "I call him Freud Patterson. He is vulnerable to words as well as punches." But despite being a pariah in his own camp, Cus was still tooting Floyd's horn. He saw Norman Mailer and told him, "Everything points to an upset. The other man is casual, Patterson has been working hard, all the signs are there." He talked to Arthur Daley, who was covering the fight for the *Times*. "Floyd has knocked out every man he met in a return bout." Of course, that was one guy, Ingo. Then Cus put his spin on the first Liston fight. "Floyd gave him hitting room from up close. This is really correctable. He won't do it again."

So much for "Custradamus." Floyd lasted four seconds longer against Sonny this time but that's counting the two mandatory eight counts he got after Liston floored him. Once again he ignored his game plan and froze. Despite the pitiful showing, it was Liston who was booed on his way back to his dressing room after the massacre.

Floyd and Cus each reacted to the outcome true to form. Floyd used an interview with Gay Talese that appeared in *Esquire* as another therapy session. "I think that within me, within every human being, there is a certain weakness. It's a weakness that expresses itself more when you're alone. And I have figured out that part of the reason I do the things I do, and cannot seem to conquer that one word—*myself*—is because . . . I am a coward. I am a coward. My fighting has little to do with that fact, though. I mean you can be a fighter—and a *winning* fighter—and still be a coward. . . . It's easy to do anything in victory. It's in defeat that a man reveals himself. In defeat I can't face people. I haven't the strength to say to people, 'I did my best, I'm sorry, and what not.' "

Floyd's description of being knocked out by Liston was chilling. "Suddenly, with all this screaming around you, you're down again, and you know you have to get up, but you're extremely groggy, and the referee is pushing you back, and your trainer is in there with a towel, and your eyes focus directly at no one person—you're sort of floating. It is not a bad feeling when you're knocked out. It's a good feeling. You don't see angels or stars; you're on a pleasant cloud. After Liston hit me in Nevada, I felt, for about four or five seconds, that everybody in the arena was actually in the ring with me, circled around me like a family, and you feel warmth toward all the people in the arena after you're knocked out. And you want to reach out and kiss everybody—men and women—and after the Liston fight somebody told me I blew a kiss to the crowd from the ring. . . . But then this good feeling leaves you. You realize what has just happened to you. And what follows is a hurt, a confused hurt—not a physical hurt—it's hurt combined with anger and all you want then is a hatch door in the middle of the ring that will open and let you fall through and land in your dressing room. The worst thing about losing is having to walk out of the ring and face those people."

At the press conference after the fight, Cus talked with the fabled writer A. J. Liebling. Liebling asked Cus what had happened. "It was the same as last time. He didn't move around. . . . He can still lick anybody else in the world," Cus said. The two hadn't eaten yet so Cus suggested his hotel, the Tally-Ho, a new hotel that had no gambling tables but good food. The fact that Cus was staying in a hotel rather than at Floyd's camp spoke volumes. Over dinner, which for Cus was a rare Manhattan, chicken-liver pâté, calf's liver smothered with onions, and cherry cheesecake, they talked some more. "I am always at my best when the bottom drops out," he told the writer.

With Sonny again victorious, Jack Nilon now had his chance. He immediately fired Roy Cohn and Championship Sports, whose option expired after the rematch. That was the end of the line in boxing for Cohn. He could have used the same excuse he had employed after the first Floyd–Sonny fiasco: "Why blame me for a bad fight? How did I know Patterson was going to turn yellow?"

When he got back to New York, Cus tried to patch things up with Floyd. He had someone drive him up to Patterson's training camp and knocked on the door repeatedly but Floyd, who was inside, refused to come out and talk to Cus. "I tried to see him every day," he later told Robert Boyle. "He didn't answer the door, but he was in there. I'd bang and bang on the door and call. Nothing would happen. Sometimes I'd wait half an hour, an hour. Then I'd go away. That happened almost every day for a month. We'd been through so much together. I had to see him. We had an agreement that I never was to believe anything he supposedly said until he told it to my face. He has never told me to my face that I am not his manager. I have no idea why he won't see me."

Now Cus began to worry about money. He had spent most of his money in his fight with the IBC. He was working with José Torres, but Cus had never taken a penny from Torres, since he was doing so well with Patterson. With monies still being withheld from the first Liston fight, Patterson asked November for a full accounting in the summer of 1964, but the lawyer never gave him a satisfactory one. It should have been a tip-off when November sued Cus's friend Robert Boyle and *Sports Illustrated* for libel for Boyle's article on the third Ingo fight. November claimed that when Boyle wrote that November told Cus he didn't have to show up for Lefkowitz's subpoena, they were "maliciously false statements defaming him as a lawyer and a man."

So Cus hired the high-powered Washington, D.C.–based attorney Edward Bennett Williams to help him follow the money trail. He figured that he was still owed about $250,000 from the two Liston fights. What they found was that besides the money that had been seized by the government, other money had never reached Cus because Roy Cohn had devised a deferred-payment scheme for Patterson to avoid taxes. Cohn's promotional company would pay off Floyd literally with the interest of his own money and at the end of ten years it would have paid off the obligation to Patterson and still retained the principal!

Since the payments were deferred, Cus never received his one-third but the IRS still taxed him on the amount he would have earned. It was the same way that Joe Louis had gotten screwed. To make matters worse, Cus's accounting was handled by November. Cus never recovered from this quagmire. He was broke and he had no way of making a living because he had signed that consent decree with New York State that he wouldn't manage again. Now Cus felt emotionally betrayed by Floyd and financially betrayed by November.

It got worse. On May 23, the NYSAC approved a one-year pact for Floyd's trainer Dan Florio to manage him. Cus was now officially out without a word of explanation from his greatest pupil. The next week *Sports Illustrated* came to Cus's defense in an item headed "Goodby, Cus." "Boxing has always been a harsh sport, long on bitterness and short on loyalty. But Cus and Floyd seemed different. They were more like father and son than manager and fighter. D'Amato had signed Patterson with a handshake after Floyd had won the 1952 Olympics. Four years later he got Patterson the title fight with Archie Moore that made him, at twenty-one, the youngest man ever to hold the heavyweight championship. D'Amato insisted on sharing the racial snubs Patterson had to endure. He gave up smoking and drinking to make abstinence easier for the fighter. He dedicated himself to making and keeping Patterson the champion. At times he was too dedicated; he was overly protective and too choosy in picking opponents. He may, as some critics think, have stunted Patterson's development. On the other hand, his caution may be the reason why Patterson held the title so long and made so much money from it.

"Patterson has always appeared to be an honorable man and a thoughtful man—though, for a fighter, a curiously hypersensitive one. He must have sound reasons for firing his old friend. But whatever the reasons, he did not discuss them with D'Amato, nor did he tell Cus that he was fired. D'Amato learned of his dismissal from a reporter who called to get his reactions, 'Floyd may have his reasons for doing this—perfectly good reasons. Though the facts point to a complete falling out, I won't accept it until Floyd tells me face to face. That was our agreement.'" Even after he's screwed by Floyd, he's still making excuses for him!

The next month Patterson fought Eddie Machen in Stockholm. Arthur Daley characterized the fight as "two pilgrims along the comeback trail, plodding along the weary road to nowhere." Patterson won the decision but he was criticized by many, including Johansson, for not finishing off Machen when he had him on the ropes. Patterson said, "I looked in his eyes and I saw hurt and defeat. This is a man who had a hard life. He has been broke and in a mental institution. Should I knock him down further for my own good?" Even

Florio, his new manager, was disgusted: "He wants to pick them up. He knocks them down, and he wants to pick them up."

It seemed that Floyd was missing Cus too. A man who was "close" to Patterson told *The New York Times*, "He misses Cus D'Amato. He tries to do everything himself now—run the camp, worry about the money, take legal advice, everything. D'Amato used to do all that and keep him away from everyone so that he could concentrate on fighting. And then you have to remember that he was raised by Cus. All he knows and all his attitudes he got from D'Amato, including the suspicions and prejudices and his quickness to resent. He's got all of D'Amato's craftiness, without D'Amato's background and intelligence."

Three months after he left Cus, Patterson was hit by the IRS. They claimed that he and his wife owed $41,649 for years 1957 and 1958 and that Floyd Patterson Enterprises owed $44,736 for the same period. The IRS disallowed certain claimed expenses—such as travel and training—and claimed his fight profits were higher than reported. They went after his business because they said it was a personal holding company for Floyd and not a corporation, so they should pay personal tax on that income. Floyd kept on fighting, now out of necessity. On November 19, 1965, Patterson fought Muhammad Ali, who had captured the heavyweight crown and retained it when he beat Sonny Liston twice. Cus was still estranged from Floyd but he was optimistic about his chances versus "Clay." "Floyd was a confused fighter against Liston," he told the media. "The only question in my mind is as to whether or not he has cleared it up enough to apply all his assets against Clay. I don't care what anyone says, I'm still absolutely convinced that Floyd was one of our better heavyweight champions, despite his weaknesses."

Ali battered Floyd around for twelve rounds in what some people thought was an attempt to humiliate him. Most of the boxing pundits at ringside said that Ali carried Floyd. Even Cus had to admit Ali's dominance. "The fight proved nothing except that Clay is the most beautiful, the most graceful heavyweight we ever had, certainly the best businessman, maybe someday the best fighter. The more obnoxious he becomes, the more they'll look for a white hope, a Holy Grail, and that is very good for our business," he told *The New York Times*.

Floyd kept fighting, and now, at thirty-two, he was holed up full-time at a new training camp near Newburgh, New York, in a weather-beaten building next to a lodge that had gone out of business. His wife had divorced him and moved to Massachusetts with their children. But Floyd insisted he was happy in an interview with Dave Anderson, a sportswriter for the *Times*. "I'm living the way I want to live. Nobody around me except one trainer, no one else. I love it. The smell of the gym. The long walks. The road work. The seclusion. I may never get back what I once had but it's a pleasure trying it my way, not the way others wanted me to go." Eddie Fowler was training him now and he was managing himself. "If I can be half the manager Cus was for me, I'll be okay."

By 1967 Floyd and Cus were still waiting to get paid for the first Liston fight. And that year the Justice Department formally recommended criminal charges against Cohn and Tom Bolan and the rest of Championship Sports. Eventually every agency involved, Treasury, Justice, even the IRS, dropped the charges. But still the money wasn't released yet. By 1965 Floyd had married a Swedish girl and they had a daughter. And he was telling the press that if he beat Jimmy Ellis in his upcoming fight in Sweden there was "a chance he might get together again with Cus D'Amato."

The fight went the distance, fifteen rounds, and Patterson lost a close decision that was booed by his adoring Swedish fans. Then he went home and fired Julius November, his longtime attorney. According to Floyd, November had made four large investments using Floyd's money and they all failed, including a substantial investment of "many hundreds of thousands of dollars" in Roy Cohn's company Lionel Trains. Now Patterson was suing November for a full accounting of his money.

Cus was in no better financial shape than Floyd. He told his friend Gene Kilroy that if he needed money he could go down to Washington and access the money that the government was holding from the first Liston fight. But in 1980 he did go there only to find that the funds had been released to Patterson. Cus told Joe Colangelo, his close friend in Catskill, that his share was hundreds of thousands of dollars. "Patterson stole that money," Joe told us. "And Cus still treated him like he was his son and he was going to defend him, no matter what. I used to say to Cus, 'Patterson ripped you off.' He would argue that he didn't and I would say, 'You can sit here and say anything you want, anything. But you can't lie to the guy in the mirror,' that was the old Italian expression. I went toe to toe with him on that issue many times and finally Cus said to me, 'He knows what he's done! That's all that counts. He knows what he's done!' "

WHILE CUS HAD THE HEAVYWEIGHT CHAMPION in Patterson, he began developing middleweight José Torres. Torres had won a silver medal at the 1956 Olympics, and some of Cus's fighters from the Gramercy who competed in Melbourne came back and told Cus about him. Cus then took out a full-page ad in *El Mundo* that read in Spanish: "Manager of the World's Heavyweight Champ Floyd Patterson interested in signing our champ 'Chegüi,'" which was José's nickname.

They developed a close relationship. In the first major article about José in 1958 in *The New York Times* by Gay Talese, you can sense the affection between the two. "Cus is like a second father to me," José said. D'Amato smiled and asked, "Have you ever disapproved of anything I've done for you?" "No." "Haven't I always welcomed suggestions from you?" "Yes." D'Amato smiled again. "I consider this boy extraordinary. This boy will build up boxing in New York. He will be the hero of the Puerto Rican people, and he will aid the juvenile delinquency problem." That's Cus. Always the social reformer.

José began dressing like Cus and adopting his mannerisms. Cus refused to take a penny from Torres's purses. But José's career began to be sidetracked; Cus wanted him to fight only unrated fighters and to stay away from televised fights, because he was certain that the remnants of the IBC still controlled them. And when Teddy Brenner joined Harry Markson at Madison Square Garden, Cus refused to allow José to fight there.

The situation was causing controversy in boxing circles and Cus defended his position in a front-page article in the December 31, 1960, edition of Eddie Borden's *Weekly Boxing World*. Cus went into a long history of his relations with MSG and Brenner's constant practice of bringing in out-of-town fighters who could beat and hamper the development of local talent when Brenner was the matchmaker at St. Nicholas Arena. Then Cus rested his case in the last paragraph of his piece, noting that Brenner's ties to the mob had been established in sworn testimony from a "paid IBC confidant. Now tell me Eddie, how can I do business with the Garden or Teddy Brenner?"

Cus never mentioned that the mob associates Norris met with and who put Brenner into the Garden were Frankie Carbo and Blinky Palermo.

The debate over Cus's handling of José raged on. Cus found a defender in a veteran boxing writer named Max Yeargain, whose letter was published by Eddie Borden. Yeargain wrote that he was an early supporter of Cus's battles with the IBC and that most boxing minds couldn't begin to comprehend Cus's strategy of nurturing José. He compared Cus to the then richest man in the United States, J. Paul Getty. "Men like Getty and D'Amato, who dare to be different in thought or action or deviate from the mediocre norm, will be branded as a Bolshevik, a Bohemian, a crank or a crackpot. The General in the Army does not confide with the Private, what his battle plans are, nor does an astute boxing manager map out his strategy to a young protégé, how he will climb to the top in boxing's jungle of crosses and double crosses."

The inactivity began to take its toll on José, both physically and mentally. Pete Hamill, then at the *New York Post*, was a friend of

Cus's and a roommate of José's, and he wrote a moving letter to Cus on March 9, 1961.

In the letter, Hamill showed concern about the caliber of fighters Cus was matching against José, especially since a year earlier there was word that Torres was to get a title bout. Pete, who knew Torres very well, told Cus that José was into boxing more for the glory than the money. "Torres is a supreme egotist . . . a guy to whom the noise of the crowd is very, very important." Hamill warned Cus that if he continued to match Torres in out-of-town venues away from his rabid Puerto Rican following, then "you will break his spirit."

Hamill then had some suggestions for Cus, which included getting Torres a fight at St. Nicholas (and Hamill even offered to get a promoter's license to put it on), giving him some good opponents, putting him on TV for one sensational fight, and having him in training camp with Floyd. But his last suggestion was the most telling: "Come down to the gym at least once a week to look at Torres." Word was being spread in the Puerto Rican boxing community that Cus was so concerned with Patterson that he had lost interest in José's career. If he was present in the gym, Hamill told him, he "could head off any further changes in [José's] attitude."

Of José's next seven fights, the closest he came to New York was the Plaza Ballroom in Paterson, New Jersey. Torres won them all. Cus had felt that José had lost the fire that he had when he first started out. But on July 27, he knocked out Obdulio Nunez in Puerto Rico to win the Puerto Rican middleweight title. Nunez was unconscious for twenty minutes. Now both Cus and José thought that he was ready for a title shot even though he was unranked, thanks to Cus. Paul Pender was the middleweight titleholder then. To get the fight, Torres called Pender in Boston in August of 1962 and impersonated a sportswriter for the newspaper *El Diario*. "We hear rumors that you have been offered $100,000 to fight José Torres," Torres said. "I never heard about that," Pender replied. "In other words, you refuse to fight Torres?" "Listen, I don't care who my opponent is, all I'm interested in is money. I want money."

Now all they had to do was raise the money. Cus was broke and told the press that the fight had to be called off because the IRS still had his Liston purse. But Torres went to the press with the real story. Cus had gone to Patterson and asked him to lend him the money and Floyd had turned him down. Patterson still seemed to be harboring a grudge against Torres because when he was sparring with Patterson in preparation for the Harris bout, Torres hit Patterson and he either slipped or went down from the punch and the publicist used it as PR to make Harris look like he had a chance against Floyd. Patterson still resented that.

By the end of 1964, José had moved up to light heavyweight and he was on a roll, winning all six of his bouts that year. On November 27, he fought in the Garden against Bobo Olson, with the winner being guaranteed a shot at Willie Pastrano's light heavyweight belt. Torres knocked him out in the first round and now he was finally about to challenge for a title. Again José had to put up a $100,000 guarantee for the fight. By then he had acquired a business manager, a black real estate developer named Cain Young.

Cus and Young didn't get along at all. They were at a Torres fight in Puerto Rico and Cus attacked Young and someone had to separate them. So Young told José that the only way he'd put up the hundred grand was if Cus released José from his contract. José was incredibly loyal to Cus and he didn't want that to happen, so José went over to his friend Norman Mailer's house and explained that he needed money to fight for the title. Mailer called his father, who was also his accountant. He cupped his hand and whispered to José, "How much money can we lose if the worst happens?" José said, "I don't know. Maybe $90,000 at the most." Mailer checked with his father and said he'd put up the $100,000.

José then called Cus. But Cus was adamant. "We could lose. I don't want you to screw up your head worrying about your friend's money." And three weeks later, Young apologized and put up the guarantee. Torres then refused to fight unless Cus sat ringside and called out the numbers that they had developed using Cus's Willie (Pastrano) bag system.

The fight was set for the Garden on March 30, 1965. Cus, of course, was predicting that José would knock Pastrano out, even though Pastrano had never even been knocked down in his whole career. José's fellow Puerto Ricans jammed the Garden and the attendance, 18,112, produced a record gate of $239,956. One of the spectators was a black man wearing a false mustache and goatee and sitting in the balcony. It was Floyd in disguise. Some of the press speculated that Patterson didn't want to see Cus, but when he was approached he said he wanted to concentrate on watching the fight.

Torres was the aggressor the whole fight and some reporters gave him every round. In the sixth, Cus, who was sitting ringside, yelled out, "Five," which was a body shot to the liver, and José nodded. There was some speculation that Torres would target the liver because the rumor was that Pastrano was a boozer. José got in a vicious left hook and Pastrano crumbled into the ropes and went down for the first time in his career. He got up at the count of nine. The doctor examined Pastrano in his corner and they let him continue, but after the ninth round the referee stopped the fight.

There was a near riot in the Garden as fans rushed into the ring. Norman Mailer was one of the first to congratulate José but cops stopped Cus from climbing into the ring. Don Dunphy, who was calling the fight for TV, said he had never seen such bedlam in the Garden. One reporter wrote, "When Pastrano fell it was as if every Puerto Rican present felt that he personally had done it."

José and his entourage went to Toots Shor's restaurant to celebrate because Torres and Pete Hamill had gone there years earlier and the bartender had looked suspiciously at José, as if he didn't have the money to pay for his drinks. Then at two forty-five in the morning they all drove to Brooklyn to party all night at Mailer's apartment. Mailer had won $600 on the fight and he had hired a three-piece rock 'n' roll combo to entertain the guests. It was an eclectic mixture at Mailer's—James Baldwin, Ben Gazzara, Leslie Fiedler, George Plimpton, Pete Hamill, Senator Jacob Javits, and Archie Moore. When Torres finally arrived, one guest actually said, "Who is he?"

The party raged on for hours. At one point, Cus commanded the attention of the room. "Nobody in that place could be as happy as I was, nobody. You see how happy you are? You and all of them, couldn't be as happy as me. I want them to know, because if I was in that corner, you know what I would have said to you, Joe? Joe, you won that championship, you and you alone. I helped in different ways, yes, but you and you alone did that and now you're going to be twice as good a fighter as you was before, do you know that? You were great before, you're twice as good now that you know you're the champion of the world. You're going to win the heavyweight championship too."

"Yes, sir," José agreed.

"You've got to admit one thing, I'm not often wrong, am I, Joe?"

"No."

"And you see, the way I say things that's the way they come out. I tell you now, Joe, I'm going to say it in front of your wife, you have the best wife in the whole world. I'm telling you, that's the truth."

José was good, but he didn't want to take any punishment in the ring. He was never the same after Florentino Fernández dropped him in Puerto Rico in 1963. Cus was wary after that and never put him in with big punchers. That's why he put him in with Pastrano. Willie was a masterful boxer but he was a little bit over the hill and he couldn't punch hard.

One night I was in a club and I met Willie Pastrano's granddaughter. Once I see somebody and they tell me they're related to a fighter, their night is ruined because they've got to listen to me fire off question after question—I want to soak up as much as I can about the greats. "Tell me about him, what kind of guy was he?" She told me that Willie was poisoned before the Torres fight. Somebody put something in his drink and he felt drugged that whole fight. It's funny because Dunphy was talking during the whole fight about how Willie looked sluggish and couldn't find his rhythm.

Now Cus was back and he wasn't shy about it. His friend Robert Boyle wrote a big article in *Sports Illustrated* called "Svengali Returns!" It was vintage Cus. He scorned the doubters who, he said, "penalize me for their ignorance." He defended his peekaboo style. He told Boyle that he gave José his release because Markson and Brenner wouldn't let José fight for the title if Cus controlled him, then went after them. "As far as I am concerned, the fight is not over until I win. I may not win the battles, which I look upon as only temporary advantages to my opponent, but I'll win the war! And the war will go on till I win out, till Teddy Brenner and those characters go."

Then he went after the press and the pundits. "If every newspaperman, every commission, thinks my fighter should fight some fighter of a better class, that doesn't impress me. I alone have the responsibility for the development of the fighters. These so-called experts are ignorant. They think a fighter should fight a certain fighter, and if my fighter loses, who gets blamed? The critics? No. Me. I didn't let Torres fight at times, and the reason I didn't is secret. To reveal the reasons is to make the fighter susceptible. I could avoid all this criticism by sitting down and educating the critics and after I got through, they would agree with me. But I let the results speak for themselves."

Cus told Boyle he had some "tremendous surprises planned, but I can't say what they are because they wouldn't be surprises if I did. These surprises may very well make headlines." Then he landed the knockout punch. "There is no man in the whole world who knows as much about the whole boxing picture as I do. I don't say that I'm smarter than other people, but I had the opportunity available to me in the last 10 years, and I was almost alone. It's like a doctor given the chance to study under a great surgeon way ahead of everybody else. That's not bragging. That's simple fact."

After the fight, Torres immediately announced that he was going after the heavyweight crown. In an article he wrote for *Boxing Illustrated* in November 1965, he vowed to fight and beat Patterson. "We were once very good friends. But, when he had a chance to do something big for me, he let me down and he let Cus down. . . . Against him, I'll be double mean. . . . I have my ambition to become heavyweight champion. I have my ambition to get even for Cus with

Patterson, and I have my ambition to make myself a better, and a cleverer, voice to help my people in the future, whatever way it's possible."

None of that happened. The day after he won his crown, José told Pete Hamill that he couldn't believe he was champ, that it was like a dream. But something was strange. "It still didn't feel right," José said. He defended his crown successfully three times yet he never had the same fire as when he was young.

Cus blamed Torres's decline on his friendship with famous writers. Cus was interviewed for a book about Norman Mailer and said, "The only change I noticed in José after he became friends with Mailer was a definite loss of interest in boxing. José would go out to bars, stay out all night, and so forth. It was all the writers that Torres used to meet when they'd go and drink—Hamill, Budd Schulberg, Harvey Breit, Gay Talese. And since José was interested in writing, he looked up to these people."

José lost his title in December of 1966 to Dick Tiger, then he fought three more times before retiring and, after being mentored by Hamill and Mailer, became a writer. He stayed loyal to Cus for the rest of his life.

Now Cus was a go-to analyst again, popping up all over the media. In April of 1965 he was quoted in *Sports Illustrated* commenting on the upcoming second fight between Ali and Liston. "If I had Liston, he could beat Clay. Liston is confused by mobility. I would show him how to neutralize Clay's mobility. That may make me sound conceited, but I'm not." Liston lost that second fight, getting knocked out for the first time in his career by "a punch of dubious velocity," as Arthur Daley called it. Six months after he lost the rematch, Liston reached out to Cus to manage him for his comeback. Cus thought that it would be a challenge but he said that there was a "distinct possibility that I could make Liston the heavyweight champion again if he divests himself of the people around him." Sonny agreed, saying, "It's the onliest way." But that was the last anyone heard of that union.

Cus's image was so rehabilitated that he was called to Washington to testify at hearings on introducing legislation to create a federal boxing commission. He appeared alongside Marciano, Dempsey, and Tunney, who all supported the bill. On July 8, 1965, he appeared before the House of Representatives Committee on Interstate and Foreign Commerce to talk about boxing regulation. After introducing himself, he talked about his struggle to fight the boxing monopoly.

"Once [Patterson] became champion of the world, I tried to influence the situation by introducing promoters who were not affiliated with those that controlled boxing. I wanted the boxing people to know by dealing with these promoters that a heavyweight championship fight could be conducted without the people who controlled boxing, that this was possible; and . . . I had hoped to influence the managers who had other fighters who, being encouraged by my success, would follow. This did not happen. But in the process of doing this, Floyd Patterson, the heavyweight champion of the world at that time, made more money than any other fighter in the history of boxing. He made that money because I dealt with people who were willing to pay because we had competition in boxing for the first time; a monopoly did not exist. I had hoped by my example to influence the others and to stir up a spark so that they would fight too. But they could not and they would not."

At one point Cus was interrupted by Representative Torbert Macdonald of Massachusetts.

MACDONALD: At that juncture, Mr. D'Amato, I would like to make my position clear. I have never met you, but I have admired you for a number of years for your fight against the monopoly of boxing, and also for the care that you gave to your fighters. I think when you say that Floyd Patterson has made more money than any boxer ever has, I think that is a tribute to you for which you have been criticized and how you handled him or not that is a testimonial to you. I think one thing should be said for the record that you, perhaps, would be too modest to say, is that after you developed the now light heavyweight champion of the world and the one who might indeed be the heavyweight champion, in my judgment, you gave him his release . . . D'AMATO: I did. MACDONALD: After you had expended a number of dollars in developing him. D'AMATO: Many thousands of dollars.

MACDONALD: I would think that your example in the boxing field is not only exemplary but extraordinary, and I personally would like to congratulate you on your conduct in the area.

Cus must have eaten that up.

Cus seemed to be back but he began spending more time upstate. Cus had always had an upstate retreat where he would secretly meet Camille. It was the house in Fishkill that was referred to in the NYSAC hearings. Everything about Cus was complicated and this house was no different. The house was in his brother Tony's name. But the first mortgagee was Einer Thulin, Cus's Swedish fight-reporter friend. And the fire insurance policy was addressed to Cus c/o Robert Melnick, Cus's old trainer friend.

During the Ali–Patterson fight in Vegas on November 22, 1965, Cus was interviewed and talked about moving upstate. "It was very tough coming up here to live, because I was very bored and the loneliness and the quietness was something," he told a CBS television program. "I couldn't sleep, I just couldn't sleep. I had to get used to everything, the idea of dying. It's something a person gets used to and accepts it." Little did anyone know that the following year I would be born and our mission for world domination would be destined.

But he kept trying to keep busy. He devised a scheme to get the great basketball player Wilt Chamberlain to fight Muhammad Ali. Cus offered Chamberlain a contract to turn pro and Ali and Wilt even did some promotional interviews together but in August of 1965 Chamberlain used the offer as leverage to sign a three-year deal for $110,000 a year with the Philadelphia 76ers.

Around the same time, he tried to sign Buster Mathis to a pro contract. Mathis was a promising amateur who had beaten Joe Frazier in the Olympic Trials but couldn't compete for a gold medal at the 1964 Tokyo Olympics because of an injury. He was six feet, three and half inches tall and weighed 290 pounds, and he was surprisingly light on his feet for such a heavy guy. But on August 17, 1965, Mathis signed with Peers Management, a syndicate that included two sons of the owner of the New York Jets. They named Al Bachman as Buster's manager and Charlie Goldman as his trainer. At the press function to introduce Mathis, Cus was giddy about him. "He's a monster who performs like a little lightweight," Cus said. "He has more ability, coupled with audience impact, than anyone in boxing today, and that includes Cassius Clay."

The boys at Peers must have remembered those kind words seven months later when they fired Bachman and Goldman and hired Cus to train Mathis. Cus wanted to manage him but took the lesser position on two conditions—that he would have complete creative control over Mathis's boxing and that he himself would work for free until the Peer Group recouped its initial $50,000 investment. After that, they would split their share of Mathis's annual earnings.

Cus's first move was to pull Mathis out of a fight with Jerry Quarry at the Garden because of a last-minute "injury." Brenner then vowed to hold Mathis to his original contract. That led to a new feud with Brenner and more fights being canceled by the Garden.

In April of 1966 Cus took Buster up to Pawling Health Manor, the holistic health retreat in Rhinebeck, New York, started by Cus's friend Dr. Bob Gross and his wife, Joy. People from all over the country came to the Manor to lose weight, eat well, and rejuvenate. They had a small gym on the property and Bob told Cus he could put his boxing ring in the gym. Buster was put on a high-protein, low-carbohydrate diet and he dropped fifty-five pounds. Cus also began introducing Buster to the Willie Bag and had him box five rounds with it every day. Once, after Buster complained, he had him throw twelve thousand more punches. "When I first met Cus, I didn't get along," Mathis told Robert Boyle. "I didn't know how to hang up my clothes and clean my room. I'm not A-1 yet. He's hard to get along with, and sometimes he's miserable. But he wants to make me champion. This is the only man I met who didn't lie, and he doesn't bite his tongue for anything. There are times I get so mad at Cus I cry. But he's a heck of a man. I have learned more from him than I have from anyone," Buster said.

One of the first things Cus did was to win over Buster's girlfriend, Joan. "Cus, he was really a good man. I'm just a country farm girl, so when Buster introduced me to Cus, Cus looked at Buster and said, 'If you don't marry this woman, I'm going to disown you,' " she told us. "And Buster said, 'Why would you say that, Cus?' Cus said, 'I am a very good judge of character and this woman will stick with you, whether you make it or not.' "

Cus knew he'd need an ally to get to Buster. Cus had a keen perception about people and he used it to his advantage when needed. Before long he had Joan working as a spy for him!

"Cus could just read people," Joan said. "Sometimes Buster would come home on breaks from camp and Cus would call me, 'Did he run this morning?' I said, 'No.' Because I would tell Cus exactly the truth, because that's the only way I know how to do it. Cus would ask, 'Is he sticking to his diet?' and I would say, 'No.' He would tell me that he won't mention it when Buster comes back to camp. He never knew that Cus was checking up on him that way."

I can just picture him doing that.

Buster's son, who was named Buster D'Amato Mathis, remembers his father telling him that Cus was a "militant" trainer and everything had to be done his way. He mentioned that all of Cus's fighters had to fight going forward. It was hard for them to go backward, he said. But that was all about entertainment. If you're going forward, you're entertaining the crowd. Backing up meant you were retreating. No action. No entertainment value. Cus encouraged Buster to be a showman. He liked it when Buster danced a jig on his way to his corner. He encouraged him to blow kisses to the crowd. And he taught him to growl at his opponent as he threw a punch. Buster seemed to be happy with his new arrangement. "When I walk into the ring, I figure I gotta win," he said. "No one trains as hard as me, runs as hard as me, or has had Cus on his back."

But by May 1967 there was trouble in paradise. The *New York Post* had a big headline, "Will Buster's Backers Split over D'Amato?" Lester Bromberg reported that there were splits among the six investors in Peers Management. After a year of working with Cus, the investors thought that Buster hadn't made enough progress or gotten enough experience in the ring. Jim Iselin, the originator of the group, was spearheading the move to oust Cus. But one dissenter was willing to buy out the other five and keep Cus. Iselin refused comment.

But Cus commented on Buster and a lot more in a very revealing interview he did with Lenny Traube for the August 1967 issue of *Sport* magazine. They started by talking about Mathis.

Q: Is Mathis really a fighter? A: I think he's a potential champion providing I can iron out some of his emotional problems. He's really ready now to step out with some of the better fighters.

Then Traube asked Cus the questions most fight fans were interested in getting answers to.

Q: What was the big reason for your split-up with Patterson? A: To this day, I don't know why we separated. All I can say is it must have been due to outside influences. Patterson and I had a verbal agreement that if he ever wanted to leave me, all he had to do was come to me and I would release him, contract or no contract. But under no condition was he to accept anything said by anyone else without discussing it with me. He agreed to do this. Since he has not yet in so many words told me that we are no longer associated, I still consider that we are bound by that verbal agreement.

Q: Did you sincerely feel at the time that Liston was dominated by the underworld, or was this just an excuse to avoid making the match? A: Let's say it was certainly a means by which I accomplished my objective, which was to not let Patterson fight him until I felt that Patterson was at his best.

Whoa. Here's Cus going out of his way once again to avoid saying anything about the mob even when anyone who listened to the testimony in the Kefauver hearings knew that Liston was cut up to five different mobsters. Now he's saying that the mob owning Liston was just a tactic to avoid the fight? Then Cus lets it all hang out about his break with José, even if José didn't know they'd had a break.

Q: Torres once said that he'd like to fight Patterson to punish him for what he did to you. Has that loyalty Torres displayed then, since disappeared? A: Well, I don't know. All I know is he objected because I fired a trainer whom I caught lying and cheating. He thought that because he was champion of the world I should bow to him, but to me he was another fighter, that's all, and so I just walked away from him.

Q: You have always maintained that the fight game was gangster controlled. Do you still believe that? A: No. I don't believe the fight game is gangster controlled. At one time it was, but it is not anymore.

Q: Of all the fighters you've handled whom did you admire most as a man? A: I admired Patterson both as a man and a fighter up until the time he allowed himself to be distracted. My admiration suffered somewhat as a result of his being influenced.

Q: What's been the happiest moment in your life in boxing and the unhappiest? A: The happiest moment of my life was when Floyd Patterson won the heavyweight championship of the world. The unhappiest was when he was defeated by Liston.

Q: How does Clay compare with Louis and Marciano? A: You are picking three completely different styles. I would say that Clay is a great fighter. I do believe, however, that he has certain areas of weakness, which can be reached but which I would rather not go into until Buster Mathis demonstrates them.

"Within a month after our interview with D'Amato," the magazine pointed out, "there were rumors that Buster Mathis' backers were considering hiring another manager to replace D'Amato. According to the published reports, some of the group was dissatisfied with Mathis' progress as a professional fighter."

Well, they weren't just rumors. After a while, Cus and Buster were at each other's throats. "I'm a man," Buster told *Sports Illustrated*. "This guy takes away my pride." Gene Kilroy remembered a time when Cus got into an argument with Buster and then challenged him and Buster wouldn't hit him. "It kind of disappointed me," Cus told Gene. "But now I knew he had no guts."

At one point, the investors had to order Cus out of the house in Rhinebeck where Cus was staying with Mathis. Cus refused to leave. So the Peers guys locked the refrigerator and tried to get the electricity cut off but Cus ran down the steps at the utility workers and threatened them with a realistic-looking water pistol. They finally had to call state troopers to evict Cus, according to Mark Kram's account in *Sports Illustrated*.

Then Jimmy Iselin, one of the Jets owner's sons, gave his rationale for dumping Cus. "I just couldn't communicate with D'Amato anymore," he told Kram. "He was impossible. He'd call up at 1:30 in the morning and say, 'Jimmy, the refrigerator's locked.' What the hell am I going to do about that all the way down here in the city? He was muttering about bombs being hid in his car. He wanted a pistol to protect himself from the sparring partners, God knows why. He was always feuding with the fighters and neighbors, and finally he tried to cause a split between my partners and myself. This guy belongs in another world."

By July, Cus made it clear to Buster that is was him or the young Turks. Buster went with the money. "Well, I'd like to say this," Mathis told the press. "I had to go through a learning process, so Cus worked with me. But I was with Jimmy Iselin from when I started and I couldn't leave them, because without them, there would have been no Buster. Cus wanted me to go with him and Iselin wanted me to go with him. I've got this far, and if the good Lord's willing, I think I'll be champion of the world. Well, this is what this is all about. If I didn't think I'd be champion, I wouldn't be doing it."

Cus didn't take all this too well. He announced that he was suing Peers Management for $8 million. But some of Cus remained with Buster. He still used Cus's tapes of Cus calling out the numbers for his Willie Bag workouts. And a few months later, Mathis sounded like he was channeling Cus when he told reporters his new mantra. "C'mon, Bus, it's gonna be a good day, don't let your mind make you lazy. You're full of confidence now, Bus, 'cause you know your turn will come."

It didn't take Buster or Joan too long to realize the mistake he had made. "I think that was the most hurting thing I ever could witness," Joan said. "I did not want him to leave Cus. I don't know anything about boxing, but I liked Cus and I knew Buster was making a huge mistake by leaving him. Later Buster called Cus up and told him the worst thing he could have done was when he left him. After he left Cus, it bothered him so much I think it contributed to his death. He would always say, even during the time he got sick, 'If I only listened to Cus, if I only had stayed with Cus, I would have been the heavyweight champion of the world. I came so close.'"

Imagine if Cus were alive to hear all this. Cus was always like, "If only he listened to me." That's the thing with Cus, it always came back to him. "Because he didn't listen to me, he never became anything." Cus talked to me about Buster. He told me that Buster didn't have the fortitude or the heart. He was at a certain level, but he'd never get to that big level. But Cus still got Buster to get on my case. One time they were talking and Cus gave me the phone and Buster told me to listen to Cus. To be honest, most of these guys just didn't have what it takes. To be a great fighter you have to have humility, and some fighters can't bring themselves to that.

By 1968, with the financial help of Jimmy Jacobs, since he still had a tax lien on him, Cus left the city and settled into a small apartment a few miles outside Rhinebeck. One of the problems was that Cus couldn't drive, so Joy Gross became his designated driver. Joy got to know Cus well from his nonstop monologues on those drives. "He was a very interesting man. He was paranoid. I can remember taking him to the train station in Rhinebeck on a cold winter day. Because there were famous rich people who lived around here, it was a very fancy station. So I dropped Cus off and there was nobody else there. When I went back to my car I could look down and see the railroad tracks. Cus was down there waiting for his train all by himself. It was as quiet as a mouse, cold as hell, and he had his trench coat up around his neck and he was walking up and down the platform, and he continually looked back as if he thought somebody were following him. He was suspicious of everybody."

Brian Hamill, Pete's brother, had once been a pupil of Cus's at the Gramercy Gym and he decided to visit Cus, along with a few of his "hippy-dippy" friends. He drove into the driveway, got out of the car, and rang the bell to the upstairs apartment. Brian told us the rest of the story. "Nobody answered, so I rang it again, and he opened the door, but I couldn't see him, I just heard a voice. He said, 'Who is that?!' I said, 'Cus, it's Brian.' 'Who?' I said, 'Brian, Brian Hamill,' and he came out onto the landing and he had a rifle in his fucking hands. I said, 'Cus, it's Brian Hamill.' He went, 'Oh, Brian.' He couldn't see, he was always squinting. So he said, 'I'm sorry, Brian, I couldn't hear you.' So me and my friends went upstairs, and that was their first introduction to Cus. Holy shit, this fucking guy was ready to shoot us if we were the wrong guys."

Cus was alone again. He wasn't working with any prospects. He was upstate full-time and the Gramercy Gym had been inactive for years so he "sold" the gym to two of his boxing cronies for one dollar. Then sometime in 1970 he made a hasty exit from Rhinebeck. Joe Colangelo remembers that Cus told him that a "Norris guy" had moved into Rhinebeck and Cus "ran out of there and went to Camille's house. The main reason why they weren't living together back in the day was that he was still involved in boxing and he did not want to bring Camille around because then these guys would find out who Camille was and then they'd start strong-arming her."

Not only did Cus leave Rhinebeck in a flash, but he also immediately sold his log cabin at a bargain price. Cus's niece later revealed that her father, whose name was on the title, disposed of it to the first buyer. Cus was obviously paranoid about whoever this "Norris guy" was.

By the end of July 1971, Cus filed for bankruptcy in Federal District Court. He said he had liabilities of $30,276 and assets of approximately $500. And now, a half year away from hitting sixty-four, Cus was in total exile. To help kill time, he worked with kids in Catskill who had gotten in trouble or involved with drugs and needed discipline. And, in a last desperate attempt to forestall death, he started conjuring me up.

Cus is Cus, so it didn't take long for him to put down some boxing roots in Catskill. Shortly after moving in with Camille in 1970 he opened up the Catskill Boxing Club in a city building that also housed the police department. Cus was really doing community service because, after a while, the schools began sending over kids they couldn't control. They'd train from four-thirty to seven p.m. He had come full circle from his early days at the Gramercy Gym.

But then he began bringing some promising fighters up to the house in Catskill, guys like Joey Hadley and Paul Mangiamele, who was related to Al Caruso. And before long that big Victorian house was filled with boxers. Just like I'm sure Cus envisioned it all along. Camille used to talk about being tired and closing the house down and going to Florida, where two of her sisters were living, but Cus would tell her that when she felt tired, it was just boredom and she'd get bored a lot faster down in Florida.

Cus was exactly where he wanted to be, but he had no money to support all the fighters and that's where Jimmy Jacobs and Bill Cayton came in. By 1974 they had started managing fighters, as well as making tons of money from their fight-film business. Their first fighter was Eugene "Cyclone" Hart, a hard-punching middleweight from Philadelphia. Jimmy brought him up to Catskill to work with Cus but he drove Cus crazy. Cus told me he was a great puncher but if he didn't knock his opponent dead he had a tendency to quit. You can't do that with Cus. He used to tell me, "If you quit in the ring, you're useless as a human being. You could run a fifty-billion-dollar company but if you quit on anything, there's no reason for you to live. Why do you want to live? Facing the slightest struggle you know you're going to give in."

Hart remembers his time with Cus a bit differently. "Cus was a gentleman who believed everything he'd say and do would work," he said. "He always gave me confidence that everything he gives me will be successful. I learned all the things that he taught me to protect myself. It worked, but it didn't work that much in the ring with Cus, because when I went to fight, I had so many fights already underneath my belt that I depend on doing it the way I was doing it from being in Philly. I didn't know anything about the peekaboo style. And he learned me that I could hit that other guy, and that the other guy couldn't hit me." Cyclone said that he couldn't adapt to Cus's style and I agree. It's very complex. Most people are loose and Cus's style was very closed. And it's intimidating too, constantly moving, boom, boom, boom.

In 1977, Jacob and Cayton bought the contract of Wilfred Benitez from his father. Benitez was the youngest world champion in boxing history, having won the WBA Light Welterweight Championship in 1976 when he was just seventeen. Jacobs and Cayton hired Emile Griffith to train Wilfred and then named Cus as a special adviser. In January of 1979 they held a press conference at a restaurant in New York City to announce Benitez's upcoming fight against Carlos Palomino for his share of the welterweight title. For the first time in years, Cus was back in the boxing limelight. Michael Katz covered the luncheon for *The New York Times*. "The remaining hairs around the fringe are white, but D'Amato remains an imposing figure, a cement block in a gray suit," he wrote. Cus told him that he was seventy-one, "that's physically. Actually I'm about 40." Griffith was named as the trainer but then Jacobs laid out Cus's role. "Cus is above the trainer. Cus supervises the overall training, not just the physical aspects. He gets more into the psychological aspects."

That's Cus. Don King was at the luncheon and he announced that it was "good seeing Cus around again." Cus objected. "I've never been away," Cus said. He explained that he'd been in Catskill working with Wilfred and "paying no attention to time as it passes by. I don't think about the past except to apply its lessons to the present. What the hell, nobody wants to talk about the past anyway. My reasons for not being involved are no longer there." Cus didn't want to bring up his old battles but he did want to talk about cementing his legacy and the dozen amateur fighters he was training upstate.

"I teach my fighters how to teach," he told Katz. "It's like the *Encyclopedia Britannica*. All that knowledge inside doesn't mean a thing if nobody picks it up and opens it to read. When I die, my fighters will know what I know. I'm better than most trainers around. People say I'm egotistical. But it is not that. It is just that most everyone else is very incompetent. You don't have to be a genius to be better."

Cus was so prideful. Kevin Rooney told me about the time that Al D'Amato, then the Republican senator from New York, met Cus at a function. D'Amato was curious if they were related, but Cus completely dissed him, probably because he was a Republican.

Ali's right-hand man, Gene Kilroy, remembered the time that he got Cus a room in Vegas for a fight. Gene went in to talk to Cus but Cus wouldn't begin the conversation until he opened up the bathroom door and turned on the bathtub so nobody could bug their talk.

People would say he's paranoid. But Cus truly loved conflict and fighting. The word out there was that Cus was a nice, kind, old white man. But this guy was an irritant. Look, Cus was never really appreciated. All that hard work and he never got anything. He had Floyd for a second and those guys snatched that from him. People would marvel at his ideas and say things to him like "How do you know that?" He'd tell me, "I don't know nothing, I figured everybody knew it. I feel like I'm stupid, I don't think I'm smart." Yeah, but if you'd challenge him, uh-oh, the monster would come out. Isn't that wild? Some guy who didn't think much about himself, boom, all the energy comes back and shakes the fucking hemisphere.

I'm an extreme kind of guy, but Cus could be too extreme even for me. Cus bumped into Buddy McGirt, who was being trained and managed by this old-school boxing guy Al Certo back then. They were in a posh clothing store on Madison Avenue in the city. At that time Kevin Rooney was still boxing for Cus and it was years before Certo would be named as an "associate" of the Gambino crime family by Sammy "The Bull" Gravano, an allegation that Certo passionately denied. This was the first time that Buddy met Cus, and it was memorable. Cus walked up to Certo and said, "If Kevin Rooney's name ever comes out of your mouth again, I'm going to kick your fucking ass." "Get the fuck out of here," I said to Buddy. "Cus didn't say that." Buddy replied, "Yes, he did. That's how I met Mr. D'Amato."

Now, Buddy McGirt is as straight as they come. Cus goes into the store, gets into Certo's face, like he's some young guy, and then he's talking some gangster shit? This is the guy who's telling me that gangsters ain't shit, the mob ain't shit, the only thing they do is hurt Italians anyway. Whoa. You can't embarrass Cus. He ain't afraid of nobody. Cus is like the government. He works on people's fears.

Mark D'Attilio trained with Cus and became an FBI agent with Cus's encouragement. They were at a tournament I was boxing in up in Lake Placid in 1984. Gerry Cooney, who was undefeated until he lost to Larry Holmes for the heavyweight crown two years earlier, was managed by two guys, Mike Jones and Dennis Rappaport. One of them went up to Cus and said, "Hey, Cus, how are you?" Cus didn't say anything, didn't put his hand out, he just stared at him. "Cus, don't you remember me? I'm Mike Jones," he said, and stuck his hand out to shake. Cus just let it dangle. "Mike Jones. I remember who the hell you are. You're partners with that other thief Dennis Rappaport." Jones turned red and walked away.

But when Cus wanted to charm and persuade someone, he could turn it on. In 1979, Cus went to a party at his sportswriter friend Robert Boyle's house in Cold Spring, New York. Cus showed up with a guy who was seven-foot-two. Cus said, "Bob, see that guy? He's seven-two, he's a truck driver, and he's forty-two years old. He is going to be the oldest, tallest guy ever to win the heavyweight title. You watch." Boyle never heard anything about the guy again. Then he met up with Cus a year later. "Bob, I've got the shortest, youngest guy, and he's going to win the heavyweight championship." Boyle said, "Who is that?" Cus said, "He's a kid named Mike Tyson."

Cus put the hope in the air. Positive affirmations. The more you say something, the more it will happen. That's what happened with my crazy ass. Cus works with the crazy ones. What does Bob Marley say? The last will be first, the first will be last.

Cus was so hard to understand. How did he get Jimmy and Cayton to bankroll his training camp? Were they really hoping to find a potential champion among the Catskill Boxing Club kids? Why, when all of a sudden Cus finds me, a young kid from the gutter, doesn't he tell Jimmy and Bill about me? The day after I sparred for Cus he called up his friend Brian Hamill and told him to come over to see me. When Brian said he'd come over the next week, Cus urged him to come the next day. He told a lot of his friends about me. Just not Jim and Bill. But José Torres came up to visit to tell Cus all the gossip in the city, and he saw me spar, and ran back to tell Jim and Bill about me.

Right away they called up. "Cus, what's this we hear about a fourteen-year-old kid up there?" Cus said, "Hey, he's just a street kid. We don't know what he's capable of doing." Cus was downplaying me. He was pissed at José for opening his mouth. Maybe he was trying to get another sponsor before he had to go to those guys and then José blew it up? José was probably talking like "Oh, this young kid, his punches, I've never . . . !" Just like Cus, making it sound better than it actually is.

There was often strange shit happening with Cus. Cus was still friendly with Charlie Black and although I never met the gentleman, Joe Colangelo told me that Charlie would visit Cus often. But it was a visit Charlie made to someone else that was really interesting. Years later I was told this story. Before I got to the house, my future roommate Frankie Mincelli got a job washing dishes at a posh Italian inn. One day Frankie was washing dishes and the owner was pushing his buttons—as he was known to do—and he pushed

Frankie over the line. Frankie got mad and threw some dishes. He was wrong to do it and he offered to pay for the dishes he broke, but the owner wanted his whole check.

Frankie told Cus and then Cus asked Joe Colangelo what he knew about the place. Joe said that they acted like they were connected with the mob but he didn't know for sure. He knew that Fat Tony Salerno used to eat there a lot but that didn't mean anything. So Cus and Joe decided to pay the owner a visit and work out the problem with Frankie's paycheck. Joe went in first and the owner started getting all excited. "Listen, calm the fuck down," Joe told him. "Let me just say this to you. If I was you, I would give the kid his check. You want replacement value for the dishes, whatever he broke, then we'll give you replacement value based on what they cost. But if you push the envelope on this, you're messing with the wrong people, you are."

Then Cus walked into the office. Colangelo said that Cus gave the owner a stare that could "pierce through ten feet of solid steel. You could see him melt right then and there." Frankie's check was returned, they figured out a payment schedule, and all was good. Except that somehow Charlie Black found out about the story. The next thing you know, Charlie paid a little visit to the owner. "If you even think anything bad about Cus, never mind say it, if you even think it, you're going to be hung up on piano wire."

Charlie Black wasn't the only person from Cus's past who came up to see him in Catskill. Jacobs came up to the gym while I was sparring one day. I must have been about sixteen at the time. Jim was accompanied by an older Italian-looking gentleman. I saw him talking with Cus and then, after my workout, we exchanged a few words. The gentleman said that I looked like Henry Armstrong. He knew all those fighters from back in the day. He seemed like a sweet, retired old dude. Only while doing research for this book did I learn from Joe Colangelo's interview that that man was Fat Tony Salerno! He did live close by, in Rhinebeck, so he didn't have to go out of his way to visit. I remember other visits from some smooth-talking Italian guys who came from Cus's old neighborhood. Some of them were old fighters who trained with Cus and then turned to the mob, like Nicky the Blond. I'm no fool—even though I was a young kid, I could see their personality, the barometer. These guys come up there, they have no care in the world, you know what I mean? You don't see stress lines on their faces.

They weren't businessmen. They looked good, they had the business clothes but they didn't have no business lingo. These guys seemed harmless. They didn't have any bodyguards with them, unless they were hidden somewhere where I couldn't see them. Listen, this is tricky. Cus was paranoid about everybody. Now he's got Fat Tony and other guys hanging out in the gym on a number of occasions.

Cus was always adamant about fighting against these guys. What could he or Jim possibly owe them? There were rumors in the boxing world that Fat Tony always had a piece of Patterson's action, even after he sold his share in Rosensohn Enterprises. It could have been through Roy Cohn, who was his lawyer and who promoted the next five Patterson fights until Liston took him out of the picture. It wasn't as if Jim and Cayton needed money—they were loaded. But it was widely believed that Jim had accumulated a lot of his old fight films from mob guys.

Because of Fat Tony's undercover promotion of the first Ingo fight, Cus had been barred from getting a license in New York. You'd think he'd still hold that grudge, as he did with so many others. Cus had an enemies list longer than Richard Nixon's. Norris, Cohn, Julius November, Hoover, Cardinal Spellman, President Reagan, Bob Arum, Teddy Brenner. He'd always be talking about Roy Cohn. Sometimes when he would mention his name, Cus would then spit on the floor.

I remember us driving on the turnpike one day and a bus passed us that had FUGAZY painted on the side. "That's probably Bill Fugazy's bus," Cus snorted. Cus also hated Bob Arum. One time he said, "Bob Arum is the worst man in the western hemisphere, and if he was in the eastern hemisphere, he'd be the worst man there."

Cus sometimes talked about killing some of his foes. He'd see somebody he didn't like on TV and he'd just growl and say, "Oh, I wish I could kill that guy. The guy gives me so much trouble." He'd see an ad for Fugazy Travel and he'd go off on how he'd like to kill Bill Fugazy. Look, I came from Brownsville, everybody's got problems, everybody is always bitching and shit. We always think that the white life is so much better. So I move in with Cus, and this old man is bitter, whoa! Some of these enemies of his are dead already and he's still talking about killing them. He even had a bitter falling-out with his brother Rocco over a lawn mower! Rocco sold a piece-of-shit lawn mower to Camille, and Cus went ballistic. "You're cut off, you're not family. Family doesn't do that to family." Cus was such a rage-aholic. He'd yell at Camille if she moved his stuff while cleaning and he couldn't find it. He'd scream at people he was talking to over the phone.

Cus had a passionate opinion about everything. We'd be watching the fights on TV and the announcer would be saying what a great performance one of the fighters was putting on and Cus would be screaming, "The guy is a bum! What is this guy talking about? The guy's a bum! The other guy's not throwing back!"

Sometimes being around Cus was like being at a pity party. Usually it was just me and Cus and Camille, and Cus would start a monologue about the past. "I spent so much money fighting the IBC. I invested so much time in people who disappointed me the most. All my fighters betrayed me." And he wanted revenge. Cus wouldn't let go. I wanted to help him too with that *Count of Monte Cristo* shit. I wanted to hurt people in the ring because I knew it would make Cus happy. Isn't that some sick shit?

Yet the one person who really betrayed Cus the worst always got a pass from him. I didn't like the excuses Cus gave for Patterson. Cus never said anything derogatory about him. He always defended him. He got me up here being the killer, and he's giving this guy excuses? I didn't have any excuses. I didn't like what Patterson did to Cus at that time. I couldn't understand why Cus held him in such high regard. Cus loved him. Cus said only beautiful things about him. It pissed me off. I saw how he betrayed Cus. I wanted Cus to talk about me like he talked about Patterson. But it wasn't my time yet.

I'm not like Cus. I get too involved emotionally with this stuff and it bothers me. I hated to hear Cus talking about how good a fighter Patterson was. I want to say something kind, but Patterson couldn't fight. I'd see guys who were better than Patterson fighting and Cus would tell me they were bums. So I'm smart enough to realize what's going on. I'm a disciple, but I'm a great reasoner because of Cus. I used reason and knew Patterson wasn't better than those guys.

I was jealous of Patterson. Cus loved him so much. He never told me he loved me. He didn't tell me nothing, everybody else had to tell me. He told me to clean the fucking gym. I was respectful to Patterson only because of Cus. I never said two words to him when I met him in person, though.

Patterson's excuses for why he sold Cus out were all over the place. I think he just looked at Cus as invincible, that he could do everything for him and then he saw Cus lose in a power struggle with Cohn and November. Cus pretty much got kicked out of boxing so Floyd looked at him like, "He can't help me no more. He can't protect me." In one interview Floyd claimed that he stopped talking to Cus because Jim Jacobs ripped him off on that documentary they made that didn't sell anywhere because Patterson had no charisma. But when he spoke to Peter Heller for that great book *"In This Corner . . . !"* he blamed November for turning him against Cus. "I was blinded of many, many things. I was taken to a lawyer and he used some kind of psychology and not having a mature enough mind, he was able to make me see things other than the way they were. I began to see Cus different. Then, as time passed, this lawyer kept me aware of every move Cus was making and he distorted everything Cus was saying, doing, everything. So then it got to a point that I felt that it would be better that Cus and I separate because there was some Mafia or gangster stuff that came out and the lawyer really jumped on this and tore it up although it was just an innocent thing."

When he was interviewed for a CBS program, Floyd said, "If I had it to do all over again, I wouldn't change one bit of it, I'd keep it just the way it was, except one thing. Cus would have been there in the end. He was there in the beginning."

Sometimes Cus would actually say that he was testing Floyd, giving him enough rope to see what Floyd would do. A true test, as Cus put it. I guess I passed the test, I was with him to his end. But if he was testing Floyd's character, why did he say that Floyd wasn't responsible for his actions because his mind was "poisoned"? His mind may have been poisoned, but he still could have given Cus his half of the money.

Cus and Patterson reconciled while I was living with Cus. It was at some amateur fights at Columbia-Greene Community College. They couldn't avoid each other and they sat in the stands and talked for two hours. Tom Patti was with Cus, and when Patterson said good-bye, Tom and Cus headed for the car. Cus put his arm on Tom's shoulder and said, "I never realized how little he knew about all that I did for him. I protected him so much, I kept him in the dark about all these dangers in the sport around him. He was naive to all of it and therefore he never knew or appreciated all I did for him."

My personal opinion is that Cus was always looking for an out for this guy. He always gave Patterson excuses and that guy hurt him bad. I just don't understand human beings. The more somebody hurts you, the more you love them. It's weird. Cus would say it again and again, "The people I invested the most time in disappointed me the most." He was probably talking about Patterson. And November. Maybe José Torres. Definitely his two trainers, Dan Florio and Joey Fariello, who had both left him. He said that the biggest mistake he made was letting his feelings get involved with Floyd. He got taken and he never made himself vulnerable again. He had to detach his feelings from his work. I had to sacrifice for Floyd's betrayal. I would have had a normal adolescence, I would have had a guy showing his love and verbalizing it, instead of everything being regimented. Regimented love. But I got that unconditional love from Camille, which helped balance me. In retrospect, I realized that had I received that kind of "soft" love from Cus, I probably wouldn't be who I am now. I was always trying to be the best, hoping to prove myself to Cus.

The funny thing is that Cus was afraid that I was going to leave him. One time I got up the nerve to tell Cus that I didn't think Patterson cared about him, and that I did. Cus looked at me and said, "You don't know. They got his mind twisted up. One day maybe they'll twist your mind up and then you'll leave me too."

He'd always say that. "You're going to leave me too. Just like everyone else." I didn't know if he was giving me a mind trip, because that's what he'd do, or if this was just him feeling sorry for himself. I thought he was losing his mind. I'm sitting reading a book, and Cus was walking around the house in his robe. "Yeah, you too, they'll take you away too, you'll leave me just like everybody else, wouldn't you?" "What? Who's going to take me?" "You know, all those guys." Cus never gave me the credit I deserved for being loyal to him.

But Cus would feed my vanity. He'd feed it with love and hate and gasoline and nuclear potions. Can you believe I told people, "How dare these guys challenge me with their primitive skills? These mere mortals." I was a sick fuck! I think about this a lot. It's this old washed-up dude and this young street urchin, this fucking slum dweller. That's what I was, a slum dweller. And we're up there and the dude is telling me shit and I'm believing it. I think I'm invincible. Now I'm scared to even think the way I thought back then. Cus had me thinking I was this invincible fucking monster from another galaxy. A mean, vicious, ferocious savage, he used to call me. I'm sure he called Patterson that too. Patterson never believed it. But I did.

IN FEBRUARY 1983, I was coming off two Junior Olympic titles and continuing my amateur career. I was still only sixteen but I was rated the number eight amateur super-heavyweight in the country when I went to the Western Massachusetts Golden Gloves tournament in Holyoke. One of the tournament officials told Cus that he didn't think I could handle all the experienced fighters who were in the tournament and that I should fight in the novice class. "He'll get killed in there with those experienced fighters," the guy told Cus. Cus just laughed. "Yeah? Just watch him."

I got byes to the finals because nobody wanted to fight me, and those fights wound up as defaults. So my first actual fight was on February 12, against Jimmy Johnson, a tough kid from Springfield, Massachusetts. He was a big, muscular, tall guy, and he had brought his wife, his kids, and all his relatives to the fight. Just seconds into the fight, we clinched and when the referee parted us, I knocked him cold with a right hand. His wife, carrying his newborn baby, and his two other little kids ran into the ring, crying. I told Cus that and he laughed. "What? The babies and the mother were crying? Boo-hoo-hoo." He was so happy.

I won the New England Golden Gloves championship by default when the guy I was supposed to fight came up with a sprained ankle. I started to get some national publicity and Cus had me sparring with pros. One of them was Carl "The Truth" Williams. We drove down to White Plains to spar with him. He was the new up-and-coming guy and I was the amateur guy. Eventually I defended my title against him, but that first time I boxed with him he beat the shit out of me. I pounded him hard, I hurt him sometimes, and he hurt me. It was a war. "Michael was coming in and Williams hit him with a straight right hand," Kevin Rooney remembered. "It was like Michael wasn't hit, he just kept coming. An ordinary person would have gone down; he's not ordinary. Needless to say, we didn't get invited back."

I never fit into the amateur system. You could be rewarded the same amount of points for a harmless jab as for a punch that sent your opponent down. The amateur officials considered themselves genteel. But I was out for blood. Sometimes I'd get points deducted before the fight even started because they didn't like the way I was staring down my opponent. "We are boxers," they'd say. "I didn't come here to box. I'm here to fight, sir," I'd tell them. They didn't like my Brownsville attitude. Cus and I took on the whole amateur system. We didn't win but we fought them hard.

Sometimes Cus's reputation probably cost me fights. I made it to the National Golden Gloves finals and on March 26, 1983, I'd just beaten the two-time defending champion, Warren Thompson, and now I was going to fight Craig Payne, who had been beaten by Warren Thompson the year before. I clearly won every round. I was the aggressor, I punched more, and I should have had the decision. But I was robbed with impunity. Just watch the fight, you'll hear all the boos from the crowd. I was crying like a baby after that decision but Cus started chasing the amateur officials. Kevin and a police officer who was escorting us around had to get in between Cus and them. That made me feel so good to see Cus taking up for me. I was to find that many boxing officials favored Norris when they were younger and I felt they never gave me a fair shake my whole amateur career.

A few months later I went back to Nelson's smokers in the Bronx. I fought a tough guy named Bill Sammo and battered him around for two rounds but he wouldn't go down. So in the third I started jabbing and opened up a nasty cut over his left eye and the ref stopped the fight. Cus always liked me to jab. I don't jab much, but I have an awesome jab. Sometimes I'd knock the teeth to the back of a guy's head using my jab.

In August I won the Ohio State Fair, knocking my opponent out in the first round. Then I won the U.S. Amateur Boxing Championships later that month with another first-round KO. In September we traveled to Lake Placid, New York, for a U.S.–Germany tournament, and I knocked out Peter Geier in the first round. I won the Adirondack Regionals in October when my opponent didn't show up. Then I went on to win the New England–New York Olympic Regionals at the end of the month when my opponent didn't show up there also. Then I hit a wall. On November 8, I fought Kommel Odom in Colorado Springs in the Amateur Boxing Federation National Championships. Odom was a journeyman but I wasn't into the fight. I wasn't hurt but I held him and I was disqualified in the second round. Kevin called Cus with the news and he was as confused as I was when he talked to a local reporter. "I think they said Mike was holding, which I don't understand. This Odom was probably the weakest fighter in the class. I can't really explain it, except that Mike is out of the tournament. These things happen in boxing. Now we have to go back to the gym and work."

That fight was so out of character for me. I was always up for tournament fights. I wasn't like the rest of the guys I was fighting; this was my whole life. Those trophies were my life source. Cus would take my trophies and use them to decorate the house. When I got back to Catskill we discussed the fight and then we just kept on training, getting hypnotized, and sparring. I guess Cus knew what he was doing, because I got better.

Cus always used to say that I could become heavyweight champ barring any distractions. I'll tell you what "no distractions" meant. No distractions was going to the gym, maybe twice a day, and then when you go home you do your washing and your chores and you go upstairs and you watch fight films for ten hours. Then you do some exercises in the room. Then you go to bed, and when you wake up you go running. Then you come back from running, you go back upstairs, take a shower, and then watch some more films until it's time to eat breakfast and go to school—when I was still attending high school. At school I learn nothing and then I come back home, I eat dinner, I watch some fight films until it's time to go to the gym and train and spar. Then I come back home and take a shower and go watch some fight films again until it's time to go to sleep. That's my regimen, that's "no distractions."

Cus got a little concerned about my total devotion to fighting. I was spurning the advances of girls who were my fans because I was too in love with myself to think about anything else. Cus would urge me to go out dancing or something but I would rather curl up with a book about Benny Leonard or Joe Gans. The writers who wrote about those guys did a magnificent job of making my heroes almost human gods with flaws. That was my *Iliad*.

"They had a life, Mike," Cus told me. "You're too young not to have a life. There's something not right. I've been at this sixty years and I never saw anyone with your dedication."

I would complain about not having any girlfriends, but I wasn't the suavest when it came to girls. I had a lot of crushes on girls but I never got to second base because I never tried. I never said a word to them. They were all crushes in my mind. As I got better known in town, girls started flirting with me but I didn't know how to handle that. I didn't want to deal with that, I might start arguing with them.

But then when I was about seventeen I got my first girlfriend. Her name was Angie and she was a wonderful girl. Her parents were well educated. Her father was the manager of the J.J. Newberry variety store in Catskill. Her uncle won a national scholastic contest for Boy of the Year when he was a kid. They gave him a big parade and Cus said, "I want to do that for you too. You're going to have a parade just like that one." That stayed in Cus's mind, that they gave this guy a parade. That got Cus excited.

So Cus started pushing me to marry Angie! She was Cus's idea of a positive black person, the one who goes to church and prays. He wanted me in that family. "Her family has a very good reputation in the neighborhood." Reputation was everything to Cus, even if he acted like it wasn't. I think Cus believed that if I got married, I'd be a calmer guy and that would make me a better fighter. Cus wanted to control my life to a T, even who I married.

But Camille took my side against Cus. She told me, "You should go out with Angie but you can have as many girlfriends as you want. You should bring them all over, everybody should be friends. Nobody should get married yet." Cus would go, "Ah, Camille, he's a fighter, he just needs to focus on one woman who's his wife and be focused and determined to take care of his family." When Camille said no, I knew that wasn't good advice from Cus. When I started seeing a girl named Holly at the same time as Angie, Cus got mad and said it was the first sign of trouble with my character, although he liked Holly too.

Cus probably thought marriage would make me more mature. I wasn't having sex with Angie and wouldn't become a sexual animal until later in my career after Cus was gone. But he predicted it when he was interviewed about me once. "You don't know where sex can take him, he had a lot of potential, but he doesn't know where he's going to go. Sex can take a young man places he never can believe."

And it did. Cus knew me too well. He knew that I was an extreme person and I had sacrificed so much, including sex, because I wanted to rule so badly.

I went to my first strip club up in Montreal early in 1984. Cus and a few of the fighters drove up to see one of the Hilton brothers fight. It was always great hanging around the Hiltons. When they showed up to train in Catskill it was a fun time. So we got to Montreal and Davey Hilton took us to Chez Parée, one of the world's best strip clubs. We sat down and the waitress came over and I told Tom Patti, who was collecting the orders, to get me an orange juice. Well, Tom told her to add some vodka.

"Oh man, this orange juice!" I made a face. "Mike, this is Montreal, it's special orange juice. Drink it, or you're going to insult them," Tom told me. So I drank the first one and that one led to the second and to the third and fourth. Meanwhile, Tom went over to one of the strippers circulating in the room. "Listen, see the black guy who's with us? He's a very shy guy. I need you to help break him out of his shell." He was trying to get me laid. "Maybe you can go over and say hello, warm him up, because he's really quiet." Tom was talking to her with his back to me. The stripper took one look over his shoulder and asked, "Which one is quiet and shy?" "The black guy," Tom said. "You mean the one who's jumping on the tables?"

Tom turned around and he saw me dancing and jumping from tabletop to tabletop, flying and spinning through the air. After a few hours we left the club, and got back to the hotel about one-thirty in the morning. I was staying in a room with Cus, and Tom and Davey were in the other room. So I went to my room and I knocked on the door. "Cus, it's Mike, let me in. Come on, Cus, I'm tired, let me in." Meanwhile, Tom had run to his room because he didn't want to get blamed for taking me to a strip club. I was knocking and pleading and I heard Cus from the other side of the door. "Who is this? The Mike Tyson I know wouldn't be out this late. You must be an imposter. Go away. The real Mike Tyson wouldn't do this."

So I went over to Tom's room and begged him to let me in. "You can't stay here, I'm going to get in trouble," Tommy told me. Then he lay down on his bed and passed out. He woke up about an hour later and found me nearly levitating above the floor, trying to lie on the six inches of space on the mattress that he wasn't occupying. I guess I learned that from Cus too. He used to tell me about how he slept while standing up in the Army. A few hours later Cus knocked on the door and chewed us all out for staying out so late.

I began to train seriously for the Olympic Trials, which were scheduled for June 1984. In April, I won the National Golden Gloves with a first-round KO of Jonathan Littles. We were back in Catskill before going to Texas for the trials, when Alex Wallau, an ABC sports commentator, came up to interview me and Cus. Alex and Cus were old friends because Alex started out producing Howard Cosell. He was also close friends with Jim Jacobs, who urged him to get out from behind the cameras and be an on-air commentator. So this wasn't your usual shallow interview. In fact, it might have been the most in-depth interview that Cus had ever done. We sat down to tape it in the living room. Cus had gotten dressed up for the occasion, putting a gray suit jacket on over his plaid lumberjack shirt. I was looking fly, wearing slacks and a shirt and a white Kangol cap, embellished with a gold chain and pinky rings.

Alex began by asking Cus how he'd met me and asking me about my background. I said some heavy stuff about crime that was right from that Jean Valjean character in *Les Misérables* that I had read at the house. Alex turned to Cus now. "You talk about peeling away the layers to find out what makes somebody tick. When you peeled away the layers on Mike Tyson, what did you find?" "I found what I thought I'd find. A person of basically good character, a person who is capable of doing the things that are necessary to be done in order to be a great fighter or a champion of the world. When I recognized this, then my next job was to make him become aware because unless he knew them as well as I did, it wouldn't help him very much. So I had to make him aware by constantly bringing to his attention the little incidents which would tend to reveal himself, so to speak, to himself. And enable him to get the real solid, deep-down, inner belief in himself.

"A man who is able to do what needs to be done, no matter how he feels within, is a professional. I think that Mike is rapidly approaching that status, that important point which I consider he must do in order to be the greatest fighter in the world."

I'm sucking this up. I believe I am that fucking guy. I'm keeping it real, right? I'd been living with Cus for years, I've been used to hearing him talk, and it took me back, but that was good to hear there. Cus was a master of dropping bombs on you, even when he was talking to someone else.

"And for all we know, barring unforeseen incidents and if this continues without any interruption, I'm going to say something that most people would think, well, he's a biased person. It's entirely possible that if he gets the sparring and everything else that goes with it, whatever he requires"—do you see the crescendo coming up?—"he may go down in history as one of the greatest that we ever had, if not the greatest that ever lived in his division."

Now Alex started to get touchy-feely. "Mike, how would you describe your feelings for Cus?" "That shouldn't be hard to do, he's like my father. I never look at it as he's my trainer or my manager. I just go by the way that he has feeling toward me and it's like a father-and-son relationship. And that's mostly what I'm based on, even though he is my manager and trainer. Sometimes I forget that, because of the way we are."

Now it was Cus's turn to be on the hot seat. "Cus, how would you describe your feelings for him?" Oh God. "Well, you know, I tell these boys, all of them, when I come into contact with them, as a result of our relationship with one another, you either get to gain respect or lose respect for me and I will either gain or lose respect for you. I find the best way of teaching is by setting examples. Now, you set a good example and it appeals to them, they'll try to emulate you, and this is what I try to do. My purpose in explaining is only to let them see the logic and the value of what I have to explain and teach. But they have to have the intelligence to understand it and accept it as truth, as fact. And then this helps develop them to the point that it's necessary."

But what about his feelings? Alex kept at him. "Are you able to think of a fighter you work with, like Mike Tyson, do you ever think of him on a personal basis, as opposed to being a boxer? What do you feel about him on a personal basis?" Whoa, Alex is getting too deep with it. "First of all I am a professional, and as a professional, my judgments as to a fighter are detached. I never allow my personal feelings to get involved, no matter how much affection I might have. But as I said before, you either gain or lose respect and having watched him come from where he was, to what he is, I can say honestly I have a very deep affection for him, I do. Not only affection and admiration, because I know what it takes to be and to do what he has done and what he's doing. I'm aware of it, and, well, I feel I was a part of it, it's almost like liking yourself too. Because you never know how much you contributed to it, but the result is then you like to think you had more to do with it. So that, in a sense, I think I answered the question." That's what I've always been saying, falling in love with myself and idolizing myself. I said that. But he's saying he sees so much of himself in me, he's liking himself too. I didn't know that shit then.

Alex then asked Cus if it was hard for him at seventy-six to work with a seventeen-year-old black kid. "I never think of him as black or white, or colored or whatever. To me, he's my boy, he's with me." I'm his boy. That made me feel good. Again, he was using Alex to send me a message.

But Alex wanted answers about our age difference. "I can relate to any age, because I'm seventy-six and I lived through all those periods. I grew up in a very tough neighborhood, so that I'm aware of how they feel, so the years have gone by, people are people. And boys are boys and I know exactly how he feels. From time to time, I know when to put a little pressure down to make him aware and perhaps influence him in a particular direction. I also know when to lay off. I also know, that having been a boy myself, that pressure at the wrong time may arise a certain amount of resentment, which will delay the development."

When did he lay off? Is that when people like Atlas thought he was favoring me? They didn't see him when he talked to me alone. Cus never laid off. Cus was a contradiction, I can't believe he said that.

"I often say to him, 'You know, I owe you a lot.'"

Never! He never said he owed me anything!

"I owe you a lot. And he doesn't know what I mean. I'm going to tell him now what I mean. Because if he weren't here, I probably wouldn't be alive today. The fact he is here and doing what he's doing, and doing as well as he's doing and improving as he has, gives me the motivation and interest to stay alive. Because I believe a person dies when he no longer wants to live. Nature is a lot brighter than people think. Little by little we lose our friends that we care about and little by little we lose our interest, until finally we say, 'Well, what the devil am I doing around here,' because we have no reason to go on. But I have a reason with Mike here."

In a way he was putting pressure on me with that talk. That was the first time I ever heard Cus say that I was prolonging his life. He never talked personal stuff like that with me. He'd talk about my pain, how I was thinking, feeling, going through my hardships, my family, my people dying, but other than that it was just the mission we were on. He never talked to me about how much I meant to him.

Meanwhile, we began getting more and more media attention and the stories were always the same: a nice old white guy is saving a young antisocial disadvantaged black kid from the ghetto. Just read the way *CBS Sunday Morning* framed the story:

NARRATOR: Cus D'Amato is more than a manager of champions. He is a savior of souls. He saved Floyd Patterson and others, and he is saving Mike Tyson.

CUS: I don't succeed when I make a guy or help a guy become champion of the world. I succeed when I make that fellow become champion of the world and independent of me, that he doesn't need me anymore.

NARRATOR: But they need each other now, because someday soon they will be coming out of the country, coming hard and coming fast for the lights of the city.

But first I had to win the Olympic gold medal. The odds were stacked against me, not because I didn't have the talent, but because of Cus's disputes with Bob Surkein, the head of the amateur boxing program. Cus had known him for years, and he was convinced Surkein was against us. Actually Cus thought that anybody he didn't like was down with Norris. Cus and Surkein had butted heads earlier when Cus wouldn't let me fight in an international tournament in the Dominican Republic. Cus wasn't thrilled with me going there to begin with, but when they told him that their trainers would train me, Cus flipped out. "It is their position that Mike would have to work under their coaches," he told the local paper. "Well, I'm not about to let them mess up my fighter. I won't let him go into any international tournaments or the training camp in Colorado unless one of my coaches goes along."

Later, Cus would tell other reporters that he was worried about an international terrorist attack in the Dominican Republic. That pissed Surkein off. Then Cus wanted me to fight at my natural weight, which would have been in the superheavyweight division. But Surkein told Cus that I had to fight in the heavyweight class. "Well, how are you going to stop me?" Cus asked Surkein. According to Cus, he said, "I am the power behind the American Federation of Boxing. I make those people, the officers." He told Cus that if I were to win I'd have to do it "the hard way." Cus thought he was implying that he would try to put obstacles in our way. Cus considered letting me take my chances in knocking out every superheavyweight I faced. But then he decided he didn't want to gamble with me, so we dropped down to heavyweight.

It was fun losing the weight. I didn't eat much and I had to wear a vinyl suit all day long until I went to bed. I loved it, I felt like a real fighter, lose the weight to make the weight. I thought I was some great warrior. I was so delusional.

I was pumped when I got to Fort Worth. My first fight was with Avery Rawls. I knocked him down seconds into the fight and then I stuck my tongue out at him. Both the ref and Cus gave me shit afterward. I got the decision after three rounds. Then I fought Henry

Milligan, a Princeton boy. I knocked him out in the second round and flossed to the press. "I was a young spoiled brat in the past but my attitude in the ring has changed. I just do my thing and if an individual allows himself to be intimidated, that's his fault. I have so many styles that I don't know them all. I have more confidence than anyone on this planet. My punch can stun you, hurt you or knock you down. My opponent was game and gutsy with a heart of a lion, but I was not impressed with his punches. What round did I stop the gentleman in, anyway?"

I went into the finals against Henry Tillman convinced I would win. My previous opponent, who lasted two rounds with me, had already knocked Tillman out. The fight started and I beat his ass for two good rounds and even dropped him. But when they announced the decision, they gave it to Tillman. The whole arena was booing. I was totally distraught. When they gave me the consolation trophy I smashed it in the dressing room.

Besides the ridiculous decision, Cus was furious at Howard Cosell's lopsided call for Tillman on the television coverage. "He's a rat, I paid for his wedding," Cus yelled. But losing didn't mean I was out of the Olympics. Three weeks later there was the Olympic Boxoff in Vegas, and if I beat Tillman there, then we'd have a third fight to see who went to the Olympics. We both got to the finals and again both the crowd and I thought that I had won but again they gave the decision to Tillman. While the crowd was booing, Cus went right after Surkein. He started throwing punches and Kevin had to step in and break it up. That's why I would have killed for him. He always had my back.

We returned to New York the second week of July and days later I had a new car. I didn't want a car. I didn't know how to drive a car. I had no interest in learning how to drive a car, but Cus told me I was getting a car. And Cayton was paying for it. He sent Cus a check for $600 on July 19, $500 for the deposit on the car and $100 for the first payment on the insurance. But there was no question as to who owned the car. "Although the registration will be in your name, the car is owned by Reel Sports Inc.," Cayton wrote Cus.

Cus wanted me to get a safe car like a Volvo or something but I figured if I was going to get a car I'd go for a Caddy. So I got a brand-new Caddy even though I had never thought of driving in my life. I would have been happy with a motorcycle. But they got me a car because my friend Mark Breland, who had gone to the Olympics, got a new Mercedes from his managers. Cus was so old-school. He thought that I'd leave him for the first person who threw some money or a car at me. He believed money could turn everybody. But I was in it for the family. I was into the household and my lifestyle there and my friends in the town. Cus thought that all that conflict with Norris and Carbo and those guys could recur with new people.

Not fighting in the Olympics didn't change much for me. I kept training hard and fighting hard and visualizing myself as the champ. Everyone would come up to me and give me some great affirmations, like "You're the best" and "You'll knock all those guys out." Jimmy got me passes for the whole Olympics and they flew me to Los Angeles to soak in the atmosphere. I watched all the fights and I was just waiting for my time, I knew it would come. I knew when I turned pro I would do well. Man, I was so confident, thanks to Cus.

I went back to the tournaments. I fought in the Empire State Games in August of 1984. In the finals I fought Winston Bent. We almost went at it before the bell sounded. I got carried away a little when he stared at me "in a very aggressive way," as Cus would say later. I was dominating the fight and in the third round I put him to sleep with a right hand.

A week later, on August 25, I was fighting in Lake Placid for the Junior National Championships. I had drawn a bye all the way to the finals, where I fought Kelton Brown, who I had knocked out in the first round two years earlier to win the national championship. This time it wasn't different except that I knocked both him and the ring out. I hit him with a left to the body at the beginning of the fight and he had to take an eight count. Then he took another one after I rocked him with a right to the head. Then I missed him and hit the rope so hard that it broke. I broke the ring. Brown didn't last too much longer.

After the fight, Cus met with the press. "Well, I was very impressed. He reminded me of a modern-day Jack Dempsey, he's awesome. I think Mike is ready to turn pro. He probably will enter the European Championships in Finland in October and then turn pro in December." I used to love when he said stuff like "You remind me of a modern-day Jack Dempsey, you're just so ferocious." My dick would get hard.

In October I went to Europe for the first time. The International Tammer Tournament was in Helsinki, Finland. My first match was a walkover when my opponent suddenly got ill and refused to fight. My whole life was like that. I got a reputation as a bully. In my next fight I fought István Szikora, a veteran Hungarian fighter. I boxed the guy for three rounds and beat him real smart and easy. In the finals I fought a huge six-foot-five blond Swede named Hakan Brock. He had upset the favored Russian fighter to get into the finals. He towered over me during the referee's instructions, but once the bell rang I was all over him. I got him on the ropes and went right to his body, boom, boom, boom, boom. Somehow he got off the ropes and spent the rest of the fight avoiding me. I won the decision but Kevin was disgusted by the Swede. "The guy didn't want to fight," he told the press. "But again Michael closed the show nice."

When I got back from Europe, I started driving up to Albany and hanging out there—checking out the real estate, meeting people. I was young and vibrant and I had a white Caddy with a blue top, some money in my pocket, nice clothes. They wouldn't let me in the clubs. "Mike, I'm sorry, you're underage, you can't come in," the bouncer said. "You shouldn't be telling everybody how old you are in the paper." "Then I wouldn't be special," I said. So I started hanging out with some dope dealers, deplorable women, and street people. They were trashy girls but they were fun. I didn't know anything about girls. Nobody was going to give me no pussy, though.

Some of the guys who were training in Catskill lived in Albany and worked in Albany. They saw me out there and they remembered when I first came in at twelve and thirteen, now they were seeing me at eighteen, hanging out. They may have gotten the word back to Cus or maybe Cus sent Mark D'Attilio up to Albany on a few reconnaissance missions to track me down, because Cus confronted me. "Don't go up there fucking with those people again," Cus told me. "Stop talking to those people immediately." I kept going to Albany, but I stopped seeing those people, because that's what Cus wanted.

Now reporters were coming up to the gym and sensing a good story. In November, *The New York Times* sent a reporter to profile the Catskill Boxing Club. Cus was being rediscovered, both as a boxing guru and as a Good Samaritan who saved wayward kids from a grim future. " 'Teaching a youngster to fight,' Mr. D'Amato explained, 'does not mean raising fists in the schoolyard, on the street. It means,' he said, 'learning discipline,' a favorite word of his. He pointed to a young man who was sparring in the ring. 'He was a troubled boy when he came here. He's learning to control his emotions. He's learning discipline, which he didn't have.' 'If one could measure the contribution, one could nominate the man for sainthood,' said William F. Hagan, Greene County Administrator. 'He's instilled a sense of character in these kids.' "

At the beginning of 1985, we were fucked because we didn't win the Olympics and we had no money. Cus began to implement Plan B. He had me sign a contract with Jimmy Jacobs and Bill Cayton. I signed a standard manager's contract with Jim, four years, one-third to him. Cayton then signed me to a four-year contract for personal appearances and endorsements. Then each of them assigned half their earnings to the other so they were splitting both ends. On paper Cus got nothing. But he did manage to keep control by signing the contracts as "Cus D'Amato, adviser to Michael Tyson, who shall have final approval of all decisions involving Michael Tyson."

I think that Cus was covered because of his long-standing relationship with Jimmy. Alex Wallau told us that their relationship had changed by the time I came around. Jimmy was now supporting Cus. "By that time Cus was dependent upon Jimmy financially. At no time did Jimmy, in any way, do anything but project Cus as a god who he worships and that's the way Jimmy felt, but there was this sort of dual relationship, where on the one hand Jimmy had that love of Cus and that overwhelming respect of him and on the other hand he was supporting him. It was different than it was initially."

Jimmy didn't have any money when he first came to New York. Cus probably taught him how to get money. I think Cus saw that Jimmy had potential and Cus groomed him to be this great impersonator. I met his family and they were broke. But Jimmy always acted like he was loaded. He was probably playing Cayton big-time. I can't picture Jacobs and Cayton even liking each other.

Now that I was turning pro, Cus began to ramp up his psychological game. One day in the gym he said, "Now I work for you, Mike." I said, "You don't work for me, get out of here, if this means you work for me, I don't want to do it, then." Cus smiled. "Yeah, I don't work for nobody. You're all right, you're my boy." That's Cus. Always testing me, playing head games. Another time I was beating up a sparring partner in the gym. I saw that he was in trouble and I let him catch his breath for a second. Cus was all over me. "Look, I think you're in the wrong business. You don't want to do this, do you? I don't want to waste my time."

But the biggest dig came one night at home when I was getting the garbage together to take out. One of the reasons people were skeptical about Cus's claims that I would win the title was that they thought I was too small. So as I was tying up the garbage, I was talking about how good I was going to do as a pro. Cus just said, "I wish you had a body like Mike Weaver or Ken Norton, because people would just see you and they'd be intimidated. I wish you were big like those guys. You'd scare people."

Man, did that hurt me. I couldn't tell him, though, because he would say, "What are you, a little baby, you're crying? How can you handle a big-time fight if you don't have enough emotional toughness?" I threw out the garbage and went upstairs and cried in my room. Had Cus lost hope in me? Why was he putting it in my mind that nobody was going to fear me? Right then and there, I was determined to project the most savage, intimidating aura that boxing had ever seen. I went downstairs and I found Cus. "You wait, Cus. One day the whole world will be afraid of me," I vowed. "The whole world is going to be afraid of me." I got an old man who's nuts, and he got a young kid who's nuts.

But that was the day I turned into Iron Mike. I didn't want to let Cus down, I didn't want him to say, "I'm an old man, I'm going to die, and you wasted my time?" So I'd be the savage Cus wanted. I even began to fantasize that I'd actually killed someone in the ring. How's that for intimidation? Cus wanted an antisocial champion, and he always used to call me "the actor," so I'd act. I remembered all the bad guys from movies I'd watched, and all the villains I knew from wrestling, and I drew on that and threw myself into the role of the arrogant sociopath.

Shortly after this talk, I went roller-skating and I tripped and fractured both of my wrists. I went to the doctor in New York, he put a cast on each of my wrists, and I didn't miss a day of training. I didn't want Cus to question my commitment. Around that time, Cus and I were talking about Ali. Cus was saying that Ali had such character. He had the perfect fighting mentality, he truly loved himself, and he really believed everything he said. "I don't understand," I said. "I thought all that stuff was just a game." "No, Mike, he believes every word he says. He believes he's a god." How can a mortal be a god?

Cus was always on my ass until the day he died. After I got my license, I became his designated driver. Sometimes we'd drive for two hours so he could go to a conference. And the whole way, he'd be fucking with my head. I'm doing everything good and he makes up shit to fuck with me? He presses my buttons, he wants to see me lose it every now and then. But I see how he's trying to figure how far he can push me before I explode. By then I had realized that the way to get Cus off my back was to humor him and show him that he couldn't get to me. He'd go into his rant, "Oooooh, you're an actor, you're a phony," trying to get me mad, and it wouldn't work. So he's getting madder, because I'm not getting mad. Then he'd start in on "You're still not ready. I don't think you have received the discipline necessary to handle a real pro, Mike, a real pro, not like these tomato cans you've been knocking out. A real experienced pro is not going to get discouraged if you hit him with those punches." And I'm laughing. "No way, Cus. I'm the best fighter in the world, Cus. Cus, God can't beat me because I'm your fighter, Cus. Remember you said that, Cus?"

Then we came up to a tollbooth. I took the ticket from the lady in the tollbooth and said, "Thank you, ma'am, have a good day." Oh man, Cus went off on me. "You're a damned phony, Mike, a goddamned phony. I've been around phonies all my life." He made it like it was the worst thing in the world that I said, "Thank you, ma'am," like I was the biggest Uncle Tom in the history of Uncle Toms. That blew my mind but I just said, "Oh, Cus, come on, stop it." I'm doing my shtick. "She's a nice lady, it's such a beautiful day." While I'm doing my thing, he's calling me the worst names under his breath, but I hear it. Then he goes, "You know in boxing, you can't be doing none of that phony stuff. They'll bang it all out of you and then what are you going to do? You live your life the way you fight your fights."

It's not like he wanted me to be Sonny Liston. He wanted me to be respectful but I was overdoing it: "Yes, ma'am. Thank you, ma'am, have a nice day." You can't do any of that shit around Cus. I'm saying to myself, "How can I win?" Then he got off me for twenty minutes and started in on Roy Cohn and Julius November. "That Benedict Arnold caused me so many problems . . ." And if I tried to put in my two cents, he'd say, "What do you know? You drive this car." Then he'd get back into killing me again. "Don't tell me 'What?' You know what you did." "I don't know," I'd insist. "You know." He tried to get me to confess, but I don't know what I'm confessing to. I want to confess, but I don't know what I'm confessing to.

Then he got on me for my relationship with Bill Cayton. "You're just another phony. Yeah, you and Bill Cayton should get on real well, you should get along REAL well." What the fuck is he talking about? He knows I hate Bill. "You like that, don't you? You like people to look up to you, tell you how great you are, don't you, huh?" Meanwhile, he's coughing and wheezing the whole time he's talking, working himself up to a point where I'm worried that he's really getting himself ill. "You're just a damn phony. Who taught you that, huh? I know I didn't teach you that." I'm happy, he's not happy, so he is going to rip into me. "You're a phony, you're a faker." "But Cus, wouldn't you want me to say 'Thank you' to them if they were assisting you?" "No, that wasn't a sincere 'Thank you.' "

It took me a while but I began to get it. Cus thought I was going to suck up to Bill because Bill had money. He despised Cayton. He was always telling me, "Yeah, go back to them so they can tell you how great you are and how much they like you and you're one of them." He started putting that Uncle Tom shit on me. He knew that phrase would hurt me. He never said the words, but he implied it. He knew that concept would hurt me. Sometimes I would go into the city and hang out at Jimmy and Cayton's office. I was represented by white people who knew how to organize shit. I was programmed to be an international, sensational entertainer. But he didn't want me to be in debt to Bill Cayton or to accept anything from him. When I'd go to their office and call Cus, he'd go, "What are you doing there with him? Are you going up there kissing up to him and being a phony?" Being with Cus was like being with a wife who had you walking on eggshells. He was jealous. He thought Bill was going to win me over.

Cus had subtler ways of keeping me in check. *Sport* magazine had come up to Catskill to do an interview with me and put me on the cover. They brought up the reporter and another editorial person and a photographer and his assistant to the gym. And after the interview and the photo shoot, while the press was still there, Cus said, "Mike, take the broom and mop and clean the gym." After looking like a star, I had to clean the gym.

But then the two of us would be in the kitchen at home and out of the blue Cus would say, "We're the greatest fighter-trainer combination in the world. Take all the prophets and they have a son and their son is a fighter and they have the first connection to God. And they still can't beat my fighter, because I'm the best trainer in the world and my fighter is the best fighter in the world." That would send me to the moon. I realized that our success came from the bond we had with Cus. Me and Kevin, and even Camille and Jay, we all had a bond that none of the other fighters had. It wasn't that we had a bond with each other, although we all loved each other, but the bond was all about Cus. We all loved each other but Cus was like our guru from the fucking heavens. We're going to fucking accomplish this and succeed. We were his disciples. Yet I also learned from Cus that I could be a teacher's admirer but never their follower. I learned from following Cus not to be a follower. I didn't know back then that I had to base my life on my own standards and my own morals and not somebody else's. I didn't master it, but that's what I eventually learned from my relationship with Cus. I had to be my own guy. I guess that was Cus's idea, that he didn't succeed until he made someone independent of him.

The more I think about Cus, I realize that Cus's thing was to let you see how much pain he could take. You can't hurt him and you can't defy him and he'll fight you until the end. Cus was the kind of guy who said, "I don't care, you can cut me up in pieces, I'm never giving in." Cus doesn't want to see anybody who does what he does even appear to be more famous. He'd be talking about other trainers and say, "They're not trainers, they're more like glorified cheerleaders. You know what a trainer does? A trainer takes the kid that never had a pair of gloves on before in his life and makes him a world champion. That's a trainer." But Cus was not just a trainer, he was also a manager. He had to learn every aspect of boxing. He was an overachiever, destined to survive and win and laugh and be a big shot.

Cus told me that everybody is waiting for their moment. He also said that everybody you meet is not who they appear to be. When they meet you and shake your hand and talk to you, this is not who they are. We'll never know who they are, until the time that they have to show their true colors. Cus would tell me that we were like crocodiles in the mud in the Sahara. They are there for months or years waiting for migration, for these gazelles and wildebeests to cross the water. "Do you hear me, son? And when they come we are going to bite them. We are going to bite them so hard that when they scream, the whole world is going to hear them scream." I took all this dead serious.

Cus would always say, "God, I wish I had more time with you. I've been in the fight game for sixty years and I've never seen anybody with the kind of interest you have." He was open about facing his own mortality. When I was ready to begin my pro career he'd constantly wake me up in the middle of the night. "Remember what we talked about, remember what we practiced," he'd say. "I'm not going to be here long, but if you remember everything and continue to progress like you are, you'll be the greatest fighter in the world." I always thought Cus would be around, I never thought he would die. I thought he was talking shit. But there were subtle signs. He told me that he wasn't going to work my corner. He wanted Kevin and Matt Baranski, who was my cut man, to be there. I later learned that was because he didn't want me to come back to the corner one day and he wouldn't be there. He told the others, "I'm going to die someday, I want everything to be the same."

When I was about to start my pro career, Cus was still talking to me about my mission, but it had changed a little now. He started talking about immortality. I used to ask Cus, "What does it mean being the greatest fighter of all time? Most of those guys are all dead." "Listen, they're dead, but we're talking about them now, this is all about immortality." That fucked me up. It changed the whole game. I just thought it would be about riches, the big cars, the big mansions he used to point out to me. But now he was taking it to a whole other level. He got me hooked with the riches, but now he suddenly said, "You're going to be a god." This was the real deal, and the real deal fucked me up real good. Then he said, "Forget that money." Once he told me that shit, it blew my mind. He was talking immortality and I'm figuring out what that is.

I was all set to begin my pro career when I hurt my hand in the gym at the end of November 1984. I had previously injured the same hand at the European championships. I wasn't hurt too bad, but Cus didn't want to take any chances, so he sent me to the city to see a specialist. It turned out that I had torn some ligaments, so we had to postpone my pro debut.

My first pro fight was scheduled for March 6, 1985. But a few days before the fight, I split. It was like the feelings I had when I was about to do my first smoker. Tom Patti tracked me down. I was downtown sitting in my Caddy, listening to music, when he knocked on the window. "What are you doing?" he said. "I don't think I'm going to fight anymore," I said. "What are you going to do?" "I'm going to manage a J.J. Newberry's. Angie's father is the manager and I'm going to get a six-figure salary and be an assistant manager." Tom started lecturing me on how I'd have to start at the bottom being a floor sweeper and how I'd have to give my Caddy back to Cus. But I wasn't serious about any of that. I was whining. I just reverted to being a scared kid. Every now and then I lose my heart, boom, I lose my guts and I run. I don't know why I'm that way. If I'm in the dressing room, I'm crying and Patti is like, "What the fuck is going—" And the next thing, boom, I'm a fucking savage, I'm killing the fucking guy in the ring.

I went back with Tom, and Cus wasn't going to let me explain what I did but eventually we talked and I said, "Yes, I'm going to do this." The morning of my fight, I knocked on Tom Patti's door and said, "Tom, I want you to give me a Jack Dempsey haircut." I don't know why I thought this white kid who never cut hair before could accomplish cutting my black hair. So he got out a little Norelco flip-top razor and he replicated Dempsey's intimidating-looking bowl cut. It was a disaster of a haircut. I didn't care what people thought about me, though. I was going to be dark and a little bit antihero. I'm not a bad guy, but I'm not a hero either. I'm nobody's friend.

Cus would usually give me prefight instructions. Cus would watch the tapes of the guy's fights and then we would get together and he'd demonstrate the way I should attack the guy. "Hold your hands up, the guy fights like this, so when he comes, you slip, you jab, jab, right here." He'd tell me how the guy was vulnerable. It wasn't that he was looking to break guys' ribs, he was looking at their mistakes. Like he would watch a guy and watch a guy, and when he makes the move, he'd say, "Listen, this guy is wide-open for you to break his ribs, like that." He didn't have to tell me that, because I was looking to break their ribs anyway.

My first fight was against Hector Mercedes. His record was 0–3 but Cus didn't know anything about him, so he got on the phone to Puerto Rico the morning of the fight to see who he was, who he fought, what gym he came out of. That was Cautious Cus's way.

The fight was in Albany. Before we left the dressing room, Cus came over to me. He was totally formal and he looked stone serious. He put out his hand to shake and I shook it and his grip was vise tight. "Good luck," he said with detachment. There was no feeling at all from him. I laughed. "What do you mean, 'Good luck'? I don't need luck," I said, and he shot me a look that could kill. Cus was serious and he was totally impersonal. Okay, I thought. And then before each fight, we'd both get serious and do that Roman shit. When we shook hands it was like a fucking lock. Boom. Ice-cold. Once we shook like that, I knew what it meant. No feeling, no love, no kidding, just that coldness that meant it was time to go into the ring and do something bad.

My first fight didn't last long. I stunned him with a left and he went reeling into the ropes. He tried to cover up but I unloaded lefts and rights to the body and he crumbled into the canvas. He got an eight count but the ref stopped the fight at 1:47 of the first round. When I was interviewed afterward I said, "I feel bad fighting somebody smaller than me. It makes me feel like a bully." Cus was pretty reserved too. "I thought on the whole he did very well. The other fellow tonight fought back. He threw good punches. If Mike wasn't more elusive he would have got hit," he told one reporter. But he told another one that he thought I would break Patterson's record of being the youngest heavyweight champion. On the way back to the dressing room, Cus was quizzed by his friend William Plummer, who was following Cus around for a major article about him for *People* magazine. How did it feel to be back after all those years? Cus told him he hadn't been away at all. So he reframed his question. What difference had I made on his life? "He's meant everything. If it weren't for him,

I probably wouldn't be living today. See, I believe nature's a lot smarter than anybody thinks. During the course of a man's life he develops a lot of pleasures and people he cares about. Then nature takes them away one by one. It's her way of preparing you for death. See, I didn't have the pleasures any longer. My friends were gone, I didn't hear things, I didn't see things clearly, except in memory. The last time I had an erection was fifteen years ago. So I said I must be getting ready to die. Then Mike came along. The fact that he is here and is doing what he is doing gives me the motivation to stay alive. Because I believe a person dies when he no longer wants to live. He finds a convenient disease, just like a fighter, when he no longer wants to fight, finds a convenient corner to lie down in. It's like boxing. It's all psychological."

I wasn't there to hear him say that, but on the way home, he told me he was pleased after this fight. He had no criticisms at all. He thought I moved well and finished great. And I got a reward for the win—Cus paid for some nice clothes.

We had a little celebration at the house. The next morning, Cus changed his tune a bit. "Feeling pretty cocky, huh? Think you're tough, don't you? Unbeatable. Well, let me tell you, you're not. Oh, you did good all right, and you deserved a quick knockout, but you made a lot of mistakes too. You were too excitable, too wild. You fought out of control. A good fighter would have laid back and picked you apart. You've got to stay calm so you can think out there. You did a good job on your first fight, but now we've got to go back to the gym and work on your ring discipline."

He was always looking to rain on my parade. A little while after the fight, Cus gave me some real talk. "Mike, this is the real world. You see those people in the arena? When you lose fights and don't perform well, they don't like you no more. That's just the way it is, Mike. These people are only with you when you're doing well. Everybody used to like me. Believe me, even at an old age, I was an old man in my fifties and women would chase me all over the place, young beautiful women, and I'm an old man. But now no one comes around anymore.

"But if you listen to me, you'll reign with the gods. See the way you talk about all these old fighters? If you listen to me, the only reason people would know about these guys is because you'll keep them alive. You will make more money and have more fights than all these guys, don't worry about that. I'm older than some of these guys you are talking about, Louis and those guys. I watched them develop. I watched Jack Dempsey as a boy. They are not what you are. You are a giant. You are a colossus among men."

I was eating that shit up. But I also felt sorry for him. He'd talk about getting old a lot. "Remember I'm an old man now, Mike. I look in the mirror, I don't even know who that guy is, I get scared with what I'm seeing."

Now that I was being interviewed after my pro fights, Cus started grooming my speech. He would take me to all his interviews and I would absorb his diction. Cus spoke very properly when he did an interview, but when we were home together he would talk tough and that turned me on. Mort Sharnik, an old friend of Cus's and a boxing consultant for CBS, said, "Cus had been calling me, telling me about this kid and then when I saw him, I couldn't believe it. He really did look and sound like Cus, from the high sidewalls haircut, to the way he smiled and how he expressed himself, carefully spacing out his words, it was uncanny." I morphed into Cus. I'm just one of those people. "Philosophically he was Cus and he had Cus's passion for boxing."

Now that I was fighting pro fights, Cus began to redouble his efforts to get me to control my emotions. He was schooling me on discipline. He had me practice getting used to people saying provocative things and not getting mad.

My next two fights were also in Albany. On April 10, I fought Trent Singleton. I entered the ring and bowed to all four corners and raised my arms like I was some Roman gladiator nigga. I was really getting into character. I knocked him down three times in the first round and the referee stopped the fight at fifty-seven seconds. Then I sauntered over to his corner, kissed him, and rubbed his head. "Little boy, you okay? Oh, I'm sorry." Cus couldn't complain, he'd seen

Jack Dempsey do that. After the fight I told the press, "I was so confident in this fight. I don't think anybody can beat me because I'm the best fighter in the world. The fans may not know it yet, but my peers know it." Whew. I was asked whether I was scared when Singleton tried to stare me down during the referee's instructions. "I was scared . . . scared that I might kill him."

Cus seemed pleased when he talked to the press after the fight. "Anything can happen at any time in prizefighting. Mike proved that tonight. Even though Mike's fighting stiffs, somebody like Larry Holmes would react the same way. It's so hard to get somebody in the ring with him, though. Professionals with decent records are afraid to get hurt, and up-and-comers are just looking to win big. I'm even having trouble finding people to spar with Mike. The ones that agreed to do it charge me a fortune."

I was back in the ring on May 23 fighting Don Halpin. It took me four rounds but I knocked him into the ropes and then chopped him down and left him a bloody mess. He couldn't meet with the press afterward because he was being treated for a broken nose and a huge gash over his right eye. But I could talk. "I can't feel bad the way it ended. If I do, then I shouldn't be a fighter. This is how I make my living, this is how I put clothes on my back. Outside the ring, I'm a nice guy, but not once I go in." Cus put a good spin on the fight. "The first three rounds we wanted to get Mike to open him up a little so he could get a clean shot. I thought Mike showed more poise and was more relaxed than he had ever been before."

Now I was starting to get a local fan following. People were bringing signs that had a big "KO" written on them, a takeoff on the Mets fans holding up "K" signs for Doc Gooden. Cus was thrilled with all that. "You're the greatest fighter the world has ever seen. I just need you to believe it," he'd keep telling me. He thought so highly of me as a fighter, it was like he was worshipping me. And I understood that, and I started worshipping myself. I started getting groupies coming to my fights but I didn't take them up then. I was too in love with myself at the time to think about caring about anybody else like that.

That's what it was all about, what Cus created for me, circling the world around myself. *Love yourself, look in the mirror, shadowbox, and look at your work. It's magnificent, what you're doing, it's never been done in the annals of fight history.* He always dropped those charged words.

I wasn't making too much money for these first fights. The promoter lost money on my first fight and Jimmy Jacobs paid me $500 out of his pocket. He took $50 of that to pay Kevin and then put the $350 in a bank account for me, so I walked away with $100. After a few fights I was supposed to go up to ten-round fights and get paid $20,000. Then Jimmy called me and told me that I was too young to go ten rounds. I was pissed because I thought I wouldn't get the twenty grand. Cus found out and he thought I was mad because I wasn't fighting a ten-round fight. When I called Jimmy again, I asked him if I'd still get the twenty grand. "Oh yeah, of course! Don't worry about it." When I got the money, I put it into a knot right in my pocket, because Cus was going to put that shit into a trust fund or the bank.

Cus was concerned that Jim would lose a lot of money on these first fights so he had Joe Colangelo counting all the people who came in with a clicker. Cus told him, "Look, Joe, I don't want Jim Jacobs to lose one penny more than he has to, so you've got to make sure of that because he's my friend."

On June 20, I traveled down to Atlantic City to fight Ricky Spain. I knocked him out in one round. When we went through Cus's files, there was a strange letter that Cus got on July 8, a few days before my next fight. It was from the NYSAC, where José Torres had recently been named the chairman. It included an application for a manager's license that Cus had requested. Cus had told people in Catskill that he was probably going to be my manager. There's no evidence that Cus applied for that license, though.

I was back in Atlantic City on July 11 for a fight with John Alderson. He was a big country guy, six-foot-four, a miner from West Virginia. We had identical records going in, 4–0 with four knockouts.

But this was another quick one, a TKO at the end of the second, when the doctor stopped the fight after I knocked Alderson down three times that round. The Jersey crowd loved the fight. When I was hot, I was really hot. I'm a ham and I played the role. I watched movies and read books about how the gladiators went into the arenas, how they acted before the crowd. They expected to sit on the fucking throne without even fighting, that's how arrogant they were.

On July 15 the *People* article came out. The reporter covered my first fight but he also went into a long retrospective look at Cus's career, including his fight with the IBC. And again, Cus said that he wouldn't have been able to fight the IBC until he found a "kid" who was not only "good but loyal." Another whitewash of Patterson. Cus's whole thing was to make Patterson look good. Patterson had some form of diabolicalness. He played the role, but if he could he'd beat you.

Cus was pissed after my next fight. I fought Larry Simms in Poughkeepsie and it was the only one of my fights that Jimmy and Cayton didn't film. It was a hard fight for me, Simms was slick. The guy was hitting me hard. The guy was moving, giving me problems, moving, jabbing, awkward, and the next thing you know, I switched to southpaw and I hit him with a right jab and then with a right hook. The punch came out of nowhere. Everybody thought it was beautiful. He was dead, cold, sleeping, out. They had to give him ammonia to wake him up. But Cus was furious because I didn't do it the way he wanted me to do it. "Who taught you that southpaw crap? It might be hard to get you fights now. People don't want to fight southpaws. You're going to ruin everything we created," he yelled at me afterward. "I'm sorry, Cus," was all I could say. I never practiced going southpaw in the gym. I was watching people doing it on television and I said, "That looks cool." I was just a dick trying to emulate stuff and Cus was so pissed. A lot of boxing people thought that I was naturally left-handed because I had so many powerful knockouts with a left hook or a left jab.

Cus kept that criticism between us. After the fight he told the press, "I'm a sculptor. I can picture the ultimate fighter and I keep chipping away until I have created that fighter. I don't know how long it will take Mike Tyson to become the champion, but if he maintains his discipline and dedication, he can become champion before he's 22. Mike believes in himself so much, his actions in the ring become intuitive. And once they're intuitive, nobody can beat him. He can take anybody out. If he hits Holmes, then Holmes will go down too."

A month later I was back in the ring in Atlantic City against Lorenzo Canady. A one-round TKO and my record went to 7–0, all KOs. Jimmy and Cayton were sending videotapes of all my spectacular knockouts to the boxing press. They were talking to columnists they knew, like Dick Young, and they were even getting me into the gossip sections of papers. I would go into the city and they'd set up interviews for me. I had been finishing Cus's sentences for years so I knew how to handle the press, the way Jimmy and them wanted me to. Cus thought the whole thing was so phony. It's crazy that this guy had such affection and love for me and he'd fight to the death for me, then he'd come up to me and say, "You know, you're a phony."

Cus was always keeping me in check. When I'd talk to the reporters in my dressing room after a fight, Cus would stand in the back, with his arms folded, observing. One day a female reporter asked me a question and I answered, "Nah, baby." Oh shit! On the way home, he was fuming. "Who taught you to talk like that? I never talk like that around you. Who are you around? 'Nah, baby'—what does that mean?"

As my confidence built I started talking trash around the house. "I'm the top fighter. How can anybody beat me?" Cus would say, "Listen, there were fighters like Jim Jeffries, Sonny Liston, when they walk in the room, they don't say a word, they just walk in the room and people die of a heart attack. If you start doing that, then you're something."

Cus was way ahead of his time when it came to protecting fighters. I'm not being egotistical, but Cus used to tell me, "All your fights have been easy, no-risk fights because there's no one who can compare to you, because of what I've taught you. What I taught you is innovative to any thinking in the boxing world today. You've been fighting only a couple of months and you've got more press than all the Olympians. People are talking about you fighting the champ already. Listen, we're doing the right thing. These people, they're out of their league trying to compete with me. I've been in this business for sixty years, I've seen no one who even comes to my standards when it comes to the peerlessness of this particular genre that we are performing here."

Three weeks later I was back in Atlantic City again to fight Michael Johnson. Check out the ring announcers' account of the first round:

RING ANNOUNCER: And his opponent in the red corner wearing the white trunks with the green trim, undefeated with seven wins, all of them by knockout. Hails from the Catskills in New York. Please welcome, weighing two hundred nineteen and a half pounds, Mike Tyson!

FIRST TV COMMENTATOR: I was about to say when Stefan Herreria made the announcement, Mike Tyson really, vocally sounds just like Larry Holmes. I mean, I thought I was back in eastern Pennsylvania talking to the champ.

SECOND TV COMMENTATOR: He does sound like him. He's meaner, though. Look at the size of him—he looks like the Incredible Hulk.

FIRST COMMENTATOR: In that case, I'm glad I'm not Michael Jack Johnson.

SECOND COMMENTATOR: We want to point out it's the first fight for Michael Jack Johnson in two years.

FIRST COMMENTATOR: I'm glad you pointed it out, because down he goes. Michael Jack Johnson went good-bye. That left hook just caught him and sent him right to the—

SECOND COMMENTATOR: A right to the head and it's all over. Good-bye.

FIRST COMMENTATOR: I hope he's not hurt.

When I knocked Johnson out, his two front teeth were lodged in his mouthpiece. I stood in my corner laughing at the guy, like an ar-

rogant kid, high-fiving Kevin. "Look at this dead nigga, Kevin."
Everybody hated both of us—we both talked nasty. Cus didn't comment on our celebration but he did defend his matchmaking to the
press. "People have been saying that he's been knocking out ordinary
guys. He isn't. This guy [Johnson] was chosen because the promoters
felt he could do something with Mike. But the same thing always happens. When he hits them, they go down. You've seen the destructive
effects his blows have. It doesn't matter who he hits; it could be [IBF
champion] Holmes in there, and the same thing would happen to
Holmes." Cus hated Holmes. I had said something complimentary
about Holmes after he beat Cooney, and Cus was all over me for that.
"You have to reign solely supreme. Anything you like, you have to
despise."

By now I was 8–0 and everyone was ecstatic about my progress. I
fought three times in less than a month starting on October 9 when I
KO'd Donnie Long in the first round. Sixteen days later I knocked
out Robert Colay in thirty-seven seconds of the first round. On November 1, I took out Sterling Benjamin in one round. But all these
achievements were under a big black cloud. Cus was in the hospital
fighting for his life.

I knew something was up with Cus, going back to that Alex Wallau interview we did before the Olympics in 1984. While they were
setting up the lights, Cus was coughing and he told Alex that he had
pneumonia. Alex asked him how he got it and Cus said he knew he
had it in 1983 when he was in St. Louis. But then when we fought in
Lake Placid in September of 1983 he told Wallau, "I developed a condition that I went to the doctor for that had nothing to do with pneumonia, I learned about the pneumonia inadvertently. I had a condition
known as hiatus hernia, which is extremely painful. I woke up in the
middle of the night, about two o'clock in the morning—it felt like a
red-hot iron. I thought it was a heart attack, but I didn't want to say
anything, but by twelve o'clock I decided that this might get worse. So
I decided to go to the doctor. And at that point he told me he thought
I had a hiatus hernia. Then he sent me for X-rays and the X-rays revealed I was recovering from pneumonia." "So you had walking

pneumonia before?" Alex asked. "Probably, but it had a very bad effect on my stamina. It took me a while to recuperate."

He never did recuperate. Cus was taking some pills and he would go to a doctor every now and then. They put him on a diet and he couldn't eat certain things he liked and he was mad. He'd still eat that stuff. He always thought he knew more than the doctors. He had no respect for them. But in early October of 1985 he fell ill after I drove him to a seminar on boxing head injuries that was conducted by the NYSAC and the American Medical Association at a Catskill hotel. They took him to the Albany Medical Center and he stayed there for about a week. I saw him there and he seemed okay to me. He was in a small room and it was clean but it had that medicinal smell of castor oil combined with mildew. We were talking about my last fights. Jimmy had sent Cus tapes of them and Cus then told me the things that I was doing right and pointed out the things I did wrong. One of the things that was worrying Cus was that he was afraid of losing the gym. He said that followers of Teddy Atlas were trying to get Cus kicked out of the gym so that Teddy could come back to Catskill and take over. Cus was working on getting a long-term lease for one dollar a year.

Tom Patti visited Cus up in Albany and Cus asked him if I had been training. "Yeah, Mike is looking good, he's fighting actively," Tom told him. Then Cus asked about Kevin Rooney. "Well, what about that Rooney guy?" Tom didn't know where Cus was going with this. "What the hell has that Rooney been doing, has he been coming around?" "Yeah, Cus. Kevin has been there," Tom said. So he was quiet for a moment and then he said, "I'm very disappointed in Kevin. Tommy, the worst combination in boxing is a gambler who is a drinker. They make decisions that can jeopardize not only their own future, but their fighters'." Tommy was being trained by Kevin and he told Cus that Kevin was fine. But Cus said, "When I get out of here, I'm going to have to replace Kevin."

Look, Kevin did gamble and drink, but as far as training goes, Kevin was an animal. We had a great understanding. He's an awe-

some person. Atlas was a great psychologist because he got everything he knows from Cus. Kevin didn't get the psychology. But he
loved hurting the opponent. After our fights, we'd laugh at the guys
who wound up picking their teeth off the canvas. We were dedicated
and focused on hurting people.

When Bonnie, Kevin's wife, visited Cus in the hospital, he asked
her about Kevin. "He's gambling and drinking again." That was the
straw that broke the camel's back. Kevin knew he was in trouble. He
went over to the hospital with his daughter on his shoulders and
walked into Cus's room and Cus yelled, "Get out, I never want to see
you again, get out!" He kicked him out of the hospital room. Now
Kevin was in jeopardy. And I knew that without Kevin we were
fucked. Without him this was all going downhill, I don't care who
Cus wanted to bring in. Nobody could have the chemistry that Kevin
and I had built up. Kevin was a total street guy, even more than me.
So I went to Cus and begged him, "No, Cus, don't do that, man. It's
not happening if he leaves." Kevin was one hell of a soldier for Cus to
the end. If you were Cus's enemy, you were his enemy. Kevin had
to be with me. When we worked together, our brains were two peas
in the same pod. We were the same person. Who else was I going to
be with?

Cus wasn't getting any better, and it turned out that he had been
misdiagnosed and they were treating him for the wrong thing. When
Jimmy went up to Albany to visit Cus he was appalled, and he moved
Cus to Mount Sinai in the city, where his doctors could treat Cus.

After Cus was evaluated at Mount Sinai by Dr. Eugene Brody, a
friend of Jimmy's, the doctor told the press that "Cus is a very sick
man" and they listed his condition as "serious but stable." He said
that Cus was suffering from interstitial pulmonary fibrosis, a lung
disease formerly known as Hamman-Rich syndrome. Dr. Brody said
it was a "life-threatening" disease. But Cus seemed to be in good
spirits. When José Torres went to the hospital to visit him, Cus looked
up at him and smiled and said, "Don't worry. I'm not going to die—
not here. I won't give my enemies the pleasure."

Cus was in the hospital for about a week when I got a call from Jimmy. He said that Cus was not doing well and that I should come down to see him. When I walked in the room it was like night and day compared with his room in Albany. He was in a private, much bigger room. I saw that Cus had a catheter because he couldn't get out of bed.

But Cus was sitting up, eating ice cream. To me that was a good sign. He used to buy his ice cream, eat a little, and then mark the container, just to see if I would have some of it because he knew I loved ice cream. When I didn't eat his, he knew I was getting disciplined. That's my adoptive father. He was the food police too.

Then Cus asked the people in the room to leave because he wanted to talk to me alone. As soon as they left, I started crying. Then Cus told me that he was dying from the pneumonia. I started getting angry. We had so much together. I'm a little street kid with this old guy who's in exile and we'd talk about these grandiose dreams and making money and buying mansions and how there was nobody in the world who could touch us. They couldn't do anything but gawk at us. We were the most magnificent gift boxing had ever witnessed. And now it was over before we had reached our ultimate mission. I couldn't go on with it without Cus.

"If you die, I'm not going to fight anymore," I said, sobbing. Cus looked angry. "Now listen, if you quit fighting, then you're going to find out if people can come back from the dead, because I will come back and I will haunt you for the rest of your life. You have to fight."

Then Cus started talking about some regrets he had. "The people I have invested the most time in disappointed me the most," he told me again. Was he talking again about Patterson? His trainers Florio and Fariello? I didn't know. But as I got older and dealt with life on life's terms, I realized that Cus's morals are hard to live up to. And if you didn't conduct your life with a certain kind of morality, the one that Cus believed in, then he wouldn't have respect for you.

But then he lost it. He started crying like a child and sniffling. I was floored. I'd never seen any emotion out of him before. Even when his hero Joe Louis died he just went up in his room and stayed there the whole day. But this was something else. I was crying too. Then Cus told me that he was crying because of Camille. He was upset that he never was able to marry her. When he went up against Norris, Cus sacrificed his personal life. He kept Camille hidden. His own nieces, who loved him, never understood why he hardly ever came around anymore. Cus relinquished his personal happiness to achieve his professional goal. And then, after beating the IBC, he still couldn't marry Camille because of the treachery of November and Cohn and he wound up bankrupt and didn't want to jeopardize the house if Camille took on his tax debt. I used to hear Cus say, "I wish I had taken care of Camille when I had money." Cus had stopped crying by then and he put me on a second mission—to take care of Camille for the rest of her life. That's what he wanted me to do—fight and pay the rent.

Then we were interrupted by a doctor who was on his rounds. He was wearing glasses and he had a high-pitched voice. "Hi, Mr. D'Amato," he said. "How are you feeling?" Cus smiled. "Come here, Doc. You're in the presence of the heavyweight champion of the world. This is the heavyweight champ." "Oh really? Is that so?" the doctor said. He must have thought Cus was going in and out. I was mad. In my head, I'm saying, "You heard what he said, motherfucker. I'm the heavyweight champ." What a megalomaniac Cus made me into.

The doctor left and Cus started talking to me about moving my head. That was his mantra, move my fucking head. "A more experienced fighter would have hit you that last fight." I'm thinking, "Cus, I knocked the guy out in thirty seconds." That was my last conversation with Cus. After he boosted me all the way up, he brings me down, pointing out my flaws. Then he told me to leave. "Go now," he said. "Go take care of Camille." I wanted to hug him good-bye but he just didn't give me that energy, even though he was dying. But death didn't mean anything to Cus. I'm at his bedside and by now nobody's crying. If I tried to hug him he would have gone, "Mike, stop that, we got business. You've got to be disciplined, you've got to be professional and disciplined. Mike, you have to control your emotions." The last thing he said to me was that he was going to bring a good pro fighter upstate to spar with me. So I got up and left and did what he told me to do. Fight and take care of Camille.

After I left Cus's room I met up with Jimmy because we had to deposit my last purse in my bank account. There was a female teller there I was interested in. I was a young up-and-coming guy, I'd come in the bank, and the teller was very attractive, and we used to flirt all the time. And we'd call periodically. Now I'm coming in and you'd think someone beat me with a whip, I was screaming and crying so loud. "Is everything okay?" the bank officials asked. They were frightened that something was drastically wrong, and Jimmy coldly said, "Well, a friend of ours is not doing well. He won't live through the night and Mike is distraught." After that teller saw me like that, I never talked to her again. I never stepped foot into that bank again. I was so fucked-up. I was in a dark, almost suicidal hole.

Cus survived the night. They tried to sedate him and he put up a fight and tried to pull the tubes out but he was too weak and then the drugs kicked in. Camille had called Tom Patti and asked him to be by Cus's side that night. And in the morning, Cus passed peacefully. Within a half hour Jimmy showed up and he was as emotionally detached as he was in the bank the afternoon before. Then José Torres came by. Jay Bright thought he was just visiting Cus when he came an hour later and found out that Cus was gone. He went numb. I couldn't bring myself to go to the hospital again when I got the call that Cus had died. I was still in that dark place, just ready to kill everybody.

So I went back to my old Brooklyn neighborhood to re-situate myself. I walked around and talked to some people I grew up with. When I hit Amboy Street, I saw my old friend Buck. "Hey, man, I'm sorry you got bad news today." He had heard the report on the radio. He left and I was sitting on the stoop and everybody knew because hardly anyone was coming up to talk to me. Normally everyone who passed by would give me a greeting. I was the up-and-coming superstar. I sat there from eight o'clock at night until four in the morning. After a few hours somebody would sit down and talk to me, smoke some weed or share a drink, and then go home. A few strangers even came up to me and said, "What are you doing here, Mike? You still come back here?"

They didn't know me like the older people—their fathers or older brothers. I'm packaged different, but I'm one of those guys. The old ones knew that I had to be down there. So I stayed there for hours, just chilling, eating take-out Chinese food that people brought me. Whenever I had a crisis, I had to go back to Amboy Street. That was how I healed.

went back home to Catskill and hung with Camille and Jay Bright. Cus's brothers and his nieces and nephews came around the house, along with Camille's sisters. I was in a daze. There was no Cus to talk to, so I started rereading the *Boxing Encyclopedia* and stayed on our mission to be great. Tom Patti stepped up now and did a 180-degree turn. Him and Cus used to butt heads, Cus would be on his back all the time. But when Cus died, he took control. I was watching him handle the whole funeral situation, thinking Cus would have been so proud. They started becoming closer as Cus got older. Cus made a soldier out of Tom. Cus used to tell me, "You see this guy? He's come a long way, hasn't he?" He would never tell Tom that. He would have killed me if I had told Tom he said that.

Tom selected the pallbearers—Patterson and Torres, Jimmy, Jay Bright, me, Tom, and Jerry D'Amato, Tony's son. He arranged for the rosary to be done at the funeral parlor and then services at a Catholic church. I was trying to hold it together but the night before the funeral, at the funeral parlor, I had to go into the bathroom and I started crying hysterically. Tom walked in and he grabbed me and we hugged, both of us just bawling. I didn't speak at the service the next day. I was a dazed-out, fucked-up zombie. After the service we went to the grave site for the burial and then we headed home.

In the limo with Camille, I broke down crying. "Camille, I never knew what love was until now," I told her. "Cus taught me so much." It was the first time that I had ever cried in front of her.

I was still wearing my suit when we got back home and I went out to the yard and started playing with my birds. They were another connection between me and Cus. After a while I drifted back into the house. I saw Cus's old friend Mort Sharnik and he asked me how I was doing. I told him that I felt rootless without Cus but that I knew where I was going and that I would achieve our goal. Then I went over to Camille, who was sitting in her easy chair. I sat on the arm and put my arm around her and started stroking her hair. "Don't worry, Mom. I'll take care of you. You never have to worry, I'll look after you, Mom." She smiled and said, "We've got to take care of each other now." She told me later that Cus had made her vow to take care of me after he died. And that's what we did. We were truly together. If she needed anything—money, medicine—I would work on it. We started working without anybody really saying anything. We knew we had each other. Camille mourned Cus for a long time. She was not a wimpy woman, she was a strong Ukrainian.

Cus died penniless. He had a will and his brother Tony was made executor. In his mind, that meant that he was in charge of everything—in charge of the gym, in charge of me, in charge of everything that Cus was involved in. He started going around talking like he was going to take over my career and that started pissing people off. Camille had to call up his daughter Betty, who knew how to talk to her father better than anyone, and she was able to get him to back down. Betty and Tony went over the will. The only possession Cus had was that ragged old station wagon that had gone through God knows how many transmissions. And Cus had willed that to Kevin to drive the fighters around in. So Tony was the executor of nothing. After Betty explained it to Tony, he retreated gracefully. But I guess it was nice to have people fighting over me.

After Cus died, I shut down emotionally. I got mean. I wanted to prove myself. I wanted everyone to think I was a man, but I was just a boy. At first I lost my spirit, my energy to do anything good. I began to blame myself for Cus dying. I realized that the reason Cus always stayed loyal to Floyd, despite all of Floyd's treacherous acts toward Cus, was that Floyd gave Cus his championship, he gave him that feeling that Cus always wanted. So Cus was indebted to him. Patterson made him a champ and that was his life's dream, so he's like, "I ain't gonna say bad things about him." Now I wanted to help put Cus back, I wanted to be there for Cus, and he gave me a platform. Now I had to take it to another level. If I had taken it to another level sooner, then Cus would have stayed alive. That was my thought process. I didn't feel I was good enough. I wasn't progressing fast enough. Maybe if I had won the Olympics he would have had more hope. All that talk about him wishing I was built like Mike Weaver, in my mind, I thought that showed a little bit of doubt in me.

Then, soon after he died, all of a sudden it just clicked. It happened overnight. As soon as I thought he had doubted me, I went to that other level. Maybe it was because I was fighting for his legacy as well as mine. I was fighting to stick it in the face of all those who doubted him, who'd say, "That stupid old Italian didn't know what he was talking about." Cus's whole strategy was about manipulation, about confusing the enemy, taking advantage of people's characteristics. He believed the character makes the person. He said you could have ten Harvard law students who all had the same professor. But when they become lawyers and they go into the courtroom, they are all going to conduct law differently. And they won't all be great lawyers: it is only character and personality that will make some transcend. A lot of people were trained by Cus, but only certain people can grasp who he was. It's not that I am any more special than anyone else, it's just that I understood where he was coming from because he spoke to me in my language.

Jimmy Jacobs tried to fill the huge hole when Cus was gone but that was impossible. Jimmy was a good guy and I totally respected him but he wasn't Cus, even though he had become Cus-tomized. When he talked to the press, he talked very dispassionately, like an actor, saying the same things over and over again. I didn't want to have anything to do with Cayton, because Cus had hated him so much, so I always dealt with Jimmy. He was a warm guy in private. As I got older I realized that he was a smooth operator, a hustler, making up stories about his past. I thought that was beautiful.

After Cus died, I was interviewed and I said, "I used to be bored only part of the time but then I spoke to Cus and he kept me in suspense. But now I'm bored all the time. I have nothing to do." Jimmy must have heard that and he knew that as I got older and with Cus no longer there to keep me in check, I'd need something to keep my mind occupied between fights. Jacobs had once told a reporter, "Cus was rigid and had his own high set of standards. I could understand in the future, when Mike is eighteen, nineteen, it would be very difficult for Mike to spend 24/7 at camp. The problems are not with fifteen-year-old Mike, but eighteen when he wants to be out in the world." So he started teaching me how to edit fight films for Big Fights. I learned how to splice and dice, all that shit, and I was good at it too.

When it came to the fighting, Jimmy followed Cus's blueprints to a T. Who I fought, how I fought, it was all Cus. And it had results. "Mike has had fifty-six pro and amateur fights and he's never had a bloody nose, never had a cut, never had a lump on his face," Jimmy told a TV interviewer. "When he's toweled off after a fight you'd never know what his profession is." So Jimmy and Cayton followed Cus's plan after he died. This blueprint had been in Cus's head ever since he'd been involved with those IBC guys. Cus invented all this—the house I'm sitting in now, the cars, it is all his projection.

I fought again against Eddie Richardson in Texas on November 13, just nine days after Cus died. I was fine with that. I was going to fulfill the D'Amato prophecy. Now I was focused. It was like taking Adderall. But I was also bitter and unhappy. I'd been miserable all my life. And I would think, "If I get mad, I'll fuck the world," that's my mentality. Maybe I was partly motivated by feeling sorry for myself. I lost my mother, I lost Cus. Maybe it all came back to me not wanting to be poor again, or be a nobody again. Cus was gone and I'm nothing.

Even when I was doing bad, but doing good doing bad, people said that I was good at something. I never thought I was good at anything. But I was good at robbing and snatching and knocking people out. My sister said, "He's the greatest pickpocket in Brooklyn." I took pride in that, being that guy, I took pride in fighting. It was weird, people said, "You're bad." Even though I was snatching purses and stuff, I got a big souped-up head and it was like Cus, he would soup me up to this shit. And that's what it was, he pumped up my ego. I fell in love with myself because Cus told me I was a god. I'm more superior than them because I had the greatest trainer in the world.

Cus hated the rich but he wanted me to be privileged. He never wanted me to work a day in my life. He'd say when reporters asked me where I had worked, "I want you to say, 'I never worked a day in my life, sir.' " I wanted to work at a barbershop and he said no. I said, "Cus, you hate the rich people who never broke a sweat but you want me to tell people I boxed all my life and never had a job?" I didn't have to worry about paying any bills. I had no restraints, I was totally free to train and fulfill our prophecy. I used to think I was the golden child. Now I was the golden orphan.

I brought along a photo of Cus to the Richardson fight. I put it in my hotel room and I talked to Cus. I could hear him tell me to move my head and punch in combinations. Constant aggression, throwing punches with bad intentions. And I did my affirmations out loud. "I'm going to become champ of the world." "I'm the greatest fighter God created." "How dare he challenge me?" I'd say that to the mirror in my hotel room with the picture of Cus propped up.

Richardson didn't challenge me much. I knocked him out in the first round. Then I talked to the press about Cus. "People don't think I'm emotional because of the way I am in the ring, but I'm emotional when it comes to family. Now I'm alone. There's no Cus to tell me how I did. There's no mother to show my clippings to. No matter how I did, Cus would always find something wrong, something I needed to work on. He never let me get cocky. With Cus gone, I have to take my job more serious now out of respect for him. When I was seventeen or eighteen, I was very cocky. I thought I was so good I didn't have to train, but Cus tried to keep me on track. I used to go into fights five or ten pounds overweight and still win. I had a bad attitude then, but Cus straightened me out. Now I have more discipline. I know that when two guys get into the ring together, anything can happen."

They had a memorial for Cus at the Gramercy Gym on November 19 but I didn't go. Besides boxing people, all his old literary friends were there lauding him. Norman Mailer said, "I never knew a man who was not a writer who thought more like a writer. . . . His influence upon boxing in terms of style was probably as great as Ernest Hemingway's influence upon young American writers has been." Gay Talese spoke about how Cus's teachings transcended a boxer's career: "He also sensed that there was something beyond winning. It's called living beyond your days as a performer. And I think that that was a quality that I appreciated most when I had the honor of knowing him." Jim Jacobs reminded everyone about Cus's long struggle with the IBC. "Cus D'Amato was violently opposed to ignorance and corruption in boxing. While Cus was unyielding to his enemies, he was understanding, compassionate, and incredibly tolerant with his friends." Tom Patti was there and he didn't like the fact that Jimmy promoted me a lot at the memorial. But knowing Cus, that's exactly what he would have wanted. But it was Pete Hamill who talked about how Cus's teachings could transcend boxing: "He taught me so many things not just about boxing, which was a craft and could be mastered, but about living and about life, which is not so easily mastered."

Jimmy and Bill's idea was to keep me busy, so just nine days after Richardson, I fought Conroy Nelson, the former Canadian titleholder who had lost to Trevor Berbick a year before. Nelson was a real test for me but I went to his body in the first and broke his nose with a right in the second and won by a KO. That fight was upstate and I realized that with Cus gone, there were no more celebrations after every victory, even if it was just a cake. Camille later thought that Jimmy and Bill started to lose touch with me because they didn't give me that prestige. It was true. Even if it was a simple celebration Cus made it big. Cayton never even visited me once in Catskill. That was all right. I didn't want him to. He once sent me a book on pigeons and I threw it right in the garbage.

Two weeks later I fought at the Felt Forum at Madison Square Garden. My opponent was a 250-pound Kentucky good old boy named Slamming Sammy Scaff. Two left hooks to the head in the first round bloodied him badly and earned me another first-round KO. "Damn, he hits hard," Slamming Sammy told the press afterward. "I thought it was all hype, but man, he hit me good." Without Cus there, I slowly began to develop my post-fight Iron Mike persona. "I was so anxious," I told the reporters. "I wanted to get my hands on him, because he went four rounds with Tim Witherspoon. I don't want to sound like a Neanderthal man, but I wanted to get my hands on him, chew him up." When I was asked if the fight was work, I said, "Yeah, it was work. I had to walk to the ring. I wasn't impressed with him. If he had stayed around, he would have gotten a worse beating."

I achieved two more first-round KOs in my next two fights against Mark Young and Dave Jaco. Both fights were upstate and I partied after both of them. But after the Jaco fight I didn't get back to Catskill until early the next morning. Camille asked me how I made out. "I did good in the fight, Camille, but I was lonely. Cus wasn't there. Everybody tells me I do good, but nobody tells me if I do bad. It wouldn't make any difference how good I did. Cus would always find something I did wrong. I'm trying to get Cus's death out of my mind, but it's difficult. I used to talk to him before every fight. Now, when I start to get nervous or scared, I have to deal with it myself," I told her. It was true.

And I was getting a little cocky with Cus not around to check me. I fought a big Irishman named Mike Jameson on January 24, 1986, and I told a local reporter, "When you see me smash someone's skull, you'll enjoy it." It took me five rounds to get a TKO over Jameson because he was a wily veteran and he knew how to hold and stop my momentum. On February 16, my next opponent, Jesse Ferguson, took holding to a new level. This was my first national TV appearance and I wanted to look good because Ferguson was the ESPN heavyweight champ and I wanted that distinction. He held me for the first four rounds but in the fifth I unloaded a vicious right uppercut that broke his nose. He barely got out of that round and in the sixth I had him in trouble again and he enveloped me and stopped the action. The ref disqualified him, but a few minutes later they changed the decision to a TKO because a disqualification would have stopped my knockout streak. It was good to have José Torres as the NYSAC chairman.

But the real shitstorm came after the fight. When the reporters asked me about finishing Ferguson off after I had broken his nose with the uppercut, I said, "I wanted to hit him on the nose one more time, so that the bone of his nose would go up into his brain. . . . I would always listen to the doctor's conclusions. They said that any time that the nose goes into the brain, the consequences of him getting up right away are out of the question." The next day a lot of the papers questioned whether I was a thug. I even got a letter from my old social worker Ernestine Coleman and she advised me to be "a man, not an animal." But what they all said didn't matter. I had a job to do. I wasn't going to be heavyweight champion Mike Tyson, this great fighter, by being this nice guy and saying I'm going to do it in Cus's name. No, that's just not going to make it. They have to know that they're going to have to pay with their life or, at the minimum, their health, and that fighting me was going to be a very stimulating experience.

This is what Cus told me to do. He'd say to rival managers, "You want to fight my boy? All right, listen, he won't even hit you, he'll walk around you in a circle until you fall dead of a heart attack." He was a shit-talking guy. When I was a kid, Cus would say, "I want you to break this guy's arm. Hit him in the lower ribs, there's no protection there, hit him there, bring it up to his nose. Try to ram the bone through his nose into his brain." And he's saying all this so calmly. So after the fight my mind is all Cus D'Amato, I'm just his disciple, and so I got there and repeated all of it. I didn't know how barbaric it was; that's how we talked in the gym—we talked nasty and macho. Now I'm starting a whole new age in televised interviews.

Cus would never have me say that in public, but I would, that's the whole thing. Without Cus around, I didn't have a filter. The next day Jim and Bill told me what to say after a fight but that's why I ultimately didn't work with them. You can't suppress me. I wanted these people to see the savage that was within me. When Cus died, I started fucking people up and Kevin and I would delight in it.

I also started hitting the bottle more. Look, I've been an alcoholic my whole life. I think I'm a drug addict, a cool drug kid, but I'm a fucking sloppy drunk. You don't even know you're an alcoholic. I can't be pulling out cocaine in front of somebody, I can't be smoking weed, but you can drink wherever you're at. I drank when I was nine years old in Brownsville and I drank beer when I was doing amateur tournaments, but with Cus gone I began to drink more, mostly Bacardi and blueberry brandy. I was scheduled to fight James Tillis on May 3 and I got way out of shape because I was drinking too much. That never would have happened if Cus were alive.

We fought in upstate New York and it was a brutal ten-round fight. I got hit with some great body shots. I didn't even go home that night. I stayed in the hotel because my stomach was hurting so bad. That was the first time one of my fights went the distance but I floored him once and that was the difference. I may have been drinking a little bit too much, but still I beat the guy, even though it was tough.

With Cus gone, the punches seemed to hurt me more. Sometimes I wanted to quit after some of my fights, because I didn't like how some of those punches felt after Cus died. But I didn't quit because I knew I was going to be champ. I had a total of sixteen fights after Cus died before I got my chance. I was beating everybody and looking good doing it and a big buzz was forming. "Wow, when can we see Tyson again?"

And on November 22, 1986, I was matched against Trevor Berbick, the WBC heavyweight champion. *Sports Illustrated* previewed the fight and gave a great nod to Cus. "Tyson has no illusions about the availability of ghostly assistance this Saturday night at the Las Vegas Hilton, where he means to punch the WBC heavyweight title away from Trevor Berbick and thus fulfill D'Amato's prediction that he will become the youngest-ever heavyweight champion. 'I believe when someone dies, he dies—that's it,' the challenger said in his quiet light voice a few days ago. 'But I'll take everything he taught me in there, all the lessons, all the principles.' That rational appreciation of his inheritance would have pleased D'Amato. It may also go some way toward diluting the concern of those who have been asking if Tyson's boxing career (and indeed his life) could be distorted by its being seen as essentially a tribute to the extraordinary mentor who died of pneumonia at the age of 77 in a Manhattan hospital a year ago this month." Jimmy was quoted tooting Cus's horn. "It's no coincidence that Floyd Patterson and José Torres both became world champions with Cus and each, in turn, became commissioner of boxing in New York. This incredible man, this great scholar and definitive teacher, did far more than educate those he worked with in how to box and how to manage. He prepared people for life. They became champions out in the world as well as in that 20-foot square ring."

By now I managed to control my trash-talking persona and came off as a straight-shooting choirboy. "What bothers me the most is being around people who are having a lot of fun, with parties and stuff like that. It makes you soft. People who are only interested in having fun cannot accomplish anything." Jimmy summed up our position. "I have zero trepidation," he said. "This is the best heavyweight in the world, and he is about to prove it."

The only problem was that none of those proclamations of avoiding party people were true. I was drinking like a fish right up until going into training camp. And I caught a raging case of the clap from a disreputable young lady who wound up dying of AIDS. But now I had six weeks to clean up and get a shot of ceftriaxone. By the end of training camp I was in the best shape I'd been since Cus was alive. I knew I was going to destroy this guy, but I didn't know how it was going to happen. I didn't have a plan, I was going to keep moving my head, avoid punches, and blast him. Going into that ring, it was me and Kevin against the world. It couldn't have been any better. With Matt in the corner, we were a hard-core boxing group.

I had additional motivation to win because Berbick was trained by Cus's old rival, Angelo Dundee. I always liked Mr. Dundee but Cus had a vendetta against him. Before the fight Dundee was telling the press that Berbick had "a style to do a number on Tyson" and that he was "licking his chops." Of course, if Cus was around, Angelo never would have said anything like that. Cus would have said, "Hey listen, Angie, I know you. Don't act like you're a genius. You're a glorified cheerleader."

I couldn't sleep the night before the fight. I was on the phone talking with girls I liked but had never had sex with. I was like Nietzsche, the first time he gets some pussy, he gets syphilis and dies. I get some pussy and I'm about to fight for the title and I get the fucking clap. It didn't matter. As I prepared to walk to the ring, I was dripping like a Good Humor bar in July. In the dressing room it was as quiet as a funeral service. There was no emotion, no love, just nothing. I had done my affirmations all day long in my head, even when I was talking to people, so I was stone-cold ready. Nothing could distract me. I was supposed to enter to that Phil Collins song "In the Air Tonight" with that line "I've been waiting for this moment for all of my life, oh Lord," but they switched it up on me and played some lame Toto song. During the introductions of the celebrities Ali came into the ring. He came over to my corner and whispered, "Get him for me." Berbick had beaten Ali in the last fight of his career. "That's going to be easy," I assured Ali. This is how out of whack my ego was then. I thought that I'd become a part of boxing history because I would avenge my hero's loss. Like Sugar Ray Robinson avenged Henry Armstrong by beating Fritzie Zivic. I wanted to get ahold of Berbick so bad but I stayed controlled. I knew that once I hit him, it would be over. Now Berbick came into the ring and I thought he was already beat. He was disciplined enough to have a tough guy's face on but I could see through it.

The ref called us to the center of the ring and gave us the instructions and I couldn't wait to get my hands on him. He was looking like a big roast beef sandwich. We went back to the corner to await the bell and Kevin kept saying Cus's mantra, "Move your head, move your head. Don't forget the jab." I wasn't one bit afraid of Berbick. I knew I could walk right through him. Nothing he did could affect me. Nothing. The bell rang and I was too anxious in the first round but I got a lot of heavy punches through. I wanted to get that mother-fucker. Back in the corner Kevin told me, "Good round. Relax, calm down more. Good round."

Ten seconds into the second round I dropped him with a right hand but he got right back up. He was retreating for the rest of the round. But with half a minute to go, I hit him with a right to the body and then missed an uppercut. But then I followed that with a left hook to the temple. I thought I missed that left but it was one of those punches that are so clean you don't realize they've landed, like when baseball players say a pitch hit their bat so cleanly they didn't even feel it but it's a home run. There was a delayed reaction to that left hook and then Berbick crumbled to the canvas. He got up and he started lurching around but he couldn't keep his balance and he went down again and again. I knew he wasn't getting up but I kept saying in my mind, "Get up again!" I wanted to hit him again and knock him out cold. I wanted him sleeping.

The place erupted. It was all a blur but I remember pointing at Camille and hugging Kevin and kissing Jimmy. José Torres came over and I said, "I can't believe this, man. I'm the fucking champion of the world at twenty. This fucking shit is unreal, champ of the world at twenty! I'm a kid, a fucking kid." Then I asked Jimmy, "Do you think Cus would have liked that?" Then I talked to Cus. "We did it, we proved those guys wrong. I bet Berbick didn't think I'm too short."

I knew that Cus wouldn't have liked the way I fought. I was trying to take him out, I wasn't fighting smart. He couldn't hurt me so I didn't care if I got hit. "Everything else you did in the ring was gar-bage," I heard Cus say in my head. "But the ending was so resound-ing it's all people will remember." I would have given up my whole purse just to hear what kind of shit he would talk.

Larry Merchant interviewed me after the fight.

Q: How does it feel wearing this belt?

A: It's a moment I've waited for all my life. Berbick was very strong. But I was calm. I was timing my punches, and I threw every punch with bad intentions in a vital area.

Q: How were you prepared for this fight?

A: I anticipated a knockout because I had so much confidence, so much belief in myself. My trainer, Kevin Rooney, and I sacrificed so much, we couldn't fail. My plan was to stick my jab in his face, and every punch I threw with bad intentions. Now I'm the youngest champion in the history of the sport. My record will never be broken. I want to live forever.

Q: Did he hit you with anything?

A: He hit me with a few glancing punches, but even if he connected, I refused to get knocked down. I refused to lose. There was no way I was gonna go outta this ring walking. I woulda hadda been carried out. There was no way I was gonna leave this ring alive.

Q: He looked like he was just trying to survive as early as the second round.

A: I don't know about that. If that was so, that was his problem. I came to destroy and win the heavyweight championship of the world, which I done. I want to dedicate this fight to my great guardian, Cus D'Amato. I'm sure he's up there, and he's looking and he's talking to all the great fighters, and saying his boy did it. Now I want to unify the title.

Q: When Cus first saw you at 13 years old, he said, "Stay with me and you can be the heavyweight champion of the world." And you said, "How do you know that?"

A: That's not what I said. I said, "He's a crazy ol' white dude." But he was a genius. Everything he said happened. Isn't that true? Everything he said happened. . . . I'll fight any man alive. I can beat any man in the world. And I'll take on all comers.

After seeing Camille in her room and spending some time at the postfight function, Jay Bright, Matthew Hilton, Bobby Stewart's son, and I got drunk at a dive bar in the Frontier Hotel right across the Strip. The place was empty except for a few old, beat-down hookers. I was drinking vodka straight and I truly got smashed. After Matthew passed out, I went around to some different girls' houses, showing them my championship belt. I couldn't have sex with them I was so drunk. In the morning I finally returned to the hotel and kept looking at myself in the mirror, wearing that belt that Cus and I had sacrificed so much for. Winning it was like finding the Holy Grail. But Cus wasn't there so I didn't know what to do with it. I felt empty. Now what the fuck do we do? Despite what I said in the postfight interview, winning that first belt was more important than unifying the titles.

I stayed upstate for a few weeks after I won the crown. One night we went to Cus's grave and poured a bottle of Dom Pérignon, his favorite champagne, over him. Every time from then on when I'd win a fight I'd get a bottle and celebrate with Cus. I went all over town, to the ice cream store, to the local pizzeria, everywhere, wearing the belt. Then I took the belt back to Brownsville and celebrated there. I'd get some cognac and hang out on the corner and play craps while dope dealers chilled with me. Everybody gravitated to me and they were laughing, crying, happy, the whole gamut of emotions in Brownsville. By now my childhood friends had become neighborhood drug kings, tying people up and burning up motherfuckers. They were very ominous-looking people and the people I was hanging out with would whisper to me, "Whoa, you know this motherfucker?" I'd say, "Yeah, I taught him how to steal."

By the time I won the belt I was a wrecked soul. I was lost because I didn't have any guidance, I didn't have Cus. All I knew was winning the belt for Cus. We were going to get that belt, because that was our goal. We were going to do this or else we were going to die. That was the payoff for all that sacrifice, suffering, dedication, sacrifice, suffering, dedication, sacrifice, and suffering. After we won the title, I didn't care about glory anymore. Sometimes I even question all that. What was in my mind that made me work so hard for that belt, made me think that I'd cut off a hand for that cheap tin piece-of-shit belt? At least in the 1950s it was a gold belt. But I broke bones all over my body, I'll probably be crippled later in life, I can't remember shit sometimes, all from fighting for that belt.

Look, I wasn't Cus. Even though I sound like Cus, I don't think like him. No one thinks like him. I was an unfinished project, twenty years old. One of my sons is almost twenty and he thinks he knows everything. I must have thought I knew everything because I was champ. I think I still had some of that Iron Mike in me because I still felt I could beat any opponent and I was still dying to fight people, but now I slacked off my training because Cus wasn't there to make me train. I always hated training. I'm a lazy fuck. I needed Cus to prod me. Once I was in the gym, I was a monster. But it was all about getting me in there. Cus was still in my life, though. I thought about him a lot. I was still watching my fight films in Camille's house. Even though I had my own apartment in the city, I spent a lot of time with Camille.

Now that I was champ, Jimmy and Cayton tried to mold my image. I did PSAs for the police department and the FBI. They wanted me to be like Joe Louis but I wasn't that guy. I felt like a fake. I didn't become champion to kiss people's asses. "Yes, ma'am. Yes, sir. I'm going to be the best fighter in the world." I heard Cus in my head: "Did you become heavyweight champ of the world to be a peasant? You think people work hard to become peasants? They work hard not to be peasants." I liked being the champ and I felt that nobody could do the job of being heavyweight champ better than me. I knew that guy. Let others play the role of being the people's person. Not me. I'm the heavyweight champ and I will destroy anything in front of me. Anybody with the same occupation and the same weight, you're dead. I don't want to say anything about caring about people in order to get people to like me. I have to kill you, that's what I was taught. My whole job was destroying people, that's what I wanted to do, and in the process, people just might like me.

Cayton was an advertising guy. They wanted to tone me down. But I wanted to be a cantankerous, malevolent champion. I used to watch television and I watched these comic book characters and I loved this guy named Apocalypse from the X-Men comics. He said, "I'm not malevolent, I just am. That's who I am, I'm not a bad person, this is just who I am." Bill Cayton and those guys wanted me to be friendly with everybody, be sociable, but a man who is friendly with everyone is an enemy to himself. You have to keep it real, that's what people like. But this is what I learned from Machiavelli: The man who is constantly honest with everybody will lose the respect of the people. People don't want to be confronted with honesty constantly, so you have to be careful with your honesty. For a long time, I never said what I felt and for a long time I never believed what I said. When the time came that I did say the truth, I hid it under so many lies it would be hard to find. If I was giving an interview about my life and there were some things I didn't want to talk about I'd say, "I was raised by a lot of prostitutes and women of disrepute," but I didn't say that my mother was a prostitute.

All Cus and I ever thought about was getting that belt and all these benefits I'd get. But I hadn't gotten those benefits he promised me yet. Do you feel me? I wanted them. I wanted people at my feet, I wanted people to cater to me. I would have any woman I wanted, I'd have to beat the women off with a stick, this is what this man told me, and I'm not getting this. I wasn't getting it to the degree Cus told me I was going to get it. I was just pleasing people. I'm a good, submissive guy, kissing ass, but it's my time in the ring now, and Cayton and Jimmy aren't letting me near the ring, I'm still sitting in the bleachers. I'm making millions of dollars and these guys got pissed off because I went out shopping and bought a $12,000 stereo system. After that Berbick fight, I started fighting just for money. I didn't have a dream anymore. Now I wanted to get some wine, have some fun, party, and get some pussy. A lot of pussy.

Once the money started pouring in, they couldn't stop me. I'd go up to Cayton's office and pick up $25,000 in hundred-dollar bills. I told one of the guys who worked for me that I didn't let all that money get to me. "What's important is caring about people. Even if I got a billion dollars, I'm still going to be known as Little Ike." That's all Cus's Robin Hood shit. I was into redistributing the wealth. I'd drive back to Brownsville and stop the car and get out and give money to winos and homeless people. One day I stopped at Lester's sporting goods store and bought ten dozen pairs of sneakers in different sizes and gave them away to kids on the street.

But back in my white world, I didn't know what to do with myself. I stayed in the house and watched a lot of TV. I had been away from society for a long time, just training and talking with Cus and wanting to be a fighter, I didn't know what the hell I wanted to do with my life. My head was so far up my ass. Now I had to deal with all the fake celebrity bullshit. I felt like a trained monkey. Everything I did had to be premeditated and then was critiqued. When Joe Namath interviewed me for a show after I won the title, I told him, "If Cus was alive, he'd be enjoying this more than me."

After the longest layoff of my career, I went up against James "Bonecrusher" Smith for his WBA title on March 7, 1987. Before the fight, Kevin told the press, "Mike is only about fifty percent now. There's a lot of little things we learned from Cus that he hasn't done yet and if he keeps the interest and fights long enough then you'll see that." That may have been true but I walked into that arena like I owned that place. I just thought, "This is my home and this is where I live and I'm totally comfortable in this circumference here. I can do this sleeping." I wasn't seasoned, even though they thought I was. This is something that people never knew, that Cus would say even though I would become champion of the world, I still wasn't a seasoned fighter. A lot of people looked at me and thought, "Oh, he's a killer." But I was still a baby, very immature. I still had sixteen-year-old friends.

I was so fairy-tale-ish about being champion of the world. "There's no man alive who can beat me." What the fuck? "I'm champion and now they've got to bow down to me. I served all these years, now I'm going to rule." Cus used to say that in order to rule, you have to serve. He said, "If you met a champion, you wouldn't know how to treat a champion, so when you became champion, you wouldn't know how to be treated. So you have to serve a champion, you have to know how to serve. When you meet a champion, you have to show them respect. Show them respect and then you'll know, when you are champion, how you receive respect."

Despite all my bravado, without Cus around, I found it hard to deal with all the pressure. Strangers would come up to me and say, "I bet my life on you. You gotta win because I'll lose my house and then my wife is gonna leave me." Oh boy. To yourself you say, "I can't let myself down but I definitely can't let these people down either." I developed a nervous condition where my hair fell out of my scalp in one spot from all the stress. So I had a barber friend of mine carve out two lines on either side of that hole in my scalp and he made a championship belt out of it. If someone didn't know that I had alopecia, I'd tell them that it symbolized my belt. I also developed a nervous tick that was the beginnings of sciatic nerve damage. Now it's in my arms and legs.

I didn't have to worry, though. Bonecrusher didn't show up to fight. I won a twelve-round decision that most of the boxing writers panned. They said I didn't show any of my usual aggressiveness and I only threw one punch at a time. Everybody's talking shit, but they didn't fight him. He was hard to fight. His arms were long and he was a tall guy, like six-foot-six, extremely strong. Plus I was in pain the whole fight from the nerves in my neck. I was confident that I would win but I didn't expect a fight like that from that guy.

I got more depressed after that fight. I was interviewed a month later by Alex Wallau for the *Greatest Heavyweights* show on ABC, and when he asked me how it was not having Cus around, I said, "I used to keep a lot of things inside and Cus and I would talk about them. Now when those things come up, I keep them inside." That was a sign that I was getting ready to lose it. I felt alienated from everyone around me. Alex tried to lighten it up. "Come on, you mean there aren't a ton of girls after the heavyweight champ of the world?" "They don't want me, they want the cash," I said. "I look in the mirror every day and I know I'm not Clark Gable. I wish I could find a girl who knew me when I was broke and thought I was a nice guy. Cus never told me it would be like this. He told me I'd make a lot of money and I'd have a lot of girls and I was going to be happy, but he never told me life would be like this." I was a misfit from Brownsville who couldn't handle all that adulation.

While I was waiting to unify all three titles, Cayton and Jimmy put me in with Pinklon Thomas. Before he died, Cus wanted to work with me more on certain things. But my management didn't care, they just threw me in with anybody now. Cus would have controlled who I fought and how I fought them. Cus might have said, "No, I don't want you to fight Thomas right now, I want you to fight this guy. I want you to look real good when you fight him." I beat Pinklon, but I didn't look good. The knockout in the sixth round made everything because the knockout was resounding. But Cus would have been angry at me after that fight. I didn't have that no more, so I didn't have to listen to nobody. You know how much that shit can make you relax when you don't have to give a fuck?

I was scheduled to fight the unification bout against Tony Tucker, the IBC champ, on August 1, 1987. But about four weeks before the fight I left our Vegas training camp and went home to upstate New York. I went right to Septembers, my favorite bar in Albany. Everybody who saw me there did double takes. "Mike, what the fuck are you doing? You're supposed to be training." "Nah," I said. "I'm retired. I don't want to do this shit no more." I was tired of the stress and I started getting scared. I was afraid that I'd get hurt. But after two weeks I thought, "Hey, are you fucking stupid? If anybody is going to get hurt, it's going to be the opponents. If you don't want to do this, you don't want to do this, but they're the only ones who are going to get hurt." So I flew back to Vegas.

The night of the fight I was back in my immortal mind-set. My time had come. In my sick head, all the great fighters and the gods of war would be ascending and bestowing their blessings upon me to watch me join their company. I still heard Cus in my head but not in a morbid sense. He was more supportive. "This is the moment we've been waiting for. We've trained for this moment since you were fourteen. We went over and over this again. You can fight this guy with your eyes closed."

I hadn't gotten into shape and it showed in the first few rounds. But from the fourth round on I dominated, and I won a unanimous decision. After the fight Don King, the promoter, threw a hokey "coronation" for me. He put a chinchilla robe around me and then a crown on my head studded with "baubles, rubies, and fabulous doodads,"

King said. Then he presented me with a jeweled necklace and scepter. He was taking shit from Cus's playbook, trying to get close to me. Later he even set up a parade for me in the Jersey town where I had moved after I got married to Robin Givens, but I didn't bother showing up. I felt pretty stupid wearing that crown and the robe, but deep down inside I felt like a motherfucking mad master. I was thinking, "Whoa, I'm the king!" People criticized me for eventually going with Don King but they forget that it was Cayton and Jimmy who first got him involved with me. They were the ones who signed those deals.

I fought on. I punished Tyrell Biggs for seven rounds until I TKO'd him. Then, on January 22, 1988, I took on Larry Holmes, the fight that Cus always wanted me to have. I'll never forget Cus screaming, "He's a bum! He's a bum!" after Holmes beat Ali. So when I was asked why I hadn't welcomed Holmes to the press conference I said, "Because I don't want to. I don't like Larry Holmes." When he put out his hand, I refused to shake it. I had issues.

By now my fights were occasions. Pimps and hos were seated next to mayors and senators. I'd devastate my opponent and afterward I'd strut through the lobby of the casino hotel and it'd be saturated with people, both those who couldn't get into my sold-out fights and those who did. And the security guards would carve out a path for me and I'd be looking mean and arrogant like Dempsey. "Oh, oh, look, look, look, the assassin, the killer!" I could hear everybody saying, and with each move I made I controlled the whole atmosphere. Nobody had ever seen anything like that before.

People were trying to say, "Mike, Mike, my man, my nigga," and I'd look at them with disdain. I would remember getting picked on as a kid and I'd think to myself that if anybody would try doing that then, I would rip their soul apart. That extended to my ring walk. I was a hundred percent aware of the audience with my every move, my every thought, my every sigh. I wanted to be one with that audience. It was like that out-of-body shit. This was all Cus. So when I got into the ring, I'd lift up my arms, like a benediction, and the crowd would go fucking nuts and I knew I had them. Any move I make, wild applause. I'm in total control and I see my opponent's energy leaving him slowly. This is all a psych job—I'm scared to death also. But when I control my opponent, I can do my job.

I projected that image to the press too. "I love to hit people. Most celebrities are afraid someone's going to attack them but I want someone to attack me. No weapons. Just me and him. I like to beat them and beat them bad. When I fight someone, I want to break his will. I want to take his manhood. I want to rip out his heart and show it to him."

In March of 1988, I flew to Japan to fight Tony Tubbs. It only took me two rounds to dispense with him, but I came home to horrible news. Jimmy Jacobs had died in Mount Sinai of pneumonia after secretly battling lymphocytic leukemia for nine years. It was like I had been hit with a hammer. Jimmy told me he wasn't going to make the trip to Japan because he was going to New Orleans to get some films and prints of black life there from the turn of the century. He was such a great bullshitter; he knew exactly the right thing to say. His death left me a wreck. Without Jimmy, I felt totally alone. Everybody from José Torres to Donald Trump was disrespecting Cayton and making plays, jockeying for position, trying to get close to me and hoping that I'd say some shit and get involved with them. I was married by then to that treacherous duo of Robin Givens and her mother, Ruth "The Ruthless" Roper, and they were fucking with my head on a daily basis. Everyone was pulling me in a different direction and I was getting torn apart. I tried to summon up Cus and I knew he would have said, "Get the hell out of there." Eventually I did. But first I had to fight Michael Spinks.

I was losing it. A few days before the fight I was getting some running in on the boardwalk in Atlantic City and I was interviewed by Jerry Izenberg, a boxing reporter. "What do you think about, Mike?" he asked me as I was jogging. "I think about Cus and some of the things he told me and how right he was about some things. And how he's not here anymore to help me. And then I think about certain things and it occurs to me how much more fun it used to be. It wasn't about money then so much. We were all like a family. We were together, but then suddenly they died and everything became money,

money, and I don't have anyone to talk to." Then I leaned forward and grabbed Jerry and put my head against his chest and started crying hysterically. I sobbed so much that he had to go upstairs to his hotel room and change his shirt.

I was taught that there was nothing like being the champion of the world. In my head, that was the greatest accomplishment. Something Cus and I wanted since I was thirteen, and we both participated with our blood, sweat, and tears to be involved with this. This was the first time I had accomplished any goal I'd ever set. I'd say stuff like "To be in the same breath as Joe Louis, Muhammad Ali, there's nothing like it, the whole world knows who you are." But I felt empty. I had shit going on but I went through dull moments where I'd say, "Fuck, I wish Cus was here." And then I'd say, "Cus would want me to do this, Cus would want me to do that." I wanted to enjoy it but I felt guilty that I was enjoying it without Cus. You see other people, you don't care for them, you say, "God, am I like that? Do I come across that I don't give a fuck about anybody else and I just care about this money?"

Jimmy really wanted the Spinks fight. Even though Spinks didn't hold a belt, he thought that Spinks was the real linear champ because he had taken the title from Holmes, who was in a direct line of succession to John L. Sullivan. Spinks was the people's champion. All the infighting had motivated me and I came to the fight weighing 218 pounds. The day before the fight I told the press, "I don't know how to lose and I can assure you this fight will not go the distance. There's nobody on this planet that can beat me."

I was such an arrogant prick. Like Jack Palance or Richard Widmark, I embraced the role of the sociopathic arrogant guy. For my walk to the ring at the Spinks fight I even had them play funeral music. I was so jaded and dark. But that was the mentality that Cus had promoted. He wanted a very antisocial champion. "Watch me and tremble, and I'll bring the curse of oblivion to your world."

After I destroyed Spinks in 1:31 of the first round, the infighting got worse. Robin and her mom had convinced me to sue Cayton and serve him at ringside. But the problem was that Tyson had become bigger than what Jimmy and Cayton were thinking about. It was too big for them, it was too big for Cus, I think. Everybody got greedy. They made a big thing over me, like I was some hot, pretty bitch and everybody wanted to fuck me. Cus wasn't perfect. He couldn't handle it the last time with Patterson so how could he handle it this time? He got bamboozled by Cohn and Fugazy and November and wound up bankrupt. Everybody was after me, it was just that Don King got to me, but if it wasn't Don, it would have been Bob Arum or somebody else. I was the goose that laid the golden egg and everybody was fighting for me, and with Cus and Jimmy gone, I didn't care about any of them. So I said, "Whoever gives me the highest bid, gives me everything I want, I'll go with them." It was like a game to me. Everybody was thinking about themselves, so I might as well think about myself. All my friends back in Brownsville were dying or dead anyway, so I was trying to have some fun and live. I had no anticipation of having a long life. I was never out of that life. I was in Brownsville every night.

The worst thing about the infighting was that I lost Kevin as my trainer. From where I stood, I think Cayton poisoned Kevin's mind. Kevin didn't like the fact that we were with Don King. So Kevin quit without telling anyone. He just never came to camp. I kept asking him to come back. "Why are you worrying about these guys? You're getting paid and we're still together." I heard later that Mike Marley, a sportswriter who was doing publicity for Don, put out a release that I'd fired Kevin. I never did that and never would. But once it was out, Kevin must have seen it and walked for good. He's in the hospital with dementia now. A lot of fake people are jealous that he made money, but he's a casualty of war, big-time. Nobody worked harder. He had his demons, who didn't? So he needed a drink after fights. We didn't have any help either, me and Kevin. What did we know about being single and having a lot of money? Nobody could tell us what to do.

People sometimes ask me if Don was a substitute father figure for Cus. No. King let me do basically what I wanted to do. All I did was follow his business advice. We were together and loyal to each other, and a lot of that was because Cus had taught me about loyalty. But there was no way that King had one-millionth of the hold that Cus had on my soul.

With Cayton out of the picture, I took total care of Camille. That was the only thing my friend wanted me to do. Cus forgot about the black churches, he forgot about the Communist cause, he forgot about killing those fucking Republican right-wingers. He told me, "To hell with it, Mike, just take care of Camille." He wasn't even thinking about something bad happening to me if he died. My job, even if I was boxing or not, was to "take care of Camille." So I did. Cayton was always pinching pennies with her and she'd tell me she was unhappy. And if she was unhappy, I was unhappy. Cayton was better than Robin and her mother, though. The first time that Robin came to the house in Catskill, she looked it over and then asked Camille who was holding the deed. I could guess what was going through her mind—to have the house put in my name so she could enjoy it

I was traveling a lot then but my only objective was to make sure Camille didn't stop living the life she lived. I'm an extremist—everybody has to live like me when they're around me. I had to have the best. I got Camille one of those electric lifts so she wouldn't have to walk up the stairs anymore. Camille would wait up every night for me to call her. I'd often go upstate and bring my whole crew and stay with her for a few days. When this girl I was seeing lied and said she had my baby, I told Camille I was going to bring up my baby. We stayed with her for a long time and she loved it so much. And every year when her birthday came around, I would send Camille a rose for each year of her life.

I kept fighting and winning. Frank Bruno went down in five, then I knocked out Carl "Truth" Williams in the first round. But my heart and my head weren't in fighting. They literally had to drag me on the plane to fight James "Buster" Douglas in Tokyo on February 11, 1990. By the time they convinced me to fight there wasn't enough time to train, unless you consider fucking the Japanese hotel maids aerobic exercise. I was so fat and out of shape. I was still getting hypnotized by Halpin but it wasn't the same. People who watch that fight think that I was drugged, I looked so out of it. But there was nothing wrong with my lazy ass. I was shitty that night. When I'm great, I'm great, but when I'm bad, I'm real bad—I'm so extreme. Believe me, I wanted to knock him out but I was so fucked physically. When he knocked me out in the tenth round that was the first time I had been down since that slip in the amateurs.

I never thought that I had let Cus down by losing that night. In fact, I was telling everybody that was the best fight I'd ever had because Cus would always ask me, "Could you take it? You're beating everybody now, but what's going to happen when somebody starts beating you up? Can you take it?" That Douglas fight proved I could take it. I couldn't believe I could lose, but the only thing I thought about afterward was how I could be champion again. I didn't go into a deep depression after losing. Cus always taught me not to take shit personally. I divorced myself from my emotions. I wasn't worried. I knew I'd be champ again in six months.

A few days after I got back to the States I went right back to my base and stayed with Camille. I'm back to basics once again. A writer from the *L.A. Times* came up to Catskill to see how I was coping with the loss. He asked me what Cus would have said to me after the defeat. "He would've told me, 'You didn't fight with your spirit, or with your enthusiasm!' I said. Then he would've abused me verbally for a while. Then he would have said, 'Mike, I must sit down and talk with you about your performance.' Then he'd say, 'Aw, what the hell—want some ice cream?' "

My quest to regain the heavyweight crown got derailed when I was found guilty of rape and imprisoned in Indianapolis. I've always maintained my innocence, and I present my case in my first book, *Undisputed Truth*. But being incarcerated for something I didn't do could go two ways. It could have destroyed my will and drive. But thanks to Cus, it did the opposite. This was one of Cus's true tests. And picking myself up from the ashes was what he always taught. Because you've been to prison, because you lost your fight, you lost your wife, does that mean it's time for you to give up life and give up living? We've got to grab it again, we're going to conquer the world again! And that's what it's all about. Not feeling sorry for yourself, but feeling, "They hurt me and I'm not going to let them hurt me again and to make sure of that, I'm going to kill them!" You have to make up some kind of affirmation, because if you don't, you sink into the ground and die.

Back then, I was all about fighting to the end. And even when it comes close to me dying and I'm lost, I'm sorry, I want to live. When I get well again and strong again, I'm going to fight them again. I'll fight until I win, and they'll have to kill me until I say, "I give up, I give up." And they say, "Fuck you, you don't get no quarter," and they just kill me because I never gave up. It's just who I am. I hate to be that way too. When I say, "I give," I never give, I lie. I just want to win, that's all I've known since I was a kid. I know it sounds egotisti- cal, and nobody should ever have had that at fourteen, fifteen: "You're the best, you're going to be the greatest." I should have been wishing my mother a peaceful journey to heaven, while all I was telling her was how I was going to be the most famous person in the world. I feed off my pain and suffering, because it inspires me to work hard be- cause I feel less of a person if I don't.

When I was in jail I remembered something that happened to me when I was fifteen years old. Tom Patti and I had driven down to Woodstock to get some cheap deals on stuff. For me Woodstock was legendary. When you go to Woodstock, you know what Woodstock was all about: the concert. Everybody was there at Woodstock—the Who, the Grateful Dead, Santana, Sly and the Family Stone, Janis Joplin, Jimi Hendrix. Richie Havens made his bones in Woodstock, that's how I knew who he was. I don't know any folk singers, but I knew him. When I went there, there were people who went to the concert and never made it back home. They just stayed there.

We were walking down the main street and I saw a sign for a fortune-teller and tarot card reader. I went into her storefront and she was a regular-looking chick. She wasn't an old crone, she was probably about forty-five and good-looking. She didn't look like a hippie but she dressed like one. We decided that she was going to read my palm so I put my hand out and she took it.

"Oh, whoa, whoa," she said, looking at my palm. She started laughing. "Wow. You are a rocket, a meteorite. You're going to light up the world for a short time."

I didn't believe her, because she was good-looking. Maybe that was the reason I went in there. So I'm thinking this was bullshit but she kept on.

"Oh boy, are you in trouble. You're going to endure a lot of pain, but you're strong. I can't say that nothing is going to happen to you, you're going to go through a lot but you're going to be all right, baby. You're going to get through it. You've got a long life line, but you are going for a ride. You're a mess," she said, and kept giggling.

I never told anybody about that reading. I was too scared to tell Cus, but later I found out that he did a tarot card reading to see if I would be the heavyweight champ of the world. I couldn't tell any of my friends back in Brooklyn because none of them would have believed it.

But when I was in jail in 1992, it finally hit me that she was right. When I came out of jail I was a madman, and I'd still go back to jail a couple of times later, but deep in my heart I knew I was going to survive. Even when they had people shooting at me, I knew nothing was going to happen to me. I felt like I was impervious to death.

Another thing that got me through the jail sentence was the literature that Cus had me read. Every time I'd feel down and lost, I would always go to Edmond Dantès from *The Count of Monte Cristo*. He didn't go to jail and think of revenge. He prepared for revenge and success, he learned all the arts, and he had a mentor. The only way that you can achieve success in life is if you have somebody you pay homage to and you look up to and you want to make happy. And that's what Edmond Dantès did—he had admiration for this old guy who was teaching him all the arts. That's what I always thought about when I was down or locked up. I thought about my mentor. I thought I was Edmond Dantès from the gutter. "When I'm out of prison, I'll show you. Look at me. Fuck you, look at me." That's how I survived.

As soon as I was released from jail I dropped off my stuff at my Ohio house and went right to Catskill to be with Camille. I went back to the gym there with Jay Bright, my housemate at Camille's, as my main trainer. I was already in great shape, thanks to the discipline that Cus had instilled in me. While I was in jail I didn't eat any meat and I went from 270 to 218 pounds, with the help of training hard both with weights and doing thousands and thousands of push-ups and sit-ups in my cell.

I entered the ring for the first time in four years on August 19, 1995. My first tune-up fight was against Peter McNeeley. If the name sounds familiar it's because Peter's dad, Tom, had fought Patterson back in the day. Lennie Daniels, who had trained with Cus before becoming a New York State trooper, told me that he had met Tom at a bar in Boston.

"You're one of Cus's fighters?" he asked Lennie. "Oh, the psychological things Cus did to me leading up to that Patterson fight!" Tom said. "Cus visited my camp and he went, 'This is going to be interesting. I didn't realize you were this big and strong. My guy is a little fighter, you might have to take it easy.' Then he'd watch me work out and he'd say, 'Man, I didn't know your hook was that good. I've got to get Patterson to get ready for this.' He destroyed me psychologically before I even got in the ring."

I always used to name my fights after warriors. So when I came back after prison I named my first comeback fight after King Richard, "The Return of the King." Richard came back from the Crusades and ousted his brother John. Even though Cus was dead, I'd talk to him. "Don't worry, Cus. The king is coming soon. King Richard is going to return."

Just seconds into the fight, I decked McNeeley with a right when he charged me from across the ring. He took a standing eight and charged me again and we were trading punches until I floored him with an uppercut. He was pretty out of it and suddenly his cornermen came racing into the ring. They had thrown in the towel without telling their fighter.

I didn't get much work that night, so Don King matched me up against Buster D'Amato Mathis, the son of the man Cus trained for a minute. We fought in Philadelphia on December 16, 1995. Jay Bright was in my corner, yelling out Cus's Willie Bag numbers. The only problem was that Buster's dad had been trained by Cus and he had taught his son Cus's number scheme. So for the first three rounds, every time Jay yelled out "seven-seven-two," Buster knew that a jab, jab, and right hand were coming and he avoided the punches. He knew exactly what I was going to do. I was so pissed off because I couldn't hit him the first two rounds. I kept missing all my punches and this guy was making me look stupid with my own style. Nobody else knew it but I saw him twisting and moving his head, doing my style better than I was. He made me look like an asshole until I stepped back and hit him with a vicious right uppercut with thirty-eight seconds to go in the third round. Cus would have told me, "This guy made you look like an amateur for three rounds until you hit him."

With two fights under my belt, Don put me in against Frank Bruno for the WBC heavyweight title. I know if Cus were still around, I would have had ten fights before I fought for the belt. I wasn't even out of jail for a year when I stepped into the ring on March 16, 1996. All of Cus's indoctrination poured back into me. Getting that belt back was everything. Being heavyweight champ again was more important than being president of the United States. To be champ you have to have the body, the look, the attitude, the aura, the ego. That's what I grew up believing. People may have laughed at me at first, said I was too small, but they didn't laugh when I strapped those belts around my fucking waist, did they? So I wanted that belt back. For me and for Cus.

I could smell the fear on Bruno when he entered the ring. By the end of the first round I had opened up a huge gash over his left eye. He held so much in the next round that Mills Lane had to deduct a point from him. Half a minute into the third round I rocked him with two left hooks. He was dazed and then I finished him off with two right uppercuts. He was out on his feet against the ropes, and after a few more uncontested punches, Lane stopped the fight. I had won the belt back. I started to strut and soak up all that adulation for my egomaniac ass but then I caught a glimmer of humility and dignity and I fell to my knees and gave thanks to Allah. Then I got up and started thinking about Cus and some arrogant stuff that he would have said. "One down and two to go, Cus," I thought.

The WBA belt was next. It was held by Bruce Seldon. Somehow this quest to regain the belts was nothing compared to Cus's and my original mission. The guys I was fighting after I came out of jail were clowns. I TKO'd Seldon in the first round and I didn't even connect with the punch. After the fight I asked my second wife, Monica, "Baby, did I hit him?" "Yeah, you hit him," she said. "No, babe, I didn't hit him," I told her. The crowd booed and chanted, "Fix, fix, fix," after Richard Steele stopped the fight. That was the last belt I ever won. Two months later Don rushed me into the fight with Holyfield to unify the title. I wasn't ready, and after the ear-biting incident in the return fight, I was suspended. Then I descended into the ravages of alcohol and cocaine abuse for years.

Because of some crazy spending and some back taxes that were never paid, I found myself in debt for over $100 million and divorced for the second time. In August of 2003, I filed for bankruptcy, a process that took me thirteen years to finally resolve. I was totally busted, but I lived like a king using Cus's survival tactics along with what I learned on the streets of Brooklyn as a kid. Maybe it was because early in the process, when they were figuring out my assets, my forensic accountants found an annuity that was worth $250,000. When they researched it they found out that Cus had opened that annuity for me with his last $5,000, just months before he died. Later I found out that Cus gave Camille the money and said, "In case the kid doesn't make it, put this in Mike's name." When I heard about that, I broke down and cried. I'm the kind of guy who forgets to eat if I don't have a wife. There's people out there like me who don't know how to take care of themselves. And here Cus knew that I would fuck away my life, so he was looking out for me from his grave. He cared about me. That gave me hope.

Even when I was in rehab, Cus's teachings helped me get better. In some ways, Cus taught me to become a psychiatrist. Being with Cus was like being in rehab, now that I think about it. It was always about dealing with ourselves and our character flaws, peeling away our layers of hurt. That's why I excelled at rehab. A guy like me wants so desperately for rehab to work. I accepted everything when I was in rehab. I'm a soldier, that's what I am—I fall right into formation. And that's how come I won. What did I win? I won the Rehab Dude of the Decade. I won the war. One of the ways that I succeeded was to remember that poem on the wall of Cus's gym. Sometimes when you think about giving up, just remember "Don't Quit." No matter what you do, don't give up. You'll win this situation, just don't quit.

Another important part of rehab was the notion of service, the idea that it's important to give back to other addicts who are in need. Cus's whole life was a life of service, from helping out his neighbors in the Bronx to supporting old down-and-out boxers. So I'd go out all the time with my counselor Sean and do twelve-step calls. A lot of the time we'd go to the houses of kids who were on a bad relapse and double-team them and talk them into coming back into treatment. I never once hesitated to talk to someone and help them out when Sean gave me the call.

When I was fifteen, I used to ask Cus, "Do you think I'll ever make the Boxing Hall of Fame?" He didn't think for a second. "If you listen to me, Mike, it's a foregone conclusion. You will make them forget about all the old-timers. The only reason they'll remember them is if you talk about them." Well, in 2011, I was inducted into the International Boxing Hall of Fame in Canastota, New York, only two and a half hours from Catskill. I was inducted alongside Julio César Chávez, the junior welterweight champion Kostya Tszyu, the famous Mexican trainer Ignacio "Nacho" Beristáin, referee Joe Cortez, and "Rocky" himself, Sylvester Stallone. My ego had told me that if I wasn't in the Hall of Fame, there shouldn't be a Hall of Fame. But being Mike Tyson, the insecure guy, I was always thinking they didn't like me and it was a political thing that I wasn't getting in, because guys I fought were getting inducted into the Hall of Fame before I was.

So I was surprised when I got the call. And when I got there that rainy day, I thought a lot about Cus. When it was time for me to accept the award and speak, I looked out at the audience and saw Carmen Basilio and Jake LaMotta and Ken Norton and Aaron Pryor. I realized that this was the apex of my career. This is where it ends, as far as boxing goes. It can't get any higher. So I took the mike and tried to pay homage to Cus.

"All this stuff started when I met Cus and Bobby Stewart in this reform school because I was always robbing people when I was a kid. All my life I've watched these guys"—I motioned to the fighters in the audience and up on the stage—"I look at them different. Why would I want to be like these guys, I always say. I don't know." I was having a hard time keeping it together by then. "I've got to be goofy about this or I'll get emotional up here. When I met Cus, we talked a little bit about money, but we wanted to be great fighters." With that I started sobbing softly. "Hey, guys, I can't even finish this stuff. Thank you. Thank you." I went back and sat down in my seat and the other guys came over to shake my hand. In my head, I heard Cus: "I told you you were going to be in the fucking Hall of Fame!"

Most people aren't blessed with a second act in life as I've been. Making movies, doing my one-man show, I'm thrilled to be in the great fraternity of entertainers. Even when I was fighting, entertaining the audience was always paramount in my mind. Cus had me around all these great people with magnetic personalities like Norman Mailer. I'm used to being around people who are stopped by women, stopped by men, when they're seen in the street. I learned something from these older men, lessons in charisma and getting people's attention. I learned a lot about evoking emotions from people, having them like me or even dislike me. It's all about utilizing the arts because Cus was all about the arts. Even when he talks about putting his mind in other people, that's an art. It's a dark art, but all of that is art. The art of war, the art of survival, the art of the world—I always looked at everything as an art. I'm not a good artist, but I know the arts. It's like me saying I'm not a good fighter, but I know how to fight real good. I may have a limit, but what I do is real good. It's the same with acting. It's like any other art. Ward Bond and guys like him, they were never going to be John Wayne or Errol Flynn, but you noticed when they were in the room.

While I was in the throes of my cocaine addiction I was asked to do a cameo in *The Hangover*. The movie hadn't even come out yet and I was in Vegas and some little kids jumped off a tour bus on the Strip, saw me, and started going crazy and screaming and pointing at me, "We saw you in a movie! We just saw you in a movie!" They had probably just seen the coming attractions. These kids had never seen me fight and didn't know anything about me other than I was in that movie. That was a turning point. I knew something different had happened and I didn't know why. It happened within a blink of an eye and that is real talk. I was drugged-out on cocaine, almost suicidal, and all of a sudden, in the blink of an eye, what the hell happened? It happened so fast it was uncomfortable. I'm living this life of a loser for so long and boom! Now I have an opportunity hit me in the face and I'm not even prepared for it. This is where it gets really ugly, I've got to start reprogramming my mind.

Now I'm saying stuff like "I'm going to change. I'm going to win. I'm not going to let it end like this. That is not going to be my legacy. I want to beat everybody." Then I go back to that Cus stuff in my mind: There is no one who is going to be able to stop me. My reign will be invincible. I'm thinking this shit, I'm on drugs, I don't even know what reign I'm going to have. But I know I am about to reign. I know it is not boxing, but I've got the same ideology and the same thrust and hunger. I was hopeless. I was communing with bad spirits. I had annihilated all my dreams. But one cameo and now everybody starts telling me, "Mike, you have got to keep doing the acting." Prominent actors and prominent directors are telling me this. "Mike, you have got to keep doing this funny stuff. Forget that tough-guy stuff. Funny is where you're at, Mike, because this is who you really are. You're a nice guy, Mike. All that goodness that you have is mushed down by all that dark shit that happened to you over your years in life. You've got to stay lit, because when you are in that light, you shine so brightly." They were right. That darkness was a role that Cus had imposed on me. That dark intimidation. Iron Mike. In a lot of ways Cus was using me to fulfill his own legacy. But it was a cool legacy to fulfill. If Cus asked me to do it again, I would. Only this time I'd be meaner and more vicious.

In October of 2009, my wife, Kiki, and I went to the Venetian Hotel on the Strip to see Chazz Palminteri do his one-man show *A Bronx Tale*. We were blown away, and on the ride home I realized that I was doing a version of a one-man show with my personal appearances. So we sat down and wrote a one-man show that would chronicle my life. It was also called *Undisputed Truth* and we wound up doing it in Vegas, and then Spike Lee brought it to Broadway and eventually HBO filmed it for a special. We take it on the road periodically and now we're doing a new version of it at Brad Garrett's Comedy Club in the MGM Grand in Vegas. Years ago I had some of my most exciting fights at the MGM Grand and now I'm doing a stand-up version of my one-man show here. But I wouldn't have been able to do either without Cus. Being around Cus, I learned how to tell a great story. From Cus I learned impersonality, so I can go onstage and play a character named Mike Tyson. I bare my soul onstage and it was Cus who got me to bare my soul to him so I could develop the character needed to win the crown. And I wouldn't even have a glimmer of hope that I could get onstage and entertain people if Cus hadn't bolstered up my confidence with affirmations and techniques of self-hypnosis.

Cus always told me I could succeed at anything I put my mind to and he even mentioned being an actor. I don't know if I was even meant to be a boxer. I just got caught up at a young age. Once I got around Cus, I loved that feeling of entertaining people. I loved the idea that when you come in a room, everybody rushes to shake your hand, they can't keep their eyes off you. I thought that was great. Cus used to promote that to me. "If you listen to me, every time you walk in the room, you will feel everybody watching you. You'll suck all the air out of the room." That's what this Italian man was telling me when I was just thirteen.

My acting career started with that confidence he infused in me. Thanks to him, I have enough confidence to do things I don't know anything about. Confidence applied properly will supersede genius. I just know I'm going to accomplish my goal when I walk out on that stage tonight. I don't know what's happening tomorrow, but right now I'm going to do this thing that nobody in the world ever did before. Tomorrow might be tricky, but right now this is what's going to happen.

The funny thing is that I don't think Cus would be proud of my success in showbiz. He'd say, "Boxing is what you do. Now you've got an excuse. You've got another gig. You don't like boxing anymore? You're going to focus on this?"

"But Cus, I like doing my one-man show. I like cultivating my stand-up. Someday maybe I can be as good as Eddie Murphy."

And Cus would snort and say, "Who did he fight? Who trained him? What gym is he from?"

12

One day I was walking with Cus in New York and this monster of a Dominican guy, over three hundred pounds, came running up to us. He was crying and hugging Cus. "Cus, do you remember me?" He was an older guy Cus had trained years and years ago. That's the effect Cus had on people—reducing them to tears. All the people we talked to for this book, and probably most any fighter Cus ever came across, if you had a conversation today with them about Cus, they'd start crying. That was the power he possessed. You know what Cus did to us? He exposed our biggest flaws to us, our biggest weaknesses. He'd put us to the test and then he'd try to get us to work on our flaws. He was always trying to make strength out of weakness.

Everyone who ever worked with Cus continually quotes some of his most striking insights. In fact, I'm continually quoted as saying, "Everybody has a plan until they get punched in the face." I learned that from Cus. He actually said, "Everybody has a plan until they get punched in the mouth." That's the way they talked in the forties.

But Cus was the furthest from being a dry intellectual teacher. Being around him was exciting. Again, he was another P. T. Barnum. One time after he got divorced from his first wife, Joe Colangelo brought a date over to meet Cus. His new gal was having trouble with her kids. Cus began to talk to her and after a while they were talking about out-of-body experiences and stuff like that. "When she walked out the door she was three feet in the air," Joe said. "She was ready to take on the world. Cus had built up a euphoria in her mind that she could solve all her problems."

Cus would love me talking about him like this. He always wanted his story told. There was so much misinformation out there about Cus; he wanted the truth to come out. He started on a couple of book projects when he was alive but they never came to fruition. But he was always concerned about his legacy. Part of Cus's legacy was the allegations of impropriety that surfaced after the first Patterson–Johansson fight and resulted in Cus losing his NYSAC licenses. One of the central issues that Cus was grilled on was a series of phone calls from Cus's home to the mob boss Fat Tony Salerno. Both Cus and his friend Charlie Black and his nemesis Bill Rosensohn all testified that they never made those calls. But the lingering suspicion helped the commissioners revoke Cus's licenses. During the course of researching this book, we found out who made those calls to Salerno. Near the end of our research Ratso called Cus's niece Betty, Tony's daughter, and she finally solved the mystery. "It was Emil Lence. He was the cause of all that trouble because he made the calls on my uncle's phone that got him in trouble and got him suspended from the NYSAC."

That made sense to us. Lence was the independent promoter who bucked Norris and the IBC and who helped propel Patterson's career. He was also the promoter of Patterson's first title defense after Cus publicly denounced the IBC and said that Patterson would never fight for Norris again. But we also know that Lence himself was connected. Again, it was a case where the mob-connected guys in boxing, including Carbo and Palermo, would act in their own interests and oppose Norris when it suited them. But why would Betty remember Lence's involvement in those calls after all these years?

"Lence screwed my father," Betty said. "Most of my father's earnings were from his bar and back then owners didn't have to pay into Social Security. When he closed his bar my father got a job as the manager for a bowling alley that Lence owned. But Lence illegally withheld the money he should have been paying into Social Security for my father. So when my father retired he couldn't collect on those earnings."

But other issues surrounding the first Patterson–Johansson fight and Fat Tony still remain unresolved. Could Cus really have been kept in the dark about Fat Tony's involvement by his best friend, Charlie Black? Or did Cus secretly agree to Rosensohn's getting financing from mob sources in order to make sure the bout came off? We've seen that Cus was apprehensive about making any kind of move that could potentially screw up any of Floyd's defenses of his title because that would give Norris, Cus's archenemy, a chance to climb back into the promotion of heavyweight championship fights. Cus was willing to work with mob-controlled fighters such as Roy Harris as long as Norris was shut out.

Ultimately Cus's beef wasn't with Carbo and Palermo, it was with Norris and Gibson and the IBC. Don't forget that Bill Daly, in his wiretapped conversation with Jackie Leonard in L.A., admitted that Carbo and Blinky never have any problem if you make it to the top without their help. Then they don't muscle in. It's only when they get you the fights and then your fighter wins the championship, that's when you've got to pay. And that's what Cus did, he made it to the top without their help and he outsmarted Norris, so Carbo and Palermo had no beef with Cus. It was Norris who Cus really got over on. Carbo and Palermo never controlled the heavyweight champ. Al Weill used to pay them off for Marciano's fights but they never controlled Marciano. And when Gibson and Norris put pressure on Carbo to force Cus to put Patterson up against an IBC contender for the title, they never did. They only shrugged and said that Norris could never get that match because Cus was "crazy."

During the course of doing this research on Cus, a lot of stuff about myself and Cus resurfaced. I remembered that Cus once told me that after the IBC had been dissolved, Norris came to him and asked him if he wanted to train or manage his fighters. Cus couldn't believe the guy's audacity. Cus looked at Norris and said, "What?

After all you put me through, you want me to work for you? Get the hell out of here!"

If you look closely at Cus's statements, he'd always say that he was fighting the IBC, not the mob. I think he was making a distinction there between Norris and his guys and the old-time mob guys like Carbo and Palermo. But we know that Norris was connected to mob guys who were on a whole other level beyond Carbo. It's known that Norris was connected to Capone's gang. Through his and Wirtz's involvement in casino gambling and liquor distribution to Vegas, as reported by his own employee Truman Gibson, he would have known the top mob bosses including guys like Meyer Lansky. He was close to Albert Anastasia because when Norris was in a New York hospital after one of his heart attacks, he got fresh flowers sent to his room every day from Anastasia. So when Cus was fighting Norris, Norris had access to the mob, but a whole other level of the mob.

Cus made this distinction to Paul Zuckerman, a writer who was working on a book about Cus when I was living in the house. Cus told Paul, "I wasn't fighting the mob, I was fighting the IBC. I'd rather you wrote that. I don't want to challenge these people. I got along, I never challenged them, I challenged the IBC. The IBC had undercover associates. That's how they referred to them in those days. Those fellows are still around today. I don't want to stir anything up." Sometimes Cus would go to ludicrous lengths to confuse the issue of who he was really fighting. Confusing the enemy. In a biography of Norman Mailer by Peter Manso that came out two years after Cus died, Cus was quoted about his involvement with Salerno and Carbo. "It's true, just like Norman wrote in his article, I tangled with Fat Tony—Fat Tony Salerno, the gambler. But he wasn't part of the IBC. The guy I really tangled with was Frankie Carbo. Contrary to what people assumed, Carbo wasn't Mafia, but he was the tough guy who controlled the fight managers by using the Managers' Guild, which had been a good organization, but then when Joe Louis retired, the IBC tied up all the top contenders so they weren't permitted to fight anyone else. They got control of all the titles, not just the heavyweights."

Whoa. To be clear, Mailer never said that Cus "tangled" with Fat Tony. In fact, he said the opposite. Remember? "It was discovered that D'Amato directly or indirectly had gotten money for the [Patterson–Johansson] promotion through a man named 'Fat Tony' Salerno. D'Amato claimed to have been innocent of the connection, and indeed it was a most aesthetic way for the Mob to get him. It's equally possible that after years of fighting every windmill in town, D'Amato had come down to the hard Bolshevistic decision that you don't make an omelet without breaking eggs."

Then Cus said that the guy he really tangled with was Frankie Carbo, who, he added, "wasn't Mafia." That would be news to all the guys Carbo executed in the service of the mob.

Cus would talk about his battle with Norris and the IBC to his dying day. He saw himself as a white shining knight fighting off all these bad heathens. Cus was on a mission to clean up boxing. But to clean it up, you've got to clean it up by being dirty. You can't clean it up legitimately or else somebody is going to feel some pain. If it was a case of breaking eggs to make an omelet, Cus wasn't particularly proud of that fact.

Cus knew that Norris and his friends were so powerful that if you did something to them and went to Europe, they can make something happen in Europe like they were right next door to you in America. He knew those guys had long tentacles and he knew what they were capable of doing.

After his battle with the IBC, many people believed that Cus had a huge target on his back. Jimmy Glenn, who was a trainer for Patterson and who owns the best dive bar in New York, called Jimmy's Corner, told us, "Cus needed some protection because he was a strong-headed guy. Somebody had his back, because mob guys didn't care, they'd bump him off."

We can't forget the horrible fate that befell Ray Arcel in Boston. Even Joe Louis talked about fighting the mob. In 1972, Joe Louis told a reporter, "Since 1969, I've had a little trouble with the Mafia. At one time my life was in real danger. They tried to put me out of the way. I wasn't sick at all when they put me in that hospital in Denver.

The Mafia put pressure on my wife to put me in the hospital. But it'll be straightened out." When he was asked if he felt safe right then, he said, "Oh no. They might come back at any time. One thing I know. Your best friends can set you up. Your best friends can kill you."

Several books and documentaries maintain that Sonny Liston was murdered via a hot shot of heroin by the mob. Jackie Leonard survived ratting on Carbo and Palermo because he left the country and worked as an engineer on construction projects in Saudi Arabia and Vietnam, two places where the mob's tentacles might be too short to reach.

So was Cus really in danger or was he just paranoid about the wiseguys? Cus had told me that the IBC had some hits out on him, but I was young then and I certainly didn't know the whole backstory that we've discovered doing this book. Now that statement is very meaningful to me. He said that's why he never walked home the same way. But it's probably also why he tried to never sleep in the same place two nights in a row. It's also why he kept Camille in a secret apartment in Queens that he would sneak away to.

One question that kept eating at Ratso and me was Cus's relationship with Charlie Black. The fact that Cus stayed friendly with him till their dying days suggested that Charlie had done some great things for Cus that far outweighed the trouble that Charlie got Cus into, if you want to give Cus the benefit of the doubt and say it was Charlie who got Fat Tony involved in the Patterson promotion without Cus knowing about it. Well, near the end of the research for his book, we finally found out the depth of their involvement. Ratso had called Rocco D'Amato's daughter Carole D'Amato Rothmund, Cus's niece. After talking to her for a half hour, Ratso had a hunch. "Does the name Charlie Black mean anything to you?" he asked. "Yes, it does," she replied. "I remember my father mentioning his name all the time." "Do you remember the context in which his name was mentioned?" "He said that Black stopped the mob from killing my uncle. They had him marked down to take his life. I would believe it too, because my father would never tell me a lie."

Now it gets really interesting. By 1966, Cus began retreating to upstate New York, and by the late sixties he had moved permanently from the city. When we talked to Nick Beck, a close friend of Jimmy Jacobs's, Nick reported that when he visited Cus and Jim at their apartment and was a bit shocked at Cus's shoddy housekeeping, Jim told him, "We're thinking about trying to get something better for Cus." The next thing Nick heard, they were talking about getting Cus out of the city. "Cus had made a lot of enemies in his lifetime," Jimmy told Nick cryptically.

Cus himself confirmed that his move upstate was related to his dealings with the mob. Lisa Scott, writing for Fightnews.com, interviewed Kevin Rooney, who told her that Cus said of his move upstate, "I wasn't paranoid. I just assumed that they would hurt me if they could and I acted accordingly." And when Ratso called Nick Beck again to dig into the circumstances of Cus's leaving New York, Nick remembered that Jacobs had told him that he got Cus out of town because they were worried about a mob hit. So Cus moved to Rhinebeck, New York.

Here's where Charlie Black comes in. Black's close friend and associate, the man he "dragged" into the Patterson–Johansson fight and who saved the fight with his infusion of cash, was Fat Tony Salerno. It just so happened that Fat Tony had a huge estate in Rhinebeck. In fact, Joy Gross, wife of Dr. Gross, whose health retreat was in Rhinebeck, told us that a lot of gangsters congregated in that area "but it was kept quiet. There was a group of gangsters and Fat Tony was one of them and they would meet in hidden places. That was part of the gang that I think was helping Cus."

Mike D'Attilio, a student of Cus's who went on to work for the FBI, confirmed that Cus was friends with a close relative of Fat Tony's, but he "kept that very confidential. There's another example of Cus being manipulative. He stayed away from those guys, but when it would serve his purpose, he'd get in there and manipulate them."

Cus's involvement with Salerno was no secret to many in the boxing world. Don Majeski, a fight agent and matchmaker, told an interviewer that he was sitting in Patsy's Pizzeria in East Harlem with Bill Daly, the fight manager who brought that message to Jackie

Leonard to play ball with Palermo. Daly pointed out a guy with a big-brimmed hat and told him that he was the "real manager" of Patterson. It was Tony Salerno. He said the rumor was that Fat Tony bought a house for Cus in Rhinebeck. "He just had his own mob that protected him," Majeski said.

Cus stayed in Rhinebeck until 1970, when he moved almost overnight to Catskill after an IBC "associate" turned up in Rhinebeck. So when Jimmy brought Fat Tony to watch me spar in Cus's gym in Catskill shortly after I started living with Cus, was this a mere social call? Or was Salerno coming to get a piece of me for a very big favor he had done for Cus years earlier? By then, Fat Tony was an underboss of the powerful Genovese crime family and had been designated the "front boss" to take the heat away from Vinnie "The Chin" Gigante. "I think Salerno wanted a small piece of the action," said Joe Colangelo, who was there. "I believe that they came out with some sort of working arrangement. There was no way of stopping Salerno if he wanted to muscle in. So you had to work something out."

Train your thoughts just like Cus D'Amato
Your guts is hollow

—Proof, from Car Freestyle by Eminem and Proof, 1999

For Cus, boxing was a metaphor for living. You prepare a plan whether you're in the ring, in a war, or going to work in a factory. When you strengthen your will and build up your character, you can persevere and face up to whatever challenge you face. It's hard to explain the impact Cus had on me. How can I explain Cus to my kids? I was a bad kid, went to institutions, and then I met an old guy who trained fighters. And this guy gave me the blueprint for the rest of my life. I always knew I had a special destiny even when I was growing up in the gutters of Brooklyn. But when I met Cus he told me what that destiny was and it all clicked in my mind.

I came from such despair. My kids can never relate to that. They don't have that hunger to the core. And they don't have that pressure to succeed that I did. That pressure always followed me, way after I became champ. Even today, everything is a big championship match to me. Getting the kids to school on time is a big test and if I fail it's just a disaster. Everything has to be right, I have to win all the time. If we're watching movies in our home theater and I do something stupid like forget the popcorn, fuck! I own the theater but I forgot the popcorn so I'm a loser in my mind. I learned to live with that pressure when I was with Cus. I learned to be comfortable being uncomfortable. Cus's idea of striving for perfection transcended the ring and went into every aspect of my life. Because Cus said I was that person. He said, "That's who you are. Everybody gives me what they are, this is what you are. I can bring out certain things, but this is what you are." Sometimes when we left the gym to go home, he'd be like, "Where are the gloves?" "Shit, I forgot the gloves," I'd say. "You forgot the gloves?" He'd get on me and that would eat at me.

Before I do my show or before I do a speaking engagement, I read over my script again and again and again. I might have a teleprompter but I still commit it to memory. I may see a word that I don't know and it may fuck with my head, even though I read it over and over again. So I memorize everything. I'm always on, always in a state of agitation to avoid a state of failure.

Cus once said, "I sell people dreams." That's exactly what he did. Cus sold me a magnificent story that I bought. I never thought of myself as the heavyweight champ, I never even looked like one. The heavyweight champion was big and strong. I fell in love with myself and the idea of me executing this mission. Cus taught by example. He led the life of a monk, denying satisfaction, sacrificing for success. That's what I did then and that's what I am now. But it all worked on me because I had that extremist personality. And I had such abysmally low self-esteem. What a volatile combination: low self-esteem and a sky-high ego that Cus cultivated in me.

And why wouldn't I buy Cus's dreams? Enthusiasm is contagious. And Cus was the best confidence man I'd ever met. I always ask myself, "How did this old man know?" That's the only thing that's missing from my life, that knowledge. But maybe he didn't know. Cus had spent over forty years honing his skill, so he was good. Maybe he just willed that lightning to strike twice. Bottom line, it was destiny. That's what I believe in my soul.

Cus addressed my deep inferiority complex by building up my ego and telling me I was superior to everyone around me. I don't think Cus lived long enough to balance that out and it got kind of out of hand. He never got the chance to tell me something like "Well, Mike, you have to conduct yourself like this. You're better than them, but you can't tell these people that." I offended so many people. Cus had brainwashed me with that arrogance and viciousness. It was in the marrow in my bones.

It was the best time of my life, plotting and scheming with Cus. Our goal was all about barbarian success and superiority and then, boom, it was there and he wasn't. But all that stuff isn't any good in the real world. I got older and started dating more quality women than the women I'd been dating, and they had a problem when I'd say that word "superior." That word bothers people. Cus lived for confrontation but that wasn't helpful to me as a citizen. My wife helped me break that cycle. We went to a dance show once and I got a lot of attention from the other people in the audience and my wife said, "They love you." And I said something elitist like "I expect them to love me." I saw the air go right out of my wife. Like "Man, I'm married to this shit?" She didn't say it but I felt the energy and it was the right energy. I just couldn't understand why she wasn't feeling it like I was. My wife is a humble lady and I can't be with my wife if I've got that superior mentality. That's why I never had a good relationship before Kiki. When I think back, it was the same with Cus. No one could live with him but a woman as strong, humble, and dedicated as Camille. I learned over the years that people never really left me. Like Cus, I chased them away. I'm just grateful that I finally broke that cycle.

Cus made me feel that hurting people was noble. Somebody should have shot me. I would have shot me if I would have said that shit to me. I'm just doing what this guy said to do and everything he said worked. And Cus was so dramatic. Remember that story where the mob guys came to see him in the Gramercy and they were threatening him and he inched his way to the door and threw it open so the kids in the gym could see what was happening? Cus wanted to die on the stage. He wanted to be worshipped like some noble revolutionary martyr like Jean-Paul Marat. I'm just like Cus too. If I go to my demise, I want the world to see me die. I don't want a few nobodies on a corner see me die and throw a fucking nickel on me, I want the world to see me die. Cus was just a little guy, but he was like a general. I'd do anything he told me to do. It was really dark stuff but it was awesome. I don't think like that no more. I think it was the best time in my life. Imagine being fourteen, fifteen, sixteen, and no one is going to fuck with you because your dad is the general?

Cus had the art of intimidation down to a science. He may have feared someone, but he wasn't intimidated by anybody. He'd say, "I may fear him, but I'm not afraid to kill him." I learned a lot from that wise old man. I loved going through life with him then, but it's not like I don't have any resentments now. Why did I have to work so fucking hard that I have arthritis throughout my body? I worked like a total animal because my self-esteem was so low. Now I can't walk without pain. I have broken bones in my feet and my back. I didn't even know those bones were broken because I was so active, fighting all the time. I can still work out now but I'm a wreck.

And he was always picking and probing at me. "What are you up to? You're up to something. I know something is going on." He always had me on pins and needles. Cus would be badgering me and then right in front of me, like I'm not there, he's telling guys how I'm the greatest fighter. I don't know what to do, I'm confused. This guy read me the riot act and now he's on the phone, laughing and smiling and talking about how great I am. "My boy is pretty reckless, isn't he? He's destructive, isn't he?" So proud. Then he'd hang up the phone and look at me and say, "You're a phony."

I'm fifty years old now and I'm still trying to figure it out.

Cus always talked about the people who betrayed him. They were all Benedict Arnolds. Cus believed that if you didn't take all his shit, you were a bad person. The people he antagonized were the closest people to him. But I never left him. I learned to talk like him and finish his sentences. He wanted me to think like him and I did. That's why people left him, because they couldn't appreciate the mind of a manic genius the way I could. At times Cus did drive me nuts, but I always remained loyal to him.

Cus could never be at peace with himself. He was the kind of guy who has to be the light, he wants to be seen, he wants to have great accomplishments. I understand Cus more as I get older. He wanted respect from society. Then, when he got the respect after Patterson won the title against all odds, Cus became one of the most powerful men in boxing. And he got addicted to that power. He alienated so many people who would have been his allies. The independent press, the smart sportswriters, they wanted to like him, but he was too proud. And he was too stubborn to see past his own way. He had so many legitimate enemies that he got paranoid that everybody was his enemy. When you don't know who your enemy is, you treat everyone as though they are your enemy. I'm like that. When I go through my paranoid stages, I would think my wife and my kids were against me.

But I understand Cus. Like me, he had a tough life. There was never a lot of happiness. Italians faced a lot of discrimination when Cus was growing up in the Bronx. There was pressure from the Italian mob. He never had a mother, his father died in anguish in his arms, and his favorite brother was murdered by a cop. Cus had been done dirty. Then people stole his fighters, his friends betrayed him, and he finally finds a guy like me and he dies before I make it. I was the biggest fighter in the world at that time. His progeny, his guy. Cus needed to be there. I was a fucking maniacal, malevolent heathen. "Look at me, motherfucker, I'll bite your fucking nose off." I wanted to be that guy, I wanted to be like Cus.

When I was fifteen, I would look at my opponent like I was ready to eat that fucker. I was so on my game then—never smiling when I was introduced to him, wouldn't shake his hand. That was my mindset, for real. Cus used to tell me about fighters who did that and those were the kinds of guys I wanted to be like. I had to read the history books about Harry Greb and John L. Sullivan and Jim Jeffries, because before Ali came, they were the fighters who were idolized. But they didn't talk as slick, they just talked about hurting motherfuckers. They talked the kind of shit I liked: "Hey, let's not fight in a ring. Why don't we lock the door from the inside and whoever comes out with the key is the fucking champion?"

When Cus died, I'd lost my spirit. I don't think I ever did get over his death. I felt cheated by destiny when he died. I don't even like talking about it now. Sometimes I think it was a waste of love. I can't explain it. All this stuff is his creation—the big house and the big cars, people respecting me, me being somebody, the family, the kids. The whole big facade is his creation. I don't know if I'm like this or not. I just wanted to be the big fucking guy, the heavyweight champion of the world—known around the world—with everybody wanting to be my friend. I had no choice, this was the way stuff was going to happen. Kill anything in the way, sacrifice everything. The fact that nothing is going to stop you, that was the dark side of the moon. I wasn't going to let anything stop me, my family, my mother, my sister, brother, babies.

Then I achieved that goal. I'm twenty and famous all over the world. But I'm just a trained monkey. You're famous and you disregard what people feel. And people start laughing at your ignoramus, buffoon gestures. Then you get somebody in your crew to whip their ass. What idiocy! It was all too much. You walk outside and you've got a thousand crazed fans within a one-block radius. Cus always said, "Don't let your fame or your money give you a false sense of security that you can't die."

Sometimes I wonder what my life would have been like if Cus had lived longer. For one, we would have monopolized the boxing business. People always say that if Cus had lived longer he would have worked on my character. Fuck my character. You know what my character would have been? Putting people in comas and at the end of the day saying yes to Cus's decisions. Imagine the stuff Cus would have been talking? The deals he would have made? Nobody could have turned me away from him, they couldn't trick me into believing Cus was a bad guy. I wish Cus would've seen me fighting in those big fights, but it wasn't meant to be. I know I wouldn't have been as opinionated if Cus were with me. I wouldn't be talking that crazy stuff about eating babies. Cus wanted me to be a silent killer. He wanted to do all the talking.

Here's the way it would have gone: Everywhere I'd go, Cus would be behind me. I wouldn't be talking to people, Cus would be running the show. When Jim died, Cayton would have had a problem. Cus would have come at him full blast. Cus might have even physically attacked him. And there would have been no Don King, for sure. Cus was his own promoter. Listen, I beat all Don's fighters and he was basically out of business. Then Cayton started working with him. But with Cus around, Don would be totally broke and out of business.

When I beat Berbick, Cus would have berated some people, to show how superior his thinking is. "This is just a boy, he's twenty years old. He just knocked out this heavyweight champion in two rounds." And he would go on and on and on. "He would have been the Olympic champion if they didn't rob him."

Can you imagine what he'd have been like with the press? He'd talk to only the one or two guys he trusted. He'd be vicious to everyone else. Buster Douglas? Never would have happened. Plus I would have stopped some of the guys who went the distance like Bonecrusher. Everybody was a bum to Cus. Even the good fighters. "Fucking bum, he's a goddamn tomato can," he'd say.

All this didn't happen for a reason. You know why? Because if somebody would have said something disrespectful about Cus in front of us, I would have killed him. I was too emotionally attached to him. Cus believed in dying in the ring, dying on your shield. You don't quit. It's first-class pedigree fighting. I still think that too, but I realize now nothing is more important than life. There is no trophy, there is no glory, more important than life and the people you love. I'd be the first to want to die with honors in the ring back then, but not now. That is a sucker's game. And I was probably the biggest sucker who ever came into this game.

If Cus was around now, he'd take over everything. He'd have all my kids fighting. Amir would have quit school, and he'd be a pro by now with twenty-five fights. Miguel would be in fighting in the amateurs. Rocco would be training for the Silver Gloves tournaments. He'd talk to their mothers, he'd convince them to let him handle them. "I'll get your children triple what Mike gives you."

He just had that gift of gab. If he would have been a motivational speaker he'd be bigger than Tony Robbins, bigger than that lady who wrote *The Secret*. When he spoke to an old friend's investment group in Albany a few months before he died, he wowed them with his message of positive thinking and overcoming your fears. He used his battle with the IBC to talk about how the word "impossible" shouldn't be in your vocabulary:

"You've got to overcome fear, that's how I fought the IBC. The Norris family was worth maybe fifty to five hundred million dollars in those days. They had tremendous power. Now, I was considered crazy to even dream I could oppose them, but I had one advantage: I knew I had the experience and the knowledge and the desire. Without desire, you're nothing. People are under the impression you have to be intelligent, but the most important thing is the motivation, the drive. Getting back to my fight with the IBC, by the early fifties, Norris had it so completely organized that if you didn't get work from him, you didn't get any work. So trying to buck people like Norris was considered impossible. That's why I have no respect for the word 'impossible.' You must know your mind well enough to know that, given a set of circumstances that are threatening, your mind will find excuses to avoid and evade, not to accept a confrontation of any kind.

"See, but I always say it's like crossing a suspension bridge going from one side to the other. Now when you cross to the other side, knowing what you have to cope with and knowing all that could be dangerous to you, you chop the bridge down so you can't retreat. So when you take one step forward, two steps forward, make sure you chop that back one so you constantly have a chasm there where you can't retreat. Then whatever you have to do, you can only think of one thing: accomplishment. Don't be afraid to put yourself in that position. You'll be amazed at the things you can do when you're forced to. Nobody really knows his capabilities until he tries."

You come to Cus weak and he makes you strong. When he makes you strong, you get addicted to that power and you don't want to leave him because he's the source of that strength. My whole life people have said, "How come Cus didn't make another guy like you? It was you, Cus didn't do it." But that's bullshit. I wouldn't have been that guy. Cus was the only guy who could touch me to the core. I don't like saying this shit but if Cus looked at me the wrong way, like I disappointed him, I wished he would have shot me. I would have wanted him to beat me and stop looking at me like that. I wanted to be his star pupil. I wanted to outwork everybody and shine so he could see me and pay attention to me. I know what Patterson meant when he told a reporter, "Cus makes mistakes, but the more they try to turn me against him, the more his quality comes out. Lucky he isn't a woman. I might have married him."

Cus was like those stern Zen masters. He had read all those books on Zen. The master would seem to be acting harshly and irrationally yet the disciples would completely want to submit to that kind of behavior. That's the reality of life. The human ego needs to be crushed, but the ego is so powerful it raises you to so many great heights. But then again, it's only the ego. It's an illusion but it's real. Cus didn't want to work with well-adjusted people. He wanted people who were flawed. Then he peels off the layers of trauma, which is a painful process, and then he builds up your ego. But so much of that ego came from the power he had over us. That's why when he'd say, "I don't feel I've done my job until I make a fellow independent of me," that wasn't happening. I was never independent of Cus. I can't think of anyone who became independent of him. Floyd tried to and then years later he said, "The biggest mistake I ever made was to leave Cus." And my biggest mistake was thinking that Cus would never leave me.

How far the pupil will go is not the concern of the teacher and Master. Hardly has he shown him the right way when he must let him go on alone. There is only one thing more he can do to help him endure loneliness: he turns him away from himself, from the Master, by exhorting him to go further than he himself has done, and to "climb on the shoulders of the teacher." Wherever his way may take him, the pupil, though he may lose sight of his teacher, can never forget him. With a gratitude as great as the uncritical veneration of the beginner, as strong as the saving faith of the artist, he now takes his Master's place, ready for any sacrifice.

When I asked the Master how we could get on without him on our return to Europe, he said: "You have now reached a

*stage where teacher and pupil are no longer two persons, but
one. You can separate from me any time you wish. Even if broad
seas lie between us, I shall always be with you when you practice
what you have learned. I need not ask you to keep up your regular practicing, not to discontinue it on any pretext whatsoever,
and to let no day go by without your performing the ceremony,
even without bow and arrow, or at least without having breathed
properly. I need not ask you because I know that you can never
give up this spiritual archery. . . . I must only warn you of one
thing. You have become a different person in the course of these
years. For this is what the art of archery means: a profound and
far-reaching contest of the archer with himself."*

*In farewell, and yet not in farewell, the Master handed me
his best bow. "When you shoot with this bow you will feel the
spirit of the Master near you. Give it not into the hands of the
curious! And when you have passed beyond it, do not lay it up
in remembrance! Destroy it, so that nothing remains but a heap
of ashes!"*

—Eugen Herrigel, *Zen in the Art of Archery*

So it's futile to keep asking, but one last time: Why me? How did
Cus know after those three rounds of sparring back in that musty
old gym? What if I didn't fuck up at Spofford and they never sent me
to Tryon? What if Bobby Stewart hadn't taken that job in Elmwood? What if Cus hadn't been run out of Rhinebeck by that face-
less Norris associate? I got to Cus because it was ordained by God.
Cus told me, "I've been waiting for you," and I believe he had been.
Sometimes I lie in bed with my wife, and in the middle of a conversation, I stare off in deep thought and say, "When I was born, Cus
was fifty-eight years old. I'm fifty now. I could be doing bad, but by
the time I'm fifty-eight my savior could be born. So I have to wait a
little longer, even if I have to suffer some more until that time
comes."

Cus bet his whole life on me. He put forty years of reputation on the line for me. When he told them I was going to be one of the greatest heavyweights of all time, they laughed in his face. They would say, "Cus, he's too small. He's not even six feet tall and he only weighs one hundred ninety pounds. This won't work." But it did. The whole world knows my name because of this man and he never got to enjoy any of it. Cus told me, "You'll walk into a place and people will give you a standing ovation." And one day I went into a restaurant in Chicago and the whole place stood up and applauded me.

I used to read articles about Jack Dempsey and he was so well-known and beloved. They even named a tough, boisterous fish after Jack Dempsey. When pilots named the approach into the airport in Vegas the "Tyson route" because it used to pass over my old house, I didn't want to let on that I was excited. Around other people, I denied that it was for me, but when I was alone I'd say to myself, "I'm catching up with my heroes."

A few years ago the sportswriter William McNeil published a book about me called *The Rise of Mike Tyson, Heavyweight*. McNeil is a major statistics guy and at the end of the book he compared my record over my first thirty-five fights to the records of Dempsey, Louis, Marciano, Ali, Holmes, and Foreman. George Foreman and I have the best records. "Mike Tyson's record for his first 35 fights compares favorably with the top heavyweight champions of all time," McNeil wrote. "His record is on a par with that of George Foreman, who was also a devastating puncher, but in Tyson's case, his 35 matches included seven with world champions or former world champions, while Foreman's record did not include any world class boxers." It's true, nobody beat more world champions than me in the heavyweight division. Dempsey lost three of his first thirty-five fights. Joe Louis lost one. This proves that Cus knew what he was doing and I knew what I was doing. They couldn't beat us. We had too much pedigree for them. After I KO'd Berbick I said, "I'm the youngest heavyweight champ and this is a record that will last forever." So far I'm right.

Can I be honest with you? And this is not from an egotistical perspective; this is from a rational, analytical look at the game of boxing. It's going to be difficult to find a guy like me who could generate the money and income like I did, even though nowadays they might gross more money. But no other boxer understood the sport the way I did. Most boxers today don't understand psychology, they don't know what people want, they aren't inspired enough to go to the past, and not only to find out about the fighters but to research their associations. Which ones hung out with Dickens? Do they know that Gene Tunney and Benny Leonard were friends with George Bernard Shaw? Mickey Walker palled around with Hemingway. A lot of young boxers don't understand the history of the sport. They're fighting for money but if they're fighting for glory too, they don't understand what and who they're representing. Regardless of what anybody says about me—I was "horrible," I was "a bum," I was "overrated"—I represented all the old-time fighters. I never let people forget who they were. If I hit a guy with one of the punches I learned from Benny Leonard or Harry Greb or Ray Robinson, I'd always explain that it was that fighter's punch I'd used.

Even at sixteen years old, I believed that all the heroes and gods of war—Achilles, Ares, and all these gods, and all the old fighters— were watching me and I had to represent them, I had to be bloodthirsty and gut-wrenching. I realized through Cus that we were fighting for immortality. Nothing else mattered than being worshipped by the entire world. When Cus talked to me about immortality he wasn't just talking about me, he was talking about himself too. I wasn't just fighting for my glory, I was fighting for his too. Nobody loved boxers and boxing more than Cus. He devoted his whole life to service, first to the poor Italians in his neighborhood in the Bronx and later to all the wayward kids like me, and Patterson and Kevin Rooney and Joe Juliano and on and on and on. We trained hard, we fought hard, but it was worth every minute.

Cus's friend the CBS boxing consultant Mort Sharnik wanted to do a program about Cus before he died. In one of the interviews for the show, he asked Cus if he thought about his legacy and the whole point of his life. Cus said, "All I want to do is make one small scratch on this big rock before I go. I want them to know that Cus D'Amato was here." You got it, Cus. Now there are two scratches on that rock, side by side. And whenever anyone remembers Mike Tyson, they'll know the name of Cus D'Amato too. Until the end of time.

ACKNOWLEDGMENTS

Mike would like to thank:

My inner circle of friends and family who have always been there to support, encourage, and inspire me. The list, although small, is still too long to name specifically, because in doing so I will definitely forget a name or two. But I do want to acknowledge my children, Morocco, Milan, Miguel, Amir, Rayna, Mikey, and Gena. All that I do is for you guys. Also, thank you to my wife, Kiki, for always being there: I love you.

I do need to specifically thank my man Larry "Ratso" Sloman, for all of the tireless hours and the labor of love and research he put into this book. Without your vision, this book would have never happened. Thank you, brother.

Larry would like to thank:

Michael Gerard Tyson. This second collaboration was as much a labor of love as our work together on *Undisputed Truth*. In that book Mike touched on his complex and rich relationship with Cus D'Amato, his mentor and adopted father. Everyone associated with that book felt that the relationship deserved more attention and that Cus himself had never gotten his due for his groundbreaking work in boxing even before he even encountered the young Tyson. So we decided to go deep: deep into Mike's years with Cus, and deep into the mysterious and largely undocumented life of Cus D'Amato.

I spent the first few months scouring various archives. In the City Clerk's Office in Manhattan, I found microfiche with the transcripts of the proceedings of Cus's lawsuit against the New York State Athletic Commission, which had gone untouched for decades. The transcripts were a revelation. I then pored over the transcripts of the Senate subcommittee that investigated the influence of organized crime on boxing. One prominent figure emerged from these transcripts: former New York City assistant district attorney and special counsel to the Senate subcommittee John Bonomi. Mr. Bonomi died in 1999, but his widow, Patricia, and daughter, Kathy, graciously allowed me to visit with them and photograph his archives.

The transcripts of Frankie Carbo and Blinky Palermo's trial in L.A. gave tremendous insight into the way the mob worked mostly with, but sometimes against, James Norris, boxing's premier impresario at the time. But the most amazing find was in a spare bedroom of an apartment in Jersey City. Mario Costa is a longtime friend of Mike's, and some of Mike's pigeons still reside on the roof of Mario's Ringside Lounge complex. Mario had been close to Camille Ewald for years, and after her death he managed to salvage more than forty boxes of Cus's that had been stored in his room in the Catskill house. What a treasure trove! The boxes contained what was left of Cus's files, old boxing memorabilia, newspapers from the years he managed both Floyd Patterson and Mike, and books from Cus's private library. Thank you, Mario, for your diligence in preserving Cus's legacy.

All writers stand on the shoulders of the scribes who precede them. For this work several books must be cited: The late, great sportswriter Barney Nagler wrote a fascinating book, *James Norris and the Decline of Boxing*, which chronicled both Norris's and Carbo's influence on boxing in their day. Norris's aide-de-camp Truman Gibson exposed his former boss in a self-serving memoir, *Knocking Down Barriers: My Fight for Black America*. There were myriad books about Floyd Patterson that proved useful, including his autobiography, *Victory over Myself*. Two friends of mine produced books that were exemplary in dealing with two of the most compelling heavyweights in history. Nick Tosches wrote the definitive tome on Sonny Liston: *The Devil and Sonny Liston*. And there is no finer book about Muhammad Ali than David Remnick's *King of the World: Muhammad Ali and the Rise of an American Hero*. Jeff Lieberman, my friend and collaborator in our company Shallow Entertainment, produced an award-winning HBO documentary, *Sonny Liston: The Mysterious Life and Death of a Champion*, which provided great insight into the Big Bear.

Thanks must also be given to the *Sports Illustrated* writers who covered Cus and "got" him, much more than the beat reporters and columnists from the newspapers. It was an honor to interview Robert Boyle and Gil Rogin and document their remembrances of Cus. In the previous book, we acknowledged Paul Zuckerman, a young journalist who had actually moved into the Catskill home with Cus and Camille and produced hours and hours of tape, which Mike and I listened to with fascination. I tried to track down Zuckerman at that time, to no avail. I'm happy to report that he is still around, and our conversations about Cus (and other matters) are always illuminating. Paul is still working on his book about Cus, and we hope this will surface soon.

Special thanks to Bill McNeil, who wrote a book titled *The Rise of Mike Tyson, Heavyweight*. Besides offering documentation of the years that Mike and Cus spent together, Bill generously made available the tape of Cus's speech to a meeting of the First Meridian Planning Corporation, which was owned by his old friend Roger Sala. It was Cus's last public appearance, and his motivational talk to a group of investors and investment counselors was illuminating.

We can't thank Joe Colangelo enough. Joe is Cus's last living close associate, and the two of them worked tirelessly to keep Cus's gym open in Catskill. Largely because of Joe's efforts it remains open to this day. His memories of Cus and his anecdotes of their time together were wonderful.

Two very special people assisted us in making sense of Cus's behavior and the mystery of his involvement with Fat Tony Salerno.

Cus's nieces Carole D'Amato Rothmund, Rocco's daughter, and Elizabeth (Betty) D'Amato Quintano, Tony's daughter, went out of their way to communicate priceless information to us; Betty even wrote up some remembrances of her father and uncle. Carole and Betty, you both helped us put the final puzzle pieces together!

We also would like to thank everyone who sat down for interviews to talk about Cus. Thanks to Al Caruso, Alex Wallau, Anthony Patti, Billy White, Brian Hamill, Burt Young, Buster D'Amato Mathis, Gene "Cyclone" Hart, the inimitable Gene Kilroy, Greg Walsh, Jimmy Glenn, John Halpin, Joan Mathis, Joey Hadley, Joy Gross, Lennie Daniels, Mario Costa, Mark Medal, Mark D'Attilio, Matthew Hilton, Nelson Cuevas, Nick Beck, Paul Mangiamele, Bobby Stewart (without whom . . .), Tommy Gallagher, Tom Patti, and Scott Weiss. We owe a debt of gratitude to Paul Friedman at the New York Public Library, who tracked down key reports and documents for us.

While I was in Vegas, I was always happy to be in the company of Mike and his extended family. His wife, Kiki, to my eyes, is the best thing that's ever happened to Mike. She was instrumental in helping this book along every step of the way. It's wonderful to watch as Milan and Rocco blossom into young people! All the rest of Mike's children are wonderful too, and as they filter in and out to visit their dad, they invariably bring good cheer with them. Kiki's mom, Rita, and dad, the Imam Shamsud-din Ali, and her brother Azheem and his lovely wife, Jahaira, always make me feel at home.

But home for me in Vegas is *chez* Penn Jillette. It's always a joy to crash with Penn, his lovely wife, Emily Zolten, and their two aptly named children, Moxie and Zolten. After a hard day's work with Mike, it's also a pleasure to scoot over to the Penn & Teller Theater at the Rio casino and be continually astounded. Thanks also to Mike's able assistants David Barnes (aka Farid) and David Malone for all their help.

Once again thanks to the Blue Rider publishing titan David Rosenthal, who is a joy to work or eat pastrami sandwiches with. Thanks also to our UK publisher, Adam Strange, for his upbeat enthusiasm about this book. Kudos to Brant Rumble, our editor at Blue

Rider. This is our second book together, and he always is an absolute pleasure to work alongside. A shout-out to the Blue Rider peeps who shepherded this book along: Aileen Boyle, Jason Booher, Claire Vaccaro, Linda Cowen, Terezia Cicelova, and especially Anna Jardine. And now we get to work with über-publicists Jo Mignano and Brian Ulicky, who do an outstanding job of pushing our books out into the world.

Thanks to our longtime agent, David Vigliano, and everybody at AGI Vigliano Literary. Also to my literary lawyer, Eric Rayman, and my personal lawyer, Charles DeStefano.

Finally, I'm forever indebted to my family, Christy Smith-Sloman and Lucy. No writer is a bundle of joy to deal with when he's in the midst of making deadlines, and Christy has put up with me for seven books now. I'm eternally grateful for her love and understanding. And I love Lucy too, even when she wakes me at four in the morning to go out.

PHOTO CREDITS